Beainnina Xcode
For Reference

Not to be taken from this room

Matthew Knott

Apress®

Beginning Xcode

ISBN-13 (pbk): 978-1-4302-5743-1

ISBN-13 (electronic): 978-1-4302-5744-8

President and Publisher: Paul Manning
Lead Editor: Steve Anglin
Development Editor: Douglas Pundick
Technical Reviewer: Felipe Laso Marsetti
Editorial Board: Steve Anglin, Mark Beckner, Ewan Buckingham, Gary Cornell, Louise Corrigan, James T. DeWolf, Jonathan Gennick, Jonathan Hassell, Robert Hutchinson, Michelle Lowman, James Markham, Matthew Moodie, Jeff Olson, Jeffrey Pepper, Douglas Pundick, Ben Renow-Clarke, Dominic Shakeshaft, Gwenan Spearing, Matt Wade, Steve Weiss
Coordinating Editor: Anamika Panchoo, Mark Powers
Copy Editor: Mary Bearden
Compositor: SPi Global
Indexer: SPi Global
Artist: SPi Global
Cover Designer: Anna Ishchenko

Distributed to the book trade worldwide by Springer Science+Business Media New York, 233 Spring Street, 6th Floor, New York, NY 10013. Phone 1-800-SPRINGER, fax (201) 348-4505, e-mail orders-ny@springer-sbm.com, or visit www.springeronline.com. Apress Media, LLC is a California LLC and the sole member (owner) is Springer Science + Business Media Finance Inc (SSBM Finance Inc). SSBM Finance Inc is a Delaware corporation.

For information on translations, please e-mail rights@apress.com, or visit www.apress.com.

Apress and friends of ED books may be purchased in bulk for academic, corporate, or promotional use. eBook versions and licenses are also available for most titles. For more information, reference our Special Bulk Sales–eBook Licensing web page at www.apress.com/bulk-sales.

Any source code or other supplementary materials referenced by the author in this text is available to readers at www.apress.com. For detailed information about how to locate your book's source code, go to www.apress.com/source-code/.

To my wife, Lisa. You're a rock, an inspiration, and the clockwork that makes this family tick.

Contents at a Glance

Contents

About the Author

Matthew Knott has been writing code for as long as he can remember; from marveling at moving pixels on a BBC Micro to writing ridiculous text adventures for his mother on an overheating ZX Spectrum 48k. Matthew has been a professional software developer for the past 12 years, six of which have been spent in the education sector where he has now entered the sometimes-scary world of management, although when they see the mess he made of the budget, that won't last long. Matthew's work and hobby are basically the same things, but when he's not working, he is loving life in a beautiful part of Wales with his wife, Lisa, and two kids, Mikey and Charlotte.

About the Technical Reviewer

Felipe Laso Marsetti is an iOS programmer working at Lextech Global Services. He loves everything related to Apple, video games, cooking, and playing the violin, piano, or guitar. In his spare time, Felipe loves to read and learn new programming languages or technologies.

Felipe likes to write on his blog at http://iFe.li, create iOS tutorials and articles as a member of http://www.raywenderlich.com, or work as a technical reviewer for Objective-C- and iOS-related books. You can find him on Twitter as @Airjordan12345, on Facebook under his name, or on App.net as @iFeli.

Acknowledgments

I'd always thought that when it came to acknowledgments, everyone thanked their family, and they possibly did so out of some idea of routine for this sort of thing. Having gone through the process myself now, I realize that it's just not possible to write a book without neglecting your family while continuing to receive their love and support.

With that in mind, I have to acknowledge the role my wife and my children played in making this dream become a reality.

I'd also like to thank Steve, Douglas, and Mark at Apress for their support over the years and specifically their belief and encouragement on this project.

Thanks also to Anamika, Mary and Felipe for keeping everything ship shape along the way.

Finally, a special thank you to my good friend and colleague Phil, whose continuous good humor, generosity, and sage-like wisdom have helped to keep me going through many tough times.

Introduction

Welcome to Beginning Xcode, the book that aims to give you all of the knowledge to start writing applications using what is probably the most powerful integrated development environment (IDE) ever, and it's free.

As with many Apple products, Xcode has simplicity and ease of use in abundance, but don't be fooled; the shiny exterior masks a workhorse of a tool, incredibly powerful with an extensive set of integrated tools for every eventuality. Xcode is the development environment that all other IDEs have a poster of pinned to their bedroom walls.

Xcode hasn't always been this shining Rock God of awesomeness; it used to be a sorry band of ragtag applications. When I first picked up Xcode 3 in 2007, I remember going through a multitude of different applications to perform varying tasks, such as the very basic Interface Builder, and finding out how to adapt my knowledge of C into Objective-C. Back then what I really wanted was something that showed me how to get the most out of Xcode and give me the understanding I needed to get going with the hundreds of app ideas I had in my head.

Fast forward six years and both myself and Xcode have come a long way. I feel as if I've gone from a kid, bumping my leaky paddle boat aimlessly around a boating lake, to a handsome sea captain at the prow of my vessel, gazing forth as I slice through choppy waves with grace and ease. Well, aside from the handsome part, the analogy is a good one. Xcode 5 is now a complete, integrated product that puts the same power in your hands as the developers at Apple who write the apps found in iOS and Mac OS X.

Throughout this book I aim to guide you through every facet of Xcode, helping you to understand the capabilities of each of the key areas as you build a number of cool and exciting projects along the way.

By the end of the book, you should be ready to turn the ideas in your head into reality, and I can't wait to see what that looks like.

Getting Acquainted

Welcome to Xcode

Apple provides Xcode to developers to help them create applications for Macs, iPhones, and iPads, namely, OS X and iOS. Xcode runs behind the vast majority of your favorite iOS and OS X applications. Arguably, without such a powerful, refined, integrated development environment (IDE), the thriving ecosystem that is the App Store would not exist as it does today.

What Is Xcode?

Every developer, regardless of the platform for which he or she is developing, has an array of tools that are used to take an application from an idea to something that is readily available to millions of people. Apple is no exception, and it provides a cultured, powerful, and polished set of development tools. These tools are brought together within one application called Xcode. Xcode provides everything you need to create, test, deploy, and distribute applications for iOS and OS X. With the release of iOS 7 and Xcode 5, Apple has radically overhauled its toolset and created powerful, new technologies that aid developers in making the process of creating an application fun and rewarding.

The purpose of this book is to guide you in becoming familiar with Xcode 5 in the hope that you'll become more than confident and embrace it to create amazing, innovative new applications for iOS and OS X. Like many other technical books, as you progress through each chapter, you will build upon your knowledge and systematically create a number of iOS applications.

Although Xcode was created primarily for developers working on iOS and OS X applications, it is also great if you work with other languages such as C, Java, and C++, among others. Xcode has a long, interesting history of releases, some having a very good reception and some less so. First released in 2003, Xcode has had five major releases and seen a couple of major interface overhauls, and after over 10 years of active development, it's safe to say that Xcode is a leading professional and incredibly powerful set of development tools. What's more, Xcode is available to developers at absolutely no cost; all you need is an iTunes account and you're good to go.

Why Choose Xcode?

If you have experience developing for other platforms, then you probably want to know what exactly makes Xcode so great. The main reason is because there's simply no other IDE like it; it's unique in the sense that Apple has created it to be simple, yet at the same time it masks a powerful interior. You have the ability to work with a range of technologies and also have a phenomenal developer toolkit at your disposal. Xcode itself contains everything you could need: an intuitive code editor, advanced debugging, seamless interface editing features, and the benefit of being constantly updated and maintained by Apple.

In addition, using Xcode is arguably the only practical way to develop applications for iOS and OS X that can truly be called native. Xcode is what Apple itself uses to produce its own innovative software, which is used by millions of people.

Aside from Xcode, it's hard to actually find a commendable alternative if you'd like to develop native iOS or OS X applications. Of course there are third-party services and tools, but oftentimes you'll find yourself battling with inconsistencies and a lack of compatibility rather than focusing on what's really important: creating great apps (and enjoying doing so). The purpose of Xcode isn't to simply be an IDE, it also helps, aids, and guides you on your quest of creating something that has the potential to reach a staggeringly large audience, and for that reason, Xcode is a fantastic choice.

Prior Assumptions

Before you dive in and start reading this book, it's assumed that you have at least some familiarity with Objective-C and Cocoa Touch. This book is geared toward those developing for iOS; however, it is possible to get a lot out of this book if you're developing OS X applications, as many of the principles presented can be applied to either platform.

It's assumed that you are using a Mac and are preferably running the latest version of OS X. Although it isn't necessary that you run the latest version of Xcode, this book is written specifically for Xcode 5, and some of the instructions may not be possible in older versions. There's also the misconception that you need the greatest and latest "souped-up" Mac, but in fact many previous generation MacBooks will work just fine.

It's also assumed that you know how to operate your Mac and how to use OS X. For example, you need to know how to use the Finder, save files, and so forth—all the basics. Finally, a couple of the chapters present scenarios in which an active Internet connection is required, and some features of Xcode perform better when you are connected.

It's also worth mentioning that the purpose of this book is not to teach you how to create applications for iOS or teach you how to program in Objective-C or C; the purpose of this book is to get you up and running with Xcode so you can apply your current knowledge of Objective-C and OS X/iOS development and use the latest version of Xcode to its full potential to enable you to work more productively and create fantastic applications.

What's Covered in This Book

Part 1: Getting Acquainted

- *Chapter 1*: This first chapter will start you on your journey into the world of Xcode and explain how to get Xcode onto your machine and prepare it for first use. You also are shown how to sign up as an Apple developer and you get a look at the wealth of resources provided by Apple to iOS and OS X developers.

- *Chapter 2*: Here, you'll start a project and get the ball rolling in terms of becoming familiar with Xcode. You'll learn the basics of how to create projects, creating and building applications, along with how to get around in Xcode.

- *Chapter 3*: Next, the focus will shift to how to choose from Xcode's different project templates, and you'll also have a guided tour around Xcode's interface along with an introduction to many of the menus, inspectors, and panels you should make use of to work efficiently.

- *Chapter 4*: This chapter focuses solely on how to design your interfaces using Xcode's built-in interface editor, Interface Builder, and gives you an in-depth look at the libraries and inspectors available.

- *Chapter 5*: Next, you're shown how to access the invaluable help resources that are built right in to Xcode and also how to make the most of its intelligent code completion feature.

- *Chapter 6*: Building on Chapter 4, you will be shown the new Auto Layout system introduced in Xcode 5, and how Xcode makes it simple to support the iPhone 5's larger display and how to constrain elements so they display perfectly on many iOS devices.

Part 2: Diving Deeper

- *Chapter 7*: This chapter shows you how to make use of a key feature for rapid development in Xcode, Storyboards, and how it can add a certain degree of logic to how you display and push views in your application.

- *Chapter 8*: This chapter explains how Xcode makes it easy to populate and create table and collection views with the addition of how to customize their appearance and functionality.

- *Chapter 9*: Here you'll learn how to add features to your application by adding frameworks and libraries. You'll also learn how to create a different version of your application in the same project with targets.

■ *Chapter 10*: This chapter will show you how to add your own personal touches to Xcode in terms of editing code. In particular, the code editor will be the focus of this chapter, and you'll be guided on how to work more productively and how to customize its appearance and behavior to suit your tastes and requirements.

■ *Chapter 11*: This chapter presents the idea of making your application run more efficiently and faster. This is done by looking at the range of different tools and methods included within Xcode, for example, breakpoints, and stepping through your code systematically.

Part 3: Final Preparations and Releasing

■ *Chapter 12*: Here you'll learn how you can protect your code and work effectively as a team by using Git, Xcode's integrated version control software.

■ *Chapter 13*: This chapter examines the idea of localization and how to use Xcode to accurately support multiple languages in your app.

■ *Chapter 14*: This chapter looks at the Organizer, what it's for, how to navigate around in it, and how to keep your developer assets in good standing order.

■ *Chapter 15*: To conclude, you'll make final touches on the application, build it for release, and then share it either as an IPA file or via the App Store using either Application Loader or the Organizer.

Getting and Installing Xcode

Before you can download Xcode, there are a couple of things you need to do. First, you'll need an iTunes account (or an Apple ID) that allows you to download content from the Mac App Store, and then you're good to go. If you do not have an Apple ID, you can sign up for one at no cost at `http://appleid.apple.com`. This book is written for Xcode 5, and to run it you'll also need a Mac that's running the latest version of OS X or at least OS X 10.8.4; however, if you have an older version of OS X with an older version of Xcode, many of the lessons here will still apply.

Once you're equipped with an Apple ID and a Mac running OS X 10.8.4+, you can actually begin downloading Xcode. As with many other Mac apps, you simply download it from the Mac App Store at no additional cost. Open the App Store on your Mac and select Categories from the top bar of the window and then click the Developer Tools category. Usually, you'll be able to find Xcode right away, either at the top of the window or in the sidebar on the right displaying the top free apps. Alternatively, you can use the Search bar in the top right and enter "xcode". Xcode's icon is an apt hammer over an "A" blueprint, as shown in Figure 1-1.

Figure 1-1. Xcode within the Mac App Store

Note If you don't have access to the latest version of OS X or are running an older version that isn't supported, you can download previous versions of Xcode from the iOS Dev Center, but for this you'll need to have a registered Apple developer account. This is all explained later. However, this book covers the latest version of Xcode (which is 5.0 at the time of writing).

Select the icon and you'll be taken to Xcode's App Store page. Here, you can view all the features of Xcode along with the latest additions to the current version of Xcode (at the time of writing, this is 5.0) and also preview some screenshots of Xcode. To download Xcode, just click the gray Free button, enter your Apple ID e-mail address and password, and your download will then commence. Xcode is about 1.5GB, so you can go and make some coffee while you wait for the download to finish, as shown in Figure 1-2.

Figure 1-2. Xcode's page within the Mac App Store—ready to be downloaded

With Xcode downloaded, open it from your Applications folder and you'll be prompted to install some additional packages, chick Install and enter your user password. This installation should take a matter of seconds, as shown in Figure 1-3.

Figure 1-3. *The installation of additional tools required by Xcode*

Firing Up Xcode

Once you've successfully downloaded and installed the additional components, you can now begin using Xcode. In Chapter 2, you'll actually create your first project and become familiar with the basic areas of Xcode, but for now, just make sure that everything is in good order so you don't encounter any problems later on.

When you first launch Xcode, you're presented with a Welcome splash screen, and from here you can create a new project, connect to an external repository, open documentation, visit Apple's developer portal, and also browse a list of your recent projects. For some, this screen will cause irritation, and you can prevent it from appearing each time you open Xcode by simply checking or unchecking the Show this window when Xcode launches box, as shown in Figure 1-4.

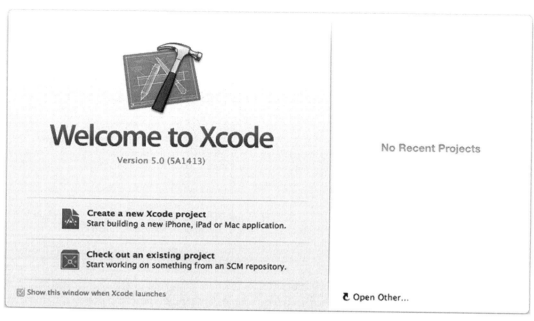

Figure 1-4. Xcode's Welcome window that's displayed optionally each time you open Xcode

To create a new project, you can simply click the Create a new Xcode project button on the Welcome screen or you can navigate to File ➤ New ➤ Project where you'll be presented with a range of templates provided by default by Xcode.

If you have gotten to this point, it's safe to assume you've successfully installed Xcode correctly and that you're ready to start creating projects. However, I'll save this for a deeper explanation in Chapter 2 and for now look at the variety of resources provided to developers by Apple.

Apple's Resources for Developers

At this point, you now have Xcode downloaded to your machine and you've fired it up to make sure it runs. If there's one thing that makes Apple stand out from its competitors it's the wealth of knowledge, resources, and tools that are made just for developers. There are thousands of documents, thousands of samples to download, and dozens upon dozens of videos you can watch. Currently, you have Xcode installed, but that alone isn't going to make you a great developer of iOS and OS X applications. You also need to make use of the vast library provided by Apple. To gain access to Apple's resources, I urge you to sign up as a registered Apple developer. To do this, all you need is an Apple ID, and you can create a new one or use the same ID you used to download content from iTunes or the App Store.

First, head over to http://developer.apple.com. This is the central web site for Apple developers. On the home page of the site, click iOS Dev Center. The iOS Dev Center is the central location for all the resources provided to those who create iPhone, iPad, and iPod touch applications, as shown in Figure 1-5.

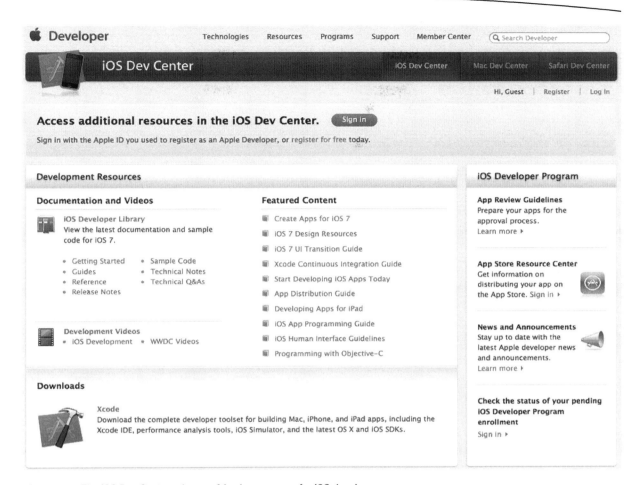

Figure 1-5. *The iOS Dev Center—home of Apple resources for iOS developers*

You aren't required to sign up in order to gain access to many of the resources including the Developer Library, an overwhelming wealth of example source code, release notes, and many more things. You can happily browse through the iOS Dev Center right now without having to sign up.

However, there are great advantages to signing up as a registered Apple developer, and it will become essential at some point if you're planning on distributing applications via the App Store. Therefore, it's a good idea to sign up right from the start. To begin the process of signing up, simply click the Register for free text just below the Log in button; alternatively, you can visit http://developer.apple.com/programs/register/. In order to sign up, you'll need to have a valid Apple ID; if you don't have one or would like to dedicate an Apple ID to your developer account, create a new one (don't worry, none of your purchases or downloaded content from the App Store or iTunes Store will be affected if you use your current one).

Once you're happy with your Apple ID, go to the link above and sign up for an account. In order to complete the process of signing up, you'll need to create a personal and professional profile; don't worry, you can change these at any time if you need to.

Next, you're required to complete your professional profile by telling Apple any previous platforms you've developed for along with your primary markets and experience with Apple's platforms. This information is used by Apple simply to get an idea of the spectrum of people who are signing up as developers. Again, once you have completed this, simply click the Next button. Also, it's important to note that what you select when updating your professional profile doesn't bind you to anything, and that you are able to develop and release applications to any of the App Store's markets. Furthermore, you can, if needed, make any amendments to your professional profile (and personal profile, for that matter) after you've signed up, as shown in Figure 1-6.

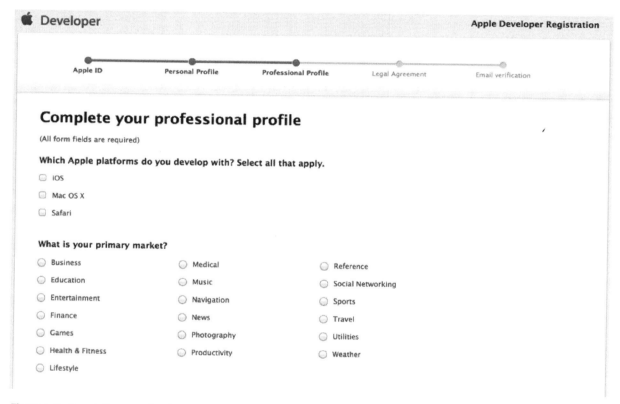

Figure 1-6. Completing your developer professional profile

Finally, you will come to the tiresome agreement that comes with many of Apple's products; simply read, click to agree, and then continue with the process. To finish, all you need to do is verify that the e-mail address supplied is valid; you do this by opening the e-mail sent to you by Apple and entering the verification code contained within.

The Dev Center

As mentioned previously, Apple really does like to take care of its developers. As a developer, your first port of call is the Developer Library, as this houses most of the resources provided by Apple. If you select the iOS Developer Library link under Documentation and Videos, you're taken to an invaluable section of Apple's developer web site. The Developer Library is a rather simple and straightforward site: simply use the links on the left-hand side to navigate around and to filter the results, either search for specific keywords or sort the results using one of the column titles, as shown in Figure 1-7.

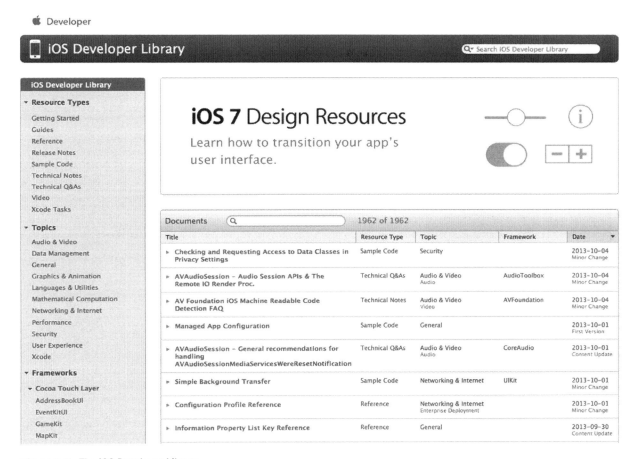

Figure 1-7. *The iOS Developer Library*

Aside from the iOS Developer Library, you also have access to an array of getting started videos that explain core Objective-C and Cocoa Touch concepts. You're also given access to a direct link to the latest version of Xcode on the Mac App Store and the ability to download previous versions of Xcode if you're not running the latest version of OS X or would like to target older versions of iOS.

Your Developer Account

Currently, your level of membership is that of a free account, meaning you have access to a staggeringly vast amount of resources but not to all the resources you need if you're planning to release applications to the App Store. Although this isn't necessary at this point, it's a good idea to sign up as a paid developer as this gives you access to the Apple developer forums, prerelease versions of iOS before they're available to the public, prerelease versions of Xcode, the ability to test your applications on your iOS devices, and, of course, the ability to submit applications to the iOS App Store. The cost of signing up at the time of the writing of this book is $99 per year, and it is required for some of the concepts presented toward the end of the book.

As mentioned previously, it isn't necessary to sign up this instant, but it is recommended that you do so at some point. To sign up for a paid account, visit `https://developer.apple.com/programs/ios/` and click the Enroll Now button. You'll then be guided through the process of signing up; it's rather straightforward if you follow the steps on screen, as shown in Figure 1-8.

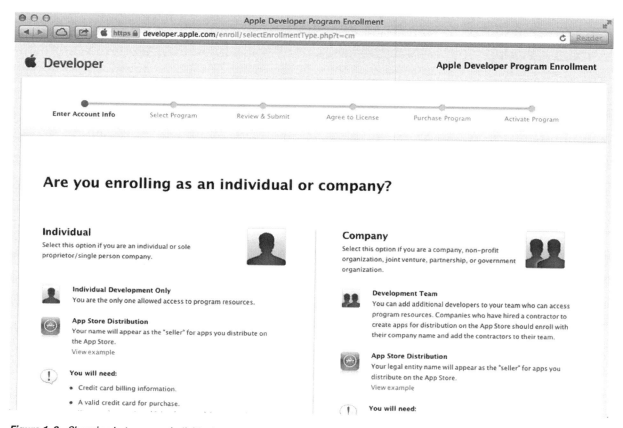

Figure 1-8. Choosing between an individual or a company developer account

It's useful to note that when you're prompted to choose between an individual or company account, if you are planning to operate under a name other than your own, you will have to register as an official company (this will be verified by Apple) and then acquire what's called a DUNS (Data Universal Numbering System) number, which uniquely identifies your company; this takes around 7 days to process, so plan ahead. If selling applications under your own name suffices, then go for the simpler option of signing up as an individual; both accounts are essentially equal in terms of the resources you're able to access. It mainly determines the name with which you'll operate under on the App Store.

Again, this can be done at a later date, but it's essential if you're planning on releasing any applications on the App Store (free or paid) or even if you'd like to test your apps on an actual iOS device. Toward the end of this book, we will look at using Provisioning Profiles and deployment onto actual iOS devices as opposed to the virtual iOS Simulator, so you will then need access to a paid developer account.

Additional Resources

Apart from Apple's own resources, there's an extensive amount of third-party resources available and on hand if you ever have a burning question or get stuck somewhere.

Forums: Forums are a great way to ask questions, learn from other people's questions, and also to help other people. In particular Stack Overflow (`http://stackovervlow.com/`) has been invaluable to the entire developer spectrum for years and has a vibrant active collection of iOS developers. There are also the Apple developer forums, which are available to those with a paid Apple developer account.

Mailing lists: There's a handy Xcode users mailing list that I'd recommend you subscribe to and periodically check over. Many other developers, including myself, participate in answering questions relating to Xcode. You can subscribe at `https://lists.apple.com/mailman/listinfo/xcode-users`.

The Xcode User's Guide: Apple provides a handy user's guide that's always being updated to accompany the latest release of Xcode, so it's a good idea to refer to it when there's a new update or if you'd like to follow up on something. It is available at `http://developer.apple.com/library/ios/#documentation/ToolsLanguages/ Conceptual/Xcode4UserGuide/000-About_Xcode/about.html`. Similarly, it's also handy to glance over the latest release notes when an Xcode is updated. This is available at `http://developer.apple.com/library/ios/#releasenotes/DeveloperTools/RN- Xcode/_index.html`.

Search engines: It's easy to underestimate the power of a simple Google search (and it's apparent many people on online forums don't have access to them), and it can save a lot of time as someone, somewhere, at some point will have undoubtedly had the same question you do, all you need to do is find where they asked it!

Videos: If you type Xcode into iTunes U search, there are a couple of good university courses that not only focus on Xcode but also iOS development in general. Similarly, type Xcode into YouTube search and you'll be amazed at what you can learn from the short screencasts that have been uploaded.

Summary

In this chapter, you have:

- Successfully downloaded and installed Xcode

- Had a look around the iOS Dev Center and also looked at the resources provided by Apple to aid developers

- Signed up and registered as an Apple developer and are aware of the option of signing up for a paid developer account

Chapter 2 will explain how to actually create your first project and help you become more familiar with Xcode's interface and the basic concepts.

Diving Right In

In Chapter 1, you downloaded Xcode, made sure it was correctly configured, and you also signed up for a developer account and explored the wealth of resources provided by Apple to help you get started with not only Xcode but also some of its fantastic new technologies. This chapter will actually explain how to create a working application using Xcode's visual interface building tool, aptly named Interface Builder, and its built-in code editor and then run it on your machine.

As mentioned, as you progress through this book, the ultimate goal is not only to get a grip on the latest and greatest version of Xcode but also, by the end of the book, to have a fully featured application that you will systematically build as you progress through the chapters. The application that you will build in this chapter will give you a flavor of what it feels like to develop with Xcode and won't be part of our final app; you will begin that in Chapter 3. For now you will develop a very simple application that has a custom background color and a label and also programmatically update the text in the label.

You should also be forewarned that in this chapter, a lot of the concepts will be new and therefore require a little more explanation to do them total justice. As a result, you'll notice that on several occasions you're told that you'll revisit many of the concepts presented in later chapters. This is because the main goal of this chapter isn't to turn you into an Xcode pro, but rather to get you started and give you the confidence to believe that Xcode really isn't as overwhelming as it may first appear. In Figure 2-1, you get a glimpse of the very simple application; although simple, it will make you at least a little familiar with the workings of Xcode.

Figure 2-1. *The application that will be created as in this chapter*

Creating Your First Xcode Project

First, you need to bring this project into existence. To do this, click Create a new Xcode project from the Welcome Screen or go to File ➤ New ➤ Project … (⌘+ Shift + N) and you'll be presented with a new window asking what kind of project you'd like to create. Apple provides, by default, a variety of different project templates for both OS X and iOS, each of which is useful for different types of projects. Chapter 3 will cover each of them in more detail, but because you're creating a basic one-view application, it seems appropriate to choose Single View Application, which can be found within the Application category underneath iOS on the left-hand side of the dialog. Once you've selected the Single View Application project template, click the Next arrow in the bottom right-hand corner. Figure 2-2 illustrates the template screen.

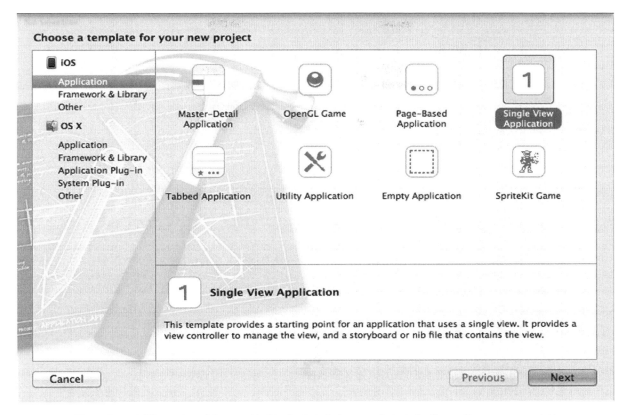

Figure 2-2. The variety of different templates provided by Apple to help you get started with creating your app quickly

With your project template selected, you need to specify a couple of different things before you can actually get started. Once you select your project template, a screen identical to that of Figure 2-3 will be displayed. Below is a brief overview of each of the values required to proceed, but bear in mind, more information on them will be provided later in this book:

- *Product Name*: The product name is essentially what you would like to call your application, for example, if you wanted to create an application called Chocolate Recipes, you'd specify the Product Name to be something along the line of ChocolateRecipes. Although not required, it's generally good practice to omit any spaces and instead capitalize each new word. The Product Name can be amended during the development of your application, so you're not obliged to stick with what you specify, but regardless, the Product Name is a rather important detail that you're required to specify at this stage.

- *Organization Name*: Whether you're working independently or you're part of a software development company, you are required to specify an Organization Name. For now, your own name is perfectly adequate, but if you're looking to submit an application to the App Store, it would be in your best interests to specify the correct name; although not required, it is recommended. Furthermore, when you create a new file, your Organization Name will automatically appear along with copyright details at the top; something to bear in mind if you plan on working in a team or handing your project off to someone else.

■ *Company Identifier*: This, like the Bundle Identifier, is only really required if you're planning on distributing your application in some capacity. For example, to distribute an app via the App Store, you're required to specify an App ID along with a Bundle Identifier, which is created by Xcode depending on what you input as your Company Identifier. The company identifier is written in the style of reverse domain name notation; my web site, for example, is `mattknott.com`, so my Company Identifier is com.mattknott.

■ *Bundle Identifier*: You cannot edit this here, but its value depends on the Company Identifier, in order to avoid confusion (I won't focus on this too much right now).

■ *Class Prefix*: A Class Prefix is something that is added to the start of every file you add to your project along with classes you create. This is a great idea if you're creating your own class library, something you'll look at later on in this book. For example, if I were to input my initials as the class prefix (MK), then every file I create via Xcode would have MK at the start, more specifically, if I were to create a UIViewController subclass, it would have MK at the start: MKViewController.xib.

■ *Devices*: Possibly the most simple part of getting up and running with your project is specifying what device you'd like your application to run on. You have three choices: iPhone, iPad, or Universal. The iPhone and iPad choices are self-explanatory, however, a Universal application is one that would be compatible with both the iPhone (and iPod touch) and iPad.

If you are using an older version of Xcode, you may see some additional options at this stage. In Xcode 5, Apple decided that using these features should be best practice, so for the majority of their project templates, it includes them by default. Even though you may not see these options, let's take a look at what they do.

■ *Use Storyboards*: Storyboards were introduced to Xcode along with iOS 5 and they allow you to systematically lay out your application in terms of how the user would navigate around it. I will touch on Storyboards in this chapter, but Chapter 7 focuses in greater depth on how to use Storyboards.

■ *Use Automatic Reference Counting*: As with Storyboards, Automatic Reference Counting (sometimes referred to as ARC) is a relatively new feature for Xcode. Apple introduced ARC to automate memory management, automatically disposing of controls and objects when they're no longer needed by the view. This can cause some problems when using older third-party libraries that haven't been optimized for ARC.

■ *Include Unit Tests*: Unit testing is when individual parts of source code are tested to determine if they are fit for use. Again, Apple includes this functionality by default in all Xcode 5 projects.

Now that you vaguely know what each of these values are for and what they correspond to, you are probably wondering what exactly you should input to create this project. As shown in Figure 2-3: you will specify HelloWorld as the Product Name; input your own first and last name as your Organization Name; use com.LASTNAME as your Company Identifier (obviously change LASTNAME to your actual last name), keep the Class Prefix value empty for now; and, finally, specify iPhone as the device.

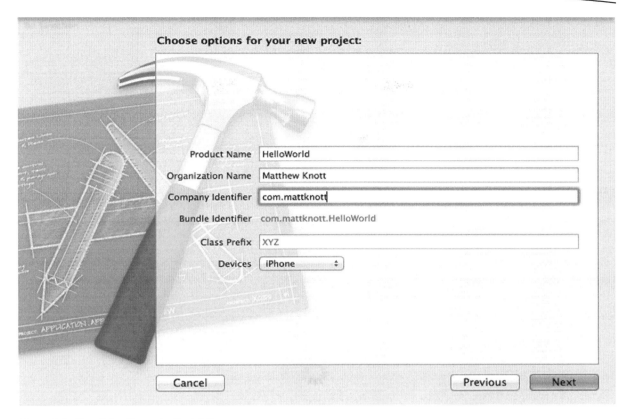

Figure 2-3. Specifying the project's details

Once you've made sure all of your values are correct, click Next and you're required to save your project to disk. When prompted to, use the familiar OS X dialog to find a location and make sure the box for Create local git repository for this project is unchecked; then click Create.

> **Note**   Git is a popular system used for version control and source code management. You can integrate a local Git repository with a web site such as GitHub or Bitbucket if you want to back up or share your code online, but if none of these things are familiar to you, Chapter 12 will explain everything.

So far you've given Xcode all the relevant details and specified what kind of project you're looking to create. As a result, Xcode has conveniently created an application for you and this is your starting point. Xcode has produced a flawless, full application that you can run right now if you like. Go to Product ➤ Run and you'll find your application builds successfully and the iOS Simulator pops up with your application running, as shown in Figure 2-4. Granted it's nothing spectacular nor will it be reaching the top 25 of the App Store anytime soon, but nonetheless, it's still an application created by Xcode itself. Return back to Xcode and click the Stop button in the top left corner.

Figure 2-4. The initial application created by Xcode

Tip   With the high resolution of modern iOS devices, unless you have a top-of-the-range Mac, it's possible that the simulator is too large for your computer screen. If this is the case, then with the simulator selected, go to Window ➤ Scale ➤ 50% or use the key shortcut ⌘ + 3. The scale menu also gives you the option to go to 100% of 75% scale using ⌘ + 1 and ⌘ + 2, respectively.

The Project

In order to make the app a little more interesting than a simple white screen, you need to actually open up some files that have been created by Xcode. As with previous versions of Xcode, the way in which Xcode organizes your project's file is somewhat strange. Upon returning back to Xcode, if you were to look to the left of the interface, you should be able to see what would appear to be an arrangement of folders and files. These are the files that make up your project (Figure 2-5). This part of Xcode is called the Project Navigator. If you're unable to find this, go to View ➤ Navigators ➤ Show

Project Navigator (⌘+ 1). It's important to note that when you create a folder in the Project Navigator, it does not correspond to the structure in which the files are saved within the Finder. Folders and the organization of the Project Navigator are purely to help you locate different files within Xcode. If you create a folder within the Navigator, you'll find that the same folder isn't present within your project when browsed within Finder. I'll revisit this when you add a file to your project later in this chapter.

Figure 2-5. The Project Navigator

With that in mind, select Main.storyboard from the Project Navigator and Xcode will open its built-in graphical user interface design tool, usually referred to as Interface Builder. As Xcode 4.0 was a major overhaul of Apple's developer tools, Interface Builder, which was previously a separate application, was conveniently integrated into Xcode, making it easy to switch between the built-in code editor and interface design tool all within one application, as shown in Figure 2-6. One warning though that is probably worth mentioning, the more you become familiar with Xcode, the more you'll pine for a larger screen!

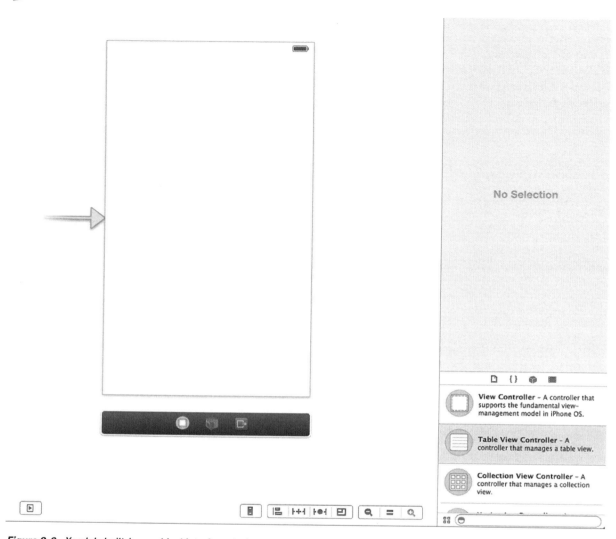

Figure 2-6. Xcode's built-in graphical interface designer

Designing the Interface

As noted previously, the app's interface is neither exceptional nor revolutionary, and here you'll be creating something very simple. However, the basics presented here will be echoed later in the book in much more detail. To begin with, let's look at the Attributes Inspector. You'll can find this by selecting the fourth tab in the sidebar on the right-hand side of Xcode's interface, alternatively you can go to View ➤ Utilities ➤ Show Attributes Inspector (⌘ + ⌥ + 4). The Attributes Inspector will play an important role when it comes to layout and fine tuning interface elements. First, you'll simply change the background color of the application, making sure the view is selected by clicking the white area with an arrow pointing to it (Figure 2-6), under the View heading of the Attributes Inspector, select the color picking option for the background and then use OS X's default color picker to choose a background color, as shown in Figure 2-7. In this example, I've used the RGB sliders and chosen a background of Red: 88, Green: 98, and Blue: 255, although you're free to choose whichever colors you wish.

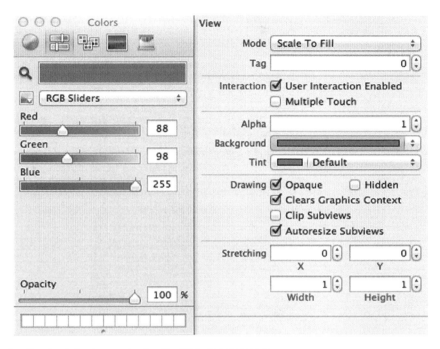

Figure 2-7. *Changing the view's background using the Attributes Inspector*

Next you'll add a label to your view. To do this, you'll need to open the Object Library (shown in Figure 2-8) and drag a label object to your view. Generally, the Object Library is right below the Attributes Inspector and accessible by selecting the third tab, however, you can access it via View ➤ Utilities ➤ Show Object Library (^ + ⌘ + ⌥ + 3). With the library open, use the small search bar and search for "label." Once you've found the label object, drag it to your interface, at the top of the view.

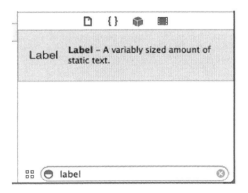

Figure 2-8. *The Object Library*

When you drag the label to your view, you'll notice that Xcode helps you align the label. I've aligned it to the top and expanded it so that it spans the whole width of the view (shown in Figure 2-9) and then used the text alignment properties within the Attributes Inspector to *Center* the text and also changed the font to Avenir and the color to white, as shown in Figure 2-10.

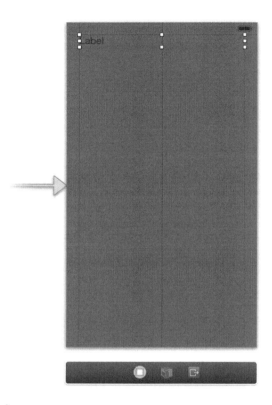

Figure 2-9. *Xcode's autoaligning feature*

Figure 2-10. *The Attributes Inspector's font property*

At this stage, you can use the Attributes Inspector to actually specify the text that will be displayed within the label; however, Xcode isn't just about creating graphical interfaces. It also houses a very powerful code editor, so as you progress in this chapter, you'll actually update the contents of your label programmatically as opposed to graphically.

Making Connections

Before you leave Interface Builder and move on to focus on Xcode's code editor, let's look at a powerful feature that allows you to use both simultaneously. Open the Assistant Editor by selecting the shirt and bowtie icon in the top-right corner of Xcode, as shown in Figure 2-11, or by selecting View ➤ Assistant Editor ➤ Show Assistant Editor (⌘ + ⌥ + Return).

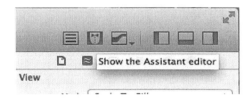

Figure 2-11. The button to select the Assistant Editor looks like a shirt with a bowtie

This will split your screen, with Interface Builder occupying the left frame and the code editor occupying the right, unless you have customized this appearance, which is something I will show you later in the book. Before you continue, you'll need to make sure Xcode has opened the correct file. You want to open `ViewController.h` (the header file), but you may find that in the tabs directly above the code, it says `ViewController.m` (the implementation file). To correct this, select `ViewController.m` to show a list of options and then choose `ViewController.h`, as shown in Figure 2-12.

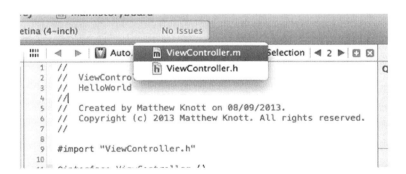

Figure 2-12. Selecting the right file in the Assistant Editor

Once you have loaded the header file, `ViewController.h`, in the Interface Builder window, click the label you added to highlight it. Now, you're going to create an IBOutlet property for this label. In older versions of Xcode, the process of creating an outlet and then wiring it into Interface Builder was quite long-winded, but Apple has simplified this greatly over the past few versions of Xcode by allowing us to drag connections directly from Interface Builder into the code.

Holding down the Control key, click the label and drag a connection over to the header file, positioning the cursor and releasing the click just below the line `@interface ViewController : UIViewController`, as shown in Figure 2-13.

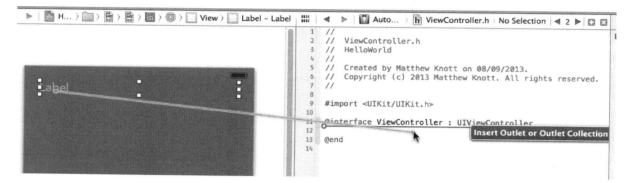

Figure 2-13. *Creating an outlet using the Assistant Editor*

When you release the click, a connection dialog will appear, asking for a number of values, as shown in Figure 2-14. The two key options you need to be aware of here are the Connection drop-down list and the Name text field. The Connection list has two options: Outlet and Outlet Collection for a label, but for an object that can be interacted with such as a button, there will be an option called Action.

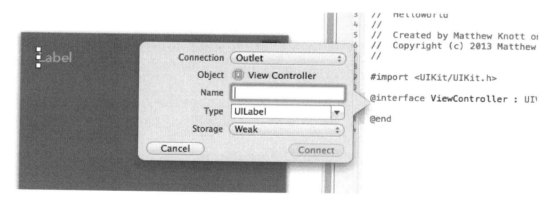

Figure 2-14. *Creating an outlet for your label*

I've already stated that you will want to create an outlet, so the default option for Connection is correct. The Name text field value will determine how you refer to your label in code, so for now, type in `lblOutput` and click Connect.

If everything's gone according to plan, you show now see the following code:

```
@interface ViewController : UIViewController

@property (weak, nonatomic) IBOutlet UILabel *lblOutput;

@end
```

You're finished with the Assistant Editor for now, so let's switch back to the Standard Editor by selecting the icon from the toolbar with three lines in a box to the left of the Assistant Editor icon (Figure 2-11).

You've finished with Interface Builder for this project, so now you'll need to look at writing some code to manipulate your label. Go to the Project Navigator and select ViewController.m, which will open the View Controller's implementation file in the code editor, as shown in Figure 2-15. Within this chapter, I'll touch upon many of the areas and concepts that I'll explain throughout the book; but at this point you are going to start using Xcode's powerful code editor and see some of the intuitive features that make Xcode one of the best IDEs ever made.

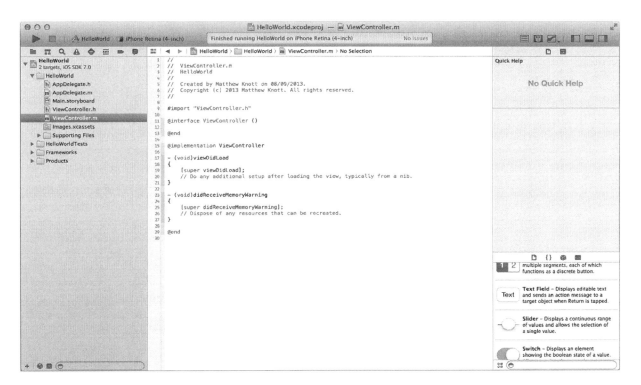

Figure 2-15. Xcode's built in code editor with our ViewController.m file open

With the implementation file open, you'll notice that it has a number of lines of code by default. This boilerplate code gives the application a starting point you can build on.

Within the code of the implementation file, look for a line that starts with - (void)viewDidLoad, this is the start of the viewDidLoad method. To complete the very simple code for this application, you need to tell the View Controller that when the view loads it should set the label's text to Bonjour!. Add the highlighted code into the viewDidLoad method as shown:

```
- (void)viewDidLoad
{
    [super viewDidLoad];
        // Do any additional setup after loading the view, typically from a nib.
    _lblOutput.text = @"Bonjour!";
}
```

Here, you can see Xcode's powerful code completion feature in action, which is able to assist you in writing code much more efficiently. As you type _lbl you'll see a pop-up appear that says UILabel *_weak _lblOutput; when this is highlighted, press the Tab or Return key, which will complete the word _lblOutput for you. Next type .te and again Xcode's code completion will snap into action and show a number of options, but the first one in the list is the one you want: NSString * text. With that item selected, press the Return key and continue typing the code. You can easily see from this example how Xcode's code completion helps you become a really efficient programmer, as well as helps you cut down on errors.

To recap, what you've done here is to declare a property which is linked to the UILabel you added to the view in Interface Builder using the Assistant Editor. You then added a single line of code to the viewDidLoad method to set the text of the label programmatically—well done!

Running and Testing

It's hard to stress just how important it is to test your application thoroughly before even thinking about submitting it to the App Store. There are many reasons for this. First, the App Store review process is very thorough, that is, if your app isn't up to par, Apple isn't afraid to let you know in the form of a rejection. So testing means that not only do you reduce your chances of being rejected by Apple, but also when you submit your app, if you're rejected, you'll have to make the amendments and then resubmit your application, all of which is time consuming—time that could otherwise have been used to sell your app. Second, when someone downloads your application, they're parting with their money and expect a certain standard. So when they purchase and download an app, it's would be very disappointing to find that it's slow and hard to use. Finally, it makes you a better developer, that is, by smoothing out the creases in your applications now and building good habits, you carry these on and they become second nature, so testing can seriously save a lot of time when working on larger, more demanding projects.

Now that you have your application ready to be run, the quickest way to check if it will build successfully without crashing is to go to Product ➤ Build (⌘ + B). If everything's in order, then you should see a small dialog stating the build has completed successfully. It's now time to run your application; similarly go to Product ➤ Run (⌘ + R), and Xcode will build and then run the application using the target specified, which is, by default at this stage, the iOS Simulator.

Once the build has completed, your application will open in an application that accompanies Xcode, iOS Simulator. The iOS Simulator is invaluable when you need to test your application quickly or to test a feature that you've recently implemented. However, it's important to note that testing your app using the iOS Simulator is not the same as testing your applications on an iOS device, that is, an actual iPhone/iPod Touch or an iPad. This is because applications may not perform the same on a device as they do on iOS Simulator because the simulator does not simulate all software and hardware functionality. To change the type of device you'd like your application to be tested on via the iOS Simulator, go back to Xcode and click the Stop button in the top left-hand corner. With the application now not running, go back to the iOS Simulator and choose Hardware ➤ Device and then choose from the list of devices available. Figure 2-16 shows both a device with a 4-inch screen, such as the iPhone 5, and a device with a 3.5-inch screen, such as the iPhone 4S.

Figure 2-16. *The iOS Simulator running the app on a 4-inch screen (left) and a 3.5-inch screen (right)*

Additionally, within the iOS Simulator you can also change the orientation of the device, the scale in which the device displays, and a whole array of other options covered later in this book. What's recommended now is that you browse through the menus of the iOS Simulator while your app is running and play around with the different options to at least get slightly familiar with the different features.

Adding Files

One final thing that's worth mentioning at this early stage is how to actually add your own files to your project. Applications are literally made up of hundreds upon hundreds of files, ranging from images to sounds, so what you'll do finally is add some images to your application. First, let's change the app's icon without writing any code, and then add an image to the main view.

Before you add an icon file, you're going to have to create one or you can download the source code for this book from the Apress web site and use the included files. Because this isn't a book on iOS design, or even iOS development, I won't digress on how to create perfect iOS app icons, instead I'll just state that you'll need to create a PNG file that, in this instance, I'm calling Icon.png with the dimensions of 120 px by 120 px. Include whatever you like as the actual graphic, just make sure it conforms to the above specifications. For our purposes here, simply create the file with a basic gradient with a speech bubble saying Hi! in the middle; that will be used as your icon.

You're going to be working with a feature that's new in Xcode 5, Asset Catalogs. From the Project Navigator, select Images.xcassets. This is where you set the application icon in Xcode 5, not in the project as with the previous version of Xcode. Drag your icon file to the right-hand box labeled iPhone App Icon iOS 7 60pt, as shown in Figure 2-17.

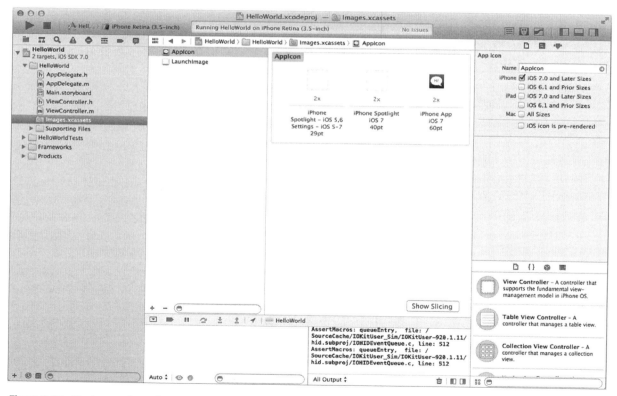

Figure 2-17. The Images Asset Catalog where you set the application icon in Xcode 5

Now let's run the app and see the icon in action. Once the application is running, click the Home button, or Hardware ➤ Home (⌘+ Shift + H). If you've done everything right, you should see something like the image in Figure 2-18.

Figure 2-18. *The application's new icon within the iOS Simulator*

Note   With the new icon formats for iOS 7 applications, the required resolutions for icon changed from what you may have known with iOS 6 and Xcode 4. If your app is going to support older versions of iOS, open the `Images.xcassets` file, highlight the app icon entry, and in the Identity Inspector, mark the box that says iOS 6.1 and Prior Sizes. This will allow you to add two icons of 57 pixels and 114 pixels, respectively.

With the icon successfully set, let's look at another way of adding files to the project. You could expand on your Asset Catalog knowledge for this example, but I'll explain this in more depth later in the book. For now, let's look at the more traditional way of adding files to your project. They say there's more than one way to skin a cat, and the same could be said for Xcode's Add Files dialog. First, you could go to File ➤ Add Files to "HelloWorld"… (⌘ + ⌥ + A), or you could right-click in the Project Navigator area and choose Add Files to "HelloWorld". But the method I would like you to use is to click the plus icon in the bottom left corner of the Project Navigator and then click Add Files to "HelloWorld"…, as shown in Figure 2-19.

Figure 2-19. *The Add Files dialog available from the Project Navigator*

The Add Files dialog will instantly be familiar to any user of OS X; locate your file (I've simply used a photo from my iPhone), select it, and then make sure Copy items into destinations group's folder (if needed) is checked, as shown in Figure 2-20, and then click Add.

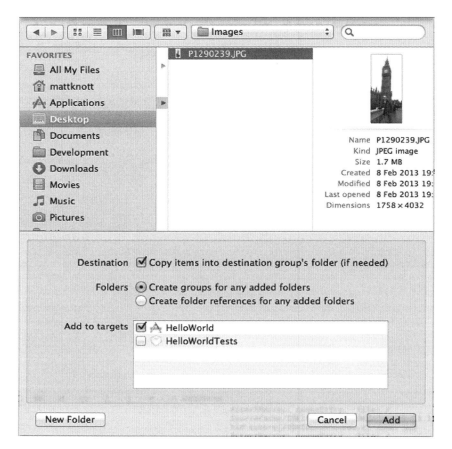

Figure 2-20. The Add Files dialog; note Copy Items into destination ... is checked

At this point you will return to Xcode, and if you look at the Project Navigator, you'll see that your file has been added to the file structure of the project. When I asked you to add the file, I also asked that you ensure that Copy items into destinations group's folder (if needed) was checked. The reason for this is that if you don't check this option, the file will appear in the project structure as it does now, but it isn't copied into the project. Hence, if you were to send the project to someone or to archive it, the image would be omitted.

Before you proceed and make this image appear in your view, let's talk about organizing files. As I mentioned earlier, Xcode gives the illusion of organization, a kind of faux folder structure that in Xcode is actually called Groups. Let's start by moving the file you added to the Supporting Files group by clicking it and dragging it until Supporting Files is highlighted. Now if you look at Figure 2-21, you can see a comparison of the structure of the files within Finder compared to the structure of the files in Xcode.

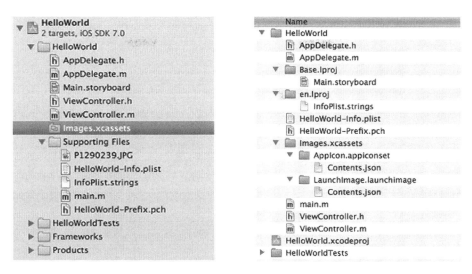

Figure 2-21. The structure of the files in the Project Navigator within Xcode (left) compared to those in Finder (right)

You've done the hard work of adding the file into Xcode, now let's do the fun part—adding the image to the View Controller using the Storyboard. Start by selecting Main.storyboard from the Project Navigator. Now, from the Object Library, select an Image View (UIImageView) control and drag it to your View Controller. If you're having trouble finding it in the list, remember you can filter the list by typing "image" in the search field. Resize the Image View so it fills the entire view controller; your screen should now look something like the image in Figure 2-22.

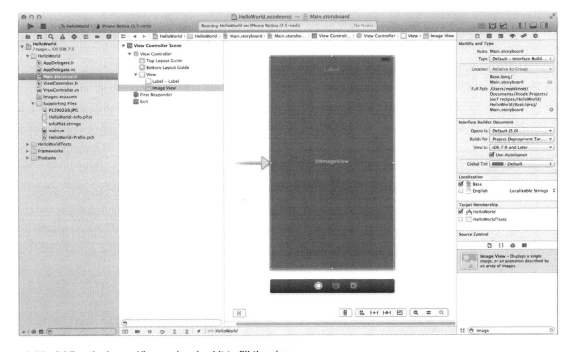

Figure 2-22. Adding the Image View and resized it to fill the view

> **Tip**   Remember, if you can't see the Object Library, you can access it via View ➤ Utilities ➤ Show Object Library (^ + ⌘ + ⌥ + 3).

With the Image View positioned, it's time to tell it which image to use. With the Image View selected, go to the Attributes Inspector on the right and from the Image drop-down, select the file you added. You'll find that the image fills the Image View, but it may have been distorted in doing so. What you want is for the photo to fill the Image View but to maintain its ratio; to achieve this, click the Mode drop-down list and select Aspect Fill. Your image will still fill the Image View, but the ratio is maintained, preserving the original look of the image.

So you're finished, right? Not quite. With the Image View filling all of the available space, you can't see the label you added at the start of the project! This is because of the way these two items are ordered, with the Image View being rendered in a layer above the label. To resolve this, let's look at the Document Outline. If you can't see the Document Outline (the column to the left of the View Controller in Figure 2-21), then click the Show Document Outline button in the bottom left corner of the Storyboard design area.

Expand all of the items in the Document Outline and, beneath View, you should have your Label, followed by the Image View. Now drag the Image View carefully to move it above the Label, as shown in Figure 2-23. Because of the hierarchy of the view, the Image View will now be rendered beneath the label, although you may want to tweak the color of your label to make sure it's visible against the background of your image. Now you're ready to run your app! Figure 2-24 presents the finished product.

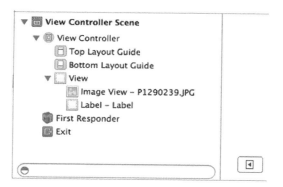

Figure 2-23. *The Document Outline after rearranging the order of the elements within the view*

Figure 2-24. *The finished app*

Summary

You've learned a lot in this chapter, specifically you have:

- Set up a new Xcode project and found that Xcode generates a functioning, yet boring, application.

- Designed an interface using Xcode's built-in graphical interface builder and used the Attributes Inspector to change some basic properties of the objects you added to your view.

- Used the Assistant Editor to visually create connected outlets quickly and efficiently with drag and drop.

- Looked at Xcode's code editor and updated the contents of a UILabel programmatically and also had an introduction to Xcode's code completion tool.

- Built and ran your application within iOS Simulator and looked at some different features of the iOS Simulator.

- Compared and contrasted the basics of the structure of your files within the Project Navigator and the structure of your project within the Finder, along with adding new files to your project, which gave your application an icon without you even having to write any code.

- Added an Image View, or `UIImageView`, to use its correct but less friendly name, to your view controller and set its image in the Attribute Inspector.

- Moved objects in the Document Outline hierarchy.

Essentially, the main purpose of this chapter wasn't to create a ground-breaking application but rather to give you at least a certain degree of comfort when it comes to working with the latest version of Xcode. It's easy to become overwhelmed with the sheer amount of menus, tools, dialogs, and inspectors; however, as you have seen, creating an app isn't too daunting when you know where to look and what to press.

Chapter 3 will introduce you to the different project templates that come with Xcode, and you will set up a new project and get a guided tour of the different array of panels, windows, and menus that come with Xcode along with how to quickly access them.

Project Templates and Getting Around

In Chapter 2 you created a very basic application and then tested it on the iOS Simulator. You were also introduced to the basics of the Project Navigator and looked at two commonly used inspectors: the Attributes and the Connections Inspectors. You also programmatically updated the contents of a label that had been placed onto the view using Interface Builder and then made it show an image file that had been added to the project. In the first half of this chapter, I'm going to take a step back from app creation and instead look at the array of different tabs, inspectors, panels, buttons, and windows that come with Xcode and also take a look at the different project templates provided by Xcode.

In order to be an accomplished app developer, it's important that you become intimately familiar with the key areas of your IDE, and there's a good chance you already knew this, which is why you bought this book. By the end of this chapter you should be a lot more familiar with many of the different interface elements of Xcode and should be able to quickly access a certain feature of Xcode. You'll also be able to choose a project template without having to worry if you've picked the right one and will have some of the key knowledge required to start creating your own applications.

In the second half of this chapter, you'll look at how to create a working multi-view application from nothing (almost nothing) without using Storyboards as you did in Chapter 2. You'll also discover how to pass information from one view to another and display that information in the ShowMe application. Although this is going to be quite involved, it will give you a better understanding of how View Controllers can share information, but later on in the book when I'll explain Storyboards in detail, you will see how much easier they can make the development process.

Without further ado, let's get started!

Project Templates

As a developer, you have the somewhat daunting task of making many, many decisions throughout the development of your application, and, with iOS and OS X apps, arguably, the first decision you need to make is choosing the correct project template in Xcode. At this point, you're optimistic, excited about the adventure ahead, and eager to get straight in there and begin writing your application, but not so fast! Choosing the right project template can have a huge impact on the direction your application takes, and that's why I'm going to go through each of them and explain in which cases you should choose a project template provided by Xcode. It's worth mentioning here that, with the main focus of this book being iOS development, I won't go into detail about the OS X templates and instead will focus more on the ones targeted at iOS application development.

To begin, you're going to need to fire up Xcode if you haven't done so already, and either choose Create a new Xcode project from the Welcome screen or go to File ➤ New ➤ Project (⌘ + Shift + N) and you'll be greeted with the screen that presents an array of different project templates to choose from, as illustrated in Figure 3-1.

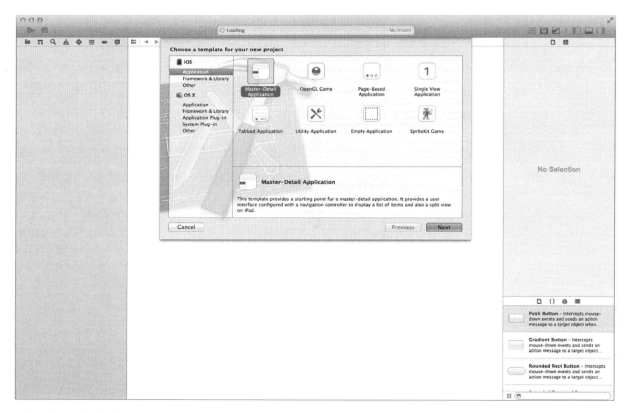

Figure 3-1. Xcode's different project templates

By default, when you first open Xcode and choose a project template, you're given the option to choose only from the ones provided by Apple; however, if you'd like to see what really goes into making an Xcode project and perhaps tinker with one yourself, the default location of Xcode's project template is `/Applications/Xcode.app/Contents/Developer/Platforms/iPhoneOS.platform/Developer/Library/Xcode/Templates/Project Templates` (this is, of course, assuming that you have Xcode located within your /Applications folder). Here, you can open the different project templates provided by Apple and dissect them. However, I recommend that before you do this you back up that folder just in case you change something that corrupts the template.

> **Note**   You'll notice that throughout this book you'll be given the keyboard shortcut equivalent whenever you are to access a menu item, open a window, or show a navigator or inspector. I strongly encourage you to take advantage of keyboard shortcuts because it can drastically improve your workflow and allow you to become a more productive developer, or, at the very least, make you appear to know what you're doing. It can also make even the more tiresome tasks somewhat bearable. What's more, many of the shortcuts that apply to Xcode can also be brought over to other applications, for example, to Finder. You could also visit Xcode's preferences (⌘ + ,) and modify some of the shortcuts if they're not quite to your liking.

Master Detail View

The Master Detail View template is a starting point if you're looking to create an application that presents the user with a UITableView and then pushes a detail view when the user taps a row. By default, Xcode creates a project that, if targeting an iPhone, has one table view that has the ability for the user to add rows when they tap the plus button in the top right corner of the navigation bar. If targeting the iPad, a new row is added to the table view, however, the layout of both the table and detail view fits much more nicely within the iPad's larger display.

Figure 3-2 displays the default project created when you specify Master Detail View as your project template, with it running universally via the iOS Simulator: iPad on the left and iPhone on the right.

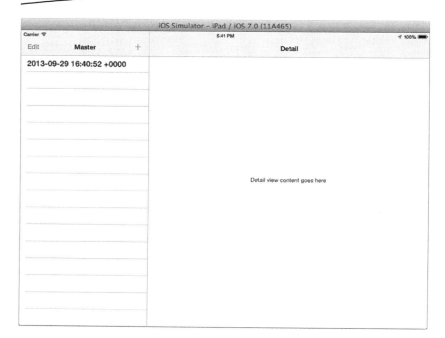

Figure 3-2. *Master detail view template running on both iPad (left) and iPhone (right)*

OpenGL Game

The OpenGL Game template is an excellent choice if you're planning to create a game using Apple's OpenGL ES and GLKit frameworks. As a starting point, Xcode creates a simple application in which two cubes, varying in color, float around the screen, detecting collisions. Furthermore, Xcode also includes two rather unique files default: Shader.fsh and Shader.vsh. Both of these are OpenGL shading language source files. Because using Xcode for game development is out of the scope of focus for this book, I won't go into too much detail.

Figure 3-3 shows the default project created for an OpenGL Game project running on both the iPad (left) and iPhone (right). It's important to note that on both platforms, the cubes are animating and detecting collisions between not only the boundaries of the device's screen but also with each other.

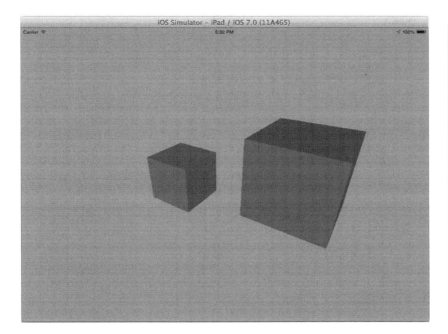

Figure 3-3. *OpenGL Game template running on both iPad (left) and iPhone (right)*

Page-Based Application

Creating an application using the Page-Based template gives users the impression they are actually swiping through the pages of a book. With the Page-Based project, Xcode gives you everything you need to create an application that displays information in a book-like format, that is, it reveals information as the user swipes the screen either left or right. By default, you're provided with UIPageViewControllerDelegate, which specifies the root view controller and initializes the view by loading PageViewModelController.

Figure 3-4 shows the default project created by Xcode when you choose to create a page-based application; on the left, you can see it running on the iPad and, on the right, it is running on the iPhone. If you were to swipe or click the left- or right-most side of the screen, the content will be pulled over as if reading a book.

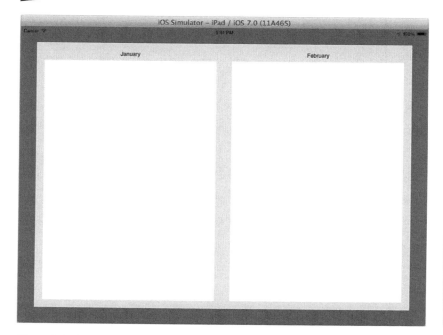

Figure 3-4. *Page-Based template running on both iPad (left) and iPhone (right)*

Single View Application

This is perhaps the most organic project template provided by Xcode and it will inevitably be the starting point for many applications. The Single View project template provides you with a single UIViewController that's loaded when the application runs. It's like a completely blank canvas, in which the application can take any shape you like. This is especially useful if you're creating a custom iOS application, if you aren't sure of the exact approach you're going to take, or if the alternative templates don't seem appropriate for your project.

Figure 3-5 illustrates what you're given by Xcode when you choose this project template and, surprisingly, you're given a blank, white view.

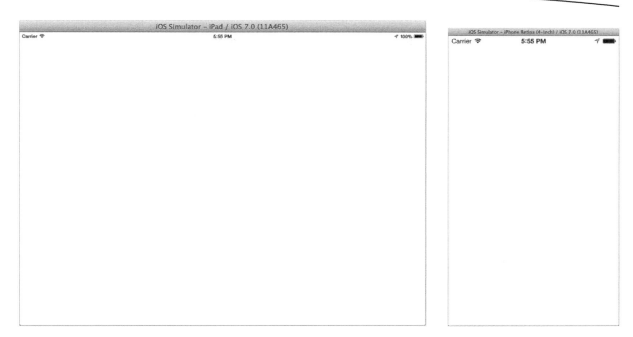

Figure 3-5. Single View template running on both iPad (left) and iPhone (right)

Tabbed Application

Because many applications use tab bars to display different parts of an application, it's no surprise that Apple has created a project template that allows you to quickly implement UIViewControllers within a UITabBarController. By default you're provided with two view controllers, each of which has its own tabs.

Figure 3-6 illustrates a tabbed application. As you can see, the application consists of a tab bar with two tabs, the first loads FirstViewController and the second SecondViewController.

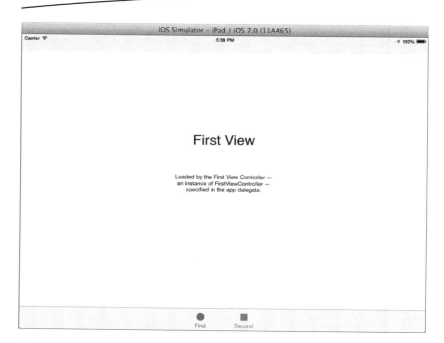

Figure 3-6. *Tabbed template running on both iPad (left) and iPhone (right)*

Utility Application

Next there is the Utility project template. When you choose this project template, you're provided with two view controllers: MainViewController and FlipViewController. The purpose of a Utility application is that it allows the user to flip the first view controller around to reveal additional settings and other information. By default when you run a utility application a gray view in the form of MainViewController is displayed along with a small information button that, when clicked, flips the view around to display whatever is within FlipViewController.

Figure 3-7 illustrates a Utility project-based application running on both an iPad and iPhone.

Figure 3-7. Utility template running on both iPad (left) and iPhone (right)

Empty Application

The penultimate template is the Empty application project template. Technically, if you were to choose this template and run the application right off, you would already encounter a problem. That problem would be that your application doesn't really have anything to load except a window and no root view controller, as generally expected by Xcode. It's easy to mistake the Single View template for the Empty application because, although both are blank, the Single View template is actually displaying a view with a view controller, albeit blank, whereas for the Empty application, as the name suggests, it isn't even displaying a white view—it's displaying nothing, just a window by itself. This template is useful if you'd like to start completely from scratch, if you don't have a clear idea where your application is going or how it will perform, or if you'd prefer to actually work from the ground up and create your application that way. The only thing provided by this template is an application delegate and a window.

Figure 3-8 displays an Empty application, both on the iPad (left) and iPhone (right).

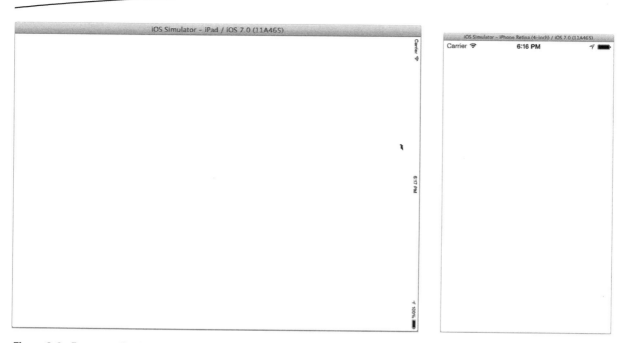

Figure 3-8. *Empty application template running on both iPad (left) and iPhone (right)*

SpriteKit Game

The Sprite Kit framework and its application template were introduced for the first time in Xcode 5. Sprite Kit is Apple's answer to third-party game engines like Cocos2D. It may not have the features of Cocos2D, but its simplicity, coupled with the powerful physics and the animation tools it provides to developers, has made it one of the hottest new frameworks in Xcode 5. In addition to giving you the tools to create your own version of your favorite 2D physics game, you can also use Sprite Kit to add complex animations to your more traditional applications (Figure 3-9).

Figure 3-9. SpriteKit Game application template running on both iPad (left) and iPhone (right)

Template Selection

Now that I've explained each of the eight default project templates provided by Apple, you can start looking at the various panels and panes you will see in Xcode. To help you with this, and for the only time in this book, you'll have a go at developing your own application entirely without the use of Storyboards. As a beginner, this is not entirely unlike taking a tightrope walk without a safety net. Storyboards make the development process much more visual, but from time to time it's good to know how to do things the old-fashioned way. For this project, which is called ShowMe, you'll use the Empty Application template.

As with any other application created using Xcode, you need to start by creating a new project, which should now be second nature to you, but if you've forgotten, it's File ➤ New ➤ New Project… (⌘ + Shift + N) or, alternatively, click Create a new Xcode project from the Welcome screen (⌘ + Shift + 1).

Once you've started the process of creating this app, you need to specify which application template you would like to use and which one would best suit this ShowMe application. In this instance, use the Empty Application template simply because it doesn't really contain anything, and you'll turn that into something useful. Ordinarily, however, when choosing a template, there is a certain thought process you would go through to make sure you start with the right template:

- *How users will navigate around your application:* If you're using a good old UINavigationController as the crux of the application, chances are you'll need a Single View application and then implement a UINavigationController manually; however, if the users will navigate using the UITabBarController, then your best choice, surprisingly, will be Tabbed application.

- *How you'd like your screens to be laid out:* Again, if screens are going to be pushed via a UINavigationController or displayed as a single UIViewController, a Single View application will suffice; however, if you're creating a book or an application in which you'd like the view to flip around to display additional settings, either the Page Based or Utility template, respectively, is your best bet.

- *Whether or not you're creating a game:* If you're creating a game, Apple has provided the OpenGL Game and SpriteKit Game templates, which give you the tools and features for almost any game project, but if they don't go far enough, you can use the Empty Application template and make use of third-party frameworks.

Because for this example I've already decided you're going to select Empty Application from the project templates dialogue, select it and click Next. Now, you're required to provide Xcode with those all-important little details such as the Product Name, Organization Name, and so on. Figure 3-10 illustrates the values to put in (remember to input your own first and last names in the relevant fields though!).

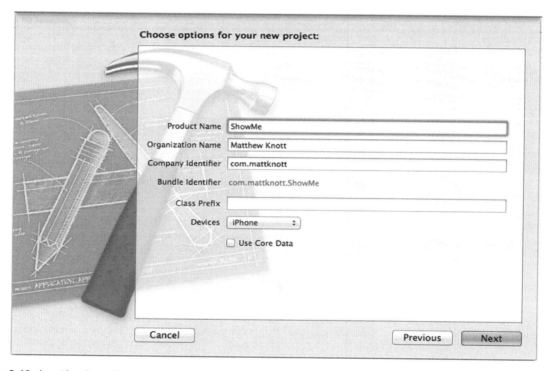

Figure 3-10. Inputting the options to create the application

For the Product Name, let's use ShowMe. For this project, you can specify your own name (that is, your first and last names) as the Organization Name, so in my case this would be Matthew Knott. In this instance, I've again used reverse domain notation and entered com.mattknott, but you could just as easily use com.YOURSURNAME. You won't be using a Class Prefix in this case, so select iPhone as the device you're targeting and uncheck Use Core Data.

To finish, simply click Next and you'll be prompted to choose a location for your project. Save your project somewhere that's easy for you to find and ensure that Create git repository on... is unchecked. Also, make sure Don't add to any project or workspace is selected from the drop-down menu and then click Create. You're now ready to explore the many different areas of Xcode.

Getting Around

Now that you have your application ready and the project set up, it'll be useful to become familiar with the main areas of Xcode's interface, that is the navigators, toolbar, editor, utilities panel, and the debugging area. Essentially, most actions you'll need to perform will be among those main areas of the interface, with the exception of the actions contained within the menu bar. In the next section, I'll focus on each of these sections so that when attention is brought to them later in the book, you'll have an idea where to look and what purpose they serve. In Figure 3-11, you can see a breakdown of the main area of Xcode's interface.

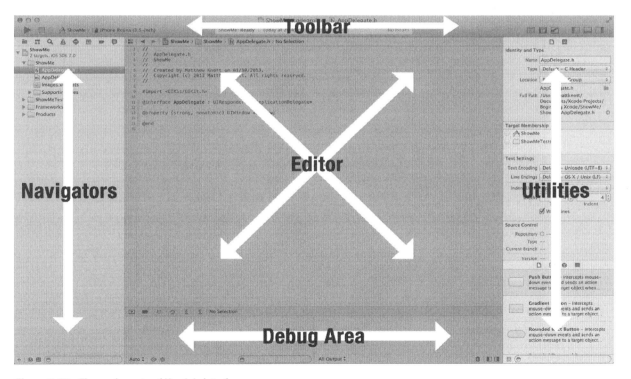

Figure 3-11. *Five main parts of Xcode's interface*

Navigators

The first focus will be on the left-most side of Xcode, the section that houses the navigators. A navigator in Xcode is something that allows you to browse various different things, whether that's files, folders, warnings, build errors, memory leaks, breakpoints, and so on. If you look at the top of the navigator's panel, you'll see that you can toggle the view using eight different tabs, as shown in Figure 3-12.

Figure 3-12. Xcode's different navigators among which you can toggle

The Project Navigator, the first tab, is perhaps one of the most important features of the whole navigator panel. It allows you to explore the files within your project and also displays what makes up your project in terms of frameworks and interface files. As previously mentioned, the file structure of the Project Navigator does not correspond to that of the Finder; things like folders are there just to make it easier for you to navigate around your own project within Xcode.

Next there is the Symbol Navigator, which is where you can browse what is classed by Xcode as a symbol within your project. A symbol is generally the name of a class or a method. If you look at the bar at the bottom of the Symbol Navigator, you can filter what's displayed and you can view Cocoa's built-in symbols or symbols that are defined within your project. The Symbol Navigator is especially useful when you have dozens of header and implementation files and you need to quickly browse them to find a certain class declaration or method.

Third, there is the Search Navigator. The Search Navigator is a very useful means of searching through your project to find a certain bit of code. If you select the small magnifying glass within the search area, you can specify certain search options such as where Xcode should look along with the ability to more accurately define what you're looking for. The Search Navigator is very useful when you need to quickly find something and you have hundreds of different files and thousands of lines of code.

Moving along there is the Issue Navigator. As you develop your application, the Issue Navigator will alert you to any issues with the application by flagging warnings and errors. The Issue Navigator will not only tell you what's wrong but also attempt to accurately pinpoint exactly where the issue lies.

Next you'll find a new tab for Xcode 5, the Test Navigator. This is where your test targets, and its test classes, can be found. From here you manage all of your tests and they're coded in a similar way to how the Project Navigator and the editor work together in that selecting a test will open the relevant code and allow you to write unit tests that ensure individual classes and methods work as they should.

The Debug Navigator, the sixth tab, is used when your code pauses and, by default, will open automatically if a pause is encountered. However, the Debug Navigator will remain dormant otherwise. Equally, the Debug Navigator will appear when a breakpoint is reached in your code. When in use, the Debug Navigator displays call stacks along with the names of nested methods. If you were to click the method name, you would have the ability to navigate through it further. In addition to this there are useful CPU and memory monitors that display the real-time impact of your code. The Debug Navigator should not be confused with the Debug Area of Xcode; I'll cover this area later in this chapter.

Note   A breakpoint essentially tells Xcode when to pause your program, and they are especially useful when you're trying to pin down an issue with your code. To add a breakpoint, open the editor and click the line number in the gray area on the left, just between the navigator pane and the editor, to add a breakpoint.

The Breakpoint Navigator, the seventh tab, is the hub in which you're able to manage your breakpoints. With a project that has dozens of breakpoints, you'll soon become accustomed to using this tab. Within the Breakpoint Navigator, you also have the ability to create different types of breakpoints, for example, symbolic breakpoints.

Finally, there is the Log Navigator. This is like the history option of your Internet browser except instead of recording what you open, it records your actions. Specifically, it lists the status of a build (whether it's failed, succeeded, or succeeded but has errors). To reveal all the details of something like a build, simply click the log item and Xcode will bring up a new dialogue within the editor showing all the necessary details regarding what you've clicked.

Now that you know exactly what each of the eight different tabs correspond to, there must be a quicker way to access them as opposed to having to click them each time. Well, first and foremost, Xcode has the tendency to spontaneously hide some of its interface elements (usually because you've clicked a button mistakenly), so if you ever lose the navigator sidebar, simply go to View ➤ Navigators ➤ Show Project Navigator and this will bring up the Project Navigator. However, to quickly switch between the tabs of the navigator, simply press ⌘ + 1 (for the Project Navigator) or ⌘ + 8 (which will bring up the Log Navigator). Again, it's useful to make use of keyboard shortcuts as they can dramatically increase your productivity, which, to a developer working through the night to get a project complete for the morning, is everything.

Toolbar

Moving on from the Navigators section, there is the Toolbar. The Toolbar is something that is present throughout many familiar OS X applications (e.g., Finder), and it houses many useful buttons and displays important information regarding build results. If you have previously used Xcode 4 or an earlier version, you'll see a number of changes, most notably the size, as the Toolbar has been compressed somewhat in Xcode 5. To tackle the Toolbar, let's examine each of the default buttons starting on the left and moving over to the right. Figure 3-13 displays the default layout of the Toolbar.

Figure 3-13. Xcode's Toolbar's default layout

First, you'll see two buttons to the left, Run and Stop; these are rather self-explanatory at this point, but clicking the Run button will start a build of your project and then launch it using whatever target is specified in the active Scheme, just to the right. In this instance, the scheme is set to ShowMe and iPhone Retina (4-inch 64-bit). Once running, you can stop your project by clicking the Stop button. Additionally, if you click and hold your mouse over the Run button, you'll find that you can choose from Run, Test, Profile, and Analyze. I'll explain exactly what each of these do later in this book, however, by selecting one from the menu, this will take the place of the Run button and will perform the specified action each time you click it.

Next there is the active scheme and device target. This is where you are able to choose a scheme, which specifies how you'd like to run your project. By selecting ShowMe, you're given the option to choose Edit Scheme, New Scheme, or Manage Scheme. A scheme essentially allows you to specify in more detail how you'd like your application to be run or debugged. If you click the iPhone Retina (4-inch 64-bit) section, a drop-down menu will appear allowing you to choose from the different platforms you can test your project on.

Next is the Activity Viewer, which tells you what exactly is happening if Xcode is performing an action. For example, if you choose to clean your project, the Activity Viewer will display the progress of the clean, similarly to when you are building an application. What's also nice about the Activity Viewer is that, if you are running the latest version of Xcode and OS X, it will display the last action performed along with when it was performed. Finally, the Activity Viewer also displays small icons toward the button that let you know quickly the number of issues or errors found within your project.

On the right of the Activity Viewer there are three Editor buttons, which change how the editor within Xcode looks and behaves. You can choose from the Standard, Assistant, or Version editor, respectively. If you click to open your `AppDelegate.m` from the Project Navigator (⌘ + 1), toggle between the three different editors and see what happens. These will be covered in the next section of this chapter.

Essentially you have three View buttons. These are very useful when you lose one of the main elements of Xcode's interface. The first button toggles the Navigators section, the middle button toggles the Debug Area, and the third button toggles the Utilities section.

> **Note**   Two of the buttons that have disappeared in version 5 of Xcode are the Breakpoints toggle and the Organizer button. The Breakpoints toggle has moved to the Debug Area, while the Organizer is now only available from the Window option on the menu bar.

As with many other OS X applications, if you right-click a gray area of the Toolbar, you're able to customize whether you'd like Icons and Text to appear, just Icons, or just Text. This isn't particularly groundbreaking, however, if you prefer to have only icons, text, or both of them together, feel free to change it.

It's also worth mentioning that Xcode does indeed support full-screen mode as introduced natively with OS X Lion, and this is especially useful when working with the Assistant editor, Storyboards, or designing iPad application interfaces. To toggle full-screen mode, select the small arrows in the top-right corner of Xcode.

Editor

Perhaps the most important part of any integrated development environment is its code editor. Xcode's editor is exceptional in many ways. The editor has three different view options—Standard, Assistant, and Version editor—each of which will be covered shortly.

If you open `AppDelegate.m`, you'll see that the editor is front and center. Simply click where you'd like to begin coding and then code away. As you type code, Xcode's code-completion feature appears. To choose an option from the code completion dialogue, simply use the Arrow keys on your keyboard and press Return or Tab.

Moreover, you'll notice that just above the editor window, there's a small jumpbar. You can use this to open files, see method declarations, and more efficiently navigator through your project and your code. I will revisit this in a later chapter.

Standard Editor

The Standard editor displays a single window and focuses on what has been selected from the Project Navigator on the left (Figure 3-14). This is will be our preferred way of coding mainly because of its simplicity.

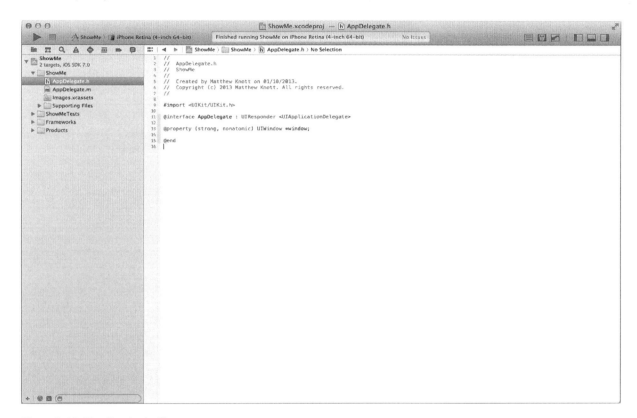

Figure 3-14. The Standard editor

Assistant Editor

The Assistant editor is a much more interesting approach, and chances are this editor will make you want to go out and purchase a larger display. The Assistant editor displays separate windows and contains logical contents depending on which file you're working with. For example, in Figure 3-15, I have the AppDelegate.m open on the left and as a result, Xcode opens AppDelegate.h on the right. This allows you to work simultaneously on both files without having to worry about switching constantly.

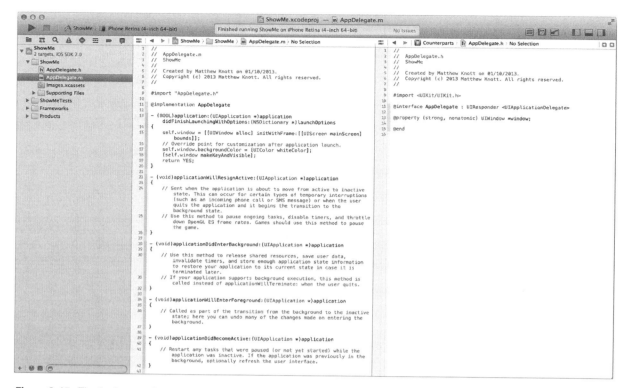

Figure 3-15. The Assistant editor

What's more, if you notice on the far right of Xcode along the jumpbar, you'll find a small button with a plus symbol on. If you click this, Xcode allows you to have multiple editors open, in fact, as many as you and your display can handle.

Version Editor

Because you haven't made use of version control yet, the Version editor won't be too significant right now, so for now all you need to know is that, as you can see in Figure 3-16, on the left the most recent version of a file was selected and the right Xcode would open up another version of that file and allow you to track and view changes that had been made to this file.

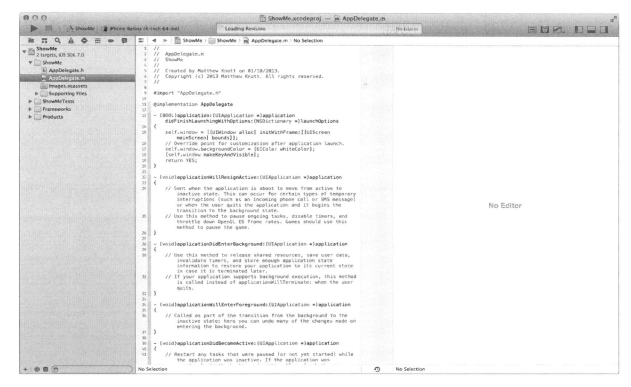

Figure 3-16. *The Version editor*

Utilities

The Utilities area provides you with essential tools for your project. What's useful about the Utilities area is that it varies in terms of what it displays depending on what you're using. Like the Navigator area, the Utilities area consists of different tabs along the top but also includes tabs toward the bottom or middle of the Utilities area.

Let's first focus on the main tabs along the top; providing you have AppDelegate.m open, you'll find that two tabs are present along the top, as shown in Figure 3-17.

Figure 3-17. *The tabs within the Utility area of Xcode with a code file open*

First, there is the File Inspector. The File Inspector allows you to manage attributes of a file, for example, its name, type path, and location within your project. As with many other inspectors within the Utilities area, you'll see that additional options can be changed if you were to scroll down. The File Inspector is one of two inspectors that is always present within the Utilities area, regardless of which file you're working with.

Second, there is the Quick Help Inspector. Here you can easily access information about a symbol within Xcode. This is especially useful when you'd like to know where something has been declared, how it was declared, and the scope and parameters. Again, this is the other tab that is always present within the Utilities area.

The Utility Navigator really comes into its own when working with Interface Builder. Interface Builder was introduced in Chapter 2 when we used it in conjunction with the `Main.Storyboard` file. One of the key things to note about a project started with the Empty Application template is that it has no Storyboard or Nib files that can be opened in Interface Builder, so before you go any further, let's do something about that.

> **Note** Before Apple introduced Storyboards with iOS 5, the visual composition and construction of views was done using Nib files. Nib files are a bit of a misnomer as there are no files with the .nib extension, rather it is a term that actually refers to .xib files. Although the Nib (or .xib) file is edited individually, the process of constructing the view is identical to when using Storyboards.

Let's start by subclassing `UIViewController`; start by going to File ➤ New(). Select Objective-C class, as shown in Figure 3-18, and click Next.

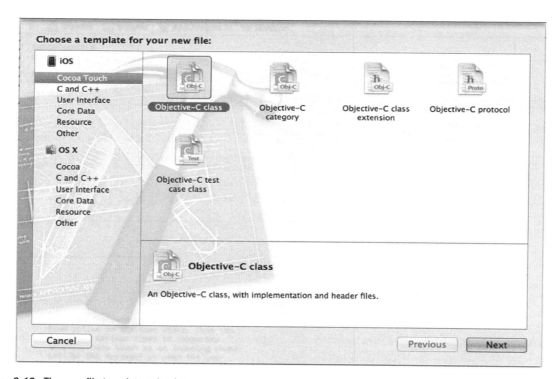

Figure 3-18. The new file template selection

On the next screen, you're asked for two values: Class and Subclass of. The class value is largely up to you; this is the name that you'll use to instantiate this view controller. When naming classes, always try to make them semantically accurate, that is, they should describe the function of the class. This will be the main view controller, so I've given it a name of `MainViewController`.

For the Subclass of value, you'll need to tell Xcode which class your new class will be based on. If you were creating a class to hold custom properties such as a Car class or an Animal class, you would use NSObject, but in this instance you need a view controller, so set the value to `UIViewController`. Finally, ensure that Targeted for iPad is unchecked, but that importantly, With XIB for user interface is checked. Check that your values match Figure 3-19 and click Next.

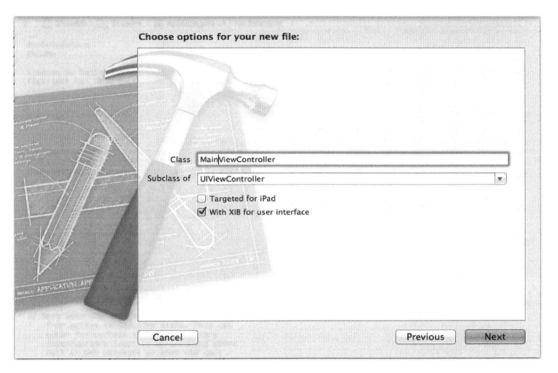

Figure 3-19. Subclassing UIViewController

On the next screen you will be prompted for a save location for your new file, just stick with the default settings and ensure that in the Targets box, ShowMe is ticked and then click Create. You should now have three new files in your Project Navigator:

- `MainViewController.h`
- `MainViewController.m`
- `MainViewController.xib`

You're now ready to start putting the interface for the first View Controller together, so select `MainViewController.xib` from the project navigator. Before you start adding anything to your view, click the view in Interface Builder, and then look back to the Utilities Navigator. You should see that the two tabs have now become six tabs, as shown in Figure 3-20.

Figure 3-20. The Utility Navigator tabs in Interface Builder

I've already covered the first two tabs, so let's look at the remaining four:

■ *Identity Inspector:* Here you're able to change details regarding an object, similar to the File Inspector. You can change and access the class name, accessibility details, runtime attributes, among others. The Identity Inspector will only be active when you have an object selected, with `MainViewController.xib` open, select the view and you should find that the information within the Identity Inspector becomes visible. You'll find you use this tab often when adding views to your Storyboard, but I'll cover that later on.

■ *Attributes Inspector:* A very useful and handy inspector to work with when you're designing interfaces graphically. With the view selected, you'll find that you can change many properties, such as background color and so forth. Without this tab, you'd have to make changes programmatically, which would not only be time-consuming but would become tedious and tiresome. You'll find that all of the different objects you can add through Interface Builder have different properties that can be configured.

■ *Size Inspector:* The Size Inspector allows you to specify the positioning of objects that are selected, along with the ability to specify minimum and maximum sizes and so on. This is also one of the places you can view and manage constraints, which are covered in detail later in this book.

■ *Connections Inspector:* This allows you to connect outlets to interface objects as well as make new connections and break existing ones. The Connections Inspector is essentially an overview of which parts of your code the visual elements are connected to, so when a label is populated, what is the name of the outlet that you would call in code, or in the case of a button, which action it triggers when pushed.

Like the Project Navigator, each of these tabs are accessible via View ➤ Utilities ➤ Show File Inspector and, more important, can be accessed using similar keyboard shortcuts. To access the File Inspector with a keyboard shortcut, simply press ⌥ + ⌘ + 1 or for the Attributes Inspector it would be ⌥ + ⌘ + 4.

If you look just below the Inspectors, you'll find that there are four more tabs: the File Templates Library, Code Snippets Library, Object Library, and Media Files, as illustrated in Figure 3-21.

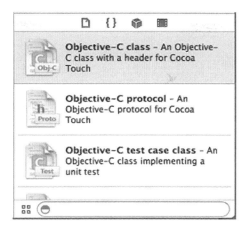

Figure 3-21. The File Template, Code Snippet, and Object Libraries along with the Media Files tab

- The File Templates Library contains templates for common classes, heads, protocols, and so forth; to add one to your project, simply click and drag it to the Project Navigator.

- The Code Snippet Library contains short pieces of code that you can use by clicking and dragging into the editor with a code file open.

- The Object Library is where you find the standard Cocoa controls for applications. You'll make extensive use of this library throughout this book. With this you can simply click and drop an item onto a view with Interface Builder open.

- Finally, there is the Media Files tab, which contains useful graphics, sounds, and icons you can use within your interfaces, again, simply drag and drop onto your interface.

Again, these four tabs are accessible via View ➤ Utilities ➤ Show File Template Library or with the keyboard shortcut of ^ + ⌥ + ⌘ + 1. Also, these tabs are always visible, regardless of what file type you're working with, however, you'll pay most attention to it while working with Interface Builder.

Before adding any objects to your view, you need to take into account that later on in this example you'll be using a navigation bar. Select the view in Interface Builder, and from the Attribute Inspector (⌥ + ⌘ + 4) you need to select Opaque Navigation Bar from the Top Bar menu. You'll see a navigation bar appear on the view, although it's important to note that this is essentially a placeholder, a visual reference that allows you to position the objects on your view accordingly.

From the Object library, you'll want to add three items to your view. First, drag a label onto the view and position it toward the top of the view in the center. Once you've positioned the label, click it once to select it, then select the Attribute Inspector. Here you can really appreciate the range of minute customizations available to you. The second property in the Attributes Inspector for this label is a text field that says Label. Change this to say "Text to send". You can edit labels by double-clicking them on the view also, but this method helps you see some of the minute adjustments you can make with the Attributes Inspector. Finally, click the T in the Font box, and select Headline from the font list, as shown in Figure 3-22. You will probably find that once you changed the text the label truncated most of the text. Rearrange the label by dragging one of the small boxes in the corners of the label until all of the text is visible.

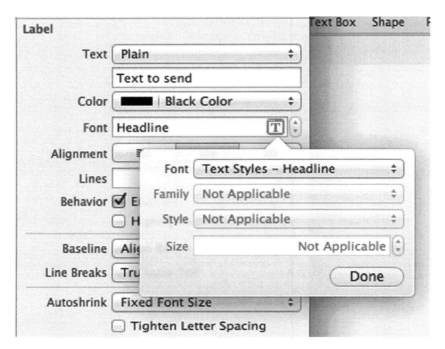

Figure 3-22. Selecting the Headline text style for your label

Now that the label is in place, drag a Text Field from the Object Library onto the view and position it below the label. As you move the Text Field in place, you should get a feel for the vertical positioning as the object snaps into place below the label. Drag the sides of the Text Field out until a blue line appears on the side of the view.

Finally, drag a Button onto the view. Position it a little below the Text Field. Once it's placed, double-click the button and change its text to "Show Me". That's it! You have now built your interface, and you should now have something resembling Figure 3-23.

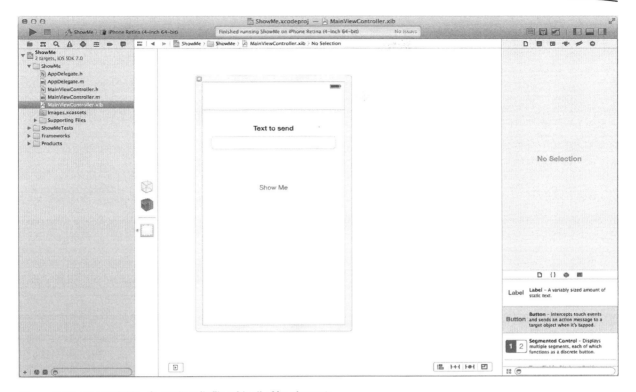

Figure 3-23. *The MainViewController.xib file with all of its elements*

The last step here is to link the objects from Interface Builder into the View Controller code as outlets and actions. For these next steps, you'll be reusing knowledge and skills you've picked up in this and Chapter 2, so as a challenge I'll present the steps for you without any visual aids, and then we'll see how everything matches up at the end.

1. Start by opening the Assistant editor and setting the file to MainViewController.h.

2. Select the Text Field and holding down the Cntl key, click and drag a connection to the header file, positioning the connection just below @interface MainViewController : UIViewController. Create an outlet named textToSendField.

3. Next, perform a similar action on the Show Me button. Control-drag a connection to the header file, positioning it just below the outlet you just created, but this time when you release the mouse button, specify that you are creating an action and name it "showMe."

That's it for `MainViewController.xib` for now, but before I move on, check that the code in your `MainViewController.h` file is the same as the code below.

```
#import <UIKit/UIKit.h>

@interface MainViewController : UIViewController

@property (weak, nonatomic) IBOutlet UITextField *textToSendField;
- (IBAction)showMe:(id)sender;

@end
```

Configuring the Application Delegate

I've covered a lot of ground so far in this chapter, but in terms of this application, if you were to run it now, you would see that it doesn't do anything differently than it would have after you first created the project. Don't be disheartened; you're only a few lines of code away from seeing the fruits of your labor. The reason nothing new happens when you run your application is that you haven't told the Application Delegate (App Delegate) about your new view controller.

In all of the other templates, the App Delegate has already been programmed to open an initial View Controller or Storyboard, but in an Empty Application template, you don't start with an initial View Controller. Now that you've done the hard part, let's go ahead and tell the App Delegate about the View Controller, `MainViewController`.

Switch the editor back to the Standard editor and select the `AppDelegate.h` file from the Project Navigator. If you can't remember how to switch to the Standard editor, refer back in this chapter to the analysis of the toolbar. In the header, you have three lines of code to add. Let's look at each one in turn and then the header code as a whole at the end.

1. First, you need to give the App Delegate visibility of your `MainViewController`. You do that by importing the `MainViewController.h` file, so after the line that says #import <UIKit/UIKit.h> type: #import "MainViewController.h"

2. Next, you need to declare a property to hold the instance of a navigation controller, so before the @end tag, type: @property (nonatomic, strong) UINavigationController *navigationController;

3. Finally, you want to declare another property to allow you to reference the View Controller, so type the following line after the last property: @property (nonatomic, strong) MainViewController *mainViewController;

Your `AppDelegate.h` should now resemble these lines of code:

```
#import <UIKit/UIKit.h>
#import "MainViewController.h"

@interface AppDelegate : UIResponder <UIApplicationDelegate>
```

```
@property (strong, nonatomic) UIWindow *window;
@property (nonatomic, strong) UINavigationController *navigationController;
@property (nonatomic, strong) MainViewController *mainViewController;

@end
```

What's worth noting here is that if you hadn't imported the MainViewController.h, you wouldn't have been able to create an instance of MainViewController for that last property. You're finished with the head; now you need to look at the App Delegate's implementation file, so select AppDelegate.m from the Project Navigator. Once more, you have three lines of code to add, and once more I'll walk you through them one by one before showing the full code at the end.

Unlike in the header, where we regarded the whole file, here you're interested in a single specific method called - (BOOL)application:(UIApplication *)application didFinishLaunchingWithOptions. This should be the first method in the implementation file and to start with, it should look like these lines of code:

```
- (BOOL)application:(UIApplication *)application didFinishLaunchingWithOptions:(NSDictionary *)
launchOptions
{
    self.window = [[UIWindow alloc] initWithFrame:[[UIScreen mainScreen] bounds]];
    // Override point for customization after application launch.
    self.window.backgroundColor = [UIColor whiteColor];
    [self.window makeKeyAndVisible];

    return YES;
}
```

Once you've found the method, add a few blank lines after self.window.backgroundColor = [UIColor whiteColor], as this is where you'll add all of your code.

1. The first thing you need to do is initialize your view controller, this basically gets it primed and ready to be used. Type: self.mainViewController = [[MainViewController alloc] init]; into the blank space you created.

2. Next, you want to initialize your navigation controller and tell it that the root view controller is the mainViewController object you just initialized. Drop down a line and type: self.navigationController = [[UINavigationController alloc] initWithRootViewController:self.mainViewController];

3. Lastly, you need to set the root view controller of the window to be your navigation controller (which in turn has the MainViewController set as *its* root view controller); so again drop down a line and simply type: self.window.rootViewController = self.navigationController;.

Your finished code should resemble the code listed below.

```
- (BOOL)application:(UIApplication *)application didFinishLaunchingWithOptions:(NSDictionary *)
launchOptions
{
    self.window = [[UIWindow alloc] initWithFrame:[[UIScreen mainScreen] bounds]];
    // Override point for customization after application launch.
    self.window.backgroundColor = [UIColor whiteColor];

    self.mainViewController = [[MainViewController alloc] init];
    self.navigationController = [[UINavigationController alloc]
                                initWithRootViewController:self.mainViewController];
    self.window.rootViewController = self.navigationController;

    [self.window makeKeyAndVisible];

    return YES;
}
```

Now for the good news; you're ready to run your application! Go ahead and click the Run button from the Toolbar or press ⌘ + R. If you've followed the steps successfully, the simulator should launch and present you with the view you created in Interface Builder, as shown in Figure 3-24.

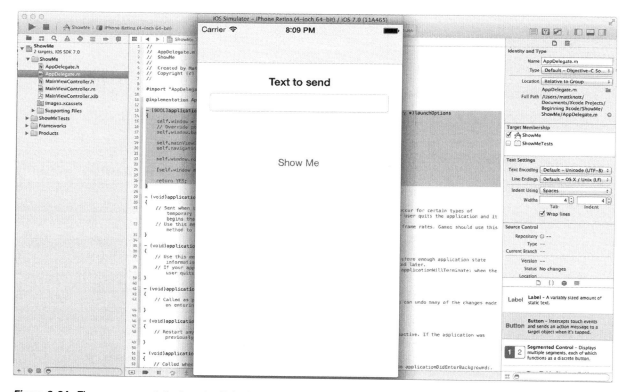

Figure 3-24. The app runs and displays the MainViewController made in Interface Builder

At this point, if your app ran successfully and you're staring at the result of your hard work, give yourself a pat on the back. You've built and configured an application the hard way, but you're not done yet.

> **Note**   If your interface was hidden beneath the navigation controller, fear not it's not your fault. At the time of writing, there was a bug in Xcode 5 that meant it ignored the fact that you told the View to account for a navigation controller. Go back to your `MainViewController.xib` and move all of the elements down. If you rerun your app, all of the elements should then appear.

Adding a Second View Controller

Hopefully, you're feeling pleased with what you've done so far, and you should be; but the application isn't finished. The idea behind this application is to type some text in the text field and have it display on another view controller, so let's go ahead and build that second view controller. Again, let's see how much you remember from creating the previous view controller.

1.   Start by creating a new file and select Objective-C Class. Name the class `MessageViewController` and ensure it is a subclass of `UIViewController`. Be sure to leave Targeted for iPad unchecked and to check With Xib for user interface.

2.   Once you have added these three files, open `MessageViewController.xib`. Select the view and in the Attribute Inspector, set the Top Bar property to Opaque Navigation Bar.

3.   Drag two labels onto the view, one below the other, and position them near the top of the view under the navigation bar placeholder. Double-click the first label and set the text to "You Said…" and then resize the second label so that it is the width of the view. Note that if you experienced the Xcode bug with the overlapping navigation bar, this is a good time to move your labels down a bit.

4.   Now, turn on the Assistant editor and, ensuring `MessageViewController.h` is selected, drag a connection from the bottom label to the header and create an outlet named `messageLabel`.

Hopefully, your view should now resemble Figure 3-25.

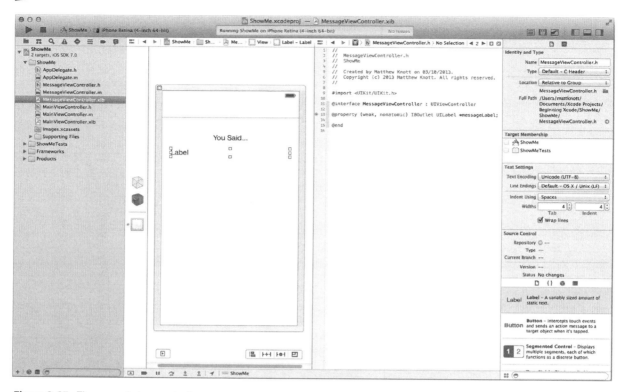

Figure 3-25. *The second view controller*

Before I go any further, let's think about what the objective is. The user should be able to push the Show Me button on the `MainViewController` and have whatever they have written in the text field appear in the `MessageViewController`. To make this happen, you need to add some code to the `MessageViewController` header and implementation files so they can receive the message from the `MainViewController`.

> **Note**   When a new view is loaded on to the screen, replacing another one within an iOS application, this is referred to as *pushing* a view.

The `MainViewController` will interface with the header of `MessageViewController`, so start by opening `MessageViewController.h` and just before the `@end` you'll declare a property to hold this message and a custom initializer. Add the following code to your header:

```
#import <UIKit/UIKit.h>

@interface MessageViewController : UIViewController

@property (weak, nonatomic) IBOutlet UILabel *messageLabel;
```

```
@property (weak, nonatomic) NSString *messageData;

-(id)initWithMessage:(NSString *)messageData;

@end
```

Here, you've added an `NSString` property, which will hold the data you pass from `MainViewController` and make them available to other methods in `MessageViewController`. You also declared an interface for the `initWithMessage` method. This is your custom initialize, so it is the method that other view controllers can see and in turn pass the message to, so that it can set the `messageData` property you've declared.

Now that you've declared the method, you need to create it. Open `MessageViewController.m` and made some room between the `initWithNibName` method and the `viewDidLoad` method. Now, type the method in the space:

```
-(id)initWithMessage:(NSString *)messageData
{
    self = [super initWithNibName:nil bundle:nil];
    if (self) {
        _messageData = messageData;
    }
    return self;
}
```

This method is very similar to the `initWithNibName` method except that it takes the `messageData` value and uses it to set the `messageData` property you declared in the header.

> **Note**   You assigned the `messageData` object that gets passed to the method to `_messageData`, but you never declared `_messageData`. Prefixing an object name with an underscore (_) allows you to reference properties that are declared in the header but not synthesized in the implementation file. Another way of doing this would be to reference `self.messageData`, and the outcome would be the same.

Although you're now able to receive the `messageData`, you're not actually doing anything to set the labels' text value on your view. You can't do this directly from your initialization method, so to do this, add the following code to your `viewDidLoad` method:

```
- (void)viewDidLoad
{
    [super viewDidLoad];
    [self.messageLabel setText: _messageData];
}
```

Here, you're referencing the outlet called `messageLabel` that you declared in the header and setting its text property to the value of the `messageData` property.

The last task, now that you've finished with the MessageViewController, is to tell the MainViewController to pass the message and display the MessageViewController. Open MainViewController.m, and below the line #import "MainViewController.h" add the following code:

```
#import "MainViewController.h"
#import "MessageViewController.h"
```

As you did with the App Delegate, you are adding the MessageViewController header so you can instantiate it and push the view controller to the screen. Now you need to navigate through the code until you find the stub for the showMe method; it will look like this:

```
- (IBAction)showMe:(id)sender {
}
```

Let's go through the three lines that you need to add, and then I'll show you how the final method should look.

1. First, you will assign the value of the text field to an NSString object: NSString *messageValue = self.textToSendField.text;

2. Next, you need to declare and initialize an instance of MessageViewController and pass in the messageValue string: MessageViewController *messageViewController = [[MessageViewController alloc] initWithMessage:messageValue];

3. Finally, you tell the navigation controller to push messageViewController to the screen: [self.navigationController pushViewController:messageViewC ontroller animated:YES];

The finished method should look like this:

```
- (IBAction)showMe:(id)sender {
    NSString *messageValue = self.textToSendField.text;
    MessageViewController *messageViewController =
        [[MessageViewController alloc] initWithMessage:messageValue];

    [self.navigationController pushViewController:messageViewController animated:YES];
}
```

That's it, you should now be able to run the application and find that you can click in the text field, type a message, and click Show Me, which takes you to the MessageViewController and shows whatever you typed, as shown in Figure 3-26.

Figure 3-26. *The finished application*

Debugging Area

The final focus is the debugging area. In order to actually see this in action, you need to add some code to the project so that it checks whether the text field is empty when the Show Me button is clicked, and you'll use NSLog to add a message to the console. Go to MainViewController.m and go to the showMe method. Modify the method by adding an IF statement that checks whether the messageValue object is empty or not:

```
- (IBAction)showMe:(id)sender {
    NSString *messageValue = self.textToSendField.text;
    if ([messageValue isEqualToString:@""]) {
        NSLog(@"No text entered");
    }
```

```
    else
    {
        MessageViewController *messageViewController =
        [[MessageViewController alloc] initWithMessage:messageValue];

        [self.navigationController pushViewController:messageViewController animated:YES];

    }
}
```

The Debug Area allows you to pin down any issues with your program. Because the Debug Area can quickly become very complex and can be used for a variety of different things, I'll only show you the basics for now and revisit it later in the book. Now run your application and try to click the Show Me button without adding any text to the text field. You should see that when you click the button, a message is added to the output console, as shown in Figure 3-27.

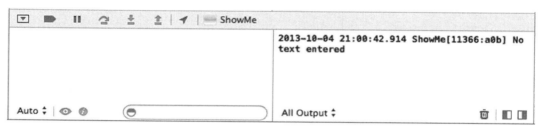

Figure 3-27. The result of the NSLog method call is displayed in the output console

For now all you need to know is that the debugger included with Xcode is the LLVM-GCC debugger, this means you're able to debug a variety of code in a variety of languages. This is especially useful as Objective-C is a superset of the C programming language, which means you're able to transfer any C programming practices and incorporate them into your Objective-C programs.

Summary

This chapter covered two rather contrasting topics: project templates and the basics of Xcode's interface. The purpose of doing so was, first, to give you the confidence to start an Xcode project and choose correctly a project template suitable for your projects and, second, to drop you in at the deep end to understand how to start with nothing and build a working application, while providing a basic familiarization with the key parts of Xcode's interface.

More specifically, in this chapter, you have:

- Created an application from scratch (Well done!)
- Passed an object from one view controller to another
- Looked at the similarities and differences between Nib files and Storyboards
- Looked at each of Xcode's default project templates and when you might use them
- Explored key parts of Xcode's interface

The next chapter will look at Xcode's graphical Interface Builder in greater detail and show you how to use this to build interfaces efficiently.

Chapter 4

Building Interfaces

A lot was covered in Chapter 3: you looked at each of Xcode's default iOS project templates, examined when exactly you should use them, and then took a tour of the main areas of Xcode's workspace, and if that wasn't enough, you created an application using the Empty Application template.

The focus of this chapter will be to delve deeper into Xcode's graphical interface design tool, Interface Builder. Interface Builder has been a key part of the Xcode set of development tools. However, with the release of Xcode 4, Interface Builder became a part of Xcode itself, as opposed to previous versions in which it was a separate application. As already discussed in previous chapters, what makes Interface Builder an attractive addition to Apple's developer tools is that it removes the need to write code in order to design great interfaces for your applications. It allows you to lay out your views and windows by dragging built-in Cocoa objects from the Object Library and placing them on the screen.

What's even more useful is that by using the Attributes Inspector, you can make many changes that would otherwise require lines upon lines of code. As a developer, this is good news for two reasons, the first being that you don't have to continuously test, build, and run your application in order to see if what you're actually designing by code looks good. With Interface Builder, you can see this right away. Second, similar to what's just been mentioned, you can make changes graphically, which saves a lot of time and effort. All of this and just the plain fact that using Interface Builder makes designing views fun!

This chapter explains how to set up an application using the Tabbed Application template. The great thing about using a Tabbed Application is that each of the tabs can act as an app within an app, each one showing a drastically different set of tools and styles. The two initial tabs you set up will showcase some of the interface elements you haven't seen yet, as well as utilize the GPS function of your device. Once you've done this, you'll set up a third tab that will allow you to demonstrate some of the important interface elements that can't be added using Interface Builder. A goal of this chapter is to show how much you can achieve while using as little code as possible, and it's important to note how little code this will be compared to how much you would need to write if Interface Builder were not a part of Xcode. The last thing you'll look it is how you can alter the interface elements with code to achieve results that Interface Builder alone cannot do but will be important in building beautiful, easy to use interfaces. Below you'll find an outline of what exactly each of our tabs will include:

1. *Track It:* Here you'll create a Text View that will display detailed telemetry from the GPS receiver, be that on a physical device or in the simulator. You'll also use a switch to turn the GPS on and off.

2. *Slide It:* As the name implies, in the second tab you'll look at how to implement the slider tab, where to build a series of sliders to alter the background color of the entire view, and how to output their values into Text Fields. On top of this, you'll answer one of the burning questions all iOS developers ask: how do I dismiss the keyboard?

3. *Alert:* In the final tab you'll look at how to use a Segmented Control to determine what happens when a button is pushed. The choice will be between an Alert View and an Action Sheet, two popular elements in many applications.

Getting Ready

Now you've had a sneak peek at the aim of this chapter, hopefully you're raring to go, so let's get to it.

1. Start by opening Xcode and creating a new project by clicking Create a new Xcode project from the Welcome screen or go to File ➤ New ➤ Project … (⌘ + Shift + N). Select the Tabbed Application template and click Next.

2. Name your project *Showcase* and ensure the targeted device is set to iPhone. Configure the other settings as you did in previous applications. Make sure the key settings match those in Figure 4-1 and click Next.

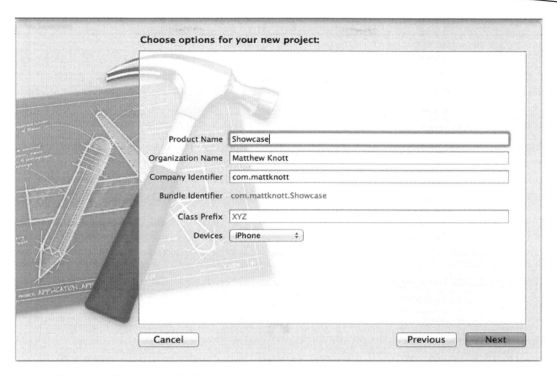

Figure 4-1. *Configuring the Showcase application*

3. You don't want to create a Git repository, so leave that option unchecked; ensure your project is going to be saved where you want it to be, and click Create.

You've now created the bare bones of your Showcase tabbed application. To see what Apple's template has given as a starting point, click `Main.Storyboard` and you should see a screen resembling that shown in Figure 4-2.

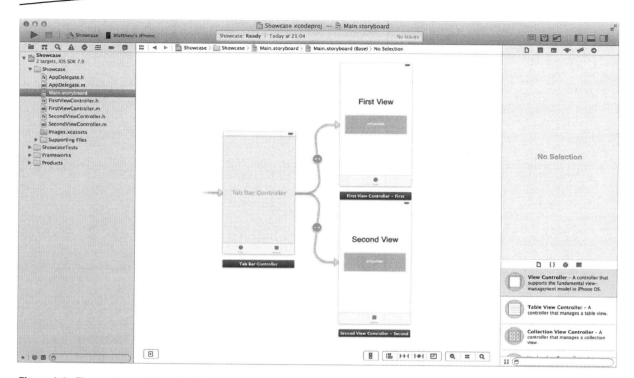

Figure 4-2. *The starting point for the Showcase application*

By default, the template gives you a UITabBarController with two UIViewControllers, attached named FirstViewController and SecondViewController. Although these names are perfectly good, tab orders can change as a project develops, so it's always better to use names that are semantically accurate. So before you add a third tab, let's rename the files to something more appropriate.

With the Project Navigator open (⌘ + 1), highlight FirstViewController.h and press Return on your keyboard. You should now be able to rename the file. Remove the text and type TrackViewController.h (you must remember to add the .h extension), then do the same with FirstViewController.m and call it TrackViewController.m. Repeat this for SecondViewController.h and use the .m extension but instead call it SliderViewController.h and SliderViewController.m. Now your Project Navigator should closely resemble what you see in Figure 4-3.

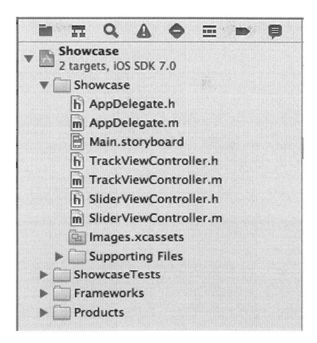

Figure 4-3. The current project's files as shown within the Project Navigator

Now you need to update your code files to make use of these new file names, and to do this you'll use the Search Navigator (⌘ + 3). You need to set up the Search Navigator to rename every instance of the `FirstViewController` to `TrackViewController`; by default you will see the words Find ➤ Text ➤ Containing above the search criteria. Click the word Find and select Replace ➤ Text ➤ Containing, as shown in Figure 4-4.

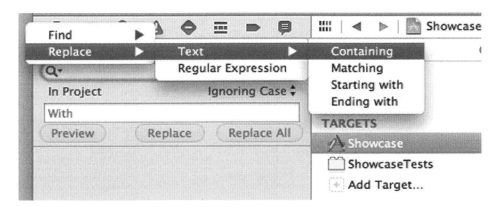

Figure 4-4. Configuring the Search Navigator to perform a find and replace task

In the first text field, type in `FirstViewController` and in the second, type `TrackViewController`. At this point you encounter an uncharacteristically poor piece of interface design in that you actually need to press Enter to perform the search, although Xcode doesn't make this clear. Click Replace All and Xcode will go through all the files listed and replace the word `FirstViewController` with `TrackViewController`. Figure 4-5 illustrates the results of this find-and-replace operation in the Search Navigator.

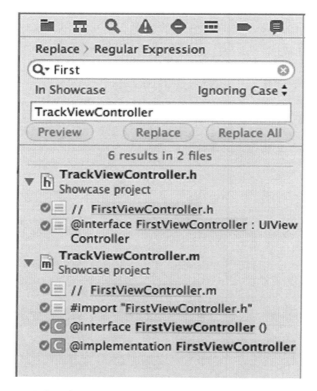

Figure 4-5. The Search Navigator updating the references to old file and class names

> **Note**   When performing a batch find-and-replace operation, Xcode may ask if you want to enable automatic snapshots. It's recommended you enable this, as there are often times as a developer where you'll perform this step in error. Having a snapshot means you can roll back in the event of a catastrophic mistake in your application. I'll cover this in Chapter 14.

Once the find-and-replace operation has completed, repeat the task but in the first box enter `SecondViewController` as the text you are searching for and in the second type `SliderViewController` as the text you want to replace it with and press the Return key, then click Replace All.

You've now updated all references to your renamed view controllers. Next you're going to create a third view controller: `ActionViewController`. To do this, create a new file (⌘ + N) and select Cocoa Touch from the left sidebar under iOS and choose Objective-C class, as you did in Chapter 3. With this selected, click Next. You should notice that Xcode conveniently adds your class prefix to the start of the class name, so specify `ActionViewController` as the class name. Type `UIViewController` in the Subclass of field and uncheck Targeted for iPad. Also uncheck With XIB for user interface and then click Next. Now create this file in the same location that all of your other files are stored and click Create.

Finally you're going to add the images that will be used as the icons in the tab bar. For this project you'll be using the free tab bar icons available for download at `www.iconbeast.com` created by Charlene. Once you've downloaded the icons, place them somewhere so you'll be able to find them easily. Head back to Xcode and select `Images.xcassets`, and you should see the four images, as shown in Figure 4-6.

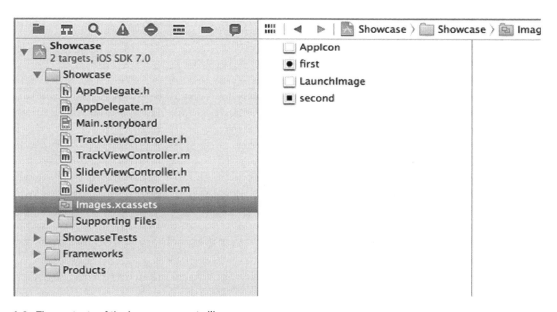

Figure 4-6. *The contents of the Images.xcassets library*

Chapter 2 briefly explained the Asset Catalogs, but here I'll go into it a little deeper.

1. Start by selecting the image named `first` and deleting it with the Backspace key, or by right-clicking and selecting Remove Selected Items; repeat this step for the image named `second`.

2. Next, click the plus symbol at the bottom of the list of images, and from the menu that appears select New Image Set, as shown in Figure 4-7. This will create a new image set called `image`.

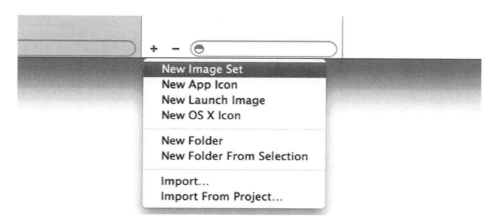

Figure 4-7. *Creating a new image set*

3. Select the new image set and press the Return key so that you can rename the file; rename it to Track. Now repeat the previous step to create a new image set two more times, naming the sets Slider and Action, respectively.

You've now created three image sets, and each one will contain the tab bar icons for the three tabs. Open a Finder window and browse to where you extracted the icons from www.iconbeast.com. Select the Track image set, and you will see something resembling the screens in Figure 4-8.

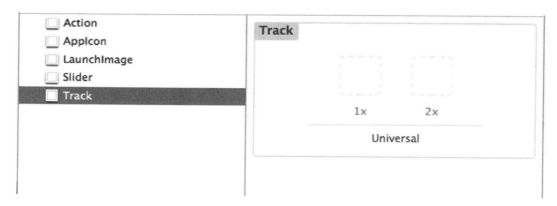

Figure 4-8. *The three new image sets*

One of the benefits of using Asset Catalogs for storing images is that they make it easy to group different resolution images together. Here you have a 1x container and a 2x container. Traditionally, in the 1x container you would place the standard resolution image, and in the 2x container the retina, or higher resolution image. However, unlike the AppIcon image set, there are no restrictions on image size here, so you'll be adding the same image into both containers.

In your finder window, locate the icon named satellite.png and drag it into both the 1x and the 2x containers. Repeat this step for the two remaining image sets, dragging paint.png into the containers for the slider image set, and window-app.png into the Action image set. Your Asset Catalog should now resemble that shown in Figure 4-9.

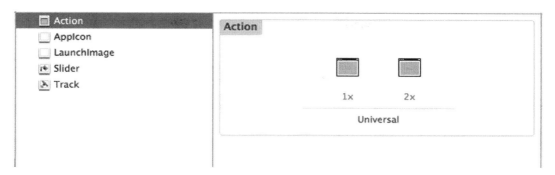

Figure 4-9. *The three image sets with the icons in place*

A great benefit of using Asset catalogs for managing images is that you're left with a much neater project in the Project Navigator! Now, you're all set up and can actually begin working with your interfaces using Interface Builder.

Before You Start …

You'll notice that, unlike in Chapter 3, your project has no .xib files; instead you'll be working with `Main.storyboard`. Storyboards were discussed briefly in Chapter 2, and I'll explain them in increasing detail as I progress through the book, but here let's stop for a minute and take a closer look at what is involved in a Storyboard.

Storyboards are a relatively new feature to Xcode that allows you to logically lay out how views are pushed and managed as a user navigates through your application. Although they may seem to be rather unnecessary, they can greatly simplify your application, not to mention add a degree of logic to how you develop your projects.

Because you'll be working with them a little in this chapter, it's important to know the basics because, after all, they are a part of Interface Builder. Open `Main.storyboard` and let's take a look at the key controls. Conveniently, all of the controls for your storyboard are located at the bottom of the storyboard design area and are separated into four groups, as shown in Figure 4-10.

Figure 4-10. *The storyboard controls*

Let's look at the groups and their icons:

- *Document Outline toggle:* This first button, located by itself in the bottom left corner of the design area, hides and displays the document outline, which I'll cover in more detail later in this book.

- *Form Factor toggle:* Located on the right-hand side of the design area with the other icons, this button switches the view controllers in the storyboard between 3.5-inch and 4-inch form factors. This is incredibly useful for testing the positioning of your elements on the view and ensuring your constraints are set correctly.

- *Constraint controls:* These will be described in greater detail in Chapter 6, but for here these four buttons grouped together allow you to control the behavior of the elements in your view when faced with differing resolutions or different screen resolutions.

    - *Align:* Allows you to position elements in relation to the view, letting you set a range of alignments including centering and aligning to the top of the view.

    - *Pin:* Fix an element in place by manually setting its constraints.

    - *Resolve Auto Layout issues:* One of the most useful buttons in Xcode 5, you will often use the powerful auto layout functions offered from this menu to do all of the hard work for you.

    - *Resizing behavior:* Use this to control how the views handle resizing, choosing from one, none, or both of the options available.

- *Zoom controls:* The last three buttons control zoom. The zoom in, zoom out magnifying glass icons will be familiar to you. The center button is the Zoom toggle. When moving around large storyboards, this becomes an invaluable tool, as you can snap zoom in and out just by clicking this one button.

This concludes our brief look at the storyboard design area controls. Chapters 6 and 7 will look at all of these in intimate detail, but for now let's move on and build the interface.

Building the Interface

Now that you're familiar with the storyboard controls, you can start to get your interface in order. To do that, you're going to remove the two views that were added by default. With `Main.storyboard` selected, you will have two view controllers, as was shown in Figure 4-2. Beneath each of these view controllers, you will see a black bar with three icons on it; select this black bar, as shown in Figure 4-11, and press the Backspace key to delete it.

Figure 4-11. *The view controller, outlined in blue after selecting the black bar*

Repeat this step for the other view controller so you're left with only a Tab Bar Controller. All of your views are going to be based on standard view controllers, so from the object library locate the view controller object and drag three of them to the design area. Position them as shown in Figure 4-12.

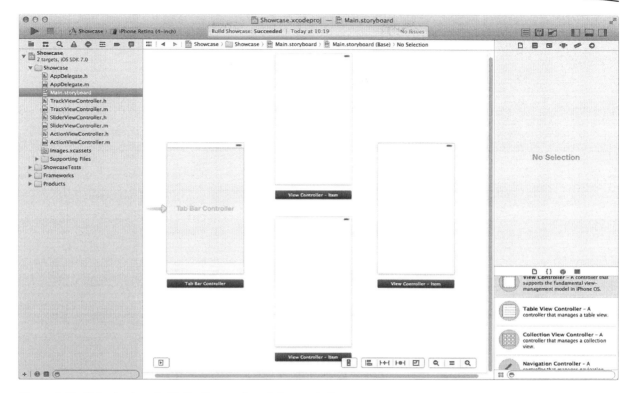

Figure 4-12. Main.storyboard with the three orphaned view controllers

Although you've added the three view controllers, they are currently orphans, that is, there is no relationship between your view controllers and the tab bar controller, so you need to create one. The process for creating a relationship between the tab bar controller and the view controllers is similar to how you connected objects to their actions and methods in Chapter 3:

1. Click the zoom toggle to zoom out of the canvas showing all of the view controllers, and select the Tab Bar Controller by clicking it once.

2. Holding the control key (^), click on the Tab Bar Controller, and drag a connection to the top view controller, as shown in Figure 4-13.

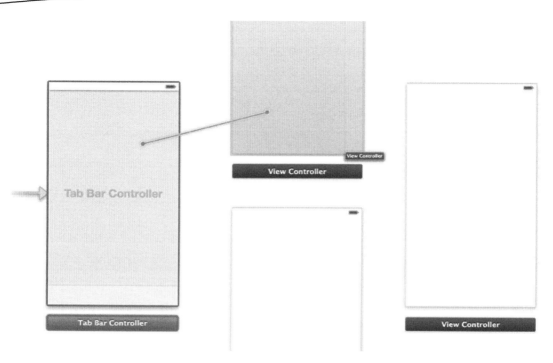

Figure 4-13. *Connecting the Tab Bar Controller to the view controller*

3. When you release the mouse button, a dialog will appear, as shown in Figure 4-14, asking you to choose the segue type. I'll cover segues in Chapter 7, but for now, select *view controllers* underneath the Relationship Segue heading, as shown in Figure 4-14.

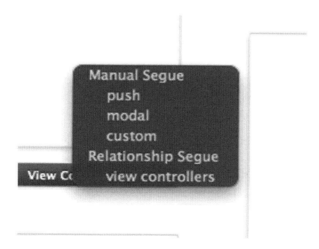

Figure 4-14. *The segue selection dialog*

Now that you've created a relationship between the tab bar controller and the view controller, you'll notice that there have been a few changes in your design area. To start with, the tab bar controller now has a tab showing on the tab bar, as does your view controller. Also you now have a line connecting the tab bar controller to the top view controller; this is called a segue and it is a physical representation of the relationship between two elements in a storyboard. Segues can link elements in several different ways, but on this occasion you'll only be choosing the branch *view controllers* to create a Relationship Segue. Go ahead and repeat this step for the remaining two view controllers, starting with the bottom view controller, then the middle view controller, until you're left with something resembling the screen shown in Figure 4-15.

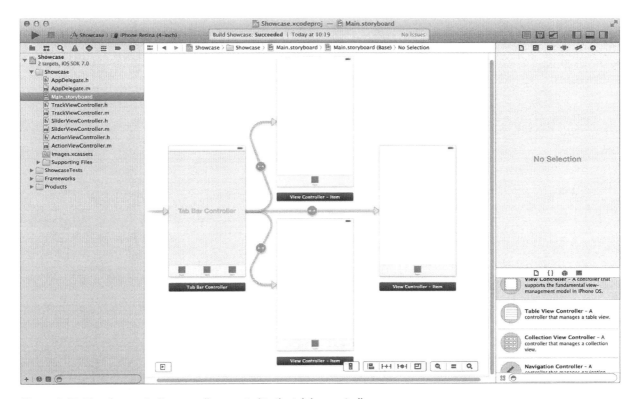

Figure 4-15. *The view controllers are all connected to the tab bar controller*

Setting the Tab Icons

You're nearly ready to start focusing on the individual views in your application, but before you do, there are a couple more tasks to complete. You need to implement the icons you added to the image asset catalog:

1. Click the Zoom Toggle control to zoom back into the design area.

2. Select the square icon above the text Item, as shown in Figure 4-16.

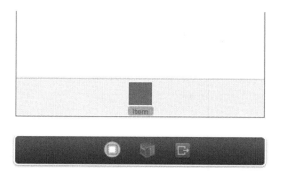

Figure 4-16. Selecting the tab bar icon in the top view controller

3. Open the Attributes Inspector (⌥ + ⌘ + 4). Set the Title attribute to Track It and the Image attribute to Track.

4. Next, select the bottom view controller's tab bar item and set the Title to Slide It and the Image to Slider.

5. Finally, select the tab bar item from the middle view controller, and set its Title to Action and the Image to Action.

Using the images asset catalog, you've successfully named your tabs and set their icons. The tabbed application is really starting to take shape, but there is one final thing you want to do before building each view. The visual relationship between the tab bar controller and the view controllers is in place, and if you want you can build and run the application in the simulator, which will work fine, however, there is one other relationship you've yet to establish.

The three views on the design area are currently using the default view controller class to control them. But you'll want to use the purpose-made view controllers that you created earlier in this chapter. In Chapter 3, you created view controllers with .xib files, so this relationship was created for you, but now you're going to have to do this yourself.

1. Select the black bar beneath the Track It view controller, as you did in Figure 4-11, and then select the Identity Inspector (⌥ + ⌘ + 3).

2. Next click the drop-down list for the Class attribute and select TrackViewController, as shown in Figure 4-17.

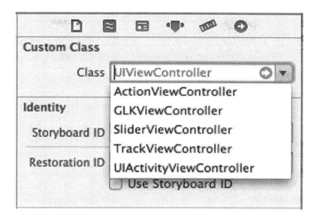

Figure 4-17. Selecting the customer view controller class

3. Select the black bar beneath the bottom view controller, and this time set the class to SliderViewController.

4. Finally, repeat the last step with the middle view controller and set its class to ActionViewController.

That's it, the preparation work is complete! So far you've renamed the default view controller classes and created an extra one, created entries in the asset catalog and populated it with some icons, removed the default view controllers from the storyboard and replaced them with three brand new ones, all before setting the classes, icons, and titles of each one. You're now ready to go on and learn more about building great interfaces.

Tracking Location with the Track It Tab

For the first tab, you're going to create a view that allows you to display some detailed information about the current location, including speed, course, longitude, latitude, and positional accuracy. To do this, you'll be adding the CoreLocation framework to the project. I will actually explain CoreLocation in Chapter 9 when I explain how to combine different frameworks in applications.

CoreLocation is used in a large portion of applications in the App Store, whether in an obvious way such as in a map-based application or in a more subtle way such as providing localized information where ever you go. The skills you learn here will give you a good grounding in applying CoreLocation within your own applications.

CoreLocation by itself isn't that useful without something to control and display its information. To do this, let's add a switch control to turn the tracking on and off and a text view to display the output information. By the end of this section, you should have created something resembling the screen shown in Figure 4-18.

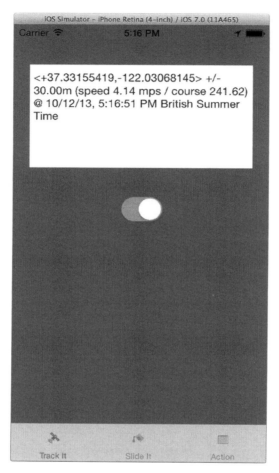

Figure 4-18. *The Track It tab in action*

Although you're working with a Storyboard file and your views are laid out in this way, you should still be able to design your views as you did in Chapter 3 with the .xib files, but with the added bonus of being able to edit all of your views in one location, without having to switch between files within the Project Navigator.

UITextViews and UISwitches

To build a simple but effective view, let's use two of the most common and useful controls provided by Apple: UITextViews and UISwitches. The UISwitch control, or Switch as it appears in the Object Library, is found throughout the Settings app on your iPhone or iPad. It has an on and an off state, and you'll use it to turn tracking on and off again.

1. Search the Object Library for switch and drag the object to the view, positioning it in the middle of the view, as shown in Figure 4-19. You'll see blue guidelines appear as you get it to the middle of the view.

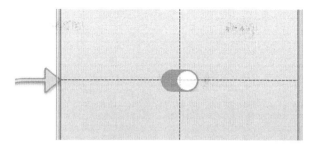

Figure 4-19. *Snapping the switch into place using the guidelines*

2. With the switch selected, open the Attribute Inspector and change the State attribute to Off.

3. Next you need to add a UITextView or Text View as it appears in the object library. Text Views can contain a large amount of text, and they allow the user to type in it, as you can with a Text Field, or scroll through it. Search the Object Library for a Text View and drag it so it appears just above the Switch (refer back to Figure 4-18 for size and positioning reference).

4. With the Text View selected, open the Attributes Inspector and remove the placeholder text from the Text attribute.

5. Finally, change the background color of the view. Select a patch of white space on the view, then in the Attributes Inspector, click the Background drop-down list and select Dark Gray Color from the list of prespecified colors.

You've added the two controls, so now you need to create the methods and outlets in the TrackViewController header that will make them come to life and give them purpose.

1. Start by switching to the Assistant Editor and ensure you have the `TrackViewController.h` file selected, *not* the `TrackViewController.m`, which Xcode 5 often selects by default.

2. Select the Text View and as you did in previous chapters, control and drag a connection from the Text View to the header file, just below the line that says `@interface TrackViewController : UIViewController`.

3. You're creating an outlet named `locationText`. Type this in and click the Connect button.

4. Repeat the last step for the Switch, this time naming the outlet `toggleSwitch`. Then drag another connection, this time being sure to create an action, and naming it `changeToggle`.

The code of your header file should now look like this:

```
#import <UIKit/UIKit.h>

@interface TrackViewController : UIViewController

@property (weak, nonatomic) IBOutlet UITextView *locationText;
@property (weak, nonatomic) IBOutlet UISwitch *toggleSwitch;

- (IBAction)changeToggle:(id)sender;

@end
```

You've created all of your outlets and actions, but before you can write any code, you still need to add the CoreLocation framework to the project to allow you to interact with the GPS features of your device.

> **Tip**   If you accidentally create an outlet instead of an action, as I often find myself doing, you may have trouble running your application after removing the erroneous line. This is because your control is still looking for that outlet. Select the control and open the Connections Inspector. You can remove the reference to the defunct outlet here.

Adding Frameworks and Libraries

To extend the basic functionality of your application, you have the option of adding Frameworks and Libraries to your application. I'll explain them in detail in Chapter 9, but for now, think of each one opening up a particular group of functionality. Some of the most common frameworks you use will be CoreData, MapKit, CoreLocation, among others. As I've already mentioned, you'll be adding CoreLocation, and Xcode 5 has made it as easy as possible to do this.

1.   From the Project Navigator, select the Showcase project at the very top of the list.

2.   From the screen that appears, ensure you are on the General tab then scroll down until you see a heading of Linked Frameworks and Libraries, as shown in Figure 4-20.

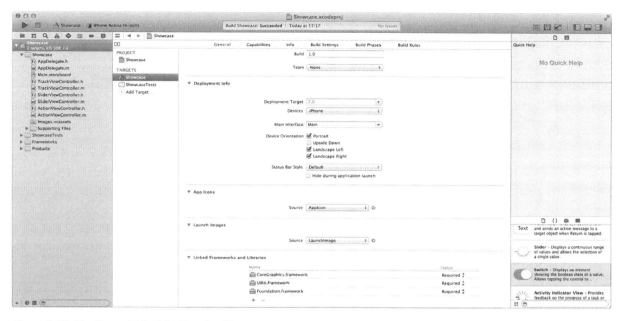

Figure 4-20. *The General tab of the Target settings area*

3. Click the plus icon at the bottom of the framework list. You will be presented with a large list of frameworks and libraries available to add to the project.

4. Browse or search for `CoreLocation.framework` in the list. Highlight it and click the Add button.

When you return to the Target settings area, you should see that CoreLocation has been added to the list. You're now ready to start coding your view controller, and although you have added the CoreLocation framework to the project, you need to import it into the header of the view controller.

1. Open `TrackViewController.h` from the Project Navigator, and ensure you switch to the Standard Editor.

2. Drop down a line from `#import <UIKit/UIKit.h>` and type `#import <CoreLocation/CoreLocation.h>`, which makes the classes, methods, and protocols of the CoreLocation framework available to us.

3. Specify that the view controller can act as a delegate for the `CLLocationManager` class. At the end of the line @ `interface TrackViewController : UIViewController` add `<CLLocationManagerDelegate>`.

The first few lines of your `TrackViewController.h` file should resemble the code shown below:

```
#import <UIKit/UIKit.h>
#import <CoreLocation/CoreLocation.h>

@interface TrackViewController : UIViewController<CLLocationManagerDelegate>
```

You're now ready to move on to the implementation file, so select `TrackViewController.m` from the Project Navigator.

The first task for the implementation file is to create an instance of `CLLocationManager` that all of the methods can interact with. After the line `@interface TrackViewController()`, drop down and add the following code:

```
@interface TrackViewController()
{
    CLLocationManager *locationManager;
}
```

The `CLLocationManager` class is the control center of all the interactions with the device's GPS features. By declaring it in the interface definition, you make it available to all of your methods, which is a really efficient way of working, and you'll see the benefits of this when you add the rest of your code.

Scroll down the implementation until you see the empty stub for the `changeToggle` method. I'll go through the code step by step before showing the final code block.

1. First, determine whether the switch was turned on or off. Do this with an if … else … statement. Start typing if, and when the code completion kicks in, arrow down to the option for ifelse and press the Tab key to create the code structure.

2. Remove the word *condition* with the Backspace key and type `self.toggleSwitch.on`. This returns a Boolean true or false value depending on whether or not the switch is on.

3. Next, remove the `statements-if-true` placeholder. Then check whether location services are enabled and available to the application. Do that with the following code:

    ```
    if ([CLLocationManager locationServicesEnabled] == NO) {
        self.toggleSwitch.on = NO;
    }
    ```

4. The next step is to check if the `locationManager` object has been initialized, and if not, initialize it. There are numerous ways of initializing a `CLLocationManager` object, but in this case you'll do four things: initialize the object, tell it that this view controller is acting as its delegate, tell it to be accurate within 10 meters, and to update when it moves more that 10 meters from the last recorded position. So, drop down a line after the last statement and add the following code:

    ```
    if (locationManager == nil) {
        locationManager = [[CLLocationManager alloc] init];
        locationManager.delegate = self;
        locationManager.desiredAccuracy = kCLLocationAccuracyNearestTenMeters;
        locationManager.distanceFilter = 10.0f;
    }
    ```

5. The last thing you need to do in this half of the if statement is to tell the locationManager object to start updating the location. You do this by sending it a startUpdating message. When it receives this message, it starts tracking your location, then every time the conditions you initialized it with are met, it fires the delegate method didUpdateLocations, which will be added later. For now, drop down a line and type [locationManager startUpdatingLocation];.

6. Now you want to code the else outcome, which is triggered when the switch is set to off. All you want to do in this instance is tell the locationManager object to stop tracking. Remove the statements-if-false placeholder and create an if statement that checks that you've initialized the locationManager object, so type if (locationManager != nil) { } and then inside the curly braces, type [locationManager stopUpdatingLocation];.

The completed method code should look like this:

```
- (IBAction)changeToggle:(id)sender {

    if (self.toggleSwitch.on) {
        if ([CLLocationManager locationServicesEnabled] == NO) {
            self.toggleSwitch.on = NO;
        }

        if (locationManager == nil) {
            locationManager = [[CLLocationManager alloc] init];
            locationManager.delegate = self;
            locationManager.desiredAccuracy = kCLLocationAccuracyNearestTenMeters;
            locationManager.distanceFilter = 10.0f;
        }

        [locationManager startUpdatingLocation];
    }
    else
    {
        if (locationManager != nil)
        {
            [locationManager stopUpdatingLocation];
        }
    }
}
```

Those few lines of code can be used as boilerplate code for anytime you want to initialize a CLLocationManager. As you implemented that code, I mentioned the didUpdateLocations delegate method that the locationManager object will be looking for every time an update is triggered. It's a very simple implementation that takes the last reported location information and outputs its description value to the text view. To do this, add the following code after the changeToggle method:

```
-(void)locationManager:(CLLocationManager *)manager didUpdateLocations:(NSArray *)locations {
    CLLocation* location = [locations lastObject];
    self.locationText.text = location.description;
}
```

That's it, you've finished the code for the Track It tab, but before you run it, you need to do something new—add an entry to the application's info.plist file. For a number of frameworks and classes, Apple likes you to add a privacy declaration. This is a message presented to the user explaining why you need access to a service, in this case, the users location.

In the Project Navigator, expand the Supporting Files group and select Showcase-Info.plist. Move your mouse cursor over the first line titled Information Property List and you will see a small plus symbol appear, as shown in Figure 4-21. Click it.

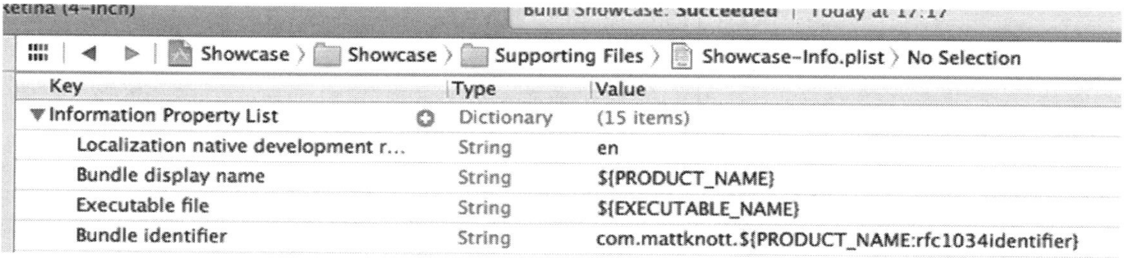

Figure 4-21. Adding an item to the application's info.plist

In the list on the left side, scroll until you see the item titled Privacy - Location Usage Description; select it and then double-click the empty Value container, and type "Testing CoreLocation," or whatever message you want to present to the user. Your finished entry should resemble that shown in Figure 4-22.

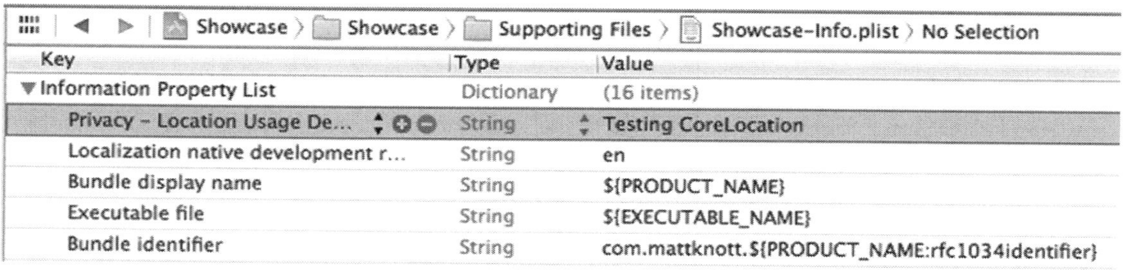

Figure 4-22. The privacy statement in the info.plist file

This may seem unnecessary because iOS will issue a default message if you don't specify one, but if your application uses CoreLocation and you don't add this description, there's a chance your application will be rejected by Apple if you submit it to the App Store. So, with the privacy message set, the last thing to do is to go ahead and test it in the simulator. When you flip the switch, you should see the privacy message as shown in Figure 4-23.

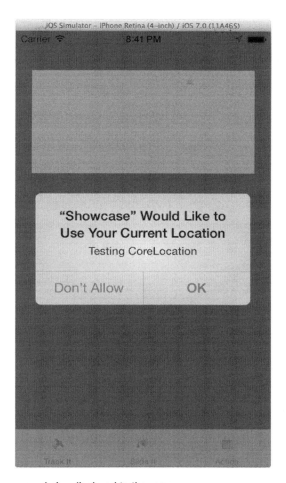

Figure 4-23. The custom privacy message being displayed to the user

Simulating Location

When you run your application in the simulator and accept the privacy message, you may find that nothing actually happens. The reason for this is simple; by default, the simulator doesn't have a location, and therefore it is unable to give you any details about it, let alone update as it's moving.

> **Note**   If nothing happens, you may not have Location Services enabled. Return to the home screen on your virtual device by going to Hardware ➤ Home and then open the Settings app. In Privacy, select Location and then ensure Location Services are enabled.

Thankfully, Apple has provided some pretty nifty tools for specifying a location, but it can also simulate a drive or bike ride, which is the preset you'll use.

In the simulator menu bar, select Debug ❤ Location ❤ City Bike Ride. All of a sudden your text view will begin filling up as this virtual bike peddles through California, near the Apple headquarters in Cuppertino. (I explain more about location debugging in Chapter 11.)

That does it for this tab! You've created a really neat app that you could deploy to your phone while you take a run to view your location and meters run per second reflected in real time, which is pretty amazing.

Mixing Colors with the Slide It Tab

For the second tab, you're going to use UISlider controls to create a RGB (Red Green Blue) color mixer that alters the background color in real time and outputs the values to a series of text fields. This is another tab with real-world practical application. RGB is a color system that defines the color by assign three values to each primary color between 0 and 255. Any web developer, or graphic designer, or even iOS app programmer, will at some time need access to a tool that gives them the RGB value for a certain color. With this tab you can play around with different combinations before implementing the one you like.

The interface for this tab is by far the most complex of the three, so let's begin. You'll create one block of elements for the red color and then repeat the steps two times for the green and blue colors.

1. Start by adding a Label object from the Object Library to the Slide It view. Position it near the top of the view, then double-click it and change the text to Red, as shown in Figure 4-24.

Figure 4-24. *The color label in position*

2. Next search in the Object Library for a Slider and drag it to the view, positioning it below the label, then resize it so it fills about two-thirds of the view's width, as shown in Figure 4-25.

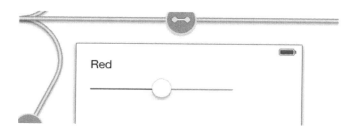

Figure 4-25. *The Slider added to the view and made wider*

3.   Finally, you want to add a Text Field to display the RGB value, so drag in a Text View from the Object Library and position it to the right of the slider, as shown in Figure 4-26.

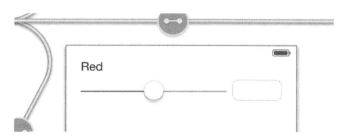

Figure 4-26. The Text Field added to the view and positioned to the right of the Slider

4.   Now, repeat steps 1 through 3, positioning each group of elements one under the other until your view resembles that shown in Figure 4-27.

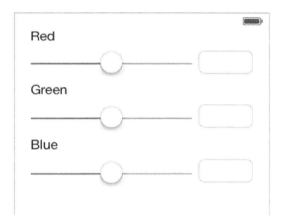

Figure 4-27. The finished interface

5.   One final step is to select the red Slider and examine its values in the Attributes Inspector. You'll see that its value range is set with 0 as a minimum value and 1 as a maximum. The instinct here might be to set it to 255, the upper value of a color in the RGB format, however, the method you'll be using expects a value between 0 and 1, so this fits your needs perfectly. You do, however, want to change the starting point for the Slider to be the upper value, so change the Current value to 1 from 0.5. Repeat this for the green and blue sliders.

This completes the interface, so now you need to create your outlets and actions before moving on to the code, which is very simple for this tab. As you did in the previous tab, start by opening the Assistant Editor and ensure it shows the SliderViewController.h file.

1. First, create an outlet for each of the UISlider controls, naming them redSlider, greenSlider, and blueSlider, respectively.

2. Next, create outlets for each of our UITextFields, naming them redValue, greenValue, and blueValue, respectively.

3. Now create actions for all of our UISlider controls, naming them changeRed, changeGreen, and changeBlue, respectively.

4. Finally, and for reasons that I'll go into shortly, make your view controller a Text View delegate by adding <UITextFieldDelegate> after @interface SliderViewController : UIViewController.

Before I move on, check that your code looks like this:

```
#import <UIKit/UIKit.h>

@interface SliderViewController : UIViewController<UITextFieldDelegate>

@property (weak, nonatomic) IBOutlet UISlider *redSlider;
@property (weak, nonatomic) IBOutlet UISlider *greenSlider;
@property (weak, nonatomic) IBOutlet UISlider *blueSlider;

@property (weak, nonatomic) IBOutlet UITextField *redValue;
@property (weak, nonatomic) IBOutlet UITextField *greenValue;
@property (weak, nonatomic) IBOutlet UITextField *blueValue;

- (IBAction)changeRed:(id)sender;
- (IBAction)changeGreen:(id)sender;
- (IBAction)changeBlue:(id)sender;

@end
```

That's it for Interface Builder and the header file of the view controller for this tab. This has been one of the most complex interfaces encountered so far. Switch back to the Standard Editor and open SliderViewController.m from the Project Navigator.

First, as with the previous tab, you need to declare some variables right at the start of your implementation. Add the following code after the line @interface SliderViewController ():

```
@interface SliderViewController ()
{
    CGFloat redColor;
    CGFloat greenColor;
    CGFloat blueColor;
}
```

Here you're declaring three floats that will store the value of their respective slider.

Next, navigate to the viewDidLoad method. You have a few lines of code to add there, so let's go through it step by step.

1. First, underneath the line [super viewDidLoad] you want to initialize your floats. Do that with the following code:

```
redColor   = 1;
greenColor = 1;
blueColor  = 1;
```

2. Next, in order to make use of our UITextViewDelegate, you want to specify that this view controller is the delegate for the text fields, so add these lines:

```
self.redValue.delegate   = self;
self.greenValue.delegate = self;
self.blueValue.delegate  = self;
```

3. Finally, you're going to call a method that you haven't written yet, so don't panic when Xcode doesn't help you through code completion and then adds a red exclamation mark next to this line. You'll call the method by adding [self updateColor]; to the viewDidLoad method.

Your viewDidLoad method code should now look like this:

```
- (void)viewDidLoad
{
    [super viewDidLoad];

    redColor   = 1;
    greenColor = 1;
    blueColor  = 1;

    self.redValue.delegate   = self;
    self.greenValue.delegate = self;
    self.blueValue.delegate  = self;

    [self updateColor];
}
```

Next, you'll write the updateColor method. This method will basically take the red, green, and blue float values and use them to set the view's background color. Underneath the viewDidLoad method, add the following code:

```
-(void)updateColor
{
    [self.view setBackgroundColor:
        [UIColor colorWithRed:redColor green:greenColor blue:blueColor alpha:1.0]];
}
```

In this code you create a UIColor object from the red, green, and blue values. The alpha property controls the opacity of the background, with 1.0 being totally opaque and 0.0 being transparent.

Now, you need to add the code into the three actions that are linked with their corresponding slider: changeRed, changeGreen, and changeBlue. All of these methods are practically the same code, with only the variable and outlet names depending on the color. So you'll set the changeRed code step by step, before you complete the remaining two methods yourself, so let's get going.

1. First, get the value from this color's slider and assign it to the redColor float. You do that by designating redColor = self.redSlider.value;.

2. Next, you want to update the text field with the correct RGB value. To do that, you need to convert your value from between 0.0 and 1.0 to what it needs to be, which is 0 and 255, so you multiply the value of redColor by 255. Finally, ensure there are no decimal places by using the stringWithFormat method and the %.0f placeholder, which in plain English means put the float value here but limit it to 0 decimal places. The number before f controls the number of decimal places shown in the string. The code to achieve this is [self.redValue setText:[NSString stringWithFormat: @"%.0f",(redColor*255.0)]];.

3. Finally, a change has been made, so you want to call the updateColor method to make sure the change is reflected in the color set in the view's background. The code for this is the same as in the viewDidLoad method, so type [self updateColor];.

The code for the finish action should look like this:

```
- (IBAction)changeRed:(id)sender {
    redColor = self.redSlider.value;
    [self.redValue setText:[NSString stringWithFormat:@"%.0f",(redColor*255.0)]];
    [self updateColor];
}
```

Now, your challenge is to go ahead and implement the remaining two methods by yourself. When you're done, check that your code matches mine:

```
- (IBAction)changeGreen:(id)sender {
    greenColor = self.greenSlider.value;
    [self.greenValue setText:[NSString stringWithFormat:@"%.0f",(greenColor*255.0)]];
    [self updateColor];
}

- (IBAction)changeBlue:(id)sender {
    blueColor = self.blueSlider.value;
    [self.blueValue setText:[NSString stringWithFormat:@"%.0f",(blueColor*255.0)]];
    [self updateColor];
}
```

There's one final method you need to write, and that's the `textFieldShouldReturn` method, which the text fields will be looking for now that they know this view controller is acting as a delegate for those text fields.

The UITextViewDelegate Implementation

Text fields are probably the most common control in an iOS app—they're everywhere. You tap inside them, the keyboard slides in, and you add your text. It's probably second nature to you that tapping the Return key dismisses the keyboard. Hold that thought; go ahead and run your application, and select the Slide It tab.

Play around with the sliders and see how the background color changes as you change the values. You've created something that can be usefully applied in the real world, which as I mentioned previously, is done by giving the RGB values so that they can be selected. Let's test this: tap in one of the text fields, as expected the keyboard slides in, great; now try to go to the Track It tab. Hmm, not so great, the keyboard is blocking the path so you're effectively stuck and would have to quit and relaunch the app to have any hope of accessing the other tabs again.

What you want to do is make it so that you can hit the Return key and the keyboard dismisses itself. This is why you made your view controller take on the `UITextViewDelegate` role. By doing this, when it comes to the point where you press the Return key, the text field will try to call the `textFieldShouldReturn` method, but because you haven't added this method yet, it doesn't do anything. Add the following code beneath your `viewDidLoad` method:

```
-(BOOL)textFieldShouldReturn:(UITextField *)textField
{
    [textField resignFirstResponder];
    return YES;
}
```

When you tap the text field, it assumes responsibility for everything that happens thereafter, or in other words, it becomes the *First Responder*. When this method is called, you are telling it to give up this status with the `resignFirstResponder` method, before returning a Boolean value, which in this case can be either true or false as the result is the same. Now rerun your application and you should find you can dismiss the keyboard with the Return key and have a fully functional color slider view, as shown in Figure 4-28.

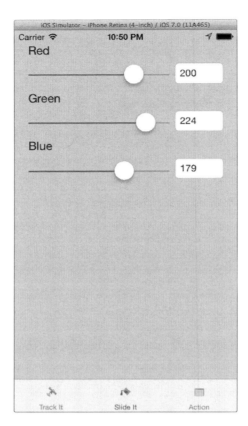

Figure 4-28. *The finished Slide It tab, complete with dismissible keyboard*

Adding "Off the Menu" Controls

You've have created two hugely different but incredible tab views so far, but for the third tab, let's look at another common control you'll add through Interface Builder—the Segmented Control. But let's also look at two important controls that you cannot add through Interface Builder: the Alert View and the Action Sheet.

UIAlertView and UIActionSheet

Before you start building your interface, let's clarify what is meant when I talk about UIAlertViews and UIActionSheets. Figure 4-29 shows how both are used in the iCloud settings area of the Settings application in the iPhone Simulator.

Figure 4-29. An example of an Action Sheet (left) and an Alert View (right)

Action Sheets, like their name implies, can be used to present the user with several options for a specific action. For example, when you tap the flag icon when looking at an e-mail, it asks you whether you want to Flag, Mark as Read / Unread, or Move to Junk. If you give the user the option to add account details to your application, you might use an Action Sheet to ask if the user wants to add an account for your site or a third-party account, such as an OpenID account.

Alert Views are coded in a very similar way to Action Sheets. Alert Views are used to draw the user's attention to an event, such as a timer ending, or confirming whether the user wants to activate a feature or delete some data. You will use them often, and the good news is that they're really easy to set up and use.

Building the Action Tab Interface

Now that you have a clearer understanding of what Alert Views and Action Sheets do, you're ready to start building the third and final tab, the Action tab. You should be left with just the middle position view controller needing to be built, so adjust your storyboard so that this is visible in the design area.

1.   Start by searching for a Segmented Control in the Object Library, as shown in Figure 4-30. When you've found it, drag it onto the view and position it in the center, at the top of the view.

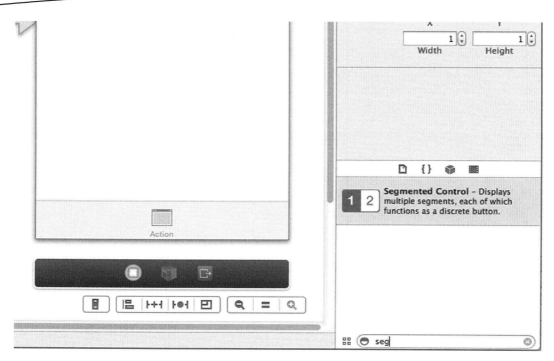

Figure 4-30. *Searching for the Segmented Control in the Object Library*

2. Now you need to change the values of the segments. To do this, select the Segmented Control you added to the view and open the Attributes Inspector. Change the segment Title attribute from First to Alert.

3. Changing the second segment's title isn't as obvious. Looking at the Attributes Inspector for the Segmented Control, you'll notice a drop-down list above the Title attribute you just changed. Click this and select Segment 1- Second.

4. You will now be able to change the Title attribute of the second segment from Second to Action Sheet, as shown in Figure 4-31.

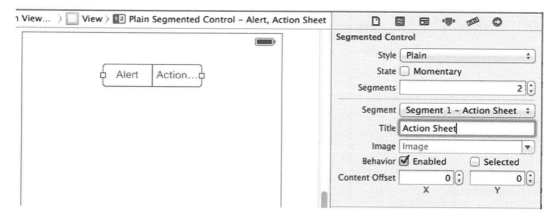

Figure 4-31. *Changing the second segment's Title attribute*

5. Next, using the square handles on either side of our Segmented Control, resize it so that you can see all of the text in the second segment, and then reposition it so that it's centered again.

6. Finally, you want to add a Button control to the view to trigger whichever option you have selected. Search for a Button in the Object Library and drag it to the view, positioning it dead center as you did with the switch in the first tab.

7. Using the Attributes Inspector, change the button's Title attribute from Button to Show Me. Again you will need to reposition it to be dead center after changing the text. Your view should now resemble that shown in Figure 4-32.

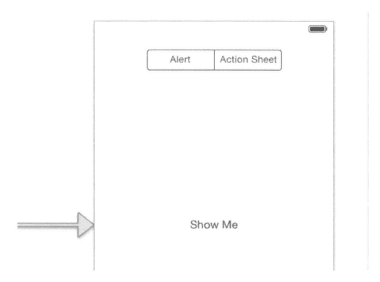

Figure 4-32. The completed interface for the Action tab

8. Now you're ready to create the outlets and actions. As usual, switch over to the Assistant Editor and ensure you have ActionViewController.h selected. Control + drag a connection from the Segmented Control into the header and create an outlet named actionControl, as shown in Figure 4-33.

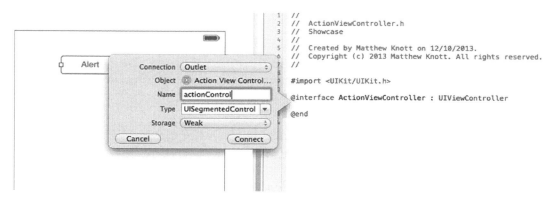

Figure 4-33. *Creating the actionControl outlet*

9. Next, create an outlet for the Button in the same way called `actionButton`, and then an action for it named `performAction`.

Your `ActionViewController.h` file should now resemble the code shown below:

```
#import <UIKit/UIKit.h>
@interface ActionViewController : UIViewController
@property (weak, nonatomic) IBOutlet UISegmentedControl *actionControl;
@property (weak, nonatomic) IBOutlet UIButton *actionButton;

- (IBAction)performAction:(id)sender;

@end
```

It's important to quickly check the official documentation when experimenting with different controls and frameworks, because quite often you need to specify that your view controller is acting as a delegate for the classes you're adding. This is the case with Action Sheets and Alert Views if you want to take advantage of any of their delegate methods. Missing a delegate reference can lead to your application failing or your code not being called in some situations. Because you won't be using the delegate methods in this example, there is no need to add them. You're now ready to start coding the implementation file, so switch back to the Standard Editor and the open `ActionViewController.m` from the Project Navigator.

All you need to look at in the implementation file is the stub for the `performAction` method.

1. Scroll down until you find the `performAction` method, and inside its braces, start typing *if* and then use the arrows to select the *ifelse* statement and press the Tab key.

2. The if statement will look to see which segment is currently selected and determine the action to perform based on that. You do this by checking the `UISegmentedControl`'s `selectedSegmentIndex` property. Remove the *condition* placeholder and type `self.actionControl.selectedSegmentIndex == 0`.

The segments are held in array and the index is an incremental number assigned to each entry. The index starts at 0, so if the selected index is 0, that means Alert is selected, if it's 1 that means Action Sheet is selected.

3. Next remove the `statements-if-true` placeholder, this is where you will initialize and show your Alert View. This is only going to take two lines of code, so for now type the code and then look at what was done at the end:

```
UIAlertView *alert = [[UIAlertView alloc] initWithTitle:@"This is an alert"
                            message:@"You've created an Alert View"
                             delegate:self
                    cancelButtonTitle:@"OK"
                     otherButtonTitles:nil];

[alert show];
```

4. Now you're going to code the *else* eventuality, so remove the `statements-if-false` placeholder and type the following, very similar code:

```
UIActionSheet *sheet = [[UIActionSheet alloc] initWithTitle:@"This is an Action Sheet"
                             delegate:self
                    cancelButtonTitle:@"OK"
               destructiveButtonTitle:nil
                    otherButtonTitles:nil];

[sheet showInView:self.view];
```

That's it; you've configured your view controller to show either an Alert View or an Action Sheet depending on the selected index of the Segmented Control. You'll notice that both controls were initialized in a very similar way, using the `initWithTitle` initializer. Because the focus of this book is Xcode, not iOS or Objective-C, I'm only just scratching the surface of what you can do with these two controls, but they are extremely easy to build upon and are a key addition to any developer's bag of tricks.

You've now coded your third and final tab, so go ahead and run the application in the simulator. It should produce results similar to those shown in Figure 4-34. Look at all the great things you've been able to achieve in this chapter, with a relatively small amount of effort and code! Hopefully this is building your confidence with the Xcode IDE, iOS, and Objective-C as a whole.

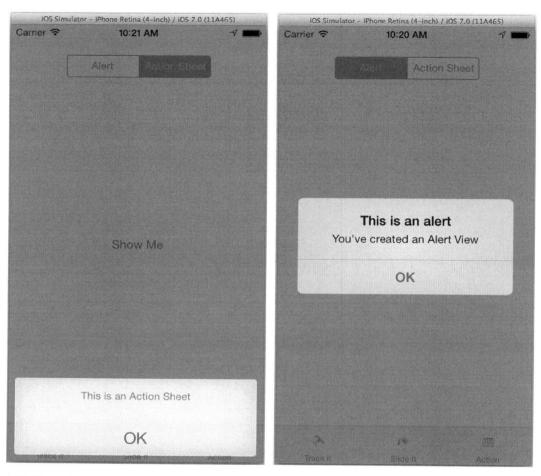

Figure 4-34. The Action Sheet (left) and Alert View (right) shown in the Action tab

Changing the Interface with Code

In this chapter, you've had a good look at how you can adjust the interface elements' attributes using the Attribute Inspector. But just as you can't use Interface Builder to add Action Sheets and Alert Views, there are some visual effects you can only achieve through code. You've already done a lot of hard work in this chapter and you won't learn any more about Xcode here. So look at this section as totally optional. However, you probably want to use the skills you would develop here to go on and build your own applications for iOS devices, in which case these examples will prove invaluable.

Buttons and iOS 7

With iOS 7, Apple introduced the most radical change in design since the launch of the first iPhone—moving away from *skeuomorphism* to a *flat* design style. The decision was controversial when announced, but many are now warming to the change and adapting their applications to fit with the new styles.

One area that has changed that many want to alter in their applications is the standard button. Figure 4-35 shows the three buttons from the Contact screen in iOS 6 and iOS 7. In iOS 6, buttons *looked* like buttons, whereas in iOS 7 they are very much shown in the same style as hyperlinks on a web page.

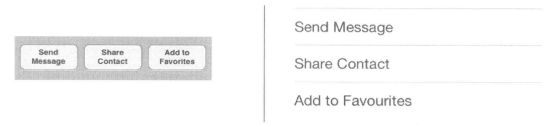

Figure 4-35. *The three buttons from the Contact apps detail view for iOS 6 (left) and updated for iOS 7 (right)*

There is no option for changing background color or rounded corners in Interface Builder, so you would need to delve into code to make these alterations.

1. From the Project Navigator, start by opening `ActionViewController.m` and scroll down to the `viewDidLoad` method. Drop down a line after `[super viewDidLoad];` and you're ready to add some custom code.

2. First, you're going to change the background color to a dark blue color. You'll do this similarly to how you changed the background color in the Slide It tab, by creating a color using RGB values, except this time, you need to convert real RGB values, which range from 0 to 255, to fit in with what the method expects, which is a value between 0.0 and 1.0. To do this you would divide your value by 255.0. Go ahead and add this line of code:

```
self.actionButton.backgroundColor =
                    [UIColor colorWithRed:9/255.0 green:95/255.0 blue:134/255.0 alpha:1.0];
```

3. Now, the button is going to be a bit hard to read with blue text on a blue background, so the next task is to change the text color to white. You could do this in Interface Builder, but then you wouldn't be able to read the button's text when looking at the storyboard. Go ahead and type the following code on the next line:

```
[self.actionButton setTitleColor:[UIColor whiteColor] forState:UIControlStateNormal];
```

4. Finally, you want to apply a curved corner to your button. You can do this easily by specifying a float value greater that 0.0 to the `cornerRadius` property of the button. You do this using the following code:

```
self.actionButton.layer.cornerRadius = 4.0f;
```

Your `viewDidLoad` method should now look like the code below:

```
- (void)viewDidLoad
{
    [super viewDidLoad];

    self.actionButton.backgroundColor =
        [UIColor colorWithRed:9/255.0 green:95/255.0 blue:134/255.0 alpha:1.0];

    [self.actionButton setTitleColor:[UIColor whiteColor] forState:UIControlStateNormal];
    self.actionButton.layer.cornerRadius = 4.0f;
}
```

Go ahead and run the application in the simulator; you'll see the difference immediately in your button on the Action tab. The problem is that the button isn't set at a suitable size to make the most of our effects. Open `Main.Storyboard` from the Project Navigator.

Make the button on the Action view much bigger and then reposition it to center it again. Now run the application again. You're button should now look great and should resemble that shown in Figure 4-36.

Figure 4-36. *The customized button*

That's it for this chapter, but as a final challenge to you, try to apply curved corners to the Text View in the Track It tab using the code you used to curve the button. If you get stuck, the answer can be found at the end of the summary for this chapter.

Summary

This has been a long chapter, but you've made it through and should be really proud of what you've achieved. The objective for the chapter was to learn more about creating interfaces within Xcode, and you did that with a mix of Interface Builder and writing custom code.

Specifically in this chapter, you:

- Created an application from the Tabbed Application template

- Renamed the default view controllers and created your own from scratch

- Removed the default Views from the storyboard and created three of your own

- Tied your new view controllers to their respective classes

- Created Image Sets in the images asset catalog and populated them

- Linked views to a tab bar controller in a storyboard

- Added a framework and accessed the devices GPS function

- Learned about `UITextView`, `UISegmentedControl`, `UISwitch`, and `UISlider` controls

- Programmatically created `UIAlertView` and a `UIActionSheet`

- Learned how to modify the visual appearance of controls using code

When you go through that list, you can see just how many new skills you've learned in this chapter. Before moving on though, I did promise the solution to how to make the corners of the Text View in the Track It tab rounded. If you did it right, you should have added the following line to the `viewDidLoad` method in `TrackViewController.m`:

```
self.locationText.layer.cornerRadius = 5.0f;
```

Very well done if you got that right, now onward to Chapter 5 where you'll begin to look at the help provided through Xcode by Apple along with how Xcode's intelligent code completion feature makes coding much quicker and efficient.

Getting Help and Code Completion

In Chapter 4 you accomplished quite a lot and you should now be starting to feel more confident with the tools and features available in Xcode, and hopefully you're seeing how this can help you in building your own applications.

This chapter will focus on the wealth of help that Xcode offers you while you create the next big OS X and iOS apps and you'll see how Xcode makes writing code quick and easy with its intelligent code completion feature. What's more, by taking a look at code completion, you will also grasp the basics of working with Xcode's code editor. The main focus of Chapter 4 was Interface Builder with a dash of storyboarding. You went from having a default tab bar application to an application that had three very different tabs. So this chapter will explain how to create the project shown in Figure 5-1 that demonstrates how you can interact with some of the built-in applications: Mail, Messaging, and Safari.

Figure 5-1. *The InTouch application*

Getting Help

Xcode provides help in a variety of different ways, not only on how to use Xcode but also how to program using Objective-C and Apple's frameworks. This section will explain the different ways Xcode provides a means of finding a solution when you're stuck, whether you're using the code editor, property list editor, Interface Builder, or if you've just encountered a problem while coding.

Creating the Project

1. Start by opening Xcode and creating a new project by clicking Create a new Xcode project from the Welcome screen or go to File ➤ New ➤ Project ... (⌘ + Shift + N). Select the Single View Project and click Next.

2. Name your project InTouch and ensure the targeted device is set to iPhone. Configure the other settings as you did in previous applications. Make sure the key settings match those shown in Figure 5-2 and click Next.

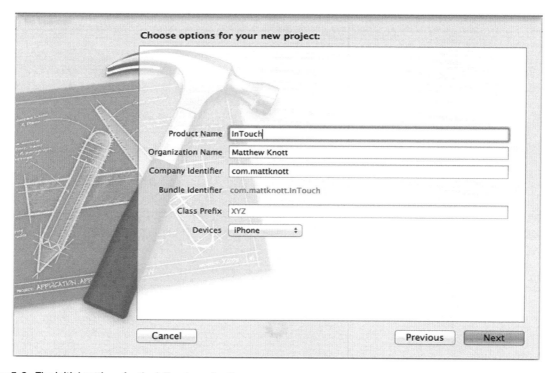

Figure 5-2. *The initial settings for the InTouch application*

3. You don't want to create a Git repository, so leave that unchecked, and make sure your project is going to be saved where you want it to be, and click Create.

That's the foundation of the project setup, and you'll be amazed how much you can achieve beyond this with very little code and effort. Before you go any further, it's important to understand that you don't have to go to your favorite search engine if you're stuck. Xcode has one of the best support systems of any IDE out there, if not *the* best.

Downloading Additional Documentation

Large parts of this chapter are dependent on you having the relevant documentation installed on your computer. Xcode often does this by default, but it's well worth checking that you have everything you need installed, otherwise you'll be missing out on some really excellent application programming interface (API) and system documentation. To check the state of your documentation, start by selecting Xcode ➤ Preferences from the menu bar (⌘ + ,). Click the Downloads tab, and you will be presented with two lists, as shown in Figure 5-3. The key documentation sets you're interested in are the *Xcode 5 doc set* and *iOS 7 doc set*. Click the down-pointing arrow next to the file size and the documentation will start downloading.

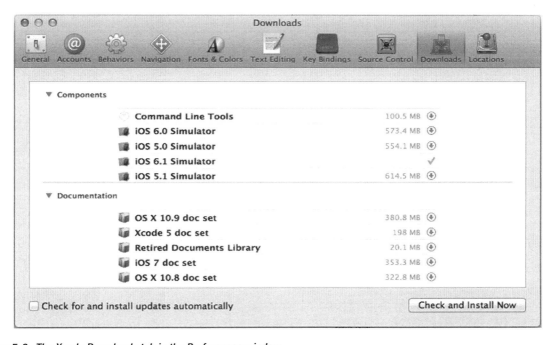

Figure 5-3. The Xcode Downloads tab in the Preferences window

Quick Help

To start off, let's focus on Quick Help. Quick Help provides a concise definition of symbols, interface objects, and build settings. The beauty of using Quick Help is that it resides within the Utilities area of Xcode and it doesn't take away your focus when you're working on a project. To access the Quick Help Inspector, go to View ➤ Utilities ➤ Show Quick Help Inspector (⌥ + ⌘ + 2). In order to see Quick Help in action, open AppDelegate.h and highlight UIResponder. You'll find that Quick Help instantaneously updates to give you useful information. Figure 5-4 shows Quick Help in action.

Figure 5-4. Quick Help showing information about the UIResponder class

You can see from Figure 5-4 that a range of information is displayed for you—what exactly is displayed varies with what you select. However, here you'll find the main entries of a Quick Help entity: Description, Availability, Declared, and Samples.

- *Description:* The description is rather self-explanatory, however, the main point of the description of a symbol, object, or setting covers how it should be used and also gives an overview of event handling.

- *Availability:* The availability states the minimum requirements in terms of the version of iOS the user can be running in order for the object or symbol to function. You'll find many classes have been available since the release of the iPhone software development kit (SDK), however, it's a good idea to keep an eye on newer technologies to ensure you don't run into any compatibility issues.

- *Declared:* Here you're given the name of the header file in which the object or symbol is defined, and upon clicking this you will be able to view the header's source code within the code editor.

- *Samples:* Apple provides a great range of sample code to get you up and running with using a certain object or technology. The Samples section provides links to relevant sample code that will allow you to further explore your currently selected entity in more detail.

If you come across a symbol, object, or setting that doesn't have a Quick Help entry, you have the ability to search Xcode's Documentation for whatever you have selected. For instance, within AppDelegate.h, if you highlight @property, you'll notice that there isn't a Quick Help entry.

With @property still highlighted, click Search Documentation, as shown in Figure 5-5, and the Documentation Viewer window will appear.

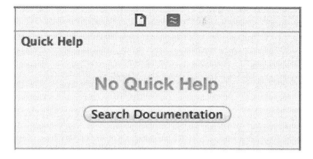

Figure 5-5. Quick Help's Search Documentation button, for when no entry exists for the highlighted entity

In Xcode 4, clicking this button would have opened the Organizer, a key part of Xcode that I'll explain in detail in Chapter 14. But for now you'll find that Xcode has placed @property into the search field and relevant documents are displayed.

Another way to access Quick Help is by pressing the Option key (⌥) and selecting a symbol within the code editor. Figure 5-6 illustrates the dialog displayed when selecting the UIWindow symbol from within AppDelegate.h. This is only accessible from the code editor, but it is very useful if you need to quickly look up a symbol. You're provided with a description of it, the version of iOS in which it was introduced, where it's declared, and a link to additional documentation (any text that's blue is a link that will open an external file, whether that is source code within the code editor or a class reference within the Documentation Viewer).

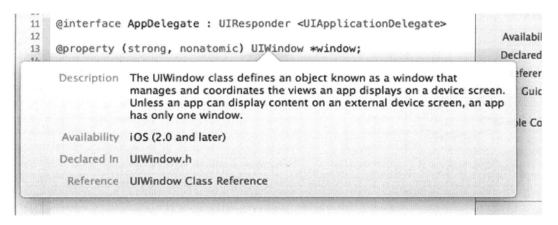

Figure 5-6. A more compact version of Quick Help displaying information regarding the UIWindow class

Documentation Viewer vs. Documentation Organizer

Before I focus on the Documentation Viewer in detail, I wanted to talk about how this facet of Xcode has changed between version 4 and 5. As previously mentioned, Documentation Viewer is a new feature for Xcode 5, having previously been integrated into the Organizer tool. If you've used Xcode in the past, you may be trying to put your finger on what's changed, specifically what's missing.

The Documentation Viewer has had a complete makeover since Xcode 4, but it still gives you access to the tools you may have been familiar with in the past as well as some neat additions.

Documentation Viewer

As you become more and more familiar with the workings of Xcode, you'll soon learn to depend on the Documentation Viewer for its quick access to documentation and SDK references, which, given the literally thousands of APIs, are remarkably detailed. Figure 5-7 displays the Documentation Viewer. To open this, go to Help ➤ Documentation and API Reference (⌥ + ⌘ + ?).

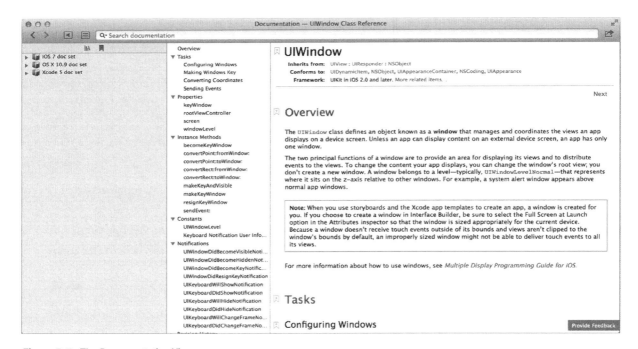

Figure 5-7. *The Documentation Viewer*

The Documentation Viewer allows you to search and browse a variety of different documents and resources, including:

- Class, framework, protocol, and object references
- Technical guides
- Getting started documents

- Technical Q&A

- Change logs and revision histories

- Technical videos

- Sample code

You'll notice that aside from the document being viewed, the Documentation Viewer has three key areas: the Toolbar, the Navigator, and the Table of Contents; I'll cover all three of these in detail in the following sections.

Note   What's really useful about the Documentation sets within Xcode is the fact that they're completely accessible offline. This means if you're working where there isn't an Internet connection, you still have access to the wealth of documentation and references.

Toolbar

The Toolbar contains all of Documentation Viewer's navigation and sharing features; I'll explain these in detail moving left to right across the bar:

- *Backward/Forward Navigation:* The Documentation Viewer works very much like a web browser in that the content is HTML based. You can bookmark pages of interest, and as you'll see here, you can navigate backward and forward through the history of your research. This can be invaluable as you dip in and out of API references trying to find how to correctly instantiate a new class or get a better understanding of the class properties.

- *Sidebar Controls:* Next immediately after the backward and forward navigation arrows are two buttons: the first controls the visibility of the Navigator, the second controls the visibility of the Table of Contents.

- *Search:* The sheer amount of documentation provided by Apple can overwhelm even the most seasoned iOS developers, and it would be absurd for Apple to assume developers would be able to find the correct documentation for the nitty-gritty details of underlying Objective-C technologies, classes, or methods. That's why the Documentation Organizer has a very useful search functionality that allows you to search for a particular term.

  To demonstrate, search for a broad term, for example, *gesture*. This can relate to a variety of different things, but luckily Xcode helps you find just what you're looking for quite easy. Figure 5-8 illustrates the results that are displayed when searching for *gesture*.

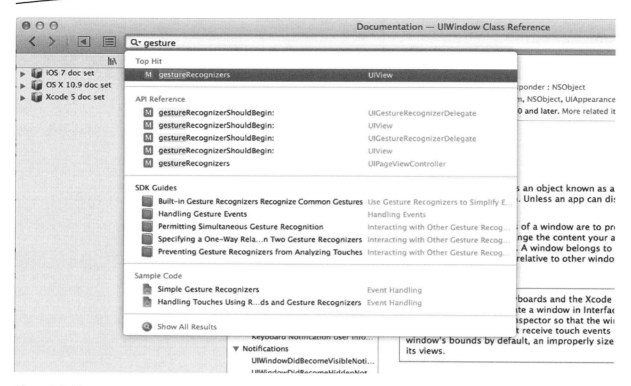

Figure 5-8. *The top results displayed when searching for "gesture"*

You'll notice that as you type, only a few results are displayed; click Show All Results to see the full set of results spread across a number of sections. In this case API Reference, SDK Guides, Tool Guides, and Sample Code are shown.

■ *Share:* A very familiar icon now to most people, and almost identical in function to its equivalent in Safari, the Share button presents a list of ways to share or export the current document: Open in Safari, Add Bookmark, Email Link, Message, and, if available, the option to open a PDF copy of the document. Because documentation in the Documentation Viewer can often be spread over numerous pages, it can be difficult to search within the scope of the entire document. This is where opening the PDF copy can be useful, and most classes and APIs support this.

The Navigator Sidebar

The Navigator provides you with two methods of accessing help and documentation. First is the ability to browse the entire library of documentation installed on the machine and the second is through access to bookmarks you have placed in various pieces of documentation. Access to each feature is controlled by two icons at the top of the Navigator, as shown in Figure 5-9.

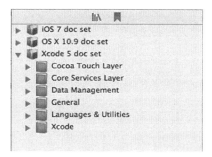

Figure 5-9. *The Navigator gives you access to browse the document library and also access your bookmarks*

The ability to browse through the documentation allows you to start out with a topic area such as file management, and then expand that topic, viewing all sample code, guides, and class references. For many developers, this is the best way to use the system documentation to approach a problem or area of development because you have all the relevant resources available to you when you reach the topic area, rather than starting with a specific class or framework.

The ability to bookmark articles, guides, references, and sample code is another heavily used feature of the Documentation Viewer. This makes it easy to refer to a piece of documentation at a later date. It's inevitable that at some point you're going to stumble upon something that may not be useful right away but you may want to refer to it at a later date, therefore, a bookmark is just what you need!

Adding a Bookmark

In order to actually bookmark a piece of documentation, Figure 5-10 shows that you have three choices. You've already seen the Add Bookmark option from the Share icon (1) on the Toolbar, alternatively you can simply click the bookmark icon found throughout the documentation (2), or you can also right-click the documentation while you're viewing it (3).

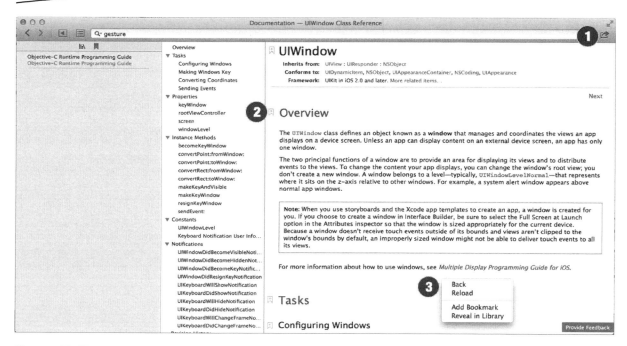

Figure 5-10. Three ways to bookmark documentation while viewing it

Viewing Your Bookmarks

Once you've bookmarked documentation and would like to access it again, you simply ensure the Navigator is active using the relevant Toolbar icon, and that the bookmarks icon is selected within the Navigator and you will see a simple list of everything you've bookmarked. Simply click the documentation item from the Navigator and it'll open. To delete a bookmark, simply select the item from the sidebar and then press Backspace, or right-click the item and select Delete.

Unfortunately, your bookmarks aren't synced anywhere, so you'll have to ensure you're on your device to access your bookmarks. It's sometimes useful to use Apple's online documentation library if you'd like to access your bookmarks on other devices, for example, your iPhone or iPad.

The Table of Contents Sidebar

The Table of Contents sits on the left-hand side of the document you are viewing and, as you would expect, it provides you with a hierarchical overview of the document, allowing you to quickly navigate a large document and see any associated source code or example projects, as shown in Figure 5-11.

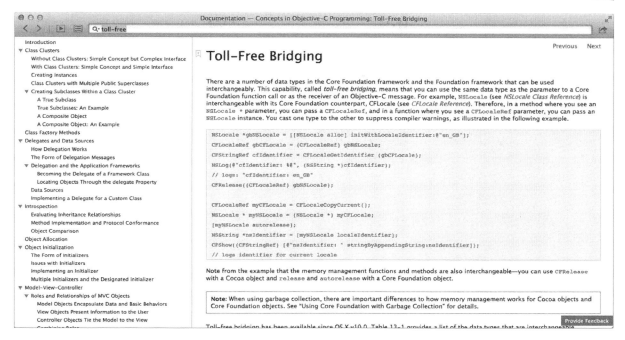

Figure 5-11. The Table of Contents allows large documents to be navigated quickly

Quickly Accessing Documentation

Xcode makes it easy to access help while you're working on your project without the need of having to open the Documentation Viewer each time you want to look something up. Simply right-click and, depending on what part of Xcode you're working with, a help menu will appear in which you can access popular documentation guides displayed as submenus. You can access these menus from the Source Editor (Figure 5-12), Interface Builder (Figure 5-13), and even the Project Navigator (Figure 5-14) along with a variety of others. When you choose an item from the help submenu, the Documentation Viewer will be displayed and will show the relevant guide or reference. These is useful when you would like to look something up quickly or want to know how to perform a task within the part of Xcode you're using.

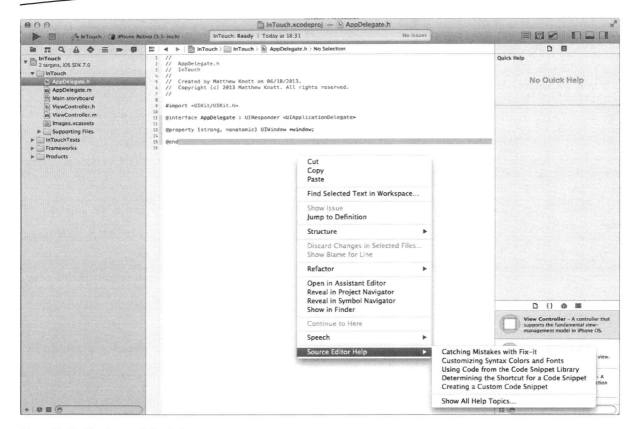

Figure 5-12. The Source Editor help menu

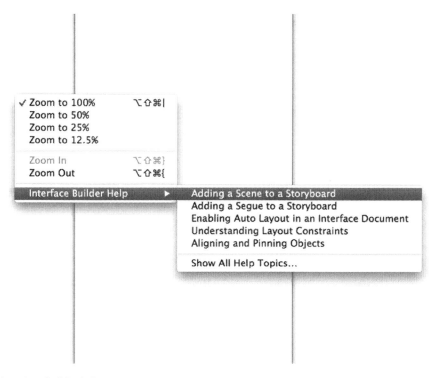

Figure 5-13. *The Interface Builder help menu*

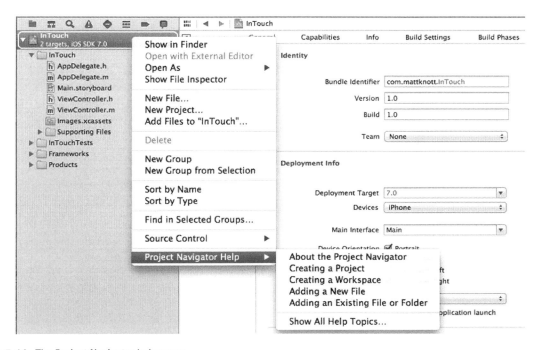

Figure 5-14. *The Project Navigator help menu*

Apple's Web Site

As mentioned previously in this chapter and also at the beginning of this book, Apple's developer web site also provides an excellent library of information. In fact, when you download a Documentation Set, you are in fact just downloading an offline version of Apple's reference library, because the Documentation Viewer is essentially a glorified web browser.

Here is a list of useful online resources that are provided by Apple, aimed mainly at iOS developers:

■ `http://developer.apple.com/` The main home of Apple's developer web site; here you can access the three developer centers available, see the latest and greatest news in the world of Apple, specifically for developers, access many other parts of Apple's developer world such as resource centers, information about copyright, and much more. I will discuss these later when it's time to build and share our application.

■ `https://developer.apple.com/devcenter/ios/index.action` The iOS Dev. Center is the main hub of all of Apple's resources that are provided to iOS developers and is immensely useful when you're developing applications. You can access the iOS Provisioning Portal, Member Center, iOS Reference Library, and also available downloads.

■ `https://developer.apple.com/library/ios/navigation/` The iOS Reference Library is what's used to populate the Documentation Organizer. The library includes technical guides, a wealth of references, sample code, and documentation. Apple really sets itself apart with the overwhelming amount of support provided to developers. If you're working with a certain technology within iOS or OS X, chances are there's a detailed guide on it. You can search the library using the search bar of the sidebar to the left. It's easy to become overwhelmed, but once you get familiar with its layout, finding what you need will soon become easy.

■ `https://developer.apple.com/library/ios/navigation/#section=Resource%20Types&topic=Sample%20Code` It's always useful to see something up and running, and seeing a working example can also save a lot of time. The sample code provided by Apple allows you to test a particular technology yourself, dissect the code, and even use the code in your own applications.

■ `https://devforums.apple.com` Something that I haven't really mentioned is Apple's Developer Forums. The Developer Forums aren't as active as other forums available online, however, the users there are much more helpful and willing to offer advice and solutions.

■ `https://developer.apple.com/videos/ios/` Apple also provides a whole host of useful videos you can watch. The videos range from low-level technologies to high-level technologies and frameworks provided by Apple. Because many developers don't have the chance to attend WWDC, Apple's World Wide Developers Conference held annually, the video coverage of the conference can also be really useful. This too can be found in the videos section of the developer web site.

Code Completion

Code completion can greatly increase any developer's productivity and can also save a lot of time, that is if you know how to use it correctly. Using code completion within Xcode can take some getting used to, depending on your prior experience, however, Xcode is much more intelligent than other IDEs.

In order to get a taste of not only code completion but also using the Source Editor as a whole, you're going to do things a bit differently this time. Specifically, you're going to code your actions and their implementation first, and then wire them up using Interface Builder, instead of using Interface Builder to create the action stubs and linkages as you did in previous chapters.

The Header File

To begin, open `ViewController.h` and just under the `#import <UIKit/UIKit.h>` line, begin typing the following:

```
#import <MessageUI/MessageUI.h>
```

As you begin typing, you'll see that Xcode starts to make suggestions of what you're trying to type, Figure 5-15 illustrates this.

Figure 5-15. Xcode's code completion

You can use the up and down arrows to change the selection within the code completion dialog and then with the correct item highlighted, simply press Enter and your cursor will focus on the end of the line and the code will be entered. You've imported the `MessageUI` framework because it gives you access to `MFMailComposeViewController` among other classes, so try out some of the skills you learned earlier in this chapter and search for it in Documentation Viewer. You'll find a wealth of information including confirmation of its parent framework.

Next, you need to tell the view controller to act as a delegate for `MFMessageComposeViewControllerDelegate` and `MFMailComposeViewControllerDelegate`. To do this, immediately next to `@interface ViewController : UIViewController`, type the following and use the code completion dialog to insert the correct code:

```
<MFMessageComposeViewControllerDelegate, MFMailComposeViewControllerDelegate>
```

Your header file should now look like the code below:

```
#import <UIKit/UIKit.h>
#import <MessageUI/MessageUI.h>

@interface ViewController : UIViewController<MFMessageComposeViewControllerDelegate,
                                             MFMailComposeViewControllerDelegate>
@end
```

Next you'll add three methods that the buttons will use to open the web site or begin composing an e-mail or text message. Begin typing the following code just below the @interface line and above the @end symbol:

```
- (IBAction)sendEmail:(id)sender;
- (IBAction)sendText:(id)sender;
- (IBAction)visitWebsite:(id)sender;
```

As you type, you'll notice the code completion dialog appears a little differently in terms of what it suggests, Figure 5-16 illustrates this.

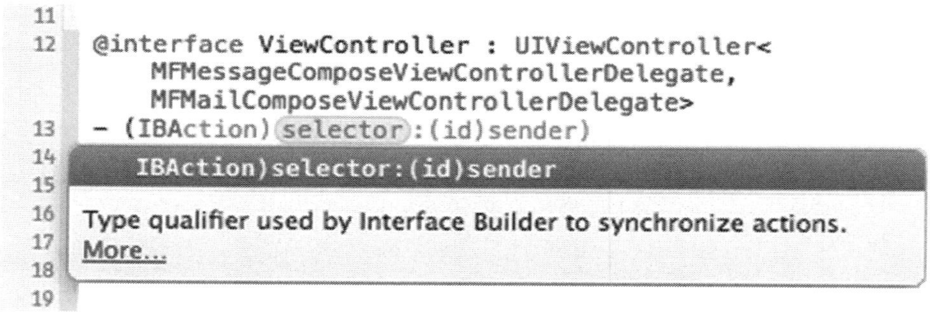

```
11
12    @interface ViewController : UIViewController<
          MFMessageComposeViewControllerDelegate,
          MFMailComposeViewControllerDelegate>
13    - (IBAction) selector :(id)sender)
14        IBAction)selector:(id)sender
15
16    Type qualifier used by Interface Builder to synchronize actions.
17    More...
18
19
```

Figure 5-16. Code completion when creating a new IBAction

This is because you're creating a method that will require you to input a parameter, in this case a selector or the name of the method that's displayed within the Connections inspector. To insert the code and jump to the first required parameter, simply press the Tab key and begin typing and then once you're done, press Enter.

> **Note**   As great as Xcode's code completion feature is, it rather lacks on the ability to add a semicolon to your code. This is because many times you will want to continue to type code once you've used code completion, so make sure you remember to add a semicolon when you need to, otherwise you'll get a nasty surprise when you try to build your application.

The Implementation File

Now you need to actually implement the methods you created within your header file. To do this, open ViewController.m from the Project Navigator and just below the viewDidLoad method, begin typing the following code to implement the visitWebsite method:

```
- (IBAction)visitWebsite:(id)sender
```

Again, Xcode's code completion will appear and display the available list of methods you can use. Use the arrows on your keyboard to select the visitWebsite method and press Enter. Insert the pair of curly braces so you have something similar to that what's displayed below:

```
- (IBAction)visitWebsite:(id)sender
{

}
```

In between the curly braces, begin to type the highlighted code:

```
- (IBAction)visitWebsite:(id)sender
{
    [[UIApplication sharedApplication] openURL:[NSURL URLWithString:@"http://apress.com"]];
}
```

Feel free to replace http://apress.com with your own URL and make sure you remember the correct amount of square brackets and the semicolon at the end.

> **Note**   Each time you add a square bracket, you'll notice that for a brief moment a little yellow box appears around its counterpart, that is, the one you're closing. This is to make sure you don't add too many or too few square brackets. This also applies to brackets and curly braces.

Next, you'll add the different methods required to make use of the MessageUI framework that allows users to compose an e-mail from within an application. Below the second curly brace that terminates the visitWebsite method, type the following code:

```
- (IBAction)sendEmail:(id)sender {
    if ([MFMailComposeViewController canSendMail])
    {
        NSArray *toRecipients = [NSArray arrayWithObject:@"xcode@mattknott.com"];

        MFMailComposeViewController *mailViewController  = [[MFMailComposeViewController alloc] init];
        [mailViewController  setSubject:@"Beginning Xcode"];
        [mailViewController  setToRecipients:toRecipients];
        [mailViewController  setMessageBody:@"I am really enjoying the book!" isHTML:NO];
        mailViewController .mailComposeDelegate = self;
        [self presentViewController:mailViewController  animated:YES completion:nil];
    }
    else
```

```
    {
        NSLog(@"This device is currently unable to send email");
    }
}

-(void)mailComposeController:(MFMailComposeViewController *)controller didFinishWithResult:
(MFMailComposeResult)result error:(NSError *)error
{
    if (result == MFMailComposeResultSent)
    {
        NSLog(@"Result: Email Sent!");
    }
    else if (result == MFMailComposeResultCancelled)
    {
        NSLog(@"Result: Email Cancelled.");
    }
    else if (result == MFMailComposeResultFailed)
    {
        NSLog(@"Result: Error, Unable to Send Email.");
    }
    else if (result == MFMailComposeResultSaved)
    {
        NSLog(@"Result: Mail Saved as Draft.");
    }

    [self dismissViewControllerAnimated:YES completion:nil];
}
```

Feel free to change xcode@mattknott to your own e-mail address and also feel free to change
the subject and presumptuous contents of the e-mail message to whatever you'd like the
user to see before they begin to compose their e-mail message to you. The second method
(mailComposeController method) is a delegate method that is required when instantiating an
MFMailComposeViewController. In this instance, you'll account for each of the possible outcomes of
trying to send an e-mail before actually allowing the user to dismiss the compose view once they've
sent their message or would like to close it because they've decided to cancel it.

Sending a Text Message

SMS (Short Message Service) Messaging is still one of the most popular systems of communication
in the world today, and just as they do with e-mail, Apple makes it very easy to send a text message
from within your application. You'll find the code is very similar to the previous two methods,
however, there is one big distinction: you have to test this on a physical device as the simulator is
not capable of simulating SMS.

With that in mind, drop down a couple of lines after the mailComposeController method and type
this code:

```
- (IBAction)sendText:(id)sender {
    if ([MFMessageComposeViewController canSendText])
    {
        NSArray *toRecipients = [NSArray arrayWithObject:@"1234500000"];
```

```objc
        MFMessageComposeViewController *smsController = [[MFMessageComposeViewController alloc] init];
        smsController.messageComposeDelegate = self;
        [smsController setRecipients:toRecipients];
        [smsController setBody:@"I am interested in your products, please call me back."];
        [self presentViewController:smsController animated:YES completion:nil];
    }
    else
    {
        NSLog(@"This device is currently unable to send text messages");
    }
}

-(void)messageComposeViewController:(MFMessageComposeViewController *)controller
didFinishWithResult:(MessageComposeResult)result
{
    if (result == MessageComposeResultSent)
    {
        NSLog(@"Text Message Sent");
    }
    else
    {
        NSLog(@"Unable to Send Text Message!");
    }
    [self dismissViewControllerAnimated:YES completion:nil];
}
```

Building the Interface

So far you've written all of the code your application needs to perform three essential communication tasks; now you need to build and connect your interface.

1. Start by opening Main.storyboard from the Project Navigator.

2. Next, drag a label and three buttons onto the view. Position the label at the top of the view and the three buttons on top of one another.

3. Resize the label so it fills the full width of the view, and then open the Attributes Inspector (⌥ + ⌘ + 4). Set the Text attribute to say "Ways to get in touch," then in the Font attribute, click the T to customize the font. Set the Font to custom; Family to HelveticaNeue; Style to Thin; and Size to 23, as shown in Figure 5-17.

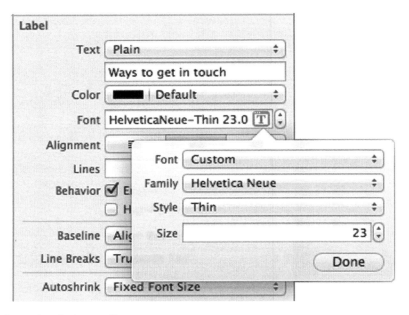

Figure 5-17. Setting the custom font properties

Next, and in order, double-click each of the buttons and name them Email, Text Message, and Website. Your finished interface should look something like that shown in Figure 5-18.

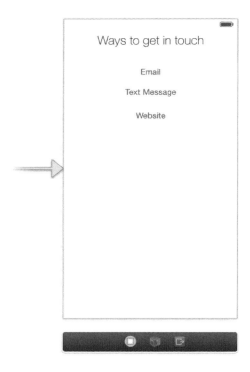

Figure 5-18. The finished interface

Making Connections

Now, you need to connect the methods you've created in the header file with the buttons you made in the previous chapter. To do this, head over to `MainStoryboard.storyboard` and open the Connections Inspector (⌥ + ⌘ + 6) with the View Controller selected from the Document Outline, as illustrated in Figure 5-19.

Figure 5-19. Main.storyboard with the View Controller selected and the Connections Inspector open

Unlike in previous chapters where you used the Assistant Editor to connect buttons to actions, here you're going to use the Connections Inspector to connect the actions to the buttons. Under the Received Actions heading in the Connections Inspector, you will see the three actions, with a hollow circle next to each one. From the `sendEmail` method's circle, click and drag a connection to the button, as shown in Figure 5-20. A menu will appear above the button, select Touch Up Inside from toward the bottom of the list.

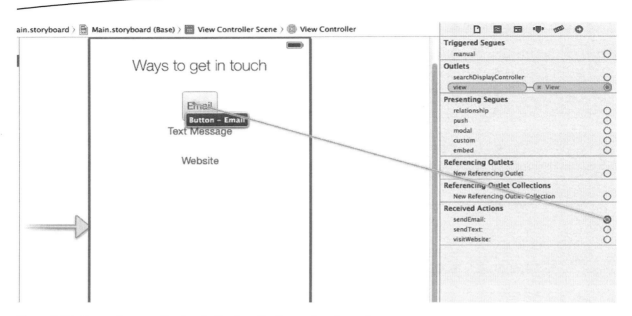

Figure 5-20. Connecting an action to a button from the Connections Inspector

Note   When a button in an iOS application is tapped, it is the Touch Up Inside event that is triggered. Therefore, by linking the action to this event, you can be sure that the code will be executed when the user taps your button.

Repeat this step, linking the two remaining actions to their respective buttons, making sure to select the Touch Up Inside event from the list.

Adding the Message Framework

Your last task is to add the MessageUI framework that will allow your users to compose an e-mail and text message from within your application. To do this, select InTouch from the Project Navigator and then choose InTouch from the list of Targets, if it is not already selected. Scroll down the General tab until you see Linked Frameworks and Libraries, as shown in Figure 5-21.

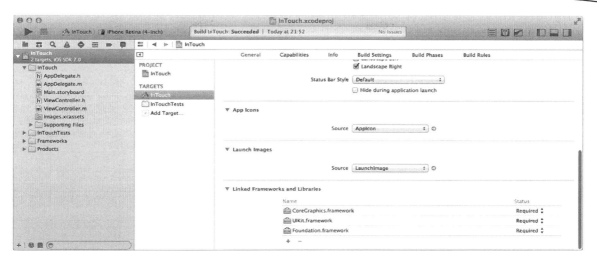

Figure 5-21. *InTouch's General tab*

Next select the small + icon in the bottom left of the expanded Linked Frameworks and Libraries section and a dialog will appear containing a list of available frameworks you can add to your project. Search for MessageUI, select MessageUI.framework, and then click Add, as shown in Figure 5-22.

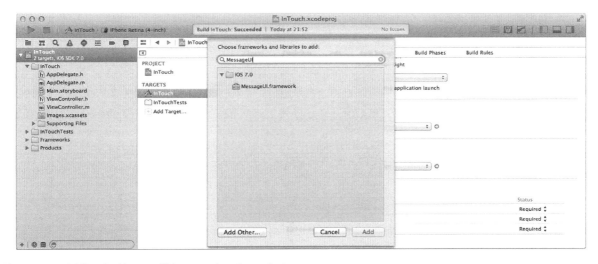

Figure 5-22. *Adding the MessageUI framework to the project*

Summary

Now, if you run your application either on your device or on the iOS Simulator, you'll find that when you tap the Website button, InTouch is placed in the background and Safari opens. Similarly, if you click the Email or Text Message buttons, a view is pushed in which the user can send an e-mail or SMS. Figure 5-23 illustrates, in order on the main view, the Email compose screen, the Text Message compose screen, and Safari with your web site.

Figure 5-23. *The mail compose view and the About tab*

> **Note**   You can't send an e-mail from the iOS Simulator and can't even see the SMS dialog, so in order
> to fully test this feature, you'll need to run InTouch on an actual iOS device that has an e-mail account
> configured. You'll commence testing on a physical device in Chapter 14, for now take my word for it and
> assume that it works.

This chapter explored quite a few different topics and you added some interesting communication features to your application. Here is what you've achieved:

- Looked at the Documentation Viewer
- Looked at how Xcode makes it easy to access help from wherever you're working within Xcode
- Learned about Quick Help
- Explored Apple's online documentation
- Became more familiar with the Source Editor
- Used code completion to speed up how you code
- Connected actions using the Connections Inspector
- Added a framework to your project

The next chapter will look at constraints. If you've been testing on a physical device or have tried rotating the simulator, you'll notice things get a little messed up. I'll explain in detail how to quickly fix this in Interface Builder, and we'll also take our first look at programmatically adding objects to the view controller and using programmatic constraints to keep them aligned.

Chapter 6

Constraints

Chapter 5 detailed the many ways Xcode gives you access to help, documentation, and guidance. You created a handy communications application along the way that could compose a text message, an e-mail, or even open a web site in another browser. You also looked at an alternative to the Assistant Editor for making connections between Interface Builder controls and your outlets and actions, and I talked briefly about how the Organizer had changed significantly since Xcode 4.

This chapter will introduce you to another significant change in Xcode—a change to the Auto Layout system. Auto Layout (or Autolayout as Apple sometimes refers to it) has been completely overhauled in Xcode 5, and in this chapter, you'll use Auto Layout to build an example application that adapts to changing resolutions and screen orientations the way you want it to. What's great is that the techniques you learn here are equally applicable to both iOS and OS X development.

Understanding Auto Layout

In Xcode 5, Auto Layout provides you with a comprehensive set of tools to automatically lay out your controls within a view and constrain how your different controls react to each other when the resolution changes or when the iOS device is rotated.

Despite the usefulness of Auto Layout, there is some stigma around it, and some developers, because of its limited control, have not always taken it seriously. Apple has worked hard to address the shortcomings of Auto Layout in Xcode 5, creating something totally new that gives developers very fine control over the behavior of the elements in the view. I'll present four different ways to add constraints to your controls in this chapter:

- *Manually*, using the Control + click-and-drag method you are familiar with for creating connections
- Using the *Add Missing Constraints* function to automatically add constraints
- Using *Reset to Suggested Constraints* to update constraints when you move constrained controls
- Using the *Pin* menu to set constraints with numeric precision

As a context for demonstrating the power of Auto Layout, you'll need to create a login dialog similar to those you will come across in many password-protected services. Let's begin!

Building an Authentication View

The authentication view you are going to create in this chapter will be a familiar sight to any user of Twitter, Facebook, or any of the countless other web service–based apps you can find in the App Store. In the project you'll be creating in this chapter, you'll be building it in a way that will teach you how to lay out the elements of your view with Auto Layout and constraints, but at the same time, it will also teach you some of the finer points of configuring Text Fields that will be crucial when you develop your own applications.

Figure 6-1 shows LoginApp, the project you'll be creating in this chapter. Here you can see constraints in action. When the device rotates, the Text Field resizes and adapts to the new orientation. I'll also explain in depth the Text Field's attributes; you can see in the finished application that you will have set placeholder text on the e-mail address, but there are a number of hidden refinements that all contribute to a rich user experience.

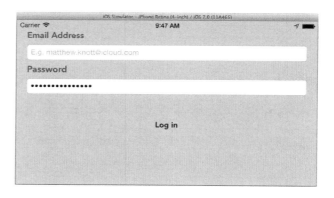

Figure 6-1. *The login page for the app resizing automatically when rotated*

You've done this several times already, so you should be getting pretty familiar with creating new projects by now, but it's always important to read the setup steps because in the next chapter you'll be trying something new.

1. Let's start by opening Xcode and creating a new project by going to File ➤ New ➤ New Project … (⌘ + Shift + N) or, alternatively, Create a new Xcode project from the Welcome screen (⌘ + Shift + 1).

2. Select the Single View Application Template and click Next.

3. Name the project LoginApp, leave the other options as default, but ensure the device is set to iPhone, as shown in Figure 6-2. Click Next.

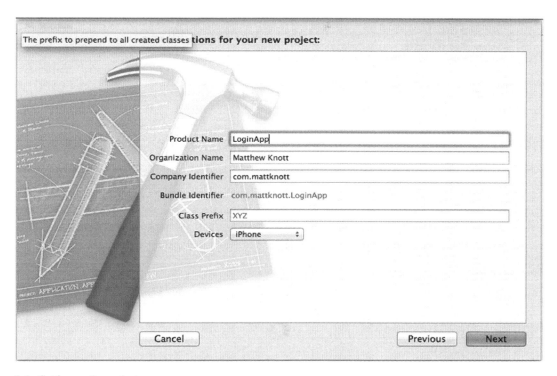

Figure 6-2. Setting up the project

4. Finally, select a location to save the project and click Create.

That's it! You're ready to start building your application, but one thing you should note before you start building up your view is that everything you do in this chapter relating to Auto Layout and setting constraints will be done purely from Interface Builder, you won't write a single line of code. You will, however, look at adding a small bit of code just to add the finishing touches to your form at the end of the chapter. With that in mind let's open `Main.storyboard` and start building the interface.

Design Considerations

If you haven't started already, I hope that after reading this book you'll start writing your own applications using Xcode, whether it's for fun, to address a problem you encounter, or maybe because of a gap you've spotted in the market. Whatever it is you do, when you're starting out, you will make design decisions that, when you run the application, make you realize you've made a terrible error of judgment in how you've arranged your layout.

The good thing is that most of the time there's a simple solution, and the whole thing becomes a valuable learning experience. Login dialogs are a potential banana skin when you're starting out because when you design a beautiful layout on your static view, it's easy to forget about the keyboard that in many cases will slide up and cover your fields, making them totally inaccessible. To address this problem, make sure that you position the Text Fields and Labels in a way that ensures the keyboard will not obscure the Text Field on either the 4-inch or 3.5-inch screen formats.

1. After you've opened Main.storyboard, start by opening the Document Outline if it is not already visible, by clicking the button in the bottom-left corner of the design area that has a box with a right-point triangle in it, as shown in Figure 6-3, indicated by a large arrow.

Figure 6-3. The Show Document Outline button in the bottom-left corner of the design area indicated by the arrow

2. With the Document Outline visible, click the disclosure triangle to the left of View Controller Scene, and then click the disclosure triangle to the left of View Controller. Now click the View item, as shown in Figure 6-4, then open the Attribute Inspector (⌥ + ⌘ + 4).

Figure 6-4. Selecting the view from the Document Outline

Note The Document Outline bar can be extremely useful when working with a large number of controls in a view because you can alter the hierarchy of the elements to make one appear above or below another, or to add them to a scroll view instead of the main view. It's also useful for creating connections between view controllers that are physically far apart in the design area, to save zooming out many times.

3. To make this view more appealing, give it a background color. I've selected a pale green color for my view, but you can select whichever color you like. Click the Background drop-down list and select either a preset color or click Other ... if you want to choose from the pallet or specify an RGB color. I've used Red 206, Green 228, and Blue 188, so you can use the same colors by using the Color Sliders from the color picker, and setting RGB sliders from the drop-down menu, as shown in Figure 6-5.

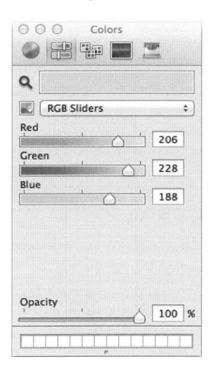

Figure 6-5. Setting an RGB color

4. Now you're ready to start adding controls to your view. Drag a Label and a Text Field from the Object Library onto the view, with the Label going in the top left corner where it snaps to the blue guidelines, and the Text Field snapping into place directly beneath it, as shown in Figure 6-6.

Main.storyboard 〉 📄 Main.storyboard (Base) 〉 No Selection

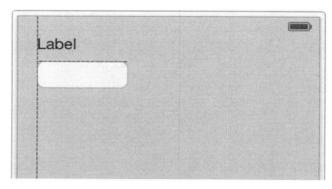

Figure 6-6. The Text Field snapping into place below the Label

5. With the Text Field added to the view, use the handle on the right of the box to resize it, dragging it to the right until, again, the blue guidelines appear.

6. Because the second row is a copy of these elements, you can duplicate them. Holding down the Command (⌘) key, in the Document Outline, click to highlight both the Label – Label item and the Round Style Text Field. You should see handles appear on both the items in the view, as shown in Figure 6-7.

Main.story... 〉 📄 Main.story... 〉 🖼 View Contr... 〉 ⑥ View Contr... 〉 ☐ View 〉 ☐ Round Style Text Field

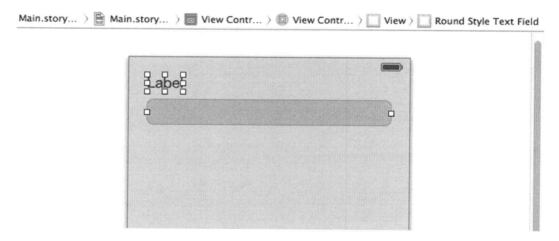

Figure 6-7. Both elements of the view selected

7. To duplicate the items, copy them with ⌘ + C and then click a blank area of the view or select View from the Document Outline. You can then paste them back into the view with ⌘ + V. When the two items appear on the view, they will be grouped together, so move them as one and snap them into place below the first Text Field.

8. Finally, you need to add a button to the view, so drag in a button from the Object Library and position it centrally in the view, a little bit below the last Text Field. If everything has gone to plan, your view should now resemble that in Figure 6-8.

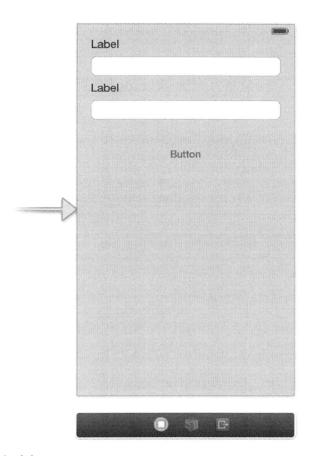

Figure 6-8. The skeleton of the LoginApp

9. With the elements all in place, you need to set the titles and text colors of the Labels and the Button. Select the first Label, and from the Attribute Inspector, set the color to Dark Gray Color from the list of presets. Customize the font by clicking the T icon, as you did in previous chapters, and set the Font to Custom, the Family to Avenir, the style to Heavy, and the Size to 16.0. Change the Text from Label to Email Address. Your attributes for the first label should now resemble those shown in Figure 6-9.

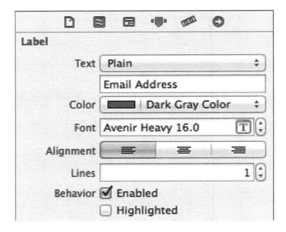

Figure 6-9. *The attributes of the first Label*

10. Repeat the previous step on the second Label, but this time set its Title to Password, and then on the Button, set its Title to Log in.

Before you go any further, let's run the application as it stands. The Simulator will open, and your view will look great, just as expected. Next, rotate the Simulator by selecting Hardware ➤ Rotate Left from the menu bar or press ⌘ + Left Arrow. Now, the problem will become apparent; as you can see in Figure 6-10, the elements stay the same size but also stay in the same position.

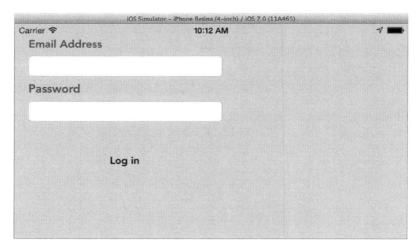

Figure 6-10. *The misaligned view, badly needing some constraints*

Ironically, if you had gone through these same steps in the previous version of Xcode, you would have had a nicely scaling view looking similar to that in Figure 6-1, so why did Apple change this system for Xcode 5? As a developer, you will want full control over how your view reacts to changes in form factor and orientation, and you just didn't have the degree of control many developers *needed* with Xcode 4.

Let's look at the various ways Apple has reworked Auto Layout to give us fine control over layouts.

Manually Adding Constraints

The first method I'll explain for adding constraints is the manual method, in which you would use the familiar control + click-and-drag technique to specify a constraining relationship between multiple elements. You should now be used to holding the Control key while clicking and dragging, you've done it a number of times in previous chapters to create connections to actions and outlets.

> **Note** Even though we're manually adding constraints, we're still using Auto Layout, which is a bit of a contradiction and can be confusing.

1. Let's start by adding five manual constraints to the layout. Select the first Text Field, then holding down the Control key, click the Text Field and drag a line to the left side of the view and release the mouse button. A contextual dialog will appear, as shown in Figure 6-11.

 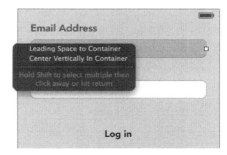

Figure 6-11. Dragging a line to the side of the view (left) and the context menu that appears (right)

2. You want to tell Interface Builder to constrain the position of the Text Field to the sides of the view so that when it rotates, the Text Field resizes. Select Leading Space to Container from the menu and an orange guideline will appear to the left of the Text Field.

3. Now control and drag a connection from the Text Field to the right side of the view, and when you release the mouse button, select Trailing Space to Container. You've now done all you need to constrain your Email Address Text Field to the sides of the view; let's do the same for the Password Text Field.

4. Repeat the process by selecting the Password Text Field, and control-drag a connection to the left side of the view and select Leading Space to Container. Next control-drag a connection from the Text Field to the right side of the Text Field and choose Trailing Space to Container.

5. The constraint for the button will be slightly different. At this point you're probably happy with the vertical position and size of our button, whatever the orientation or resolution of the device. All you want to do now is constrain the button so that no matter how the view changes, the button stays central horizontally. To do this, select the Log in button, and control-drag a line directly beneath the button, as shown in Figure 6-12.

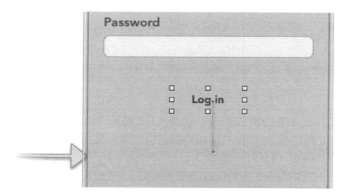

Figure 6-12. Dragging a connection below the Log in button so that you can constrain it horizontally

6. When you release the mouse button, the contextual menu appears again, this time select Center Horizontally in Container. A guideline will appear going from the top of the view to the bottom.

That's it! With a few clicks you've done everything you needed to do to make your layout respond to changes in orientation. All that's left to do is to test it in Simulator. Go ahead and click the Run button (⌘ + R). When the Simulator launches, rotate the interface by selecting Hardware ➤ Rotate Left from the menu bar or press ⌘ + Left Arrow, as you did earlier. You should find that the elements resize just as you want and exactly as previewed in Figure 6-1, with the button staying in the middle of the view and the Text Fields resizing because you've constrained them to be a fixed distance from the side of the view.

Before moving on, let's quickly look at the attributes of a constraint. Back in Interface Builder, go ahead and select the Email Address Text Field. Now, select one of the constraint guidelines by single-clicking it; it will become highlighted, as shown in Figure 6-13. Alternatively, with the View item inspected in the Document Outline, you can expand Constraints and select the first constraint in the list.

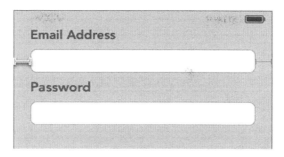

Figure 6-13. *Selecting the Constraint guideline*

If you look at the Attributes Inspector for a moment, as shown in Figure 6-14, you'll see a variety of ways to fine tune how constraint works. First, looking at the Relation attribute, which should currently be set to Equal. You can change it to Less Than or Equal To or More Than or Equal To. These two options allow the constraint to be flexible, whereas Equal is a fixed value that cannot be deviated from.

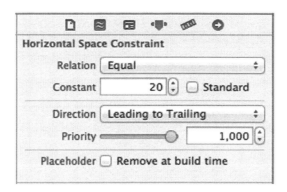

Figure 6-14. *The attributes of the constraint*

The Constant attribute contains the numerical value assigned to the constraint. Currently, if you positioned your Text Field in the same place as mine, the value will be 20. Putting these attributes into plain English, this means the Text Field will stay a distance *equal to 20* points on the leading side. Using the up and down arrows next to it, increase the constant value by clicking the up arrow. Notice how as you increase the value, the Text Field moves further from the leading edge of the view. Now set the value back to 20 and let's move on.

Specifying Constraints with the Align Menu

Because the control-drag method of specifying constraints isn't everyone's preferred way of working, let's look at how to apply the same constraints using the Align menu and then the Pin menu. The Align menu is used to specify how controls align to each other and the wider view. Because the constraint you applied to your button was an alignment constraint, you'll be using the

Align menu to constrain your button in the same way you did earlier with the control-drag method. The Align button is one of several buttons available at the bottom of Interface Builder, it is the third button from the left and resembles a small box on top of a larger one; refer back to Chapter 4 if you need to reacquaint yourself with these buttons.

Before you use either the Align or Pin menu, you need to remove the constraints you've applied to your controls. Holding the ⌘ key, click the two Text Field's and the Log in button once to select them, then click the Resolve Auto Layout button and choose Clear Constraints, as shown in Figure 6-15. Alternatively, you can select View Controller from the Document Outline, then click the Resolve Auto Layout Issues button and use the Clear All Constraints in View Controller option to remove all the constraints set in this view controller.

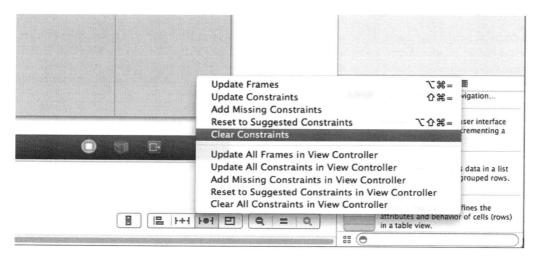

Figure 6-15. *Selecting Clear Constraints from the Resolve Auto Layout Issues menu*

The constraints you applied earlier have now been removed, and the program is ready for you to reapply them using the Align and Pin menus. First, select just the Log in button and then go ahead and click the Align button. From the menu that appears, check the box next to Horizontal Center in Container, as shown in Figure 6-16.

Figure 6-16. *Adding a horizontal alignment constraint using the Align menu*

Clicking the button currently showing Add 1 Constraint will apply the constraint to the button, exactly the same as when you used the control-drag method, but without the need to be precise with your mouse movements.

Specifying Constraints with the Pin Menu

I've shown you how you can center your Log in button using the Align menu, now it's time to constrain the Text Fields so that their leading and trailing edges stay 20 points from the side of the view at all times. This technique is known as *pinning*, because you are fixing a positional attribute of the control. Therefore, it makes sense that you would reapply the constraints to your Text Fields when using the Pin menu. The Pin menu is the fourth button from the left at the bottom of the Interface Builder design area, and is to the right of the Align button.

What's great about the Pin menu is that you can apply constraints to both Text Fields in a single action. Click the Email Address Text Field to select it, then hold the ⌘ key and click the Password Text Field to select them both, now click the Pin button and a menu will appear, as shown in Figure 6-17.

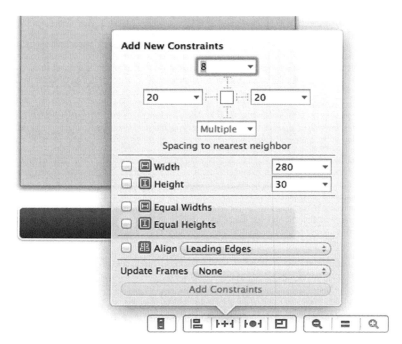

Figure 6-17. *The Pin menu*

Let's focus on the top area of the Pin menu, which is four Text Fields with a variety of values. This area is used to set the spacing to the nearest neighbor. Thinking about this specific situation, the nearest neighbor that you want to fix to is the parent view and you want to fix the leading and trailing edges of the Text Fields to that neighbor. If you remember previously in this chapter when I discussed the attributes of one of the Text Field constraints, it had a value of 20 points; conveniently, Xcode has anticipated that you might want to fix the leading and trailing edges with these values, so all you need to do here is tell Xcode you want to apply them.

It's at this point that it is easy to become confused about how to apply the constraints; the Add Constraints button is grayed out, so how do you set these constraints? Luckily the answer is an easy one. At the center of the four Text Fields in the Pin menu is a square shape with red I-bars going to each of the Text Fields; click the left and right I-bars, and they will become bright red. Also, you will notice that the button at the bottom of the Pin menu now says Add 4 Constraints, as shown in Figure 6-18.

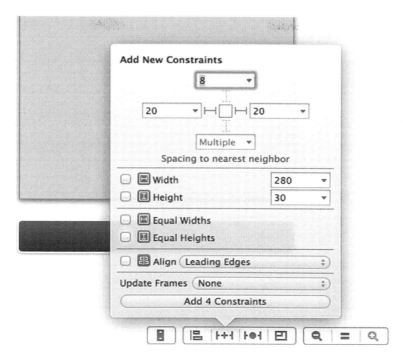

Figure 6-18. Specifying the Pin constraints for the Text Fields. Note the emphasized left and right I-bars

Now click the Add 4 Constraints button to apply the constraints to your Text Fields. This is the quickest and most efficient way of adding the same set of constraints to a number of controls, and being a great developer is all about knowing the shortcuts. If you run your app now, you'll find it reacts in exactly the same way as it did when you used the control-drag method. Well done! You now know two different ways of using Xcode to manage your layout with constraints, and although I'm now going to explain how to use automatically set constraints, there will always be a need to override or add additional constraints manually, so the skills you learned here will be extremely useful when building your own applications.

Automatically Adding Constraints

So far in this chapter the techniques you have used can definitely be classified as manual, although it was certainly not a complex process. Apple actually has gone to a lot of effort to make managing your layout even easier by giving us two great methods for automatically setting constraints. Although it's not perfect, it's the quickest way for getting the bulk of your constraints in place at the click of a button.

When adding constraints manually, you may have noticed that a warning triangle appeared in the Xcode Activity Viewer, as shown in Figure 6-19, indicating that there are four concerns with the application!

Figure 6-19. *The Activity Viewer showing four warnings*

Before adding the constraints, there were no warnings, but now that there are five *working* constraints in place, Xcode isn't happy. Thankfully, there are two ways you can find out more about why Xcode is upset. Clicking the warning triangle will take you to the Issue Navigator (will take you to the Issue Navigat + 4); alternatively, in the Document Outline in Interface Builder, click the red circle with a white arrow to the right of View Controller Scene to get a detailed breakdown of the issues, as shown in Figure 6-20.

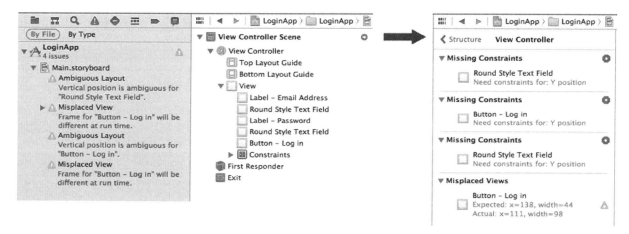

Figure 6-20. *The Issues Navigator (left) and the Document Outline (center) showing there are issues with the layout, and the detailed view of those issues (right)*

The latter option gives you the most detail about the issues that Xcode has flagged; you can see that all of the warnings resulted because all the constraints that Xcode expects for each control haven't yet been provided. All of the constraints have focused on the x axis, which is the horizontal axis, and ignored the y axis, which is the vertical axis. Let's address these missing constraints to satisfy Xcode, and luckily Apple has made this incredibly straightforward in Xcode 5.

Adding Missing Constraints

The Constraint Warning Details view accessed from the document outline allows you to automatically resolve layout issues one by one, but in many cases you will just want to let Xcode do the fixing for you. Let's try both methods.

In the Constraint Warning Details view, click the red dot next to the first constraint warning. As shown in Figure 6-21, you see that you can easily fix the constraint issue with a single click. Go ahead and fix the issue by clicking the Add Missing Constraints button.

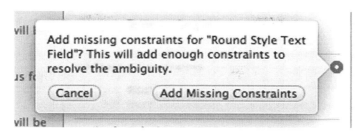

Figure 6-21. *Fixing individual issues with the Constraint Warning Details view*

Ironically, when you fix this issue, the number of issues goes up to seven! That's okay, persist and go through the remaining issues with red dots next to them adding the missing constraints until you're left with only warning triangles. With the warning triangles, when you click them, you're given several options, as shown in Figure 6-22.

Figure 6-22. *The options for fixing the constraint issues when clicking the warning triangle*

In this instance, to resolve the warnings and satisfy Xcode, you want to Reset to Suggested Constraints; select this option and then click Fix Misplacement. Repeat this step for the next warning and you should have addressed all of the issues.

If you look at the Document Outline and click the Structure button to return to the standard Document Outline view and then expand the Constraints item, you'll see that Xcode has created much more than the five constraints. Finally, run your application just to make sure everything is in place.

Tip   From personal experience, when resolving issues, start at the top of the list and work your way down, otherwise you'll have elements of your view disappearing when the dimensions of the view change.

Back in Interface Builder, note that now the previously orange guidelines have become blue! The orange guidelines are Xcode's way of telling us there is more to do.

Just as you've achieved a perfect set of constraints, let's wipe the slate clean and reset all of these constraints. To do this select View Controller from the Document Outline; now click the Resolve Auto Layout Issues button and use the Clear All Constraints in View Controller option to again remove all the constraints that were set in this view controller.

Now, reselect the Resolve Auto Layout Issues button and click Add Missing Constraints in View Controller. This will make Xcode look at every element in the view controller and add the constraints it feels that are need to make the layout adjust to a change in the shape of the view such as rotating the device or using a different form factor.

While we're on the topic of the Resolve Auto Layout Issues menu, I want to quickly draw your attention to the Reset to Suggested Constraints option. Reset to Suggested Constraints can be used in the exact same way as Add Missing Constraints can in that even if you have no constraints, you can select this option to automatically generate all of the constraints for your view. Where Reset to Suggested Constraints comes into its own, however, is when you've heavily modified your constraints and gotten into a mess; use Reset to Suggested Constraints to get back to a firm footing and start the modification process again, being more careful to test as you go.

Updating Constraints

In a short space of time, you've increased your knowledge and now know a number of ways to add constraints to a layout. Adding the constraints is all well and good, but layouts change and constraints need updating. There are two ways of doing this depending on the severity of your changes.

In Interface Builder, move the Log in button closer to the Password Text Field; this will cause the blue guideline to turn orange, as shown in Figure 6-23. The constraint is now orange because in this example, the constraint was originally set to pin the button 66 points below the Password Text Field. By moving the button closer to the Text Field, the constraint is no longer correct, and Interface Builder shows that in this instance, it's moved 16 points closer to the Text Field, as indicated by the -16 value attached to the now-invalid constraint.

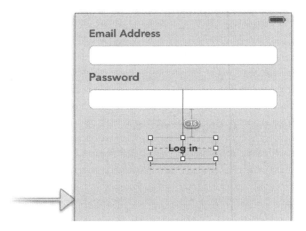

Figure 6-23. *An invalid constraint highlighted in Interface Builder, showing that the constraint is off by negative 16 points*

These types of minor interface changes happen all the time when you're tweaking your layout to be pixel perfect, and they are thankfully very easy to fix. With the Log in button selected, let's go back to the Resolve Auto Layout Issues button. This time, select Update Constraints (Shift + ⌘ + =) and the constraint guidelines will turn back to blue, happy that it is now satisfying the terms of the constraint.

If you're in a situation where you've fine tuned a number of elements in your layout and want to keep the constraints but with the updated values, go back to our best friend when using Auto Layout, the Resolve Auto Layout Issues button, and select Update All Constants in View Controller; as it implies, this will update all of the altered constraints in your view controller to their correct values.

That's it for Auto Layout in this chapter; you've learned a lot about how to apply constraints, how to fix issues with your layout, and a lot more besides that. Now let's change pace a little and examine how to Preview a layout in Xcode before moving on to customizing Text Fields to create a great user experience.

Previewing Your Layout

As you've gone through this book, you've created a number of small projects to show off the features of Xcode or iOS that you want to showcase, but in the real world, you will be potentially creating massive applications, with complex processes that you need to go through to reach a certain view, a view that you want to test for layout issues. This can take some time to do with the simulator, having to repetitively go through the application to get to your view each time. And when you're facing a tight deadline, you need to get things done as quickly as possible; this is where previewing can come in handy.

Preview Using Interface Builder

When creating iPhone-specific applications, many developers want their application to work just as well on the older iPhone 4 and 4s as they do on newer iPhone 5 models. The major difference here is the form factor, with the older phones using a 3.5-inch screen and the iPhone 5 models using the 4-inch screen, which has the same width, but is much taller.

Xcode has a great feature that lets you quickly preview either form factor in Interface Builder. To demonstrate this feature, let's say we've made a design decision to pin the button to the bottom of the view. Select the Log in button in Interface Builder and move it to the bottom of the view, as shown in Figure 6-24.

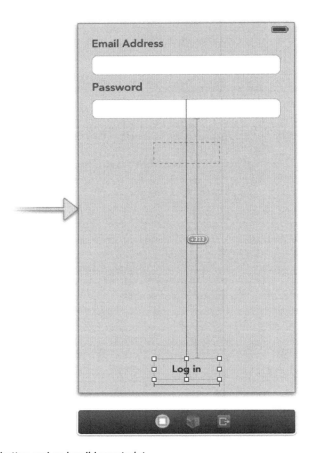

Figure 6-24. The repositioned button and an invalid constraint

Now you'll need to fix the invalid constraints and trust that Xcode knows what you have in mind. Select the Resolve Auto Layout Issues button, and then choose Reset to Suggested Constraints. That's all you need to do! Xcode has understood what you're trying to do and applied the constraints to do it. Run your app in the Simulator and rotate the device to landscape mode, and you will see the button stays central and pinned to the bottom of the view, as shown in Figure 6-25.

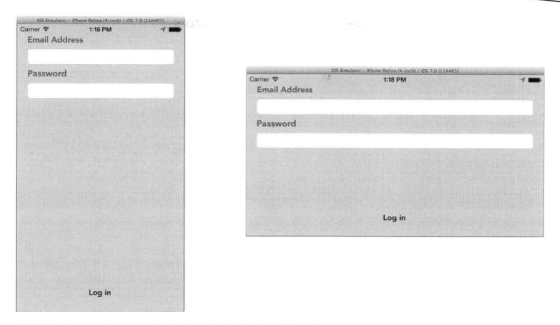

Figure 6-25. *The Log in button now nicely pinned to the bottom of the view*

First, the change worked just as hoped, but second, you didn't need to run Simulator to test it. In Interface Builder, you can easily switch between the different form factors using the Apply Form Factor button in Interface Builder, which is the first button in the right hand group of icons at the bottom of the Interface Builder design area, as shown in Figure 6-26 indicated by the large arrow. This allows you to quickly see how the view reacts to a change in form factor without having to run different versions of the Simulator.

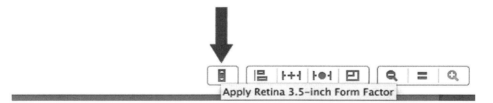

Figure 6-26. *The Apply Form Factor button for toggling between different form factors*

Click the button to see how Interface Builder toggles between the different form factors and how your layout adapts nicely to the changing conditions. This is great for testing the portrait orientation but doesn't help much with landscape orientation; for that you need the Preview Tool.

Preview Using the Preview Tool

The Preview Tool is a fantastic addition Apple built into Xcode 5, but they did not make it easy to find, which will almost certainly change in future releases. For now, to access the Preview Tool, in Interface Builder, select the Related Files button, and at the bottom of the list you will see Preview, as shown in Figure 6-27, but don't click Main.storyboard (Preview) just yet.

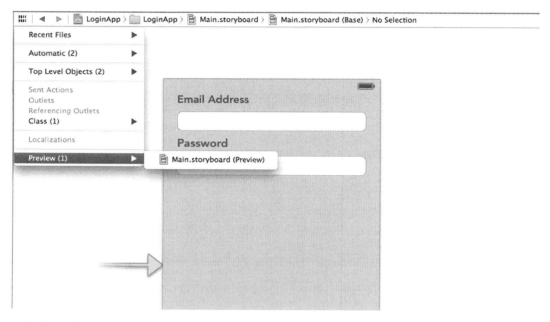

Figure 6-27. Accessing the Preview menu

First, you should ensure that your Assistant Editor is configured to display subsequent editors in the right-hand pane. There are several configurations for the orientation of the Assistant Editor, so it's important to check that your setting is correct, go to View ➤ Assistant Editor ➤ Assistant Editors on Right.

Before selecting the Main.storyboard item, hold down the ⌥ + Shift key and *then* click Main. storyboard, otherwise nothing will happen. As long as you hold down the correct key combination when clicking Main.storyboard (Preview), the screen shown in Figure 6-28 will appear. To open the Preview Tool so that it is useful, double-click the plus symbol on the right, which is highlighted in Figure 6-28, to open the Preview Tool in the Assistant Editor.

Figure 6-28. Determining where to open the Preview Tool, here opting for a new Assistant Editor window

You may have to resize your windows slightly to accommodate both panes, but the result is that you have unlocked the Preview Tool, as shown in Figure 6-29.

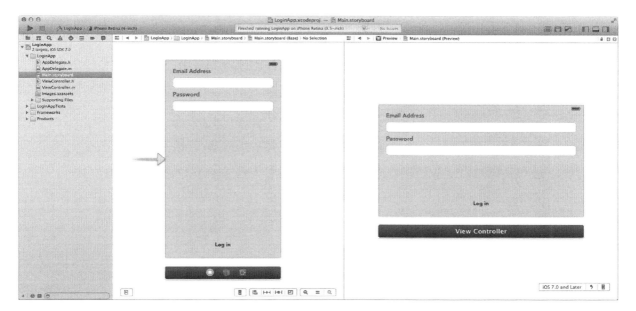

Figure 6-29. Xcode with the Preview Tool enabled

You cannot make changes in the Preview Tool, but anything you change in the left-hand pane will be immediately reflected in the Preview Tool. In the bottom right-hand corner there are several useful buttons.

- *Version*: If you are developing for current and older versions of iOS, you can see how your view will look in that version. This is useful as layouts can be rendered very differently between versions.

- *Orientation*: This allows you to change from portrait to landscape orientation and see how your layout reacts without having to launch the Simulator.

- *Form Factor*: As in Interface Builder, this will toggle between the 4-inch and 3.5-inch displays.

All of these features make the Preview Tool a necessity for all Xcode developers, but you will probably find yourself wishing it were easier to access.

Finishing Touches

We're coming toward the end of this chapter, but with the Text Fields you've added to your view, you now have an opportunity to look at how you can use Interface Builder to create a tailored experience that complements the fact that you are asking your users to fill in a form and wanting to make it as simple as possible for them.

Customizing Text Fields

Even though you only have a small number of Text Fields in your view, there are a wealth of customizations you can apply to make the form fit for the purpose in the first instance, but also add some neat features so that your users can fly through it in an intuitive manner.

Hiding Passwords

How seriously you take security in your application can make or break it on the App Store, so you need to make sure the basic features a user would expect are in place. Therefore, the first customization concerns how you set your Password Text Field to behave like a typical password field and hide the user's password as they type it, which requires absolutely no code at all.

1. Start by selecting the Password Text Field in Interface Builder, and then open the Attributes Inspector.

2. Scroll down the list of attributes until you see the Secure check box; tick the box, as shown in Figure 6-30.

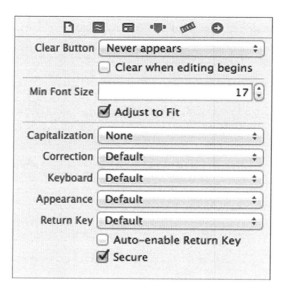

Figure 6-30. Making the Password Text Field secure

3. Run the application in the Simulator and try typing in the Password field. You'll see that as with other applications, the password is obfuscated as you type it in.

4. Another behavior you might want to add to your Password field is that when you tap into it, it clears because you can't see what you've typed, so it makes sense in this instance to clear what was typed and start again. Go back to

Interface Builder and back to the Password field's Attributes Inspector. There is an attribute section called Clear Button, and it has a check box for Clears when editing begins; check this and rerun your application in the Simulator.

5. Type in a password, then click the Email Address Text Field before clicking back in to the Password field and you should find it clears the contents, ready for you to have another go at remembering that password.

Configuring a Text Field for Email Addresses

You've configured the Password field to fit with your users' expectations, but what can you do to make the Email Address field easier to use? Quite a bit as it happens. Getting the user interface right can go a long way toward making your application a hit on the App Store. So these may seem like small changes, but in an oversaturated market, having an immaculate, intuitive interface can make a big difference.

1. Select the Email Address Text Field and open the Attributes Inspector.

2. The first thing you want to do is emphasize that you want users to type an e-mail address. You do this by adding placeholder text to guide them. In the Placeholder Text Field, I've typed e.g. matthew.knott@me.com but you can type whatever you want.

3. You will see the placeholder text you typed immediately reflected in the Text Field, as shown in Figure 6-31.

Figure 6-31. Setting placeholder text in the Attributes Inspector

4. Next, thinking back on how you cleared the Password field when editing, you should make it easier for the user to clear the Email Address field, but it shouldn't be the default action. Go to the Clear Button section in Attributes Inspector and change the drop-down option from Never Appears to Appears while editing. With this option set, the user will be given the opportunity to clear the field whenever they are focused on it.

5. Go ahead and run your application in the Simulator and type something in the Email Address field. As you can see in Figure 6-32, the Clear button (an X inside a circle) appears nicely, which is great, but what's not so great is that it's suggesting that I've misspelled my e-mail address, which is annoying.

Figure 6-32. The Clear button appearing when the user edits the e-mail address, but annoyingly it's reporting spelling errors

6. Back in Attribute Inspector, look down the list until you find the Correction attribute; select No from the list of options. Now iOS will ignore the spellings of e-mail addresses.

7. Another common feature users expect and value when entering an e-mail address is that the keyboard is set in a way that gives priority to common keys such as the @ key. iOS has a number of options for configuring the keyboard, and all are available from the Keyboard attribute, found directly below the Correction attribute. Figure 6-33 shows the great variety of context-specific keyboard options Apple provides by default, which in turn let you, the developer, make life that much easier for your users.

Figure 6-33. Choosing the E-mail Address keyboard options from a very rich list of context-specific keyboard options

8. Now, rerun the application in the Simulator and tap into the Email Address field. You'll see that the keyboard shown to the user makes it easier to quickly type an e-mail address without having to go hunting for the @ symbol.

You're now well on your way to having happy users, but there is just one more tweak I want to add to make this application as easy as possible to navigate.

Navigating Forms

A lot of what you've looked at around customizing Text Fields has focused on simplifying the experience for the user. This final example is no exception, but it requires you to write some code, even though I said this was a code-free chapter … I lied.

There are two Text Fields that don't present much of a burden to the user in terms of navigating, but with a couple of lines of code, you can add the icing on the cake by allowing the user to navigate through the Text Fields using the keyboard, making it easier for the user to complete the fields in double time. The technique learned here can be scaled up to larger forms where your users will really appreciate it.

1. To start with, open the Assistant Editor and ensure the `ViewController.h` file is loaded.

2. Control-drag a connection from the Email Address Text Field over to the header and create an outlet called `usernameField`.

3. Next, do the same for the Password Text Field, and call this outlet `passwordField`.

4. The final action for our header is to add the UITextViewDelegate protocol to the view controller, so after `@interface ViewController : UIViewController` add `<UITextFieldDelegate>`. Your header file should now look like this:

```
#import <UIKit/UIKit.h>

@interface ViewController : UIViewController<UITextFieldDelegate>
@property (weak, nonatomic) IBOutlet UITextField *usernameField;
@property (weak, nonatomic) IBOutlet UITextField *passwordField;

@end
```

5. Switch back to the Standard Editor. You need to make some changes to your interface before moving on to the implementation file.

6. When the user selects the Email Address field, you want them to see a Next button instead of the Return button so that they can tap this to move to the Password field. To set this, select the Email Address Text Field, and in Attribute Inspector look for the Return Key attribute. Select Next from its list of options.

7. Now scroll down the list of attributes until you find the View section and specifically, the Tag attribute and enter 1 as the attribute value. Tags are numeric, specifically integer values that are used to identify different elements in a layout when looking at them in code. If you have 30 Text Fields in your view, the only way in code to differentiate one UITextField from another is to examine its tag.

8. Select the Password field; change its Return Key attribute to Done and its Tag attribute to 2. Run the application in the Simulator to see these buttons in action, as shown in Figure 6-34.

Figure 6-34. *The keyboard changing depending on which field was selected*

9. As you will see, the buttons look good but don't currently do anything. Open `ViewController.m` from the Project Navigator and add the functionality needed to finish this application.

10. Go to the `viewDidLoad` method and specify that the view controller is the delegate for the Text Fields by adding the following code:

```
self.usernameField.delegate = self;
self.passwordField.delegate = self;
```

11. Next, you need to add the `textFieldShouldReturn` method as you did in Chapter 4 to understand what happens when the user hits the Return key, whether you've configured it to say Next or Done. So drop down a few lines after the `viewDidLoad` method and type the stub for the method as follows:

```
-(BOOL)textFieldShouldReturn:(UITextField*)textField;
{

}
```

12. The first thing you want to do in your method is work out the Tag for the next field assuming it's one more than the current `textField.tag` property, and assign it to an `NSInteger` for analysis, so add:

```
NSInteger nextTag = textField.tag + 1;
```

13. You then need to see if there is an element in your view with a tag that matches your `nextTag` integer value so that you can either move to the Password field or dismiss the keyboard. You do this by creating an instance of the `UIResponder` class and set it by going to the current Text Field's parent view and searching based on the tag. Do that by adding this line of code to your method:

```
UIResponder* nextField = [textField.superview viewWithTag:nextTag];
```

14. Next you need an `if else` statement to determine the course of action based on whether or not the `nextField` object was found. Start typing `if` and then use the arrow keys to select `if else` before pushing the Tab key to create a structure for your statement.

15. Remove the `conditions` placeholder and simply type `nextField`, which will return true if it exists or false if it does not.

16. Next, remove the `statements-if-true` placeholder. If true, this means the current field is the Email Address field, and that the next field, Password, exists. You want to focus the cursor in this field so that the user can type their password, so to do this you make that field the first responder. Type the following:

```
[nextField becomeFirstResponder];
```

17. Next, remove the `statements-if-false` placeholder. If you've ended up here, `nextField` was false, meaning the current field is the password and rightly there is no field with a tag of 3. In many cases you would execute your login routine at this stage, but because you don't have one, let's just dismiss the keyboard by resigning the first responder state. Type the following:

```
[textField resignFirstResponder];
```

18. Finally, after the `if else` statement, you need to return a Boolean value as to whether or not the use of the Return key should insert a line break, which it should not, so type:

```
return NO;
```

The finished implementation file code should look like this:

```
- (void)viewDidLoad
{
    [super viewDidLoad];
        self.usernameField.delegate = self;
    self.passwordField.delegate = self;
}

-(BOOL)textFieldShouldReturn:(UITextField*)textField;
{
    NSInteger nextTag = textField.tag + 1;
    UIResponder* nextField = [textField.superview viewWithTag:nextTag];

    if (nextField) {
        [nextField becomeFirstResponder];
    } else {
        [textField resignFirstResponder];
    }
    return NO;
}
```

Now run your application in the Simulator, and you should be able to tap into the Email Address field and navigate to the Password field using the Next button, before using the Done button to dismiss the keyboard. The great thing is that you can use the same `textFieldShouldReturn` method whether you have two Text Fields or 30, as long as you make sure each field has a unique tag value that is one more than its predecessor.

Summary

However you feel about constraints and Auto Layout, it's a fact of life in Xcode 5, but hopefully you enjoyed seeing the different ways you can alter the behavior of your layout under varying circumstances. Specifically in this chapter, you have:

- Learned about how Auto Layout has changed in Xcode 5

- Manually added constraints with the control-drag method as well as with the Align and Pin menu

- Learned how to add missing constraints and a whole lot more with the Resolve Auto Layout Issues menu

- Added a layer of polish to your Text Fields with the Secure and Placeholder attributes

- Used a small piece of code to take control of how the Return key works

You've covered a lot this chapter, but hopefully this is all contributing to an application you're working on, or giving you the confidence to start writing that application you've been thinking about for months. The next chapter will focus on Storyboards, the visual approach to building applications through Xcode that lets you create large portions of your application without the need to write a single line of code.

Diving Deeper

Chapter 7

Storyboards

Chapter 6, for the most part, took a break from writing code to look in detail at Auto Layout, Xcode's system for arranging layouts and specifying how they react to changes in form factor or orientation. It also explained how to craft a tailor-made user experience, customizing keyboards and Text Fields.

We're now into the second part of this book, Diving Deeper, and you will see that from the outset as we get into the nitty-gritty of building a complex multiview application using storyboards. First, I'll present the background of storyboards and the concepts behind them, and then look at the key feature of Xcode Storyboards, the Segue, and how to make the most of them when rapidly creating applications.

So far in this book, in all but Chapter 1, you've created an application as a context for your journey through Xcode, and the only difference with this chapter's project is that you will be building it over this *and* the next chapter. The reason for this is that you will be creating a functional Twitter client for iPad. So you'll start by laying out and connecting the views using Storyboard techniques, but the client is built around customized Table Views, which is the subject of Chapter 8. There's a lot to cover and I'll be relying heavily on two Apple-provided frameworks that take a lot of the pain out of communicating and authenticating with Twitter: the Accounts and Social frameworks.

Although this Twitter client won't have all the bells and whistles you might expect from a full Twitter client, you will still be able to choose from multiple accounts, see a full Twitter feed, and compose and post tweets. To get a flavor of what this application will look like, see Figure 7-1.

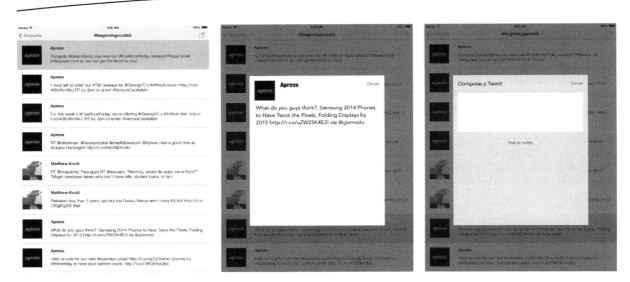

Figure 7-1. Some of the key screens in SocialApp, our functional Twitter client

A Brief History of Storyboards

Apple introduced the storyboard approach to building iOS apps with iOS 5, and it has grown from what was initially seen as a novelty to the where it is now, which is the preferred system for application development used with the majority of Xcode's iOS templates.

Storyboards are not a new concept, however, as they have been used by developers for decades. They are still used today as part of the software planning and prototyping process. When my team and I are brainstorming for a particular solution, we start storyboarding using whiteboards or flip chart pages because it's a way of rapidly expressing relationships between web pages or views in a mobile application. And it's this system for rapid prototyping that Apple has successfully captured in Xcode 5, but Apple has taken it to another level allowing for agile application development.

Outside of development, storyboards originally came from the world of cinema. They were developed by Walt Disney Studios in the 1930s to plan out animations scene by scene, which is a process that is still used today even in major motion pictures. Although there are parallels in terminology, the major difference between storyboards in animation and storyboards for software development is that in animation the progress of the story is linear—scene B will always follow scene A, but in software development, this is rarely the case, with scene A linking to scenes B and C, with scene B linking to scene D and scene C linking to scene E, which links back to scene A. It's because of the complexity of designing the user experience of a multipage application that storyboards are so valuable. The thing that movie storyboards and application storyboards share is their ability to show us the bigger picture without having all the footage or, in our case, code.

For this Twitter application, named SocialApp, which you'll be developing in this chapter and the next, I've made a basic storyboard using a graphics package, as shown in Figure 7-2.

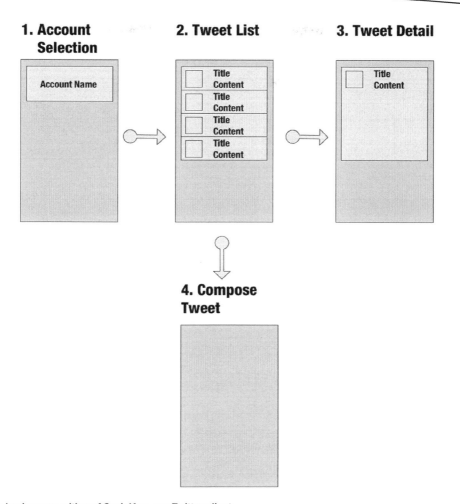

Figure 7-2. *The basic composition of SocialApp, our Twitter client*

This is the process that my team of developers and I would go through when we start thinking more about the composition of an application and knowing the functionality we want to add. We use this storyboarding process to explore ways of assembling those functions in a way that results in an easy-to-use application. When dealing with Storyboards in Xcode, Apple refers to the Views as *Scenes*. As you can see in Figure 7-2, this app has four scenes and you can see how one scene leads to the other. So before you start on the development, let's look at each scene in more detail.

1. *Account Selection:* Today people often manage several Twitter accounts, so our first scene will be a *Grouped Style* Table View Controller that lists each account available on the device.

2. *Tweet List:* Once the user has selected their preferred account, you'll want to show the 20 most recent tweets on that user's timeline. These will be displayed in a *Plain Style* Table View with a custom Table Cell.

3. *Tweet Detail:* The user can see more details about the tweet and its author in the Tweet Detail scene. This is based on a *standard* View Controller and lists the user's name, their avatar, and the full tweet content in a Text View.

4. *Compose Tweet:* Accessed from the compose icon in the Tweet List, this *standard* View Controller uses a Text View to compose a tweet, and then posts it to Twitter on behalf of the user.

If you wanted to reference the scenes in this storyboard to the actual application screenshots shown in Figure 7-1, the first screenshot is scene 2: Tweet List, the second is 3: Tweet, and the third is Detail 4: Compose Tweet.

Now that you know a little more about storyboards, their origin, and how they're used by developers every day, it's time to start putting this application together. This chapter will focus on laying out the scenes in the Storyboard and put the connecting Segues in place, as well as embedding Navigation Controllers and creating the custom classes behind the View Controllers, so let's get started.

Creating a New Project Called SocialApp

Before I get into adding in the finer details of the interface, you need to create the project and then lay out the views you'll need for this application.

1. Start by opening Xcode and creating a new project by clicking Create a new Xcode project from the Welcome screen or go to File ➤ New ➤ Project … (⌘ + Shift + N). Select the Single View Application template and click Next.

2. Name your project SocialApp and ensure the targeted device is set to iPad, not iPhone or universal. Configure the other settings as you have done in previous applications so that they match Figure 7-3 (again substituting your name for mine) and click Next.

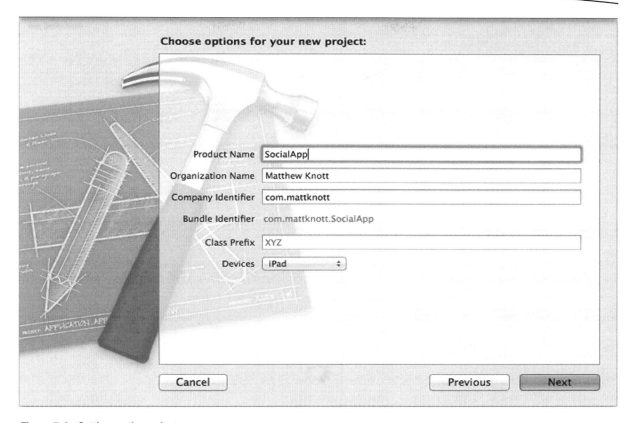

Choose options for your new project:

Product Name	SocialApp
Organization Name	Matthew Knott
Company Identifier	com.mattknott
Bundle Identifier	com.mattknott.SocialApp
Class Prefix	XYZ
Devices	iPad

Cancel   Previous   Next

Figure 7-3. Setting up the project

3. You don't need to create a Git repository this time, so leave that option unchecked and make sure your project is going to be saved in the right place then click Create.

4. Now, as should be familiar to you by now, you're ready to begin your application in earnest. As the focus of this chapter is Storyboards, it makes sense to start by opening Main.Storyboard, so go ahead and select it from the Project Navigator.

The first thing you'll notice is that unless you're working with a high-resolution screen, you might not see anything because the default view takes up the entire design area. This is one of the pitfalls of developing iPad apps using Storyboards, but in a way it's a good thing because you'll get to practice a variety of ways of linking scenes when you can't see them.

To make sense of the Storyboard you're starting with, zoom out using the negative magnifying glass in the bottom right-hand corner of the design area or by pressing ⌥ + ⌘ + Shift + {.

> **Note** When your zoom level is less than 100%, you can still create Segues between scenes and reposition them, but you cannot add controls to your views; for that you need to be zoomed in to 100% or greater.

At this point in the process, you may need to refer back to the initial layout storyboard that was created for Figure 7-2. As I explained at that time, the first scene in the application is a Table View Controller that lists the available accounts. You could add a Table View to the default View Controller that has already been added to the Storyboard, but it's easier to add a completely separate Table View Controller.

The Table View Controller is the second item in the Object Library; drag one onto the design area and drop it next to the existing View Controller, as shown in Figure 7-4. You may need to move it around a little to get a tidy design area.

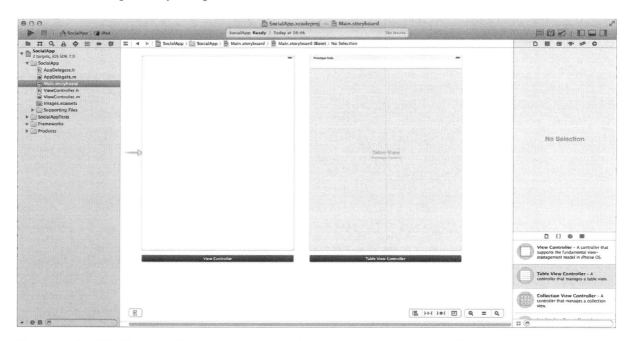

Figure 7-4. The Table View Controller scene next to the initial scene the project was created with

Before you add any more scenes, let's run the application in the Simulator. Go ahead and click the Run button in the Toolbar or press ⌘ + R. Notice that the default View Controller is loaded instead of the Table View Controller, which there is no way of accessing. Quit the Simulator and return to Xcode; the reason that the default View Controller is the starting point is that there is an arrow pointing to the left side of it, which is known as the *Starting Arrow*.

As you might expect, you can drag and drop the Starting Arrow onto the Table View Controller. When the arrow is over the Table View Controller, the scene will become highlighted in blue, as shown in Figure 7-5. The Starting Arrow will now point to the Table View Controller just as it once pointed to the default View Controller.

Figure 7-5. The starting arrow being hovered over the Table View Controller

If you run the application again, you should now be greeted with an empty Table View. It was that easy to change the starting point for this application! Before Storyboards, you would have had to modify the Application Delegate to tell it which View Controller to start with, now you can just drag and drop.

If you want to be a bit more precise when setting the initial scene and don't want to drag and drop the Starting Arrow around, there is another way to do it. Select the Table View Controller in the design area, either by clicking the scene while zoomed out or by selecting Table View Controller from the Document Outline. Open the Attributes Inspector and look down to the View Controller section. Notice that there is a tick by Is Initial View Controller, untick it and the Starting Arrow disappears altogether! You better bring it back otherwise the application will run with a black screen. While you're there, click in the Title box so that you can name the View Controller and set the title to Account Selection. A final way you could have made the Table View Controller the initial View Controller is by deleting the default View Controller, which you'll do now, as well as deleting its code files.

1. Select the blank view by clicking its scene while zoomed out or by selecting View Controller from the Document Outline, as shown in Figure 7-6.

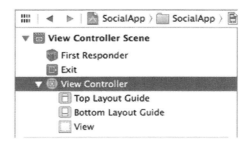

Figure 7-6. Selecting the default View Controller from the Document Outline

2. Delete the View Controller by pressing the Backspace key or by selecting Edit ➤ Delete.

3. Next, you need to remove the files Xcode added for this View Controller. Using the Project Navigator, select ViewController.m and then hold the Command (⌘) key and select ViewController.h as well. With both files selected, again press the Backspace key or select Edit ➤ Delete.

4. You will now be presented with the dialog shown in Figure 7-7 giving options for file deletion. The Remove References button removes the files from the project but leaves them in place in the project folder on your Mac, here you want to delete them altogether, so select the Move to Trash option.

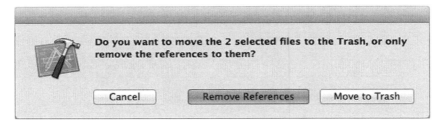

Figure 7-7. The dialog presented by Xcode when removing files via the Project Navigator

Congratulations, you've removed all of the unnecessary files and views from the project! You're now going to step away from the Storyboard for a moment to create four custom View Controllers for the views by subclassing either `UITableViewController` or `UIViewController`.

Creating View Controllers

You can add all of the View Controllers to the Storyboard that you like, but if you don't tie them to a custom View Controller class, they're effectively useless because you can't affect them in any way using code. Therefore, let's break away from the design pattern you are using called model-view-controller, more commonly shortened to MVC.

The Model-View-Controller Design Pattern

Using Xcode with the OS X and iOS SDKs is one of the most natural environments for developing using the MVC principle. First, you don't have to configure Xcode for MVC. Xcode was built from the ground up for MVC, and all of the application templates except the Empty Application template are set up using the MVC principle. Second, the terminology is completely logical, as shown below:

> *Model:* This refers to an object that stores data in a structured way. Core Data lets you create Data Models to interface with stored data, but you can also create custom classes to represent objects such as a vehicle class, which might have a type property, a wheels property, a make property, and many more.

> *View:* The view component of the MVC pattern comprises, unsurprisingly, your views, as laid out in your storyboard. The view should be all of the visual elements of an application, held in isolation from any code.

> *Controller:* The controller is the part of the model that manages the views and the models, acting as an intermediary between the two, taking information from the model and using it to coordinate changes in the view.

In SocialApp, you currently have a view, and you know you're going to add several more, but before you do, let's create all of the controllers so that when you add your views, you can tie them directly to a controller. All of your View Controllers subclass either `UITableViewController` or `UIViewController` to create individual header and implementation files for each view. You've already done this in previous chapters, but this time you need to create four of differing types.

Subclassing UIViewController

UIViewController is the class name given to the standard view controller that has been used so far in all of the applications in this book. When you declare the interface for a UIViewController, you would type, for example:

@interface UserViewController : UIViewController

This says that the View Controller called UserViewController *subclasses* UIViewController. *Subclassing* means taking on all of the attributes of another class, but with the ability to add your own methods and properties and override others. Two of your views subclass UIViewController, and I'll go through the process of creating one and then see if you can repeat the process for the remaining View Controller.

1. The two View Controllers will be called TweetViewController and ComposeViewController. First, let's create TweetViewController.

2. Start by right-clicking the SocialApp group in the Project Navigator and selecting New File …, as shown in Figure 7-8, or select the SocialApp group and press ⌘ + N.

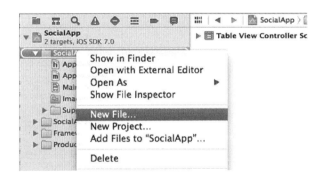

Figure 7-8. Adding a file to the SocialApp group in Project Navigator

3. You will be presented with the file template selection screen. You need to ensure that Cocoa Touch is selected from the left-hand list under the iOS heading, and then Objective-C class, as shown in Figure 7-9, before clicking Next.

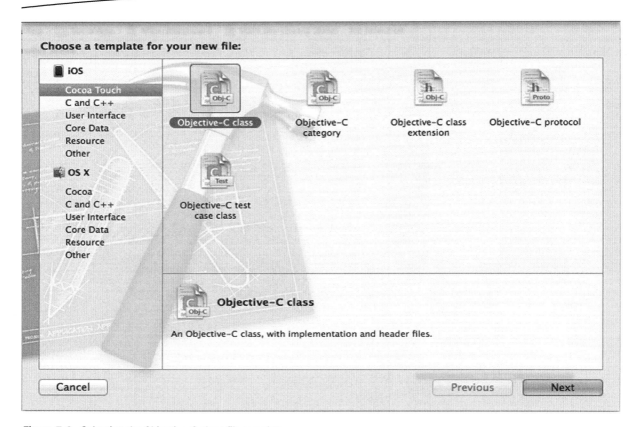

Figure 7-9. Selecting the Objective-C class file template

4. Now, start by setting the Subclass of field to say UIViewController. This will
    make life easier as it defaults the class field to ViewController, making it easy
    for you to change it to TweetViewController. Ensure that both check boxes as
    shown in Figure 7-10 are unticked and click Next.

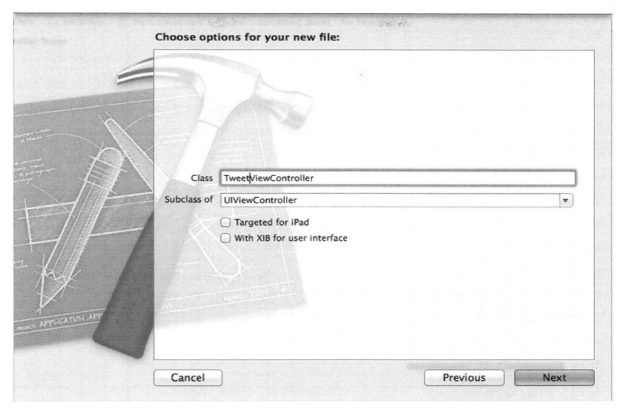

Figure 7-10. Setting the details of the TweetViewController file

5. Now you need to choose a location to save the file. Xcode will automatically suggest the project folder, which is what you want, so ensure the Group is set to SocialApp and that the SocialApp target is checked below, as shown in Figure 7-11, and click Create.

Figure 7-11. *Choosing a save location and specifying both Group and Target*

Now, you will be returned to Xcode and see that `TweetViewController.h` and `TweetViewController.m` have been added to the project. Great! That's one; now repeat this process for ComposeViewController. When you're done, your Project Navigator should resemble that shown in Figure 7-12.

Figure 7-12. The growing project in the Project Navigator

Well done! Creating View Controllers and subclassing other objects is a common task when developing applications, so you are perfecting a valuable skill. One thing you can foresee looking at Figure 7-12 is that the file list is growing, and you still have three more View Controllers to add. What you need to do now is tidy up the structure by grouping the View Controllers together.

1. At the bottom of the Project Navigator, type "View" in the Show files with matching name filter to make sure you only see your View Controllers.

2. Next, click the first View Controller file, in my case it's `TweetViewController.h`, and then holding the Shift key, select the last file, which in my case is `ComposeViewController.m`. You should now have all of your View Controllers selected, as shown on the left in Figure 7-13.

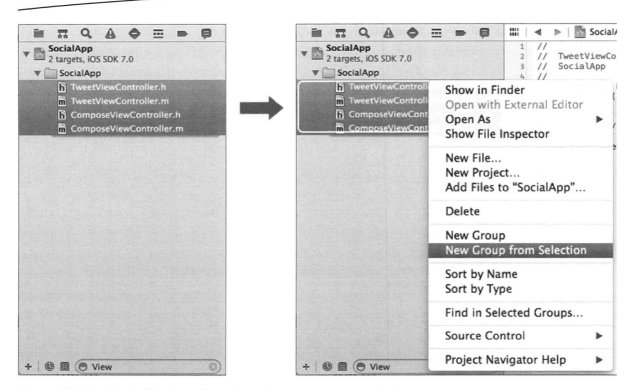

Figure 7-13. *Selecting the View Controllers and creating a new group to contain them*

3. Now right-click the selected files and choose New Group from Selection, as shown on the right in Figure 7-13.

4. When prompted, name your new group View Controllers. Now clear the filter by clicking the X at the end of the filter. You should be left with a neat project, as shown in Figure 7-14.

Figure 7-14. The View Controllers grouped neatly together

Organizing your project neatly and logically ensures the admiration of your development team colleagues. They *will* thank you for it. Organizing files in big projects means that if someone else has to work on your project, they're not hunting around for the custom classes or the View Controllers because you've applied some logic and good housekeeping to your project structure.

Subclassing UITableViewController

You've created two of the four View Controllers, so now it's time to create the others. The process is more or less the same, but there are some subtle changes. `UIViewControllers` are fairly straightforward, the views themselves are blank canvases ready for you to add controls, and in terms of their methods they are also very minimal, giving you just a `viewDidLoad` method and a handler for low memory. The `UITableViewController`, however, is a more complex system designed for displaying large amounts of data through a structured interface, and it has a number of intrinsic attributes that result in the code files containing a number of methods that are used for controlling the number of rows, sections, and more. I'll explain these in detail in Chapter 8, but for now let's just create them so you can get back to the Storyboard.

The process is largely the same as before, except this time you want to start by selecting the View Controllers group instead of SocialApp in the Project Navigator. You'll be creating the two instances of `UITableViewController` that this application will use: `AccountsViewController` and `FeedViewController`.

1. Right-click the View Controllers group, and select New File ..., as shown in Figure 7-15, or press ⌘ + N. You will be presented with the File Template selection screen.

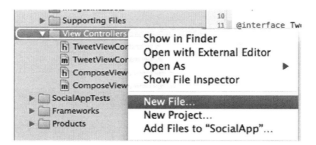

Figure 7-15. Adding a new file to the View Controllers group

2. As with the `UIViewControllers`, select the Objective-C class file template and click Next. Now, set the Class field to AccountsViewController and the Subclass of field to UITableViewController, as shown in Figure 7-16, leaving both boxes below unchecked, and click Next.

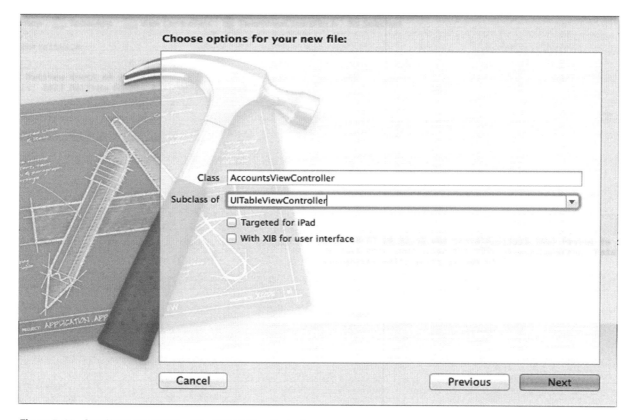

Figure 7-16. Specifying the details of the UITableViewController

3. Accept the suggested file location and click the Create button. You should now be a master at creating new View Controllers, so repeat these steps and create another UITableViewController called FeedViewController.

You've now created four View Controllers, so it's time to finish adding the views to the Storyboard and tie them to their respective controllers. Your Project Navigator should now look something like the screen shown in Figure 7-17.

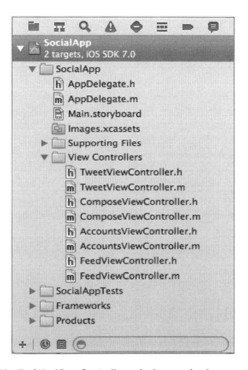

Figure 7-17. *The Project Navigator with all of the View Controllers nicely organized*

Pairing the View to the Controller

I've already explained the fundamentals of the MVC design pattern that these applications are based on. You've created the Controllers, so now you have to add the Views to the Storyboard and tie them to their specific View Controller by using the Identity Inspector from the Utilities bar.

1. Start by opening Main.Storyboard and selecting Table View Controller – Accounts from the Document Outline. When setting the class of a view, you need to select its View Controller, which is selected before you apply the class, otherwise things will get messy. That's why you use the document outline to make sure of your selection.

2. Now open the Identity Inspector from the Utilities side bar or by pressing ⌥ + ⌘ + 1. Xcode should now resemble the screen shown in Figure 7-18.

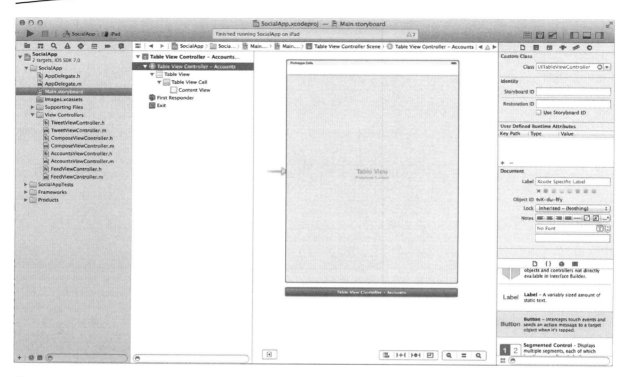

Figure 7-18. Xcode with the View Controller selected and the Identity Inspector open

3. Your focus in the Identity Inspector should be the Custom Class section. This is where you bind your View Controller's visual element to the actual View Controller. In the Class field, it will currently say that this View Controller's class is `UITableViewController`. It's grayed out because although it knows what its base type is, you haven't yet tied it to a custom View Controller. Click the down arrow at the end of the field and you should have three selections: the base class and the two custom View Controllers, as shown in Figure 7-19. Select AccountsViewController.

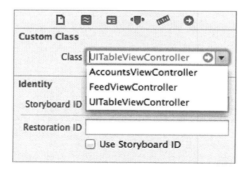

Figure 7-19. The list of available View Controllers

> **Note**   If at any time you don't see one of your View Controllers listed as an option in the Custom Class list and you have the View Controller selected in Interface Builder, either quit Xcode and relaunch it or just write the class name in yourself, but remember it's case sensitive. Sometimes Xcode loses track of which classes have been created.

You've now told the View Controller on your storyboard that it no longer complies to its base class `UITableViewController`, but now it's controlled by `AccountsViewController`. Xcode immediately reacts to the change in custom class. Now try opening the Assistant Editor; it will display the implementation file for the Accounts View Controller confirming that the class is valid and the link to the Storyboard is working.

Understanding Inheritance

Subclassing and base classes are two terms that feature heavily when describing the concept of inheritance. Inheritance is one of the key principles of object-oriented programming. It describes a link between two classes, the base or super class, and the custom class, which could be referred to as a subclass or derived class.

The best way to think about base classes and subclasses is as a parent and child; the child descends from the parent and shares the same genes, but the child will not be identical to the parent, and while the parent has their own attributes, the child has the ability to gain their own new attributes. In Wales, people are often named along the lines of David ap Gwillim, meaning David son of Gwillim. That is exactly what `@interface AccountsViewController : UITableViewController` is saying in the `AccountsViewController.h` file, that it descends directly from `UITableViewController`.

Now that you have a better understanding of inheritance and why you create custom classes, you can go ahead and finish building the Storyboard.

Building up the Storyboard

With `Main.Storyboard` open, it's time to get back to the focus of this book, Storyboards. You've created the first scene for account selection; it's now time to create the second scene, which is the list of tweets, more commonly known as the Twitter feed, which will be controlled by FeedViewController.

1. As this is another `UITableViewController` class, you need to drag a Table View Controller from the Object Library and drop it next to the first scene, as shown in Figure 7-20.

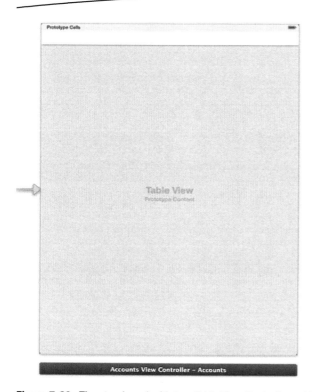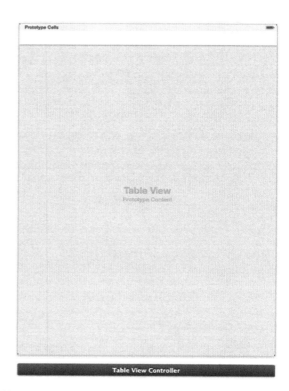

Figure 7-20. *The storyboard with two Table View Controllers side by side*

2. Select the new Table View Controller and open the Attribute Inspector. Set the Title attribute to Feed; this will help you keep track of your scenes in what will be quite a full Storyboard.

3. Now, select the Identity Inspector and click the Class drop-down list and choose FeedViewController.

4. You now have two scenes on your Storyboard, so let's add the last two so that you can move on to a careful examination of one of the key features of any Storyboard: Segues. The third scene is a regular View Controller that is used to show the details of the tweet. Drag a View Controller from the Object Library and drop it up and to the right of the Feed View Controller.

5. Select the new View Controller and open the Attributes Inspector. Set the Title attribute to Tweet. Next you need to set the class, so open the Identity Inspector and set the Class value to TweetViewController. Your growing storyboard should now resemble that shown in Figure 7-21.

Figure 7-21. The three scenes, positioned nicely ready for the fourth

6. By now you can start to appreciate how it can sometimes be challenging to work on large iPad applications using Storyboards, which is why it is best to meticulously name every scene as each is created. The next scene is the ComposeViewController, which you'll use to write tweets and post them to Twitter. Drag in another View Controller and position it directly below the TweetViewController.

7. Once it's in position, click the new Compose View Controller and open the Attribute Inspector, setting the Title attribute to Compose. As you have done previously, open the Identity Inspector and set the Class value to ComposeViewController.

You now have all of the scenes of the Storyboard laid out neatly. Each View Controller on the Storyboard is tied to its respective View Controller class. Although you now have the basic structure in terms of the scenes, the scenes themselves are largely empty. Let's focus on the individual scenes and start adding in the elements that will make up the interface. Before you move on, check that your interface resembles that shown in Figure 7-22.

Figure 7-22. *The Storyboard as it stands, all the scenes in place, but without their interface elements*

Linking Scenes and Building Interfaces

One message that should be coming across in this chapter is that building an application with Storyboards is part of a structured process. First, you plan out your application and its scenes, then you create the View Controllers before tying them into their respective visual counterparts on the Storyboard, giving you separate View Controllers that have their classes set but are ultimately strangers to one another. To address this issue you now need to progress through each scene from one through to four, building and connecting the interface with Segues.

What Are Segues?

Just as the concept of storyboards is rooted in the movie industry, so too is the term segue, which is pronounced *seg-way*. In a film, a segue is a transition between scenes, so you can immediately see how it's appropriate as a term that describes the mechanism used by Xcode to transition between storyboard scenes.

In Xcode, Segues need a start point and an end point. Typically, the start point is a button or a table cell, and almost always the end point is another View Controller. Think back to Chapter 3 for a moment; there you wrote several lines of code to push the second View Controller onto the screen; with Storyboards, a Segue allows you to do this with a couple of clicks.

To demonstrate how to create a Segue, let's start by linking the Accounts View Controller to the Feed View Controller. It's important to note that the Accounts View Controller doesn't need any specific interface work at this point, and I'll explain that in more detail in Chapter 8.

1. Start by clicking the Toggle Zoom button in the bottom right corner of the design area to zoom to 100% and move around the Storyboard so that you can get as much of the Accounts View Controller and the Feed View Controller in view as possible, as shown in Figure 7-23.

 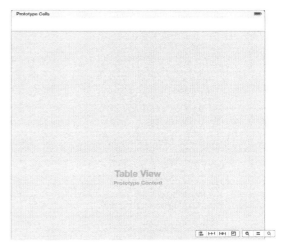

Figure 7-23. Scenes 1 and 2 side by side, the Accounts View Controller and the Feed View Controller

2. The Accounts View Controller will list all available Twitter accounts in a Table View, and selecting one of the rows will take you to the Feed View Controller. To make this happen, you need to create a Push Segue from the Table Cell to the Feed View Controller. First, highlight the Table Cell in the Accounts View Controller by clicking it, as shown in Figure 7-24.

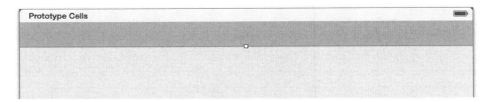

Figure 7-24. *The Accounts View Table Cell highlighted*

3. Next, hold down the Control key, click the Table Cell, and drag a connecting line from the cell to the Feed View Controller, as shown in Figure 7-25.

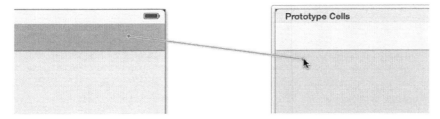

Figure 7-25. *Dragging a connecting line between the Table Cell and the Feed View Controller*

4. When you release the mouse button, you will be presented with a contextual dialog asking about the type of Segue you want to create, as shown in Figure 7-26. The dialog is contextual because depending on your start point, the options for creating a Segue will be different. The start point for this Segue was a Table Cell, so the options you are presented with are specific to this scenario. As you can see, you have two headings: one for Selection Segue and one for Accessory Action. This is because a Table Cell has two elements that support user interaction: the cell itself triggers the Selection Segue, whereas the cell accessory would trigger the Accessory Action Segue. In this instance, you want to create a Push Segue from the Selection Segue list of types.

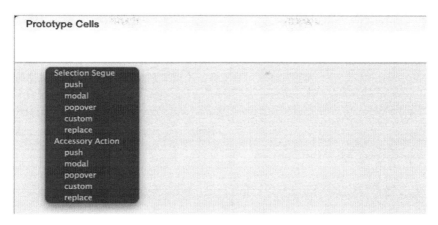

Figure 7-26. *The contextual menu presented when you create a Segue from a Table Cell*

5. A Segue will now be created between your two View Controllers. Select it, and then open the Identity Inspector, as shown in Figure 7-27. In the Identifier field, type "ShowTweets."

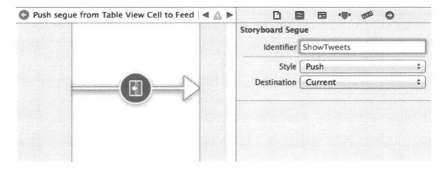

Figure 7-27. *Inspecting the Segue*

This Segue is triggered when the user taps the Table Cell for the Twitter account they want to use. When this happens, you need to pass the selected account details to the Feed View Controller. In Chapter 3 you did this by writing code that passed an object to the next view controller, but when working with Segues, you use the `prepareForSegue` method, which is called every time a Segue on the View Controller is triggered. I'll explain this method in more detail later when you write the code that performs different actions depending on the Segue that is being triggered. But to identify which Segue is being triggered, you must give each an identifier.

> **Tip** Even when you only have one Segue coming from a View Controller, as in this case, it's still a good practice to give it an identifier so that if you do add more Segues to the View Controller in the future, you won't have a situation where you're passing information to the wrong target View Controller.

Before you go any further, let's take a minute to look at the different Segue styles available to you and in what situations you might use each one.

Push: A Push Segue adds the target, dismisses the current view, and pushes the target of the Segue onto the screen. Behind the scenes, the Push Segue adds the target View Controller onto the navigation stack, which is why you always need a Navigation Controller to be present when using a Push Segue. Xcode does all the work of managing the navigation stack for you, when your Push Segue is triggered, the View Controller that is presented will automatically have a button to go back to the previous View Controller.

Modal: Modal Segues are definitely the most interesting and varied Segue you can use, especially when working with iPad applications. A Modal Segue presents another View Controller without the need of a Navigation Controller. You can slide these over the top of the View that calls the Segue with a choice of transition animations available and also a number of presentation styles, some of which I'll explain later in this chapter. Figure 7-28 shows a Modal Segue in action, presenting the Tweet View Controller from SocialApp modally with the Form Sheet presentation style.

Figure 7-28. A Modal Segue in action

Popover: Popovers are visually similar to some Modal Segues in that they cause a View Controller to appear above the View Controller that originated the Segue. These are really useful for displaying contextual information; maybe if you created an application for your online store, you could use Popover Segues to provide a quick view of your product. You can see an example of a Popover in Figure 7-29; note that the arrow at the top of the View Controller is generated by Xcode and can be configured.

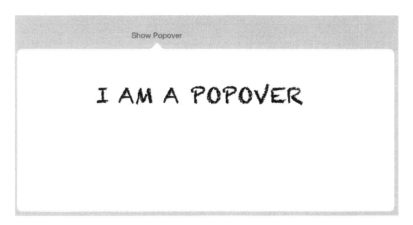

Figure 7-29. An example of a Popover Segue presenting another View Controller on top of the View

Replace: The Replace style is only available when working with an iPad Storyboard and is mainly used exclusively with Master Detail Applications. Refer to Chapter 3 if you are unfamiliar with the Master Detail Application template. A Replace Segue, as the name might suggest, takes the place of the originating View Controller on the navigation stack.

Custom: As you might expect, a Custom Segue can be anything you tell it to be. With a Custom Segue, you specify a Custom `UIStoryboardSegue` class in a similar way to how you would set custom classes for the View Controllers.

Now that you understand the different Segue styles, perhaps you've noticed from the description of the Push Segue that there is something missing from the application that is essential to support the Push Segue: a Navigation Controller.

Adding a Navigation Controller

A Navigation Controller, or `UINavigationController`, is used to manage the navigation through the various View Controllers in your application. It keeps track of where the user has been, adding each successive View Controller to the navigations stack, and provides a mechanism for the user to navigate backward through the navigation stack, all without writing any code. You first encountered Navigation Controllers in Chapter 3 where you added one programmatically to your application; however, this time I'll explain how Xcode makes this possible in just a couple of clicks.

Because the Accounts View Controller is the originator of the Push Segue, and because it is the initial scene on the Storyboard, the Navigation Controller needs to be applied here. Select Accounts View Controller – Accounts from the Document Outline, as shown in Figure 7-30, because you're applying the Navigation Controller explicitly to the View Controller.

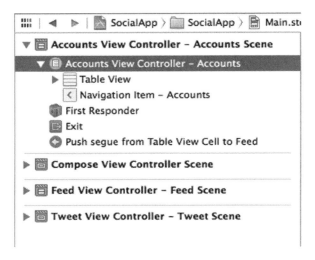

Figure 7-30. *Selecting the Accounts View Controller from the Document Outline*

1. To add a Navigation Controller to this View Controller, from the menu bar select Editor ➤ Embed In ➤ Navigation Controller. Xcode will add a Navigation Controller to the Storyboard and attach it to the Accounts View Controller for you, as shown in Figure 7-31.

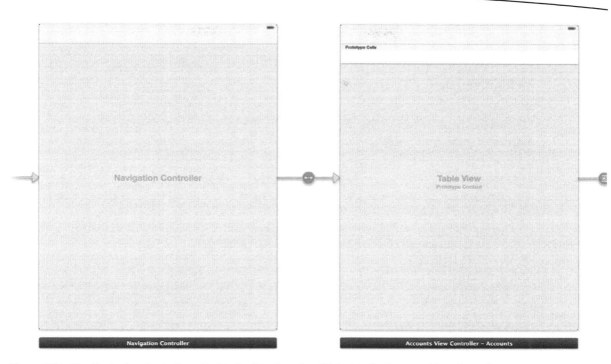

Figure 7-31. The Navigation Controller added to the Storyboard and linked to the Accounts View Controller

2. Now that you have a Navigation Controller in place, you can set a title for the View that will be visible to the user and also provide meaningful text for the Back button. Zoom back in to the Storyboard and in Accounts View Controller highlight the Navigation Bar at the top of the view or select Navigation Item from the Document Outline, as shown in Figure 7-32.

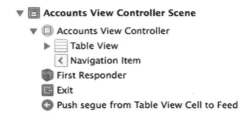

Figure 7-32. Selecting the Navigation Item from the Document Outline for Accounts View Controller

3. Now open the Attribute Inspector and set the Title Attribute to Accounts. Notice how the title appears at the top of the View Controller, as shown in Figure 7-33. What's also neat is that when you select an account and segue to Feed View Controller, the Back button will automatically be Accounts.

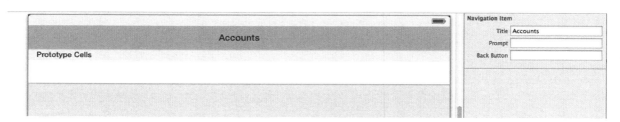

Figure 7-33. The Title attribute for the Navigation Bar in place

With the Navigation Controller in place and the Accounts View Controller complete for now, you are ready to start building the interface on the remaining five scenes, next up: Feed View Controller.

Creating an Interface for Feed View Controller

Feed View Controller is responsible for showing all of the tweets in the user's Twitter timeline. In Chapter 8 you'll be creating a custom Table Cell to display the actual tweet, but for now you need to add a button to the Navigation Bar so you can compose new tweets, and then create Modal Segues to both the Compose scene and the Tweet scene. Zoom to 100% and ensure Feed View Controller is front and center.

1.   First, let's add a button to the Navigation Bar so that you can create a Modal Segue to the Compose View Controller. To do this, start by doing a search for *button* in the Object Library, as shown in Figure 7-34.

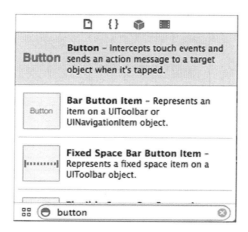

Figure 7-34. Searching for buttons in the Object Library

2.   You are looking specifically for a Bar Button Item, which should be the second item in the Object Library. Drag it onto the right-hand side of the Navigation Bar, positioning it as shown in Figure 7-35.

Figure 7-35. Adding a Bar Button Item to the Navigation Bar

3. If you still have the Attribute Inspector open, when you drop the Bar Button Item on the Navigation Bar, its attributes will be displayed, if not, open the Attribute Inspector and select the new button. You could change the Title attribute of this button to read Compose, as that is the scene it will be linking to, however, Apple provides a standard set of icons that can be used for this button by choosing one of the predefined Identifiers. Click the Identifier attribute list and select Compose, as shown in Figure 7-36. Your button will change from text to an icon with a pencil inside a box.

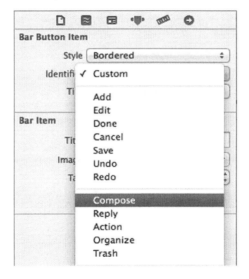

Figure 7-36. Selecting the Compose Identifier for the Bar Button Item

Note   Apple provides a number of Identifiers that can be used for many common tasks. These should be used whenever possible to provide users with icons that they are familiar with, and also to future proof your application. If Apple updates that Identifier in the future, your applications will be easy to update to the new design.

4. While you're working with the Navigation Bar and the Attribute Inspector, select it as you did for the previous scene and set the Title attribute to Feed.

5. You've created the interface for your second scene, now you need to create Modal Segues to the Compose View Controller and the Tweet View Controller. This time, because the scenes are spread out in the Storyboard, you will use the Document Outline to add an element of simple precision to the task of creating Segues. Compress all of the scenes except the Feed, Compose, and Tweet View Controllers by clicking the triangles to the left of each scene's title. Then, expand Feed View Controller, and beneath that expand Table View so that your Document Outline resembles that shown in Figure 7-37.

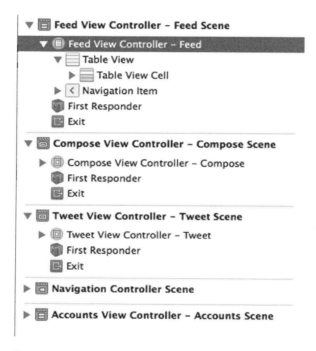

Figure 7-37. Preparing to create Segues using the Document Outline

6. The first Segue you'll create is the Tweet View Controller. You get to this scene by selecting one of the table cells, so highlight Table View Cell and control-drag a connection from here to the Tweet View Controller, as shown in Figure 7-38.

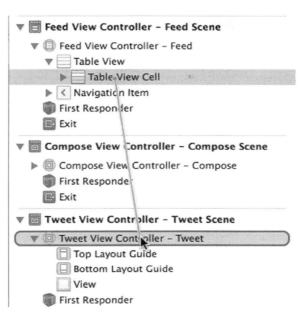

Figure 7-38. Creating a Segue using the Document Outline

7. When you release the mouse button, the contextual dialog will appear just as it did in Figure 7-26. This time select Modal under the Selection Segue heading. You now have a Modal Segue connecting the Table Cell in your scene to the Tweet View Controller, but you need to customize it slightly.

8. In the Feed View Controller – Feed Scene section of the Document Outline, you will notice you now have an item called Modal segue from Table View Cell to Tweet. This is the Segue, so select it to highlight it, then open the Attribute Inspector. Set the Identity attribute to ShowTweet, the Presentation attribute to Form Sheet, and the Transition attribute to Cover Vertical.

9. You now need to create a Modal Segue from your compose Bar Button Item to the Compose View Controller. Start by expanding Navigation Item – Feed in the Document Outline to reveal the Bar Button Item, as shown in Figure 7-39.

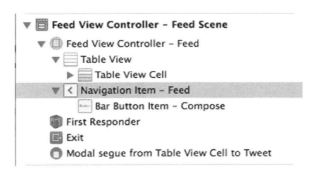

Figure 7-39. Exposing the Bar Button Item in the Document Outline

10. In the Document Outline, control-drag a connection from Bar Button Item – Compose to Compose View Controller – Compose, as shown in Figure 7-40, and when you release the button, select Modal. Notice this time how the menu is different because you're dragging from a button not a table cell.

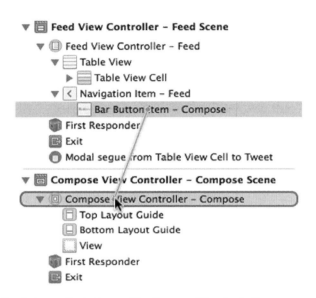

Figure 7-40. Making a connection between the button and the Compose View Controller

11. You now have two Segues listed in the Document Outline for your scene; select the one named Modal segue from Compose to Compose. Open the Attribute Inspector and set the Identifier attribute to ComposeTweet, the Presentation attribute to Form Sheet, and Transition to Cover Vertical.

Let's review where we are with the project. Zoom out so you can see more of the Storyboard, as shown in Figure 7-41. Notice how much smaller the Compose and Tweet View Controllers are since you created Segues for them. The reason for this is that they are adjusting to the presentation style you specified on each Segue, namely Form Sheet. If you refer back to Figure 7-28, you'll see the finished Tweet View Controller in action, displayed modally over the Feed View Controller.

Figure 7-41. *The Storyboard changing in appearance after setting up two scenes*

The way the View Controller reacts dynamically to the Segue means you can be fairly confident about the interface you build in Interface Builder being what you get on a physical device or in the Simulator. You're now ready to move on to the third scene, the Tweet View Controller.

Creating an Interface for Tweet View Controller

The purpose of the third scene is to display details about the tweet the user selected from the Twitter feed. You could display all types of information, but for this application you'll simply display the tweet author's name, the tweet content, and the tweet author's avatar image. Because you have done these steps a few times already in this chapter, I'll start using screenshots at key points in the process so you can verify that you haven't missed anything.

1. Because this is a modal scene, it has no Back button, so you need to be able to dismiss the View Controller when the user wants to return to the Twitter feed. Add a Button to the top right-hand side of the view by dragging one from the Object Library and positioning it as shown in Figure 7-42. In the Attributes Inspector, set the Title attribute to Cancel.

Figure 7-42. *Placing the Button onto the Tweet View Controller*

2. Next you need to add an Image View from the Object Library onto the View Controller. Position it somewhere in the view and then open the Size Inspector. This is a really handy tool for gaining pinpoint precision over your object's size and position. Set the x axis value to 20 and the y axis value to 67; these control where the top left corner of the Image View is positioned relative to the parent view. Set the Width and Height values to 82, as shown in Figure 7-43, to create a square Image View.

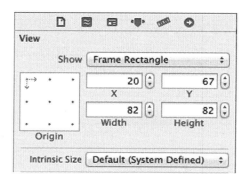

Figure 7-43. Setting the width, height, and x and y axis position of the Image View

3. Next you need to drag in a Label that will contain the tweet author's name. Drag in a Label from the Object Library and position it loosely between the Image View and the Cancel. You're going to be adjusting the size and the font, so it makes sense not to finalize the position until after you've done that.

3. Open the Attribute Inspector with the Label selected and set the Title text to User Name. Next, select the T for the Font attribute. Set the Font to Custom, the Family to Helvetica Neue, the style to Condensed Black, and the size to 26, as shown in Figure 7-44.

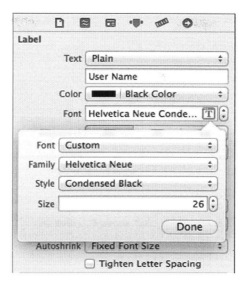

Figure 7-44. Adjusting the Font attribute for the User's Name button

5. Finally, you'll notice you can't see any text in the Label due to its size and shape. First, position the left side and top of the Label so that it snaps into alignment with the top of the Image View, then resize it so that it uses the rest of the available width in the View Controller and the height is sufficient to show the text clearly, as shown in Figure 7-45.

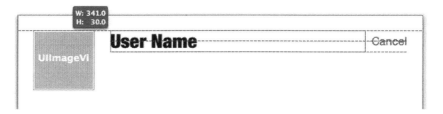

Figure 7-45. Setting the button to fill the remaining width

6. Next, you need something to show the textual content of the selected tweet; as these can vary in size, the best choice would be a Text View. Drag one in from the Object Library, snapping it into place below the Image View. Resize it to give it a generous size, as shown in Figure 7-46.

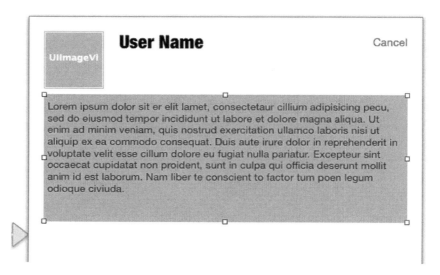

Figure 7-46. *The Text View added to the View Controller*

7. You don't want this Text View to behave like a regular Text View, because it shouldn't be editable. Open the Attributes Editor and uncheck the Editable attribute. You'll leave Selectable checked so that the user can copy the tweet text. While you're there, look at the Detection section; Twitter posts often contain links, check the Links attribute, which tells Xcode to detect links and provides a code-free way of opening the link in Safari.

8. Even though you're using Storyboards, you still need to create actions and outlets for the interface objects. Start by opening the Assistant Editor and ensure it displays TweetViewController.h in the right-hand pane. As you have done numerous times in this book, control-drag the following outlets: tweetAuthorAvatar for the Image View, tweetAuthorName for the User Name Label, and tweetText for the Text View. Next, create an action for the Cancel button called dismissView. Your header should contain the following:

```
@property (weak, nonatomic) IBOutlet UIImageView *tweetAuthorAvatar;
@property (weak, nonatomic) IBOutlet UILabel *tweetAuthorName;
@property (weak, nonatomic) IBOutlet UITextView *tweetText;

- (IBAction)dismissView:(id)sender;
```

You've now finished setting up the third scene for viewing tweets in detail, so its time to set up the fourth and final scene, the Compose scene.

Creating an Interface for Compose View Controller

The Compose View Controller provides an Interface for the user to create a tweet and post it to Twitter. You will use a Text View for the composition of the Tweet, give the user two buttons—one to dismiss the view and one to post the tweet—and an Activity Indicator that triggers when posting the tweet. Make sense? Great, let's get started.

1. To make the Text View stand out a bit, you want to change the background color of the view. Click a blank area of the view and open the Attributes Inspector. You want to choose a light gray background color, so I changed the Background attribute to one of the predefined colors: Group Table View Background Color.

2. Next, before you add the interface objects just mentioned, let's add a label to act as a title for the view. Drag in a Label from the Object Library and position it in the top left corner of the view. In the Attributes Inspector, change its Text attribute to Compose a Tweet. You also want to make it stand out, so click the T in the Font attribute and set the Font to Custom, the Family to Helvetica Neue, and the Size to 22. Resize the Label so that all the text is visible, but don't resize it to fill the width of the view.

3. Next drag a button to the top-right corner of the view; this will be the button that dismisses the View Controller. Open the Attribute Inspector and change the button's Title attribute to Cancel. Before you move on, the top of your scene should now resemble that shown in Figure 7-47.

Figure 7-47. *The Label and Button in position on the Compose scene*

4. Now drag in a Text View and position it below the Label and Button. As this is where the user will compose their posts to Twitter, you should make it a decent size. One downside is that by default, the Text View is populated with Lorem Ipsum placeholder text; open the Attribute Inspector and remove all of the default text from the Text attribute. Your scene should be progressing nicely and resemble that shown in Figure 7-48.

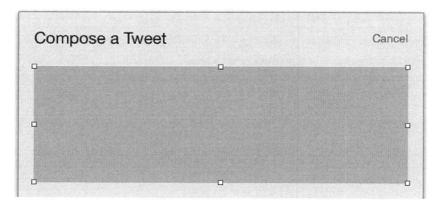

Figure 7-48. The Text View in position below the Button and Label

5. Next you need to add a second button to allow the user to post the content to Twitter. Drag in a button and position it below to the Text View. In the Attributes Inspector, change the Title attribute to Post to Twitter. Once you've changed the text, move the button toward the center of the view until the blue guideline appears and it snaps into place, centered horizontally and positioned just below the Text View.

6. This is the first time you've dealt with the next object: the Activity Indicator. The Activity Indicator is very common in applications that rely on data from the Internet. The control produces the familiar "spinning wheel" that has become synonymous with data transfer over the past decade, where it has long been used with AJAX-based applications on the web and in iOS applications since iOS 2.0. Drag one in from the Object Library and position it to the left of the Post to Twitter Button. By default, the Activity Indicator is visible and static; you want it to be hidden until it is told to start animating. Xcode provides a simple attribute to achieve this; open the Attribute Inspector with the Activity Indicator selected and check the Hides when Stopped attribute. Figure 7-49 shows the finished scene.

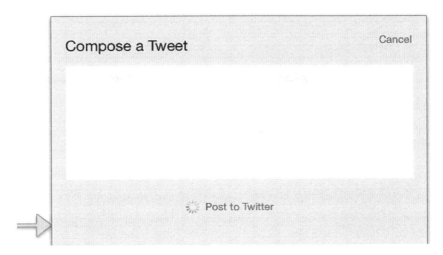

Figure 7-49. *The finished Compose scene*

7. As there are no Segues from this scene, all that remains is to create the outlets and actions. Open the Assistant Editor and ensure that `ComposeViewController.h` is showing on the right. Create an outlet for the Text View called `tweetContent`, one for the Post to Twitter Button called `postButton`, and one for the Activity Indicator called `postActivity`. Create an action for the Cancel Button called `dismissView` and one for the Post to Twitter Button called `postToTwitter`.

You should now have the following outlets and actions within your header file:

```
@property (strong, nonatomic) ACAccount *selectedAccount;

@property (weak, nonatomic) IBOutlet UITextView *tweetContent;
@property (weak, nonatomic) IBOutlet UIButton *postButton;
@property (weak, nonatomic) IBOutlet UIActivityIndicatorView *postActivity;

- (IBAction)dismissView:(id)sender;
- (IBAction)postToTwitter:(id)sender;
```

That's it for the fourth and final scene—you now have all the elements in place for your users to compose messages and post them to Twitter. You've worked really hard getting to this stage in the project, and have earned a rest before we examine Table and Collection Views in the next chapter.

Summary

It can be hard going through an entire chapter without having a completed application to show for it at the end, but in any project, you have to do preparation work, which is what you've done. In the next chapter, you will see the application coming to life in the first few pages as you configuring Table Views and take the first steps in the use of the Social and Accounts frameworks.

In this chapter, you've been shown all of the skills essential to using Xcode to build an application structure with Storyboards, which at its core is simply scenes and Segues, but specifically you've learned about:

- Organizing files in the Project Navigator using Groups
- The model-view-controller design pattern and how Xcode is built around it
- Applying custom View Controller classes to View Controllers in the Storyboard
- The inheritance principle of object-oriented programming
- Different ways of creating Segues
- The different types of Segues
- The need to specify Identifiers for Segues
- Embedding Navigation Controllers
- Using the Size Inspector to precisely position elements in the view

When you've had a well-deserved rest, move on to the next chapter to finish the SocialApp.

Chapter 8

Table and Collection Views

In Chapter 7 you started work on SocialApp, a Twitter client; I presented an in-depth look at building an application structure with Storyboards, explaining how to tie scenes together with Segues. You also learned about the principles of the model-view-controller design pattern, combining the View element with the Controller element. You also learned about subclassing and how inheritance is an import concept of object-oriented programming. Most important, you worked hard preparing the scenes for SocialApp and tying them all together with Segues.

In this age of big data, it seems in every facet of our lives we are being bombarded by more and more data, and as developers, we often find ourselves needing a way of displaying large amounts of data to our users in a concise and structured manner. In iOS, Apple has provided us with the Table View and Collection View.

This chapter will focus on the Table View and Collection View, which are close cousins with Collection View, mirroring many of the methods and properties of the more established Table View. You will explore how each view is structured and how you can use Xcode to alter their appearance. Additionally, you will learn about creating custom cells, where you will subclass `UITableViewCell` to customize the elements within your cells. As with the other chapters in this book, there will be many additional lessons learned along the way; you'll see how the Segue Identifiers that were specified in Chapter 7 allow you to share data between View Controllers, as well as learn about a variety of ways to obtain data from the Internet and display that in the application.

Because this chapter is reliant on having access to at least one Twitter account, if you don't have one, it would be a good idea to register for one at `www.twitter.com`. Ensure you have created the account and that you've "followed" some other Twitter users; whatever your personal feelings are about Twitter, remember that you don't have to use it beyond this chapter and you can delete your account when you are ready.

After you've finished SocialApp, I'll explain Collection Views and how they differ from Table Views. They are very close cousins, with Collection Views having similar methods and properties to Table Views, so much of what you learn with Table Views can be directly applied to Collection Views.

What Is a Table View?

Table Views represent an instance of the `UITableView` class; they present the user with a single column of cells listed vertically. Table Views provide developers with a great way of displaying a large number of options or data to the user, such as in a Twitter application where you can scroll through potentially hundreds or even thousands of tweets. They can also be used to neatly lay out application settings, exploiting the hierarchical structure that Table Views provide to take the user from high-level categories right down to granular details and microsettings. The flexibility of Table Views means that you will find one in nearly every application, but you might not recognize them right away. Figure 8-1 shows some of the Table Views in use through iOS and the default applications.

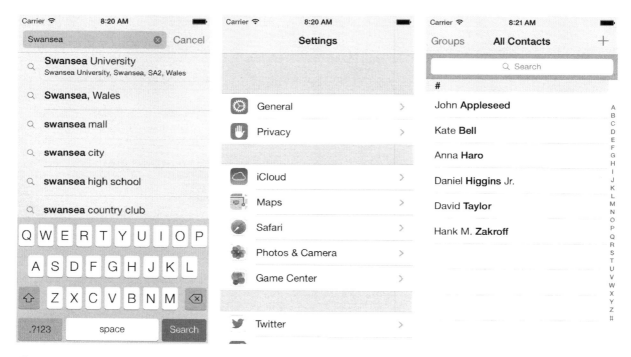

Figure 8-1. *Table Views within various iOS apps*

Because of their popularity, Apple spends a lot of time improving the flexibility and feature set of Table Views with each successive release of iOS, making it easy to add features such as Pull to refresh.

Table View Composition

Before you get into the configuration of Table Views, it's good to have a basic idea of the composition of a Table View and its key components, which are layered one on top of the other. Figure 8-2 gives you a visual breakdown of the different elements in a Table View. Let's examine the components in more detail.

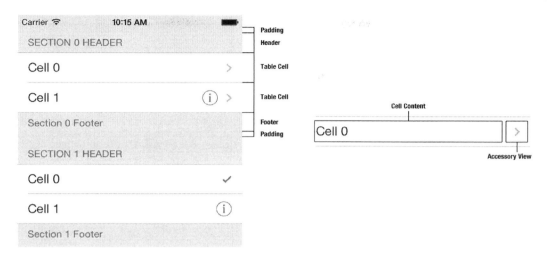

Figure 8-2. *A breakdown of the Table View anatomy*

- *View:* The Table View is the foundation in the hierarchy of elements; it sits at the bottom of the stack, coordinating all of the child components. The View element controls the overall look and feel of the table and anchors all of the delegate methods together.

- *Section:* The next item in the Table View stack is the Section. Sections are useful for breaking up tables, grouping cells together, and providing a header and footer for the group.

- *Cell:* The Table Cell represents a row in the Table View and can have varying states, such as when it is being edited, that affect the number of key areas in a cell. The two default areas of a Table Cell are the Cell Content and the Accessory View. You might think the Cell Content area is self-explanatory, but it is actually a quite varied element and, depending on the style of cell, can contain an image, a title, and a subtitle. The Accessory View can contain either a disclosure indicator, such as an arrow, a detail accessory for providing more information about the row, or both.

Table View Styles

When Apple released iOS 7, most areas that received a visual makeover were Table Views. There are two distinct styles for Table Views, but with iOS 7, they are no longer all that different. Figure 8-3 shows a Plain style Table View on the left and a Grouped style Table View on the right.

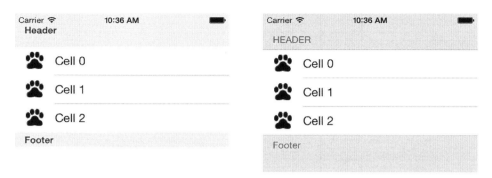

Figure 8-3. *A Plain Table View (left) and a Grouped Table View (right)*

In practical terms, you would typically use the Plain style to list large amounts of data, usually in a single section with no header or footer. The Grouped style is ideal for situations where you have a static list of data such as in a *settings* view where you group similar areas of configuration together such as in the Settings application in iOS (center image in Figure 8-1).

Configuring the Accounts View

In the Twitter client SocialApp, the Accounts View is one of the simplest to set up as it uses a Plain Table View with very little customization, however, you'll also get your first introduction to the Social and Accounts frameworks, which allow you to access details about accounts set up on the device, and then use the account to authorize requests to social media sites such as Twitter or Facebook.

This is the first time you've had to go back to work on an existing project, so if you haven't already opened the SocialApp project that you started in Chapter 7, start by opening Xcode, and then use File ä Open (⌘ + O) and locate SocialApp.xcodeproj in the folder where you created it, then click Open, as shown in Figure 8-4.

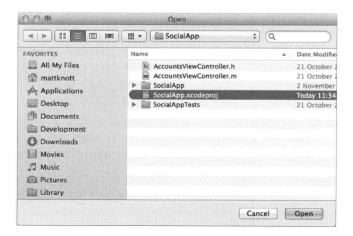

Figure 8-4. *Opening the SocialApp project that was started in Chapter 7*

Before you configure the Table View for the Accounts scene, let's explore the options available within Xcode for altering the Table View itself, and then later in this chapter you'll customize the cells. With the project open, select Main.Storyboard from the Project Navigator and position the Storyboard so that you're looking at the Accounts scene, as shown in Figure 8-5.

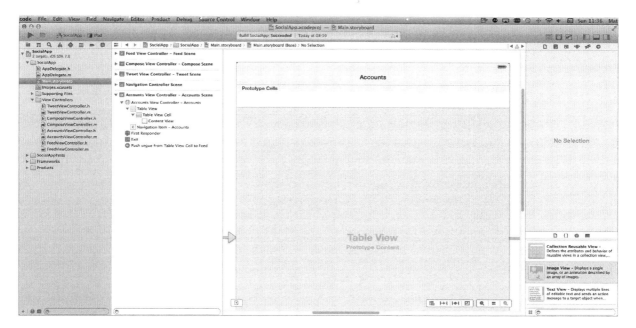

Figure 8-5. *The Accounts scene positioned and ready to go*

The Key Attributes of Table Views

Select the Table View in the Accounts scene; you can do this by either clicking the words Table View Prototype Convent in the middle of the view or by selecting Table View from the Accounts scene in the Document Outline. Now open the Attributes Inspector. If you're looking at the right object, the first segment in the Attributes Inspector will be Table View. Figure 8-6 shows the default attributes of a Table View in Xcode 5.

Figure 8-6. *The default attributes of a Table View in Xcode 5*

When configuring a Table View, most of the time you will be after one of these first five attributes as they have the largest influence of the structure and style of a Table View. Let's look at these options in more detail.

- *Content (Dynamic Prototypes):* Unlike many of the attributes you can configure in Xcode, the content type cannot be set programmatically. It's purely an Xcode thing. Selecting Dynamic Prototypes as the content type gives you a single table cell by default. The idea is that often you only have one cell style in a table, so you configure the one cell, and in code you reuse that one cell for each row. Using the Prototype Cells attribute that is available for this content type, you can increase the number of prototypes and have one for each distinct cell type. If you're using Dynamic Prototypes, you must customize the code to be able to view any cells in your view. This is the content type you will use for all of the Table Views in this application.

- *Content (Static Cells):* When using Static Cells, you use Xcode to specify how many sections will exist in your Table View and how many cells appear in each section. You can then create Segues from these individual cells to other scenes in your Storyboard. One of the biggest differences between Static Cells and Dynamic Prototypes is that although the delegate methods that Table Views use to specify the number of sections and cells *can* be used to influence the Table View, they can also be completely removed, leaving the attributes specified in Xcode as the controlling factor.

- *Style:* The Style attribute is where you choose between Plain or Grouped styles. As you can see in Figure 8-3, there is actually very little difference between the two in iOS 7. Both styles can be extensively customized using code to change sizes and colors.

- *Separator:* The separator line in a Table View is the line that appears between cells. This attribute gives you four options to choose from: Default, Single Line, Single Line Etched, and None. In reality these four options are effectively only two. The Default style is the same as the Single Line style, and in iOS 7, the Single Line Etched is now the same as None as it was deemed not compatible with the flat design approach Apple took with iOS 7, so effectively this style and its code equivalent UITableViewCellSeparatorStyleSingleLineEtched have been deprecated.

- *Separator Insets:* This is another new addition for iOS 7 and Xcode 5. In earlier versions of iOS, the separator line spanned the full width of the cell, however, in iOS 7 there is a small indent on the left side of the cell by default. By setting the Separator Insets attribute to Custom, you can specify a custom left and right indent depending on the style you want to achieve.

> **Note**   In programming, when a class is deprecated, it means that it has been decommissioned, is not supported, and is no longer considered acceptable for use. Often when a class is deprecated, it remains available for use; however, because it is unsupported, it may have consequences with other areas of your application and may cause unexpected issues with other classes.

Manipulating Static Table Views

Let's take a look at how Xcode allows you to manipulate a static layout, before going back and implementing the dynamic prototype system you will be using for this scene.

1. Select the Accounts Table View and then open the Attributes Inspector. Set the Content attribute to Static Cells; you should notice that the single cell you did have now has become three cells, and the second attribute has become Sections.

2. Let's increase the number of sections so that there are two groups of cells to work with; change the Sections attribute to read 2. Your table should now resemble the one shown in Figure 8-7.

Figure 8-7. *The static layout with two sections*

3. The number of cells in a section is controlled directly by the section attributes. Select the first section by clicking Section-1 in the view or by selecting Table View Section – Section 1 from the Document Outline, as shown in Figure 8-8.

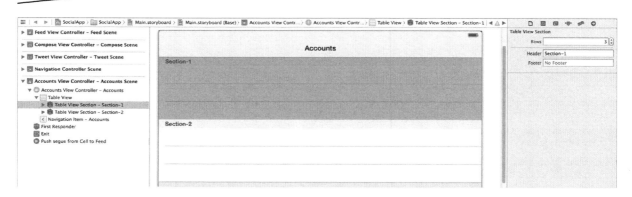

Figure 8-8. *Selecting Section-1 to access the section attributes*

4. In the Attribute Inspector, the terminology changes slightly from cells to rows. Looking at the attributes, you can see that here you specify the header and footer value of your section and also the number of rows. Feel free to try setting your own values for these attributes and see how the table changes.

5. You can also delete individual cells and move them around. In Section-2, start by deleting two cells; click on the cells individually and then press the Backspace key to remove them. Now, select the single remaining cell.

6. In the Attributes Inspector, change the Style to Basic; this will add the word Title to your cell. Double-click the word Title to start editing it, as shown in Figure 8-9, and change it to read Cell 1.

Figure 8-9. *Changing the title of the basic cell*

7. Press the Return key to commit the change and then reselect Section-2. Now increase the number of rows from one to three by changing the Rows attribute to 3. This allows you to clone your row three times. This is a really handy way of duplicating a custom cell when using static cells instead of dynamic prototypes.

8. Now rename each of your new cells by double-clicking Cell 1 and change them to 2 and 3, respectively, until Section-2 resembles those shown in Figure 8-10.

Figure 8-10. *Section 2 with three Basic style cells*

9. To demonstrate how easy it is to reorder a Static Table View, highlight Cell 3 with a single-click and then drag it to the top of Section-2, as shown in Figure 8-11. You can also move cells between sections, meaning that changing your layout needn't be a chore.

Figure 8-11. *Selecting the third cell (top image) and dragging it to the first position (bottom image)*

10. Now that you've seen the various ways Xcode lets you manipulate static layouts, you're ready to get the Accounts scene built up and working. Start by reselecting the Table View itself and changing the Content attribute to Dynamic Prototypes and ensure that the Style is set to Grouped.

11. This will leave you with a number of cells in your single section. You only want one prototype cell, so delete any excess cells by manually highlighting them and pressing the Backspace key until you are left with a single cell, ready for customizing.

12. Highlight the one remaining cell and go to the Attributes Inspector. The style should currently be set to Custom, which is fine, as you'll be setting the content programmatically. Next set the Accessory attribute to Disclosure Indicator, which will add the indicator arrow on the right-hand side of the cell. Finally, give your cell an identifier so you can refer to it in code and reuse it efficiently. Set the Identifier attribute to AccountCell. The cell's attributes should resemble those shown in Figure 8-12.

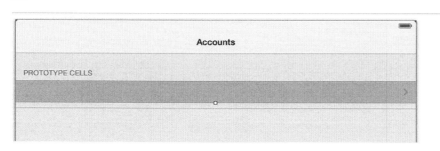

Figure 8-12. The table cell configured, ready to have its content set

You're finished with the layout and design of your Table View, so now it's time to start adding the code to access the Twitter accounts on the device and displaying them in the table. To do this, you'll need to add the Accounts and the Social frameworks to the project.

The Accounts and Social Framework

In previous chapters you've taken advantage of some of the Apple-provided frameworks, and in this chapter you'll take advantage of two: `Accounts.framework` and `Social.framework`. As with the other frameworks you've used, they make potentially complex and intensive tasks much simpler, and this is no different. Based on the fact that this is the first time you've worked with these two frameworks, it's also worth noting that the two frameworks used in this chapter work together. Accounts framework classes are prefixed with AC; in this project you'll create an instance of the `ACAccount` class, which will hold the details of a selected Twitter account. You'll then hand that `ACAccount` object to other View Controllers as you navigate through the project, and then combine that with one of the Social framework's classes: `SLRequest`, which uses the `ACAccount` object to authenticate requests with Twitter.

If you've worked with Twitter's APIs in the past, you'll know that authentication involves a process called three-legged OAuth. This involves a number of requests back and forth with Twitter, the combination of the `ACAccount` object with the `SLRequests` means that you don't have to do any of that. iOS does all of the running around so that we, the developers, are free to focus on functionality and how we handle the requests to Twitter.

I'll explain all of the ways you can add frameworks to a project in Chapter 9, but for now, let's add `Accounts.framework` and `Social.framework` in the same way you have in the past.

1. Start by selecting the project in the Project Navigator, as shown in Figure 8-13.

Figure 8-13. Selecting the project in the Project Navigator

2. Scroll down to the bottom of the General tab until you see the section titled Linked Frameworks and Libraries. Click the plus symbol at the bottom of the list of frameworks. When the list of frameworks and libraries appears, search for the Accounts framework, as shown in Figure 8-14. Select the framework and click Add.

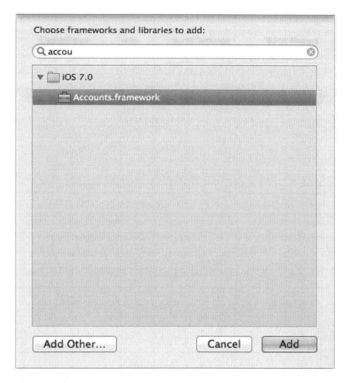

Figure 8-14. Adding Accounts.framework to the project

3. Repeat step 2, this time searching for the Social framework; select it and add it to the project. Your list of frameworks and libraries should now resemble those shown in Figure 8-15.

Figure 8-15. The final list of frameworks and libraries

Now that you have the frameworks you need added to the project, you're ready to start writing the code that will display your Twitter accounts in the Table View.

Retrieving and Displaying Twitter Accounts

To finish this scene, you need to achieve two objectives: retrieve an array of Twitter accounts registered on the device or in the simulator, and display them for the users to choose from. Let's start by setting up the View Controller's header, importing the frameworks, and creating the properties that are needed for this scene. As in previous chapters, I'll explain what needs to be done bit by bit and then review the code at the end of the process.

1. Start by opening `AccountsViewController.h`. With the header file open, you first need to import the additional frameworks that are needed for this scene. As you only access the list of Twitter accounts and do not make any requests to the Twitter APIs, you only need to import `Accounts.h`; after the line `#import <UIKit/UIKit.h>`, add the following line:

```
#import <Accounts/Accounts.h>
```

> **Note**   API stands for application programming interface. An API is a mechanism that specifies how different pieces of computer software interact with one another. In iOS Apple uses the term API to describe new classes within frameworks. When we talk about the Twitter API, we are not talking about classes within the Social framework, but rather the Twitter REST API, which you can find out more about at `http://dev.twitter.com`.

2. Next, create an array as an instance variable that will store the retrieved accounts and make them available to all methods in the class. Change your `@interface` declaration so that it looks like this:

```
@interface AccountsViewController : UITableViewController
{
    NSArray *twitterAccounts;
}
```

3. Finally, declare an instance of the `ACAccountStore` as a property. The `ACAccountStore` is the gateway to the list of Twitter accounts stored in iOS; you declare it as a property and then try to get permission from the user to access the Twitter account. If the user grants permission, the object becomes initialized. Before `@end`, add the following code:

```
@property (strong, nonatomic) ACAccountStore *accountStore;
```

That's it for the header file, you have now added a reference to the Accounts framework, created an array called twitterAccounts as an instance variable, and created an ACAccountStore property to manage the retrieval of Twitter accounts. Your final code should look like this:

```
#import <UIKit/UIKit.h>
#import <Accounts/Accounts.h>

@interface AccountsViewController : UITableViewController
{
    NSArray *twitterAccounts;
}

@property (strong, nonatomic) ACAccountStore *accountStore;

@end
```

4. Now you need to work on the implementation file, so go ahead and open the AccountsViewController.m file from the Project Navigator. Once it is open, scroll down until you see the viewDidLoad method.

5. The first thing you want to do when the view loads is initialize your ACAccountStore instance; that doesn't mean that you'll be accessing the accounts, just initializing the object so that it can be interacted with. Drop down a line after [super viewDidLoad]; and type the following line:

```
self.accountStore = [[ACAccountStore alloc] init];
```

6. Next, you'll be using the requestAccessToAccountsWithType method of the accountStore object. This method needs to be told what type of account you are requesting access to. You do this by creating an ACAccountType object and then using another accountStore method: accountTypeWithAccountTypeIdentifier. Drop down a line and add this code:

```
ACAccountType *accountType =
       [self.accountStore accountTypeWithAccountTypeIdentifier:ACAccountTypeIdentifierTwitter];
```

7. You're now at the stage where you want to ask the user for permission to use their Twitter accounts in the application using the requestAccessToAccountsWithType method. When this method is accessed, it creates an alert for the user to either grant or deny the request to access their Twitter account. Add the following code:

```
[self.accountStore requestAccessToAccountsWithType:accountType options:nil
                                    completion:^(BOOL granted, NSError *error)
{

}];
```

8. Notice that you pass the accountType object into the method to specify that it wants Twitter account access, and you handle the completion using a code block into which you'll add the logic as to whether granted returned yes or no. Because you will only want to look at the accounts available *if* access was granted, that should be the next thing you check; add the highlighted if statement inside the code block as shown below:

```
- (void)viewDidLoad
{
    [super viewDidLoad];

    self.accountStore = [[ACAccountStore alloc] init];

    ACAccountType *accountType = [self.accountStore
    accountTypeWithAccountTypeIdentifier:ACAccountTypeIdentifierTwitter];

    [self.accountStore requestAccessToAccountsWithType:accountType options:nil
                                    completion:^(BOOL granted, NSError *error)
    {
        if (granted)
        {

        }
    }];
}
```

9. With access granted, you need to populate the twitterAccounts object with all of the available Twitter accounts on the device, and here you'll use the accountsWithAccountType method of the accountStore and reuse the accountType object to restrict the request to Twitter accounts. Inside the if statement, add the following code:

```
twitterAccounts = [self.accountStore accountsWithAccountType:accountType];
```

10. Although the user has granted access, you need to check whether or not the user has added any Twitter accounts to the device. This is done by checking the twitterAccounts *count* property in an if else statement. After the previous line, drop down and add this code:

```
if (twitterAccounts.count == 0)
{

}
else
{

}
```

11. If there are no Twitter accounts stored in iOS, you'll want to summon an Alert View and tell the user that no accounts were found. Because you're running on an arbitrary thread and all interface changes need to be executed on the main thread, you'll be adding a code block to execute the displaying of the Alert View. Add the following highlighted code inside the first set of braces:

```
if (twitterAccounts.count == 0)
{

    UIAlertView *accountsAlert = [[UIAlertView alloc] initWithTitle:@"Warning"
                                                  message:@"No Twitter accounts available"
                                                  delegate:self
                                     cancelButtonTitle:@"Okay"
                                     otherButtonTitles:nil];

    dispatch_async(dispatch_get_main_queue(), ^(void)
    {
        [accountsAlert show];
    });
}
```

12. Finally, if there are accounts, then you have them in the `twitterAccounts` object and you just need to tell the Table View that it needs to reload the data showed in the table. This is done by accessing the `reloadData` method. Inside the second set of braces, add this line of code:

```
[self.tableView reloadData];
```

13. Before you try running the application, you need to go back to the AccountsViewController.h file. In the implementation file, you summoned an Alert View, and because of this you need to make the View Controller an UIAlertViewDelegate. To do this, add <UIAlertViewDelegate> to the end of @interface AccountsViewController : UITableViewController. Now go back to your AccountsViewController.m and check that your viewDidLoad method looks like this:

```
- (void)viewDidLoad
{
    [super viewDidLoad];

    self.accountStore = [[ACAccountStore alloc] init];

    ACAccountType *accountType =
        [self.accountStore accountTypeWithAccountTypeIdentifier:ACAccountTypeIdentifierTwitter];

    [self.accountStore requestAccessToAccountsWithType:accountType options:nil
                                    completion:^(BOOL granted, NSError *error)
```

```
    {
        if (granted)
        {
            twitterAccounts = [self.accountStore accountsWithAccountType:accountType];

            if (twitterAccounts.count == 0)
            {
                UIAlertView *accountsAlert = [[UIAlertView alloc] initWithTitle:@"Warning"
                                                    message:@"No Twitter accounts available"
                                                    delegate:self
                                          cancelButtonTitle:@"Okay"
                                          otherButtonTitles:nil];

                dispatch_async(dispatch_get_main_queue(), ^(void)
                {
                    [accountsAlert show];
                });
            }
            else
            {
                dispatch_async(dispatch_get_main_queue(), ^(void)
                {
                    [self.tableView reloadData];
                });
            }
        }

    }];
}
```

14. Okay, so you've added the code that pulls together a dataset for the Table
    View in the shape of the `twitterAccounts` array, so now you need to get
    those data into the cells by using two of the `UITableView` class's delegate
    methods: `numberOfSectionsInTableView` and `numberOfRowsInSection`. These
    two methods control the number of sections displayed in the table and also
    the number of table cells per section by returning an `NSInteger`, a numeric
    value that the Table View interprets. The needs are fairly simple in that you
    will only ever have one section and the number of cells is the `count` property
    from the `twitterAccounts` object. Furthermore, Apple has kindly added the
    stubs for these two methods, so scroll through the implementation file until
    you find them and then change the code in each method so that it matches
    that which is shown below:

```
- (NSInteger)numberOfSectionsInTableView:(UITableView *)tableView
{
    return 1;
}
```

```
- (NSInteger)tableView:(UITableView *)tableView numberOfRowsInSection:(NSInteger)section
{
    return twitterAccounts.count;
}
```

15. Next, because the application will try to create an instance of your prototype cell if there are any Twitter accounts set up within the simulator, it's important that you set the correct name for the prototype cell before trying to run the application. I will explain this in more detail once you have run the application, but look for the `cellForRowAtIndexPath` method, and you will see that it contains a line that reads `static NSString *CellIdentifier = @"Cell";`. You need to change the identifier to match the one specified within the Storyboard, which is `AccountCell`, so go ahead and change that to the following:

```
static NSString *CellIdentifier = @"AccountCell";
```

16. It's been a very long time coming, but you're now at a point where you can go ahead and run the application in the Simulator. Go to Product ➤ Run (⌘ + R) to launch the application. The first thing you should see is a prompt for access to the device's Twitter accounts, as shown in Figure 8-16. It's important to click OK at this point to grant access; you will then be presented with one of the two outcomes shown in Figure 8-17 depending on the number of Twitter accounts you have. The left-hand screen shows two empty cells representing the two Twitter accounts I have set up in the Simulator, the right-hand screen is what you will see if you have no Twitter accounts in iOS.

Figure 8-16. The security prompt asking for access to the Twitter accounts for our application

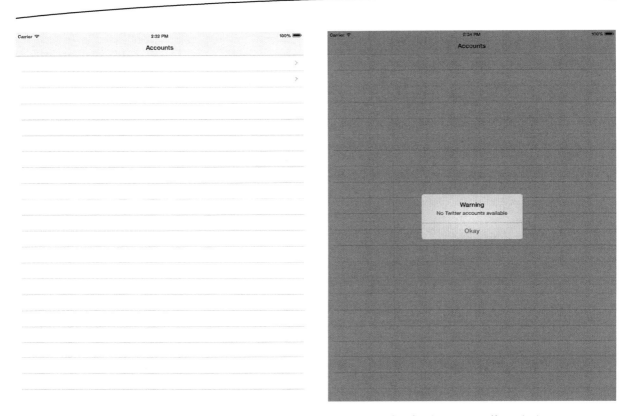

Figure 8-17. *On the left is the outcome if you have any Twitter accounts, on the right is what happens if you don't*

17.   If you don't have any Twitter accounts added in iOS and saw the second of the two screens, adding your Twitter account is very easy. In the Simulator, go back to the home screen by going to Hardware ➤ Home (⌘ + Shift + H). Click the Settings icon and then select the Twitter option from the left column, as shown in Figure 8-18.

Figure 8-18. *Selecting the Twitter settings*

> **Note**   If you accidentally refuse permission to the application, you can grant permission from the Twitter settings. You will see SocialApp listed at the bottom of the Twitter settings with a switch beside it. Turn this to the on position and permission will be granted to access the accounts.

18. Type in your Twitter account name and password and click Sign in. You can repeat this step to add more Twitter accounts if you wish. When you are done, go back to Xcode and rerun your application, this time your view should resemble the left-hand image in Figure 8-17.

19. Although the application runs, you still have to make the Table View display the account name instead of it being empty, and to do that you need to utilize another of the `UITableView` delegate methods: `cellForRowAtIndexPath`. This is the method you quickly altered before running the application. All delegate methods are called as the result of an event occurring. In this case, it's the Table View responding to the number of rows it has been told to display, and then calling the `cellForRowAtIndexPath` method to allow it to populate the specific cell's contents. Again, this is one of the methods that Apple has already created for you, and after your brief modification it should look like this:

```
- (UITableViewCell *)tableView:(UITableView *)tableView cellForRowAtIndexPath:(NSIndexPath *)
indexPath
{
    static NSString *CellIdentifier = @"AccountCell";
    UITableViewCell *cell =
        [tableView dequeueReusableCellWithIdentifier:CellIdentifier forIndexPath:indexPath];

    // Configure the cell...

    return cell;
}
```

20. Before running the application, you changed the `CellIdentifier` string to `AccountCell`. This value is critical when creating the Table Cell because it ensures that the correct prototype cell has been used. To display information within the cell, the application needs to know which row it is on. You can establish this by looking at the method variable `indexPath;`. This object has properties for section and row, with both following the array format for positioning, starting at 0 and incrementing by one. Because there is only one section, the row value will correspond to the position of elements in the `twitterAccounts` array, for example, if the `indexPath` row property is 0, it will

need to fetch the account at position 0 in the array. Remove the comment `// Configure the cell...` and in its place create an ACAccount object based on the account stored at the supplied position in our array:

```
ACAccount *account = [twitterAccounts objectAtIndex:indexPath.row];
```

21. Next, put a value in the Table View cell that shows the name of the account in the array. The table cell is currently the default `UITableViewCell`, which has three controls that can be manipulated: a Label called `textLabel`, a subtitle Label called `detailTextLabel`, and an Image View called `imageView`. Let's take the Description property of the account object and use it to set the `textLabel`'s Text property:

```
cell.textLabel.text = account.accountDescription;
```

22. Your complete method should look like this:

```
- (UITableViewCell *)tableView:(UITableView *)tableView cellForRowAtIndexPath:(NSIndexPath *)
indexPath
{
    static NSString *CellIdentifier = @"AccountCell";
    UITableViewCell *cell =
        [tableView dequeueReusableCellWithIdentifier:CellIdentifier forIndexPath:indexPath];

    ACAccount *account = [twitterAccounts objectAtIndex:indexPath.row];
    cell.textLabel.text = account.accountDescription;

    return cell;
}
```

23. Go ahead and run your application again; this time your Table View should be populated as shown in Figure 8-19. What's more, you can select an account and you will be taken to the `FeedViewController` scene, although beware, if you click on the Compose button, the view will appear and look great, but you haven't written the code to dismiss the View Controller yet and you will be stuck unless you rerun your application from Xcode.

Carrier 🗢	5:10 PM	100% 🔋
	Accounts	
@beginningxcode5		>
@codeomatic		>

Figure 8-19. *The Table View showing a list of Twitter accounts*

24. One great feature to take note of here is that as you *push* the Feed View Controller, you are automatically given a button that takes you back to the Accounts View Controller without even having to write any code.

Before we focus on the next scene, the Feed View Controller, you'll need to think ahead slightly. When an account is selected, that selection is currently kept with the Accounts View Controller; so you need to pass it on like a baton to the Feed View Controller when the Segue is performed. To do this you need to create a property on the Feed View Controller to receive the selected ACAccount object when you pass it across.

25. Open `FeedViewController.h` from the Project Navigator. In the header file, right before @end, type the following line:

```
@property (strong, nonatomic) ACAccount *selectedAccount;
```

26. Notice that Xcode doesn't like this line and will tell you it is wrong. This is because the ACAccount class belongs to the Accounts framework, which hasn't been imported yet. To resolve this, add the following line after #import <UIKit/UIKit.h>:

```
#import <Accounts/Accounts.h>
```

27. Your `FeedViewController.h` file should match this:

```
#import <UIKit/UIKit.h>
#import <Accounts/Accounts.h>

@interface FeedViewController : UITableViewController

@property (strong, nonatomic) ACAccount *selectedAccount;

@end
```

28. You now have something to receive the selected ACAccount from the Accounts View Controller; all that remains is to pass the object across when the Segue is called. Open `AccountsViewController.m` once more from the Project Navigator.

29. Because you need to pass an object to a property declared in the Feed View Controller from the Accounts View Controller, you need to import `FeedViewController.h`. After the line #import "AccountsViewController.h", add the following:

```
#import "FeedViewController.h"
```

30. If you weren't using Segues to navigate between View Controllers, you would use the `didSelectRowAtIndexPath` method to determine what to do next, but because you *are* using a Segue, you need to use the `prepareForSegue` method. Yet again, the good folks at Apple have already

written a basic implementation of the method for us, however, unlike the delegate methods used earlier, this one is commented out. At the bottom of the `AccountsViewController.m` file, you should see the method you need, but that it is commented out in green (assuming you haven't deviated from the color scheme). To uncomment the code, before the line `#pragma mark – Navigation` you should see `/*`, these two characters are used to index the start of a commented block of code; remove them. Next, look for `*/` just before `@end`; this signifies the end of the comment block, remove it as well. The method is now uncommented and ready for use.

31.   The `prepareForSegue` method is called when a Segue has been triggered. It gives developers a chance to perform any actions they need to process before the view changes. One of the parameters passed to this method is a `UIStoryboardSegue` object called `segue`; we can use this to check the segue identifier and then take appropriate action. The identifier for this Segue to the Feed View Controller scene is `ShowTweets`, so to check for this in an `if` statement, add the highlighted code to the method:

```
- (void)prepareForSegue:(UIStoryboardSegue *)segue sender:(id)sender
{
    if ([[segue identifier] isEqualToString:@"ShowTweets"])
    {

    }
}
```

32.   You'll need to find out which account was selected, create an `ACAccount` object from the selection, and pass that to the Feed View Controller's selected account property. The first task, then, is to determine which row was selected. You do this by creating an `NSIndexPath` object called *path* based on the result of the `indexPathForSelectedRow` method. Add the following line to your `if` statement:

```
NSIndexPath *path = [self.tableView indexPathForSelectedRow];
```

33.   Next create the `ACAccount` object, which you'll call `account`. This is almost an exact duplicate of when you instantiated an `ACAccount` object in the `cellForRowAtIndexPath` method:

```
ACAccount *account = [twitterAccounts objectAtIndex:path.row];
```

34.   Finally, pass the account object to the Feed View Controller. When a Segue is triggered and this method is called, the destination View Controller is stored in a property of the `segue` object called `destinationViewController`. Because you know that the destination view controller is Feed View Controller, you

cast destinationViewController from a generic ID type to be a Feed View Controller type. Finally, another brilliant feature Xcode has automatically created is a setter method for the property called setSelectedAccount. You will use this to handle the passing of the account object. All of these actions can be done in the following line of code:

```
[(FeedViewController *)[segue destinationViewController] setSelectedAccount:account];
```

That's it! You've finished writing the code for Accounts View Controller and even added a bit to the Feed View Controller. You're one down and five to go, so let's move on to Feed View Controller where you'll build on your Table View skills and learn about creating custom cells and subclassing UITableViewCell to take customizations to another level. Before you move on, check that your prepareForSegue method matches the code below and that you can build and run the application without any exceptions.

```
- (void)prepareForSegue:(UIStoryboardSegue *)segue sender:(id)sender
{
    if ([[segue identifier] isEqualToString:@"ShowTweets"])
    {
        NSIndexPath *path = [self.tableView indexPathForSelectedRow];
        ACAccount *account = [twitterAccounts objectAtIndex:path.row];
        [(FeedViewController *)[segue destinationViewController] setSelectedAccount:account];
    }
}
```

Configuring the Feed View

The Feed View is the center point of SocialApp; it lists the 20 latest tweets using some of the methods and classes used in the previous Accounts View but also many that have not been encountered in the app before. In the sections that follow, you'll learn how to:

- Use the SLRequest class to fetch the json formatted data from the Internet

- Use an NSCache object to handle some basic caching

- Use an NSOperationQueue to streamline the retrieval of Twitter avatar images

- Subclass UITableViewCell to create a custom class for the cells in the Table View

Because I really want to focus on the Table View and how to populate it, I won't be going into too much detail about the code used for retrieving the data from the Twitter API or processing them. You've already learned how to access the documentation for different classes, so if you want to know more, I encourage you to look at the documentation in the first instance, but then branch out onto the Internet if you want to know more. Figure 8-20 shows what the rows in the finished Table View will look like.

Apress

For this week's #FreeBookFriday, we're offering @TarangVC's #AtWork title: http://t.co/40fb0Km8kJ RT by 3pm to enter! #VentureCapitalists

Figure 8-20. A look ahead to a row from the finished Feed View

1. Before I get into the code, you need to build the cell's interface and link it to a custom `UITableViewCell` class. You will subclass `UITableViewCell` in the same way you did `UITableViewController`; right-click on the SocialApp group in the Project Navigator and select New File ... (⌘ + N), as shown in Figure 8-21.

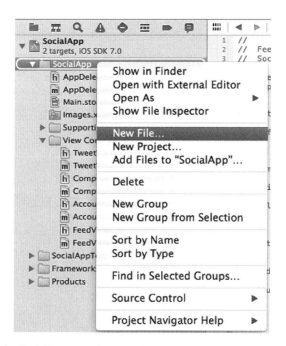

Figure 8-21. Adding a new file to the SocialApp group in the Project Navigator

2. Select the Objective-C class option that should now be selected by default and click Next. First set the Subclass of value to `UITableViewCell` and the Class value to TweetCell. Click Next. As always, you want to save the file in the project folder; click Create to create the file and add it to the project. You're now ready to set up the visual elements of the Table View.

3. Open `Main.storyboard` from the Project Navigator and arrange the view so you can see the Feed scene and are at 100% zoom, as shown in Figure 8-22.

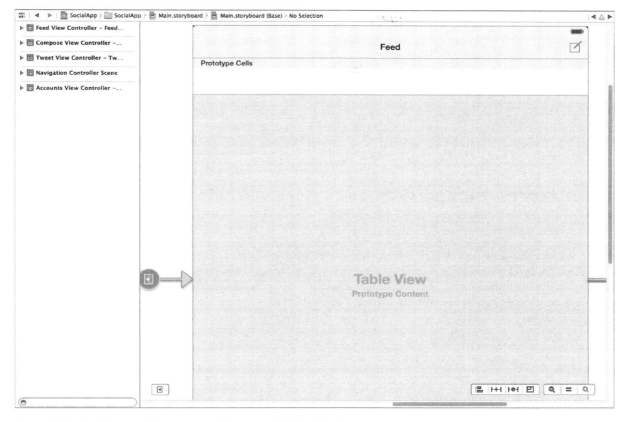

Figure 8-22. The Storyboard file open, ready for you to build the interface

4. The default row height on the cell is far too small to display everything nicely. To resize the cell, click the Table View as you did in the previous scene by clicking the view where it says Table View Prototype Content or by selecting Table View from the Feed View Controller scene in the Document Outline. Next open the Size Inspector and set the Row Height value to 120, as shown in Figure 8-23.

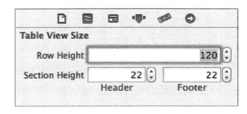

Figure 8-23. Adjusting the height of the row in the Size Inspector

5. Before you start the interface of the cell, specify that the cell is controlled by the new TweetCell class. Open the Identity Inspector and from the Class drop-down list, select TweetCell. Finally, open the Attribute Inspector for the cell. You need to specify a reuse identifier here, so in the Identifier attribute, type TweetCell.

6. Now that there is plenty of room to work in, add in the controls, which consist of an Image View and two Labels. Start by dragging in an Image View from the Object Library onto the cell. It will try to fill the view, but don't worry, put it anywhere and go back the Size Inspector. Set the x and y values to 20, and the Height and Width values to 79. The view should resemble that shown in Figure 8-24.

Figure 8-24. Manually sizing and positioning the Image View

7. Before you leave the Image View, you need a default image to act as a placeholder. In Chapter 4 you downloaded the incredibly useful set of free iOS icons called Icon Beast from www.iconbeast.com/free/. One of those icons has the file name photo.png, drag that file from Finder to the Supporting Files group, as shown in Figure 8-25.

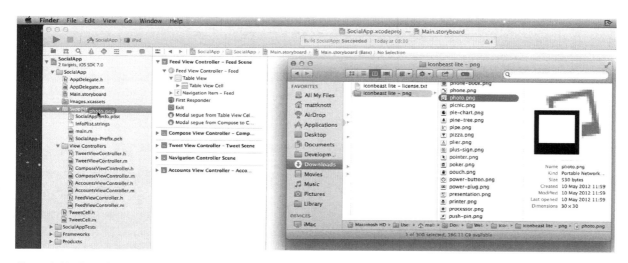

Figure 8-25. Dragging in photo.png

8. When you release the file over the Supporting Files group, the import file dialog will appear. Ensure that you select Copy items into destination group's folder and then click Finish. Switch to the Attributes Inspector and set the Image attribute to photo.png, which should now be shown in the list of available images. Because the icon looks pretty distorted, change the Mode attribute to Aspect Fit, and this will keep the original image ratios intact while making the image as large as it can be inside the Image View yet remaining fully visible.

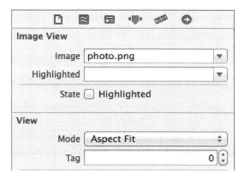

Figure 8-26. Setting the attributes of the Image View so that it has a placeholder image

9. Next, add a Label for the user name of the author of the tweet. Drag in a Label from the Object Library and align it with the top of the Image View. In the Attribute Inspector, change the Text attribute to User Name. Using the T icon, change the Font attribute to System Bold and the Size to 17.

10. With the font and the placeholder text set correctly, size the Label appropriately. It should be a single line in height and as wide as the cell, as shown in Figure 8-27.

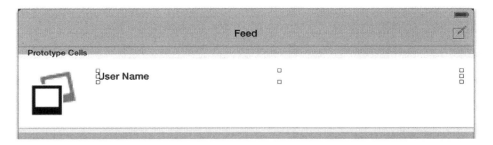

Figure 8-27. Aligning the User Name Label

11. The final object that needs to be add to the cell is a Label for the tweet content. Drag in a Label and position it just below the User Name Label. Make it the same width as the User Name Label, and then increase the height until the guidelines at the bottom of the cell show as they do in Figure 8-28.

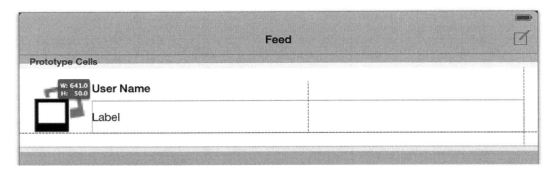

Figure 8-28. *Aligning the tweet Content Label*

12. In the Attributes Inspector, simply set the Text attribute to Content, and the Lines attribute to 2. Xcode will wrap the text onto a second line if needed. If the text length exceeds what will fit in two lines, the Line Breaks attribute will determine what will happen. The default option is Truncate Tail, which cuts the text short and appends an ellipsis or ... to the end of the text.

13. You've now built the interface for the custom cell, so next you'll need to create the outlets for the three objects. Open the Assistant Editor with the cell selected, and this time ensure that the code file that is loaded is TweetCell.h. Control-drag a connection from the Image View to the header file just above @end and release the mouse; name this outlet tweetUserAvatar, as shown in Figure 8-29.

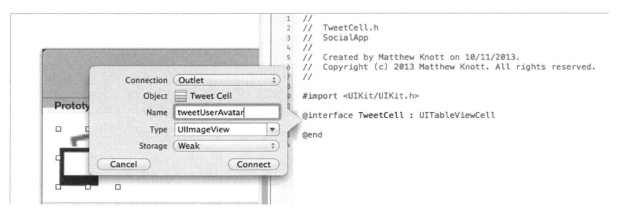

Figure 8-29. *Creating an outlet for the Image View called tweetUserAvatar*

14.   Next, create an outlet in the same way for the User Name Label, naming it tweetUserName. Finally, create an outlet for the Content Label named tweetContent. The header code of your custom UITableViewCell class should resemble the following code:

```
#import <UIKit/UIKit.h>
@interface TweetCell : UITableViewCell

@property (weak, nonatomic) IBOutlet UIImageView *tweetUserAvatar;
@property (weak, nonatomic) IBOutlet UILabel *tweetUserName;
@property (weak, nonatomic) IBOutlet UILabel *tweetContent;

@end
```

Now that you've created the interface and the outlets for the objects in the view, you can start bringing all of the different elements and classes together in the Feed View Controller header and implementation file where you'll write the code that fetches the Twitter feed and then parses the returned data before displaying it in the custom table cell.

1.   To get started, prepare the header file; switch back to the Standard Editor then open FeedViewController.h from the Project Navigator. You've already imported the Accounts framework, but for this View Controller and all the others in this project, you need to also import the Social framework, so after #import <Accounts/Accounts.h>, add the following line:

```
#import <Social/Social.h>
```

2.   You'll also need to create some instance variables for this View Controller just as you did for the last one, but this time you'll be creating three. After @interface FeedViewController : UITableViewController, add the following code:

```
{
    NSMutableArray *tweets;
    NSCache *imageCache;
    NSOperationQueue *queue;
}
```

3.   That's it for the header! Before opening FeedViewController.m, ensure your code matches that shown below:

```
#import <UIKit/UIKit.h>
#import <Accounts/Accounts.h>
#import <Social/Social.h>

@interface FeedViewController : UITableViewController
{
    NSMutableArray *tweets;
    NSCache *imageCache;
    NSOperationQueue *queue;
}
```

```
@property (strong, nonatomic) ACAccount *selectedAccount;

@end
```

You've got a lot of code to get through in this implementation file, and as I've already mentioned, I won't be going into a huge amount of detail. For the previous View Controller, you learned that in order to pass objects to other View Controllers, you need to import their headers. You also have to import the header of TweetCell so it can be referred to later, so before I get into the methods, let's start by importing all the necessary headers.

1. After the line #import "FeedViewController.h", add the following import statements:

```
#import "ComposeViewController.h"
#import "TweetViewController.h"
#import "TweetCell.h"
```

2. Next, scroll down to the viewDidLoad method. Because this method is called when the view loads, there are a few key tasks that should be performed. First, set the title of the view to the Twitter account name that was passed to the view from the previous Accounts View Controller. Next, initialize the NSOperationQueue, and finally add a call to a method that hasn't been written yet called retrieveTweets. Your viewDidLoad method code needs to look like this:

```
- (void)viewDidLoad
{
    [super viewDidLoad];

    self.navigationItem.title = self.selectedAccount.accountDescription;

    queue = [[NSOperationQueue alloc] init];
    queue.maxConcurrentOperationCount = 4;

    [self retrieveTweets];
}
```

3. Xcode will correctly flag the last line of the viewDidLoad method as being in error. This is because you haven't written that method yet. Drop down a few lines after the viewDidLoad method and declare the method stub as shown below:

```
-(void)retrieveTweets
{

}
```

4. Xcode will now be happy that everything is back in order; you'll still need to write this method's substantial code. I'll take you through each major block of code and explain the function as I go, as opposed to going line by line as I have done in the past. First, you want to clear the tweets array and declare an SLRequest object to manage this attempt at obtaining data from Twitter. Add the following code to start the method:

```
[tweets removeAllObjects];

SLRequest *request;
```

5. Next, check that you do indeed have a valid ACAccount object, and if so, initialize the SLRequest object with the URL to the Twitter API feed that provides the home timeline data that you want to display in the Table View. You then authenticate the request using the selectedAccount ACAccount object. Drop down a line and add this code:

```
if (self.selectedAccount)
{
    NSURL *requestURL =
     [NSURL URLWithString:@"https://api.twitter.com/1.1/statuses/home_timeline.json"];
    request = [SLRequest requestForServiceType:SLServiceTypeTwitter
                              requestMethod:SLRequestMethodGET URL:requestURL parameters:nil];
    [request setAccount:self.selectedAccount];
}
else
{
    NSLog(@"No Twitter Account Supplied");
}
```

For the final block of this method, you have given the request object all the parameters it needs so now you execute the performRequestWithHandler method, which accesses the supplied URL and returns the response from the request to a code block. If the request is successful, it will return a status code of 200. When this happens, you'll parse the json code into an array and use that as the contents of the tweets array. If you get anything other that a 200 response, use NSLog to make a note of the failure. Finally, you call the reloadData method of the Table View to update the information shown on the screen. Drop down a few lines and add this final block of code:

```
[request performRequestWithHandler:
^(NSData *responseData, NSHTTPURLResponse *urlResponse, NSError *error)
{
    if ([urlResponse statusCode] == 200)
    {
        NSError *jsonParseError;
        tweets = [NSJSONSerialization JSONObjectWithData:responseData
                                       options:0 error:&jsonParseError];
    }
```

```
    else
    {
        NSLog(@"http response code: %i", [urlResponse statusCode]);
    }

    dispatch_async(dispatch_get_main_queue(), ^(void)
    {
        [self.tableView reloadData];
    });
}];
```

> **Note**   If you are not familiar with `http response` codes, it may be worth looking up the possible codes online. Even if you've never heard the term before, you've almost certainly come across them while browsing the Internet. Errors 404 and 500 are two of the more visible error codes that you may have seen on a web site in the past, but there are many more and it is worth doing some research on them if you intend to use web APIs to get data into your application.

6.   The completed code for the `retrieveTweets` method should look like this:

```
-(void)retrieveTweets
{
    [tweets removeAllObjects];

    SLRequest *request;

    if (self.selectedAccount)
    {
        // Get home timeline of the Twitter account
        NSURL *requestURL =
        [NSURL URLWithString:@"https://api.twitter.com/1.1/statuses/home_timeline.json"];
        request = [SLRequest requestForServiceType:SLServiceTypeTwitter
                            requestMethod:SLRequestMethodGET URL:requestURL parameters:nil];
        [request setAccount:self.selectedAccount];
    }
    else
    {
        NSLog(@"No Twitter Account Supplied");
    }

    [request performRequestWithHandler:
    ^(NSData *responseData, NSHTTPURLResponse *urlResponse, NSError *error)
    {
        if ([urlResponse statusCode] == 200)
        {
            NSError *jsonParseError;
            tweets = [NSJSONSerialization JSONObjectWithData:responseData
                                            options:0 error:&jsonParseError];
        }
```

```
        else
        {
            NSLog(@"http response code: %i", [urlResponse statusCode]);
        }

        dispatch_async(dispatch_get_main_queue(), ^(void)
        {
            [self.tableView reloadData];
        });
    }];
}
```

7. This is actually a good point to run your application to check for errors. Your application should compile and allow you to select a Twitter account. On the feed screen you won't see anything yet, but more importantly you shouldn't see any errors. If you see No Twitter Account Supplied appear in the Debug area, check that you specified the correct Identifier for your Segue and that you referred to it correctly in AccountsViewController.m. If you see an http response code: error, check your Internet connection and that you typed the URL correctly.

8. Back in FeedViewController.m, it's time to start looking at the Table View delegate methods. Starting with numberOfSectionsInTableView and numberOfRowsInSection, you simply need to return a 1 for the single section you want to have, and the number of tweets in the array to set the number of rows in the table. The completed methods code should look like this:

```
- (NSInteger)numberOfSectionsInTableView:(UITableView *)tableView
{
    return 1;
}

- (NSInteger)tableView:(UITableView *)tableView numberOfRowsInSection:(NSInteger)section
{
    return tweets.count;
}
```

9. Now it's time to pair the data you've received and stored in the array with the custom TweetCell table cell with the cellForRowAtIndexPath method. First, delete the contents of the method so you're left with just the stub (and an Xcode warning), as shown below:

```
- (UITableViewCell *)tableView:(UITableView *)tableView cellForRowAtIndexPath:(NSIndexPath *)
indexPath
{
}
```

10. Then create an instance of TweetCell, which is similar to how you instantiated the UITableView cell in the previous View Controller. Then create two NSDictionary objects to store different parts of the Twitter feed data. One stores the main message data, the other stores the portion that relates directly to the user who created the tweet. An NSDictionary is a type of array that uses a key-value pairing system to store and access data. This means that instead of asking for the value at position 0 as you would with an array, you would ask for the value that corresponds to "name." Add the following code into your method:

```
static NSString *CellIdentifier = @"TweetCell";
TweetCell *cell = (TweetCell *)[tableView dequeueReusableCellWithIdentifier:CellIdentifier
                                                              forIndexPath:indexPath];

NSDictionary *tweetData = [tweets objectAtIndex:indexPath.row];
NSDictionary *userData = [tweetData objectForKey:@"user"];
```

11. Now let's take data from those NSDictionary objects and populate the interface. Start by setting the values of the two labels and then return the cell object to stop the error from being reported in Xcode. Note that because you imported TweetCell, Xcode knows about the outlets, and you can use code completion to quickly set their text property:

```
cell.tweetContent.text = [tweetData objectForKey:@"text"];
cell.tweetUserName.text = [userData objectForKey:@"name"];

return cell;
```

12. Because you returned the cell object, you are now error free and can go ahead and run the application. You haven't set the image yet, but you should be able to select your Twitter account and see the user and content values in each cell, as shown in Figure 8-30. If you get an exception when you go to the Feed View Controller, check that you specified the correct identifier on the cell in the Storyboard as well as in the code.

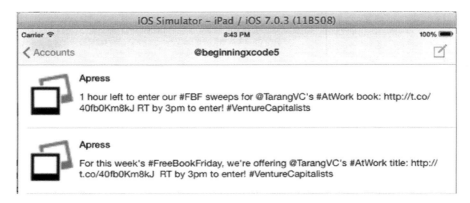

Figure 8-30. The avatar-less Twitter feed being displayed

Hopefully, you have a huge sense of satisfaction seeing your application finally coming to life this way as it reads live data from the Internet. There is one final block of code for this method that focuses on the retrieval, caching, and display of Twitter users' avatars. First, you'll try to retrieve the image from the cache, and if that fails you'll create an operation for the NSOperationQueue queue object to go and fetch the image's data and create an image from it before displaying it and then caching it for future use. Before the return cell; line, add the following code:

```
NSString *imageURLString = [userData objectForKey:@"profile_image_url"];
UIImage *image = [imageCache objectForKey:imageURLString];

if (image)
{
    cell.tweetUserAvatar.image = image;
}
else
{
    cell.tweetUserAvatar.image = [UIImage imageNamed:@"photo.png"];
    [queue addOperationWithBlock:^{
        NSURL *imageURL = [NSURL URLWithString:imageURLString];
        NSData *imageData = [NSData dataWithContentsOfURL:imageURL];
        UIImage *image = [UIImage imageWithData:imageData];

        if (image)
        {
            [[NSOperationQueue mainQueue] addOperationWithBlock:^{

                TweetCell *cell = (TweetCell *)[self.tableView cellForRowAtIndexPath:indexPath];
                if (cell)
                    cell.tweetUserAvatar.image = image;
            }];

            [imageCache setObject:image forKey:imageURLString];
        }
    }];
}
```

13. Take this opportunity to rerun your application. This time, after a brief delay, your images should all appear instead of the placeholder photo.png image, as shown in Figure 8-31.

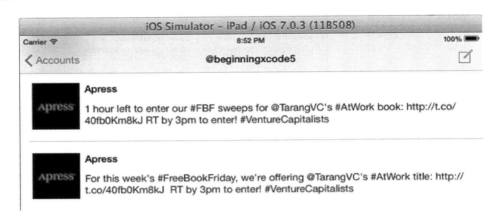

Figure 8-31. The Twitter feed, with the avatar images included this time

> **Note**   There will always be a delay when fetching data from the Internet, but because you used the NSOperationQueue object and efficiently switched between the main and arbitrary threads, there is no slowdown in the application, which would have guaranteed you negative app store reviews.

14.   Before moving on, here is the full code for the `cellForRowAtIndexPath` method:

```
- (UITableViewCell *)tableView:(UITableView *)tableView cellForRowAtIndexPath:(NSIndexPath *)
indexPath
{
    static NSString *CellIdentifier = @"TweetCell";
    TweetCell *cell = (TweetCell *)[tableView dequeueReusableCellWithIdentifier:CellIdentifier
                                                           forIndexPath:indexPath];

    NSDictionary *tweetData = [tweets objectAtIndex:indexPath.row];
    NSDictionary *userData = [tweetData objectForKey:@"user"];

    cell.tweetContent.text = [tweetData objectForKey:@"text"];
    cell.tweetUserName.text = [userData objectForKey:@"name"];

    NSString *imageURLString = [userData objectForKey:@"profile_image_url"];
    UIImage *image = [imageCache objectForKey:imageURLString];

    if (image)
    {
        cell.tweetUserAvatar.image = image;
    }
    else
    {
        cell.tweetUserAvatar.image = [UIImage imageNamed:@"photo.png"];
```

```
    [queue addOperationWithBlock:^{

        NSURL *imageURL = [NSURL URLWithString:imageURLString];
        NSData *imageData = [NSData dataWithContentsOfURL:imageURL];
        UIImage *image = [UIImage imageWithData:imageData];


        if (image)
        {
            [[NSOperationQueue mainQueue] addOperationWithBlock:^{

                TweetCell *cell = (TweetCell *)[self.tableView cellForRowAtIndexPath:indexPath];
                if (cell)
                    cell.tweetUserAvatar.image = image;
            }];

            [imageCache setObject:image forKey:imageURLString];
        }
    }];
}

return cell;
}
```

15. Finally, in this implementation file, let's create the stubs for the two Segues away from this View Controller: ComposeTweet and ShowTweet. Add the following prepareForSegue method:

```
- (void)prepareForSegue:(UIStoryboardSegue *)segue sender:(id)sender
{
    if ([[segue identifier] isEqualToString:@"ComposeTweet"])
    {
    }
    if ([[segue identifier] isEqualToString:@"ShowTweet"])
    {
    }
}
```

That's it for the Feed View Controller for now. We'll come back to this file when we need to send across any required objects for the Segue, but for now, let's move on to the third View Controller, Tweet View Controller.

Because the last two views in the application subclass the UIViewController, I'll only be focusing on adding the code. This is mainly so that you can see how the application builds up in stages and that it is rarely spit into neat chunks. But this will also give the satisfaction of building your own working Twitter client.

Configuring the Tweet View

The Tweet View Controller allows the user to see the full text of the tweet they selected from the Twitter feed. This is useful if the text in the Table View cell has been truncated. If you were making a complete Twitter client, you would have to add numerous bits of additional information, such as how many times the tweet has become a favorite or been retweeted. For SocialApp, however, you'll configure the Feed View Controller to pass across an NSDictionary object containing the data of the selected tweet; you'll then pick relevant parts of information from that object to be displayed in the view.

First, as you did with the Feed View Controller, let's configure the header of Tweet View Controller to receive the NSDictionary. Because you'll just be pulling information from an NSDictionary object and not interacting with Twitter, you won't need the Accounts or Social framework in this View Controller.

1. Open TweetViewController.h from the Project Navigator; after the line @interface TweetViewController : UIViewController, create an NSDictionary property called selectedTweet with this line of code:

```
@property (strong, nonatomic) NSDictionary *selectedTweet;
```

2. This creates the property, and because Xcode really is such an advanced IDE, it has invisibly created a setter method for this property that will be called setSelectedTweet. Now go back to Feed View Controller and pass an NSDictionary of tweet data across. Go back to FeedViewController.m and scroll down to the prepareForSegue method. You've already created the if statement that checks for the ShowTweet Segue, but inside that if statement you need to determine the selected row's index, retrieve the relevant entry from the tweets array, and pass that to the Tweet View Controller using the automatically created setter method, setSelectedTweet. Below is the if statement and all the required code, add this in now:

```
if ([[segue identifier] isEqualToString:@"ShowTweet"])
{
    NSIndexPath *path = [self.tableView indexPathForSelectedRow];
    NSDictionary *tweetData = [tweets objectAtIndex:path.row];

    TweetViewController *destController = (TweetViewController *)[segue destinationViewController];

    [destController setSelectedTweet:tweetData];

}
```

3. Now that the information is being passed across, it will be very easy to access the key information you want to display, so go ahead and open TweetViewController.m. All of the processing of data will be done in the viewDidLoad method. Also, to demonstrate the potential performance

degradation, you'll fetch the user's avatar directly from the Internet. The rest of the code you will be familiar with from the previous View Controller. Your `viewDidLoad` method code needs to look like this:

```
- (void)viewDidLoad
{
    [super viewDidLoad];

    NSDictionary *userData = [self.selectedTweet objectForKey:@"user"];

    self.tweetText.text = [self.selectedTweet objectForKey:@"text"];
    self.tweetAuthorName.text = [userData objectForKey:@"name"];

    NSString *imageURLString = [userData objectForKey:@"profile_image_url"];
    NSURL *imageURL = [NSURL URLWithString:imageURLString];
    NSData *imageData = [NSData dataWithContentsOfURL:imageURL];

    self.tweetAuthorAvatar.image = [UIImage imageWithData:imageData];
}
```

4. Finally, so that the tweet will close with the Cancel button, implement the `dismissView` method, which uses the `UIViewController` method of `dismissViewControllerAnimated`. Because it's a `UIViewController` method, and this is the implementation file for a class that subclasses `UIViewController`, you access your own methods by using `self`. Add this one line of code to your method:

```
- (IBAction)dismissView:(id)sender {
    [self dismissViewControllerAnimated:YES completion:nil];
}
```

That's it! Go ahead and run your application, select a tweet from the feed, and you should find the tweet you selected is expanded in the modal dialog and for the first time you can see the form sheet presentation style in effect, as shown in Figure 8-32. Now let's go on to the final View Controller in this application, Compose View Controller.

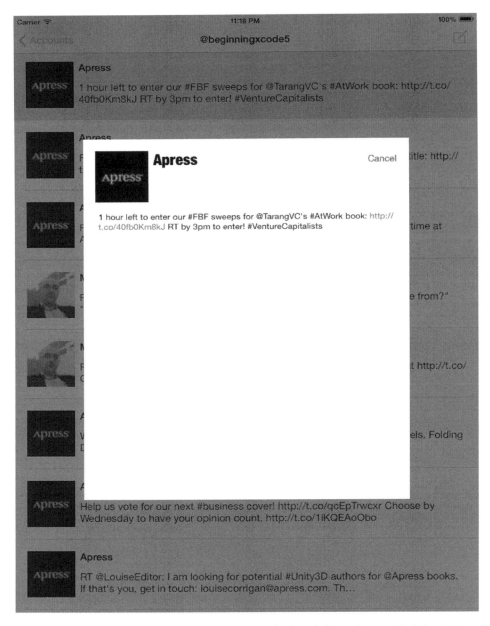

Figure 8-32. *Tweet View Controller showing the data that were passed to it and also an image pulled directly from the Internet. Notice the Link detection in effect*

Configuring the Compose View

The final view for this application is the Compose View Controller. This is where the user can compose their message and post it to Twitter. Let's enforce the 140-character limit for tweets by using a UITextView delegate method and then animate the Activity Indicator when it is sending the tweet data to Twitter.

1. The visual element has been created and the outlets have been set up, so start by opening ComposeViewController.h. As previously mentioned, you'll be using a UITextView delegate method, so the first thing you need to do is implement the UITextViewDelegate protocol; modify the @interface line so that the code looks like this:

```
@interface ComposeViewController : UIViewController<UITextViewDelegate>
```

2. Next, you'll need the Social and Accounts framework for this View Controller, so add their import statements beneath the line that says #import <UIKit/UIKit.h>, as shown below:

```
#import <Social/Social.h>
#import <Accounts/Accounts.h>
```

3. Finally, for the header file, create an object that can be passed to the ACAccount object for the selected account from the Feed View Controller; after the @interface line, add the following code:

```
@property (strong, nonatomic) ACAccount *selectedAccount;
```

4. Now go back to FeedViewController.m to pass the selected account details over, but before you do, your finished header file should resemble the following code:

```
#import <UIKit/UIKit.h>
#import <Social/Social.h>
#import <Accounts/Accounts.h>

@interface ComposeViewController : UIViewController<UITextViewDelegate>

@property (strong, nonatomic) ACAccount *selectedAccount;

@property (weak, nonatomic) IBOutlet UITextView *tweetContent;
@property (weak, nonatomic) IBOutlet UIButton *postButton;
@property (weak, nonatomic) IBOutlet UIActivityIndicatorView *postActivity;

- (IBAction)dismissView:(id)sender;
- (IBAction)postToTwitter:(id)sender;

@end
```

5. Back in `FeedViewController.m`, scroll down until you see the `prepareForSegue` method. You have an empty `if` statement set up for the `ComposeTweet` Segue, so modify the `if` statement so that it passes the `selectedAccount` object to the Compose View Controller, as shown below:

```
if ([[segue identifier] isEqualToString:@"ComposeTweet"])
{
    [(ComposeViewController *)[segue destinationViewController]
setSelectedAccount:self.selectedAccount];

}
```

6. You're now ready to tackle the `ComposeViewController.m` implementation file. You'll need to create a custom method and a delegate method as well as two actions in this file. The good news is that none of them require a great deal of code. First, scroll down until you see the `viewDidLoad` method. All you need to do here is specify the delegate property of the Text View, which as I've mentioned previously will be this View Controller, so it will be set to `self`. After the line `[super viewDidLoad]`; add the following code:

```
self.tweetContent.delegate = self;
```

7. Next, you'll create a method called `postContent`. This method will handle the transmission of the text that is sent to the Twitter account it is assigned. Start by creating the method stub:

```
- (void)postContent:(NSString *)post twitterAccount:(ACAccount *)twitterAccount
{

}
```

8. As you can see, the method takes two parameters: an `NSString` object called `post` and an `ACAccount` called `twitterAccount`. The first thing you want to do when this method is called is to start animating the `postActivity` Activity Indicator. You do this by sending the `startAnimating` message. Because of how the Activity Indicator was configured in Chapter 7, it's at this point it will appear and begin its animation:

```
[self.postActivity startAnimating];
```

9. You're now ready to start preparing the Twitter request. Just as you did in the Feed View Controller, let's create an NSURL object with the appropriate API URL for the type of request you want to make, which is used when instantiating the SLRequest object. A key difference this time is that you'll use a different HTTP method. You'll no longer issue a `get` request but instead issue a `post` request. When a `post` request is made with the SLRequest object, you supply the required parameters in an NSDictionary object. If you

refer to the Twitter documentation for the status update API at `https://dev.twitter.com/docs/api/1.1/post/statuses/update`, you will see that the only required parameter is called `status`. The `status` parameter should be the textual content of the status update, which is the `post` parameter. Drop down a line in the method and add the following code:

```
NSURL *requestURL = [NSURL URLWithString:@"https://api.twitter.com/1.1/statuses/update.json"];
SLRequest *postRequest = [SLRequest requestForServiceType:SLServiceTypeTwitter
                 requestMethod:SLRequestMethodPOST
                       URL:requestURL
                   parameters:[NSDictionary dictionaryWithObject:post forKey:@"status"]];

[postRequest setAccount:twitterAccount];
```

10. Next, access the `performRequestWithHandler` method of the `SLRequest` object just as you did in the Feed View Controller. This time, however, when you receive a successful response code, stop animating the Activity Indicator and dismiss the View Controller. Drop down a line and add the following code to complete the method:

```
[postRequest performRequestWithHandler:
 ^(NSData *responseData, NSHTTPURLResponse *urlResponse, NSError *error)
 {
     if ([urlResponse statusCode] == 200)
     {
         NSLog(@"Tweeted posted successfully");
         dispatch_async(dispatch_get_main_queue(), ^(void)
             {
                 [self.postActivity stopAnimating];
                 [self dismissViewControllerAnimated:YES completion:nil];
             });
     }
     else
     {
         NSLog(@"Post error %i", [urlResponse statusCode]);
     }
 }];
```

11. Your finished method code should look like this:

```
- (void)postContent:(NSString *)post twitterAccount:(ACAccount *)twitterAccount
{
    [self.postActivity startAnimating];

    NSURL *requestURL =
[NSURL URLWithString:@"https://api.twitter.com/1.1/statuses/update.json"];
    SLRequest *postRequest = [SLRequest requestForServiceType:SLServiceTypeTwitter
                                     requestMethod:SLRequestMethodPOST URL:requestURL
                                         parameters:[NSDictionary
dictionaryWithObject:post forKey:@"status"]];
```

```
    [postRequest setAccount:twitterAccount];

    [postRequest performRequestWithHandler:
     ^(NSData *responseData, NSHTTPURLResponse *urlResponse, NSError *error)
     {
         if ([urlResponse statusCode] == 200)
         {
             NSLog(@"Tweeted posted successfully");
             dispatch_async(dispatch_get_main_queue(), ^(void)
                 {
                     [self.postActivity stopAnimating];
                     [self dismissViewControllerAnimated:YES completion:nil];
                 });
         }
         else
         {
             NSLog(@"Post error %i", [urlResponse statusCode]);
         }

     }];
}
```

12. Next I'll address the two action methods: dismissView and postToTwitter.
    These are both one liners; the dismissView method is a duplicate of the one
    used in Tweet View Controller, and the postToTwitter method simply calls
    the postContent method you just finished writing. Implement them both as
    follows:

```
- (IBAction)dismissView:(id)sender {
    [self dismissViewControllerAnimated:YES completion:nil];
}

- (IBAction)postToTwitter:(id)sender {
    [self postContent:self.tweetContent.text twitterAccount:self.selectedAccount];
}
```

13. Finally, implement a UITextView delegate method that restricts the
    Text View's content to 140 characters. This is done by using the
    shouldChangeTextInRange, which is called every time a character is typed.
    The method simply checks that the Text view's content isn't greater than 140
    characters and that it won't exceed 140 characters if someone pasted in
    some text. If it does, it returns false and no more text can be typed. Add the
    following method to your implementation file:

```
- (BOOL)textView:(UITextView *)textView shouldChangeTextInRange:(NSRange)range
replacementText:(NSString *)text {
    int targetlength = 140;
    return !([textView.text length]> targetlength && [text length] > range.length);
}
```

That was the last line of code for this application! Go ahead and run the application and see how all the hard work you've put in over these two chapters has finally paid off. You should be able to successfully access your Twitter accounts, view the Twitter feed, see a tweet in detail, and even post your own. Your final application should resemble the four screens shown in Figure 8-33.

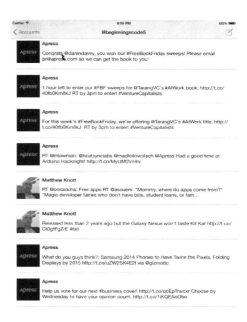

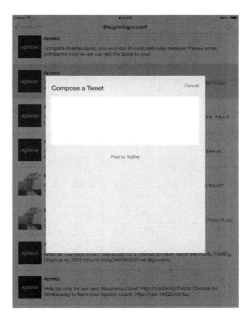

Figure 8-33. The four finished views of SocialApp

Importantly, in this chapter, you've learned all about configuring Table Views and the different methods and properties of the UITableView class.

Discovering the Collection View

Collection Views is a fantastic new feature that Apple introduced in iOS 6. They offer developers a new dimension for displaying large amounts of data just as their cousin the Table View, with the difference being that you can display in multiple columns as well as rows. Another neat feature is that they can scroll either vertically or horizontally, giving you that extra dimension as a developer.

One of the largest fundamental differences between the Collection View and the Table View is that the Collection View's layout is completely separate from the view and can either be set to default or a custom UICollectionViewLayout, giving you a massive amount of flexibility over your design.

To demonstrate the implementation and configuration of a Collection View, let's make some pretty drastic changes to SocialApp. First, let's turn it into a Tabbed application and then look at storing user preferences to automate account selection.

Embedding a Tab Bar Controller

The change I'm aiming for here is to have a feed tab and a following tab in the application, with the feed tab obviously being the Feed View Controller. Let's create the Following View Controller, which is a Collection View Controller that will show the avatars of all the users for the selected Twitter account follows. To turn SocialApp into a tabbed application, you'll be adding a Tab Bar Controller between the Accounts View and the Feed View.

1. Open Main.storyboard from the Project Navigator. Navigate around the Storyboard until you're able to see the Segue connection from the Accounts scene to the Feed scene. Highlight the Segue and delete it, as shown in Figure 8-34.

Figure 8-34. The SocialApp Storyboard with the ShowTweets Segue removed

2. Add a Tab Bar Controller, with the Feed scene as one of the tabs. You could drag in a Tab Bar Controller and manually link it up, but instead let's allow Xcode do the hard work for us. Select the Feed View Controller either by clicking it directly in the Storyboard or by selecting Feed View Controller – Feed from the Document Outline.

3. From the menu bar select Editor ➤ Embed In ➤ Tab Bar Controller, as shown in Figure 8-35. This will add a Tab Bar Controller to your Storyboard, set the Feed scene as the first tab, and arrange the views to suit you needs.

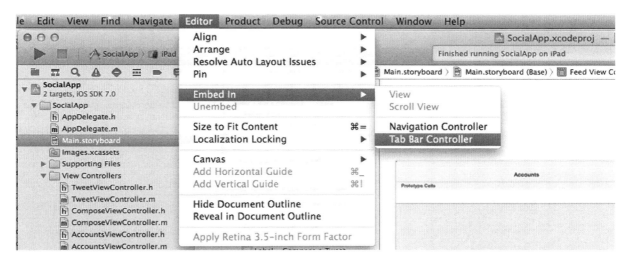

Figure 8-35. Embedding a Tab Bar Controller into SocialApp

4. You now need to re-create the ShowTweets Segue, but this time it will be from the Accounts View Controller itself to the Tab Bar Controller. This is called a Manual Segue because it is not tied to a button or table cell that can be triggered by the user, instead the Segue will be triggered programmatically. Zoom out and control-drag a connection from the Accounts scene to the Tab Bar Controller, as shown in Figure 8-36.

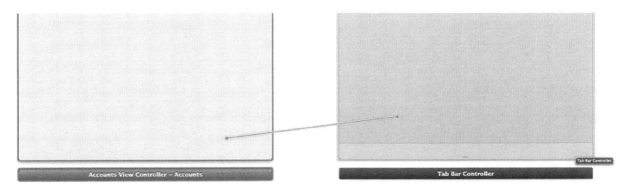

Figure 8-36. Connecting the Accounts View Controller to the Tab Bar Controller with a Manual Segue

5. When you release the mouse button, select Push as the Segue type. Select the newly created Segue and open the Attributes Inspector. Set the Identifier back to ShowTweets.

You're finished with the Storyboard for now, but before you add in the Collection View Controller, let's get the application back to a working condition. This involves executing a Manual Segue and storing the users' account selection so that whenever the application runs in the future, it will default to the account that the user selected and go straight to the feed.

Persisting User Preferences with NSUserDefaults

In a real-world scenario, a user picking up SocialApp would find it slightly annoying to have to select their account every time the application runs. Thankfully, iOS gives us a number of ways to persist user preferences including iCloud and Core Data, but in this instance you'll be using the NSUserDefaults class.

NSUserDefaults allows the app to store values or certain types of objects against a textual key and cannot be accessed from other applications. Whenever the application is closed and rerun, the preferences that are stored within NSUserDefaults are preserved but the user can access and change the saved preferences to their heart's content. The NSUserDefaults class has methods that make it easy to both store and access a range of common types such as Booleans, floats, integers, doubles, and URLs, and also supports the storage of the following objects:

- NSData
- NSString
- NSNumber
- NSDate
- NSArray
- NSDictionary

The object you want to store here is an ACAccount, so you'll have to convert it to an NSData object, but I'll get to that in a moment.

1. Open AccountsViewController.h from the Project Navigator; the first thing you want to do is create an NSUserPreferences instance variable to allow you to access the preferences from different methods without having to instantiate the method each time. After the line NSArray *twitterAccounts; drop down a line and add the highlighted code inside the brackets:

```
#import <UIKit/UIKit.h>
#import <Accounts/Accounts.h>

@interface AccountsViewController : UITableViewController<UIAlertViewDelegate>
{
    NSArray *twitterAccounts;
    NSUserDefaults *userDefaults;
}
```

```
@property (strong, nonatomic) ACAccountStore *accountStore;

@end
```

2. Next, open AccountsViewController.m and scroll down to the viewDidLoad method. The first thing you need to do when the view loads is to initialize the userDefaults object and then determine whether or not a preference that you'll call selectedAccount has already been saved; if so, then execute the Manual Segue with the performSegueWithIdentifier method. After the line self.accountStore = [[ACAccountStore alloc] init]; add the highlighted code:

```
- (void)viewDidLoad
{
    [super viewDidLoad];

    self.accountStore = [[ACAccountStore alloc] init];
    userDefaults = [NSUserDefaults standardUserDefaults];

    if ([userDefaults objectForKey:@"selectedAccount"]) {
        [self performSegueWithIdentifier:@"ShowTweets" sender:self];
    }


    ACAccountType *accountType = [self.accountStore
accountTypeWithAccountTypeIdentifier:ACAccountTypeIdentifierTwitter];
```

3. That's it for the viewDidLoad method; it's now time to address what happens when you tap on a cell. In the past, the Segue from the cell was triggered and the prepareForSegue method then passed the selected account across to the feed. This time, however, the application is going to save the selection before moving away. To do this, you will use another key UITableView method called didSelectRowAtIndexPath, which is triggered every time a table cell is selected. Before you implement this method, *delete the entire* prepareForSegue *method*; there is no longer a Segue associated with the cell and it won't be needed from here on out.

4. Once the prepareForSegue method is removed, it's time to create the didSelectRowAtIndexPath method stub. Where you deleted the prepareForSegue method, type the following method stub:

```
-(void)tableView:(UITableView *)tableView didSelectRowAtIndexPath:(NSIndexPath *)indexPath
{

}
```

5. In this method, the first thing you need to do is use the `indexPath` object to allocate an `ACAccount` object from `twitterAccounts` array based on the selected cell's index. Add the following code to the `didSelectRowAtIndexPath` method:

```
ACAccount *account = [twitterAccounts objectAtIndex:indexPath.row];
```

6. Next, as mentioned previously, you need to convert the `account` object into something that can be stored within the `NSUserPreferences`; in this case it will be converted to an `NSData` object using the `NSKeyedArchiver` class. After the previous line, add the following code:

```
NSData *accountData = [NSKeyedArchiver archivedDataWithRootObject:account];
```

7. Now that the selected account is in a compatible format, it can be saved to the `NSUserPreferences` instance, `userDefaults`. The process for saving a preference comes in two parts: first, use the `setObject: forKey:` method, which associates the `accountData` object with a key, then call the `synchronize` method, which saves the preference to the system. Go ahead and add the following code to the method:

```
[userDefaults setObject:accountData forKey:@"selectedAccount"];
[userDefaults synchronize];
```

8. Now that you've saved the user's selection, manually trigger the Segue; just as you did in the `viewDidLoad` method, you need to call the `performSegueWithIdentifier` method. Add this code to complete the method:

```
[self performSegueWithIdentifier:@"ShowTweets" sender:self];
```

That's it for the Accounts View Controller, you've removed the previous mechanisms for selecting an account and replaced them with something that will be much more appealing to the end user. Before we move on to retrieval of saved preferences, check that your method resembles the code below:

```
-(void)tableView:(UITableView *)tableView didSelectRowAtIndexPath:(NSIndexPath *)indexPath
{
    ACAccount *account = [twitterAccounts objectAtIndex:indexPath.row];
    NSData *accountData = [NSKeyedArchiver archivedDataWithRootObject:account];

    [userDefaults setObject:accountData forKey:@"selectedAccount"];
    [userDefaults synchronize];

    [self performSegueWithIdentifier:@"ShowTweets" sender:self];
}
```

Now that you've saved the users selection, you need to implement the retrieval of that selection when the application moves to the Feed View Controller.

1. Open `FeedViewController.m` and scroll down to the `viewDidLoad` method.

2. When the view loads, create an instance of `NSUserDefaults`; there is no point in creating an instance variable because this is the only time you will need to access it within this file. You will then retrieve the selected account from the preferences using the `objectForKey` method, which retrieves the object associated with the key that is supplied, in this case, `selectedAccount`. Finally, you will reverse the conversion process with the `NSKeyedUnarchiver` class, which allows the conversion of the `NSData` object back into an `ACAccount` object. After the line `[super viewDidLoad]`, add the following highlighted code:

```
- (void)viewDidLoad
{
    [super viewDidLoad];

    NSUserDefaults *userDefaults = [NSUserDefaults standardUserDefaults];
    NSData *accountData = [userDefaults objectForKey:@"selectedAccount"];
    self.selectedAccount = (ACAccount *)[NSKeyedUnarchiver unarchiveObjectWithData:accountData];

    self.navigationItem.title = self.selectedAccount.accountDescription;

    queue = [[NSOperationQueue alloc] init];
    queue.maxConcurrentOperationCount = 4;

    [self retrieveTweets];
}
```

3. Go ahead and run the application in the simulator; select an account, and you will segue across to the newly tabbed Feed view. Quit the simulator and then rerun your application. If everything has been done correctly, you should start facing the Feed view instead of the Accounts view! As a user, this is a much more favorable situation to be in. There is, however, one small issue you need to address; after embedding a Tab Bar Controller, the Table view positioning changed and now the first row renders underneath the Navigation Bar and the title has vanished, as shown in Figure 8-37. This is far from ideal, and unfortunately Xcode doesn't give us a way to fix this, it has to be done in code.

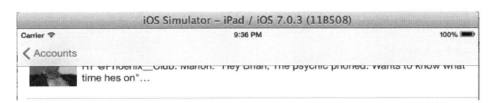

Figure 8-37. *The first table row obscured by the Navigation Bar*

4. The title no longer applies itself because when you embedded the Tab Bar
    Controller you effectively inserted another level between the view and the
    Navigation Bar controller. Ensure that you still have FeedViewController.m
    open, then within the viewDidLoad method, change the line
    self.navigationItem.title = self.selectedAccount.accountDescription;
    to the following:

```
self.tabBarController.navigationItem.title = self.selectedAccount.accountDescription;
```

5. After that, drop down another line. The issue of the table row being obscured
    by the Navigation Bar is an iOS 7–specific issue with an iOS 7–specific fix,
    but this doesn't mean your application cannot be backward compatible. Let's
    use a handy method called respondsToSelector to evaluate whether or not
    the method you are going to call exists before calling it. Add the following
    highlighted code:

```
- (void)viewDidLoad
{
    [super viewDidLoad];

    NSUserDefaults *userDefaults = [NSUserDefaults standardUserDefaults];
    NSData *accountData = [userDefaults objectForKey:@"selectedAccount"];
    self.selectedAccount = (ACAccount *)[NSKeyedUnarchiver unarchiveObjectWithData:accountData];

    self.tabBarController.navigationItem.title = self.selectedAccount.accountDescription;

    if ([self.tabBarController respondsToSelector:@selector(edgesForExtendedLayout)])
        [self.tabBarController setEdgesForExtendedLayout: UIRectEdgeNone];

    queue = [[NSOperationQueue alloc] init];
    queue.maxConcurrentOperationCount = 4;

    [self retrieveTweets];
}
```

6. Rerun your application and it should now function perfectly! You've
    successfully implemented a user preferences system that will make life much
    easier for your users. You're now ready to start creating the Collection View
    Controller.

Adding a Collection View Controller

Now that you've successfully pulled apart and reassembed your application, it's time to turn our
attention back to the Storyboard and, in particular, adding a Collection View Controller into the
application. Open Main.storyboard from the Project Navigator and position your scenes as shown in
Figure 8-38.

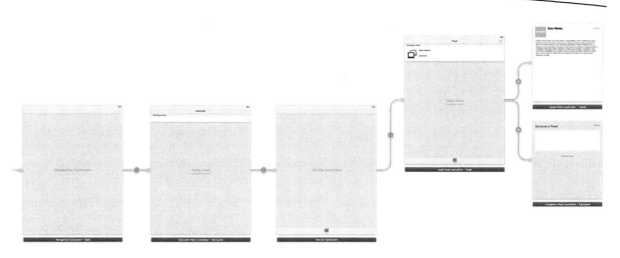

Figure 8-38. Arranging the Storyboard in anticipation of the Collection View Controller

1. Start by dragging in a Collection View Controller from the Object Library and positioning it below the Feed scene, as shown in Figure 8-39.

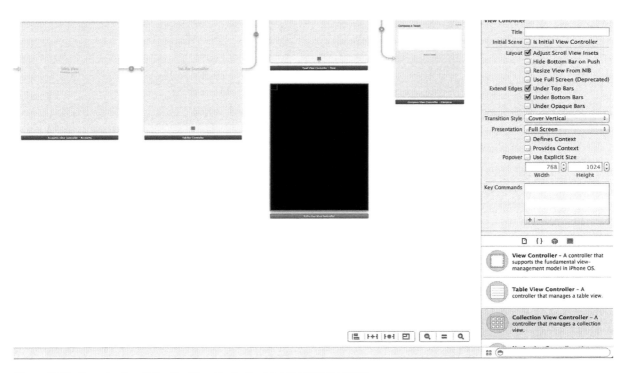

Figure 8-39. Dragging in a Collection View Controller from the Object Library

2. Next, create a relationship between the Tab Bar Controller and the Collection View Controller. To do this, select the Tab Bar Controller and then control-drag a connection to the Collection View Controller, as shown in Figure 8-40.

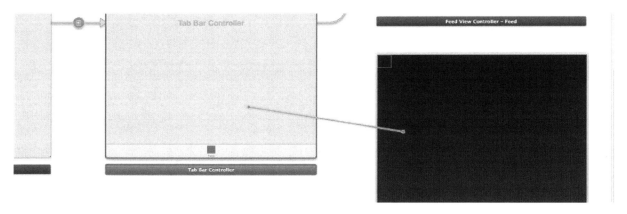

Figure 8-40. *Control-dragging a connection from the Tab Bar Controller to the Collection View Controller*

3. When you release the mouse, select View Controllers under the title Relationship Segues. You now have two tabs in the application, however, as Figure 8-41 shows, they are both called Item, which isn't much use to the users.

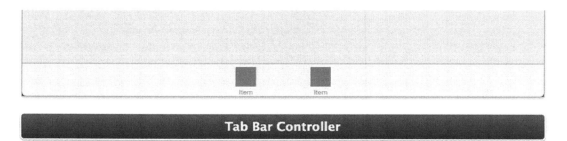

Figure 8-41. *The Tab Bar Controller, featuring two tabs called Item!*

4. To set the Feed Tab Bar button title, position your Storyboard so that you can select the Tab Bar button on the Feed scene and open the Attributes Inspector, as shown in Figure 8-42.

Figure 8-42. *Selecting the Feed Tab Bar Button*

5.   Change the Title attribute to Feed. Now repeat this process for the Collection View Controller you added to the Storyboard, setting the Title attribute to Following. Your Tab Bar Controller should now look like the one shown in Figure 8-43.

Figure 8-43. *The Tab Bar Controller featuring two correctly named buttons*

6.   As you did with the other View Controllers, you need to create a customer View Controller class file. In this instance, you'll be subclassing `UICollectionViewController`. Start by right-clicking the View Controllers group in the Project Navigator and select New File.

7.   When prompted, select the Objective-C class option and click Next. Set the Subclass of value to UICollectionViewController and the Class value to FollowingViewController then click Next. Finally, accept the default folder Xcode suggests to save the file and click Create.

Now that you've successfully created the last custom View Controller for this application, you're ready to configure the visual aspects of the Collection View before fetching the details of the users followed by the selected account from Twitter.

Configuring a Collection View

I've already mentioned how the `UICollectionView` class is very similar to the `UITableView` class in terms of the methods and also the fact that they both use cells for presenting large amounts of data to the user. They also have sections, with independent headers and footers in each one. Yet despite these similarities, the Collection View configuration within Xcode is drastically different from that of the Table View.

To start with, open `Main.stroyboard` from the Project Navigator and move the Storyboard around until you can see the Collection View, as shown in Figure 8-44. Structurally, what you are looking at here isn't really any different from what you started with in the Table View, as shown in Figure 8-27. The white-bordered box in the top left-hand corner of the view is the prototype cell.

Figure 8-44. The top of the Collection View Controller

Select the Collection View itself so that you can look at the key attributes in the Attributes Inspector. To do this, click the main area of the Collection View or select Collection View from the Document Outline, as shown in Figure 8-45.

Figure 8-45. Selecting the Collection View from the Document Outline

Open the Attributes Inspector; let's take a closer look at the key options available to us.

> *Items:* Unlike the Table View, Collection Views don't have a static mode; the Items' attribute increases and decreases the number of prototype cells. No matter how many items you have to display, if they only have a single type of appearance, then you only need one cell that you then reuse.

Layout: In a Collection View, the Layout is a separate entity from the view. The default layout is Flow, which provides a grid of items continuing uninterrupted in a fixed direction. Changing the attribute to Custom exposes a class selector whereby you can specify a custom `UICollectionViewLayout`.

Scroll Direction: As you might expect, this attribute controls which direction the cells are positioned for scrolling.

Accessories: The two options for Section Header and Section Footer allow you to add a prototype header and footer to the section. Unlike with Table Views, you can't manually specify any text into either container, they must be set programmatically.

Unlike other views, so much in Collection Views depends on the settings of the Size Inspector. When you open the Size Inspector, you will see a large number of configurable values; Figure 8-46 shows the different sizes and where they take effect. In this example, the number of items is set to 8 to help us visualize how the cells react to one another.

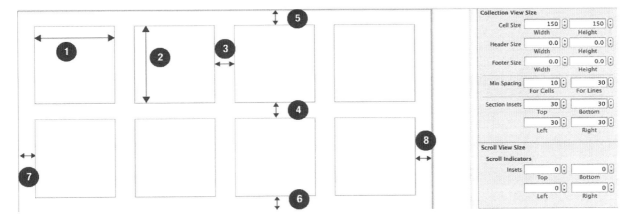

Figure 8-46. The different sizes you can alter in a Collection View

Cell Width and Height: Points 1 and 2 represent the width and height of the cell, respectively; the cell doesn't have to be square, so the two values can change independently of each other.

Minimum Spacing: The first value (highlighted by point 3), For Cells, sets a minimum value for the horizontal spacing between cells. This is useful because by default, the cells are spaced nicely and the horizontal gap is far greater than 10 points, however, we know it won't slip below 10 points should the size of the view change. The For Lines value shown by point 4 sets a minimum width between the rows of cells.

Section Insets: These four values control the spacing around the outside of the section of cells, so the cells function as a collective entity. When you increase the value of any of the sizes illustrated by points 5 through 8, you move the cells further from that side of the view. By default the Section Insets values are set to 0, which can leave content feeling squashed; set a nice inset value to bring the cells in from the edge, providing something more visually appealing.

1. For the Followers Collection View, set the Width and Height values to 75; Minimum Spacing to 10 For Cells and 30 For Lines; set all Section Insets to 30.

2. Before you start adding the code to Followers View Controller, you need to specify the class the View Controller will use. Select the Collection View Controller by either clicking the black bar beneath it or selecting Collection View Controller – Following from the Document Outline.

3. Open the Identity Inspector and set the class to FollowingViewController, as shown in Figure 8-47.

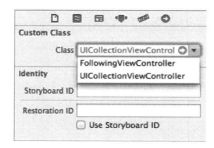

Figure 8-47. *Setting the Class to FollowingViewController*

4. Lastly, select the single cell in Following View Controller; open the Attributes Inspector and set the Identifier value to Cell.

Displaying Items in a Collection View

You've configured the Collection View in Xcode, but to finish the view you need to write the code that retrieves the list of users the app follows. I won't focus too much on the code for retrieving the list of followed users, but rather on the key methods of the UICollectionViewController class.

1. Open FollowingViewController.h from the Project Navigator. The first thing you need to do is import the Social and Accounts frameworks. After the line #import <UIKit/UIKit.h>, add the following import statements:

```
#import <Accounts/Accounts.h>
#import <Social/Social.h>
```

2. Next, declare a number of instance variables, just as you did with the Feed View Controller. You need an NSMutableArray instance called following that will store the details of each user the selected account follows, an NSCache

object called imageCache, and an NSOperationQueue object imaginatively called queue. Your completed header with these items added should look like the code below:

```
#import <UIKit/UIKit.h>
#import <Accounts/Accounts.h>
#import <Social/Social.h>

@interface FollowingViewController : UICollectionViewController
{
    NSMutableArray *following;
    NSCache *imageCache;
    NSOperationQueue *queue;
}

@end
```

3. Now open FollowingViewController.m so that you can write the implementation of for the class. Let's start with the viewDidLoad method; in this method, just as you did with the Feed View Controller, you want to initialize the queue object, set the Navigation Bar title to Following, and then call the retrieveUsers method, which you'll add shortly. Your finished viewDidLoad method needs to look like this:

```
- (void)viewDidLoad
{
    [super viewDidLoad];

    queue = [[NSOperationQueue alloc] init];
    queue.maxConcurrentOperationCount = 4;

    self.tabBarController.navigationItem.title = @"Following";

    [self retrieveUsers];
}
```

4. Next, look at the retrieveUsers method. Start by creating a stub for the method, as shown below:

```
-(void)retrieveUsers
{
}
```

5. Much of this code is the same as that used in the Feed View Controller, so I won't present the code in any detail. Start by clearing the following array and then retrieving the selectAccount from the stored user preferences, as shown below:

```
[following removeAllObjects];
```

```
NSUserDefaults *userDefaults = [NSUserDefaults standardUserDefaults];
NSData *accountData = [userDefaults objectForKey:@"selectedAccount"];
ACAccount *selectedAccount = (ACAccount *)[NSKeyedUnarchiver unarchiveObjectWithData:accountData];
```

6. Next, declare an SLRequest object and instantiate it using the URL as
    specified by the Twitter API for retrieving a list of "friends," as Twitter refers to
    the API that returns the "up to 200 users" followed by the supplied account.

```
SLRequest *request;

if (selectedAccount)
{
    NSString *targetURL =
        [NSString stringWithFormat:@"https://api.twitter.com/1.1/friends/list.json?count=200"];

    NSURL *requestURL = [NSURL URLWithString:targetURL];


    request = [SLRequest requestForServiceType:SLServiceTypeTwitter
                               requestMethod:SLRequestMethodGET
                                         URL:requestURL parameters:nil];
    [request setAccount:selectedAccount];
}
```

> **Note**   For more information on configuring the Twitter Friends/List API, visit `https://dev.twitter.com/`
> `docs/api/1.1/get/friends/list`.

Finally, for this method, call the performRequestWithHandler method of the SLRequest. Just as
before, check for a valid status code and parse the json response before picking the "users" array
from the parsed code and assigning it to the following array. Finally, call the UICollectionView
method reloadData, which causes three methods to be called. Add the following code to complete
this method:

```
[request performRequestWithHandler:
 ^(NSData *responseData, NSHTTPURLResponse *urlResponse, NSError *error)
 {
     if ([urlResponse statusCode] == 200)
     {
         NSError *jsonParsingError;
         NSDictionary *followingData =
                 [NSJSONSerialization JSONObjectWithData:responseData
                                         options:0 error:&jsonParsingError];

         following = [followingData objectForKey:@"users"];
     }
     else
```

```
    {
        NSLog(@"http response code: %i", [urlResponse statusCode]);
    }
    dispatch_async(dispatch_get_main_queue(), ^(void)
                {
                    [self.collectionView reloadData];
                });
}];
```

7. Unlike when subclassing UITableViewController, Xcode doesn't currently
    create any method stubs for the key UICollectionView methods, so you'll
    have to write them in their entirety. Luckily, the first two aren't very big.
    First, add the method that specifies how many sections there will be,
    numberOfSectionsInCollectionView, with the following code:

```
- (NSInteger)numberOfSectionsInCollectionView:(UICollectionView *)collectionView
{
    return 1;
}
```

8. As you can see, that method is extremely similar to its UITableView
    equivalent, as is the next method to specify how many cells to render,
    numberOfItemsInSection, which will return the number of rows in the
    following array, as shown below:

```
- (NSInteger)collectionView:(UICollectionView *)collectionView
numberOfItemsInSection:(NSInteger)section
{
    return following.count;
}
```

9. Finally, write the cellForItemAtIndexPath method. This method is used to
    initialize the cell and set its content, just as its UITableView equivalent does.
    Start by declaring a stub for the method, adding this code:

```
-(UICollectionViewCell *)collectionView:(UICollectionView *)collectionView
        cellForItemAtIndexPath:(NSIndexPath *)indexPath
{
}
```

10. Because the return type of this method is UICollectionViewCell, let's start
    by initializing the cell with the identifier value specified for the prototype cell.
    Go ahead and add the following code to start this method:

```
NSString *CellIdentifier = @"Cell";

UICollectionViewCell *cell =
  [collectionView dequeueReusableCellWithReuseIdentifier:CellIdentifier forIndexPath:indexPath];
```

11. Next, pull the relevant data for the current index from the following array and store it in an NSDictionary object and then extract the URL for the user's profile image, as you did in the Feed View Controller, with this code:

```
NSDictionary *userData = [following objectAtIndex:indexPath.row];
NSString *imageURLString = [userData objectForKey:@"profile_image_url"];
```

12. The next step is to set up the image that will be programmatically added to the cell using the addSubview method because no UIImageView exists in the cell, and then return the cell object, completing the method with this code:

```
UIImage *image = [imageCache objectForKey:imageURLString];

if (image)
{
    UIImageView *imageView = [[UIImageView alloc] initWithImage:image];
    imageView.bounds = cell.frame;
    [cell addSubview:imageView];
}
else
{
    [queue addOperationWithBlock:^{

        NSURL *imageURL = [NSURL URLWithString:imageURLString];
        NSData *imageData = [NSData dataWithContentsOfURL:imageURL];
        UIImage *image = [UIImage imageWithData:imageData];


        if (image)
        {
            [[NSOperationQueue mainQueue] addOperationWithBlock:^{

                UIImageView *imageView = [[UIImageView alloc] initWithImage:image];
                imageView.bounds = cell.frame;


                UICollectionViewCell *cell = [self.collectionView cellForItemAtIndexPath:indexPath];
                if (cell)
                    [cell addSubview:imageView];
            }];

            [imageCache setObject:image forKey:imageURLString];
        }
    }];
}
return cell;
```

The full code for this method is shown below:

```objc
-(UICollectionViewCell *)collectionView:(UICollectionView *)collectionView cellForItemAtIndexPath:
(NSIndexPath *)indexPath
{
    NSString *CellIdentifier = @"Cell";
    UICollectionViewCell *cell = [collectionView dequeueReusableCellWithReuseIdentifier:CellIdentifier
forIndexPath:indexPath];

    NSDictionary *userData = [following objectAtIndex:indexPath.row];
    NSString *imageURLString = [userData objectForKey:@"profile_image_url"];
    UIImage *image = [imageCache objectForKey:imageURLString];

    if (image)
    {
        UIImageView *imageView = [[UIImageView alloc] initWithImage:image];
        imageView.bounds = cell.frame;
        [cell addSubview:imageView];
    }
    else
    {
        [queue addOperationWithBlock:^{

            NSURL *imageURL = [NSURL URLWithString:imageURLString];
            NSData *imageData = [NSData dataWithContentsOfURL:imageURL];
            UIImage *image = [UIImage imageWithData:imageData];

            if (image)
            {
                [[NSOperationQueue mainQueue] addOperationWithBlock:^{

                    UIImageView *imageView = [[UIImageView alloc] initWithImage:image];
                    imageView.bounds = cell.frame;


                    UICollectionViewCell *cell = [self.collectionView cellForItemAtIndexPath:indexPath];
                    if (cell)
                        [cell addSubview:imageView];
                }];

                [imageCache setObject:image forKey:imageURLString];
            }
        }];
    }

    return cell;
}
```

That completes the Collection View and the chapter! Go ahead and run your application. As long as you're following some other Twitter users, you should find your Collection View populates with user avatars as shown in Figure 8-48. I've rigged mine to display the same image to avoid any privacy issues, but your display should be a rich tapestry of avatar images.

Figure 8-48. *The finished Collection View showing the avatars of users you follow*

Summary

There's no doubt, a lot has been covered in this chapter, but most important, you've taken SocialApp from the shell it was at the end of Chapter 7 and created a working Twitter client. This was no mean feat and hopefully you're feeling really pleased with yourself. Take a break and reflect on all the things you've learned in this chapter:

- The difference between static and prototype table cells
- When to use a Grouped or a Plain style Table View
- How to create a custom table cell
- How to fetch data from the Internet
- How to parse json data
- How to embed a Tab Bar Controller into your application
- How to persist user preferences even when the application has closed

The next chapter will look at other ways you can use frameworks in Xcode, as well as looking at libraries and how Xcode lets you create different applications with the same code using targets.

Chapter 9

Frameworks, Libraries, and Targ ets

In Chapter 8 you learned about how to configure and implement Table and Collection Views as you completed your Twitter client, SocialApp. You also used two frameworks, Social and Accounts, a topic I will explain in more detain in this chapter, to access the Twitter API. You also parsed the json formatted data and looked at `NSDictionaries` in action. I covered many important aspects of Xcode application development and hopefully you found the project useful and enjoyable, maybe even a bit exciting!

Chapter 8 had a lot of code to go through as you subclassed cells and View Controllers, but in this chapter you will see how a little code can go a long way as I explain how Xcode handles Frameworks for adding extra functionality, Libraries for encapsulating lots of classes, methods and resources neatly, and Targets for creating different versions of your application within a single project. On that matter, the project for this chapter will be a simple Map Kit application that displays pushpins on a map. You'll add the pins using a custom annotation class, which you will later move into a static library and add it back into your project to demonstrate how you can group reusable code together. You will then create two versions of your application by using targets, so that both use the same base code but with the output changing based on the version.

Map Kit is a framework provided by Apple that is centered around the rendering of an interactive map, with numerous classes for modifying and complementing the map. Whether you are adding pushpins or custom markers, plotting routes, or outlining areas, the Map Kit framework has everything you need to create a rich, map-based application.

Understanding Frameworks

Chapter 7 introduced inheritance as being one of the core principles of object-oriented programming. Frameworks embody another of these core principles: encapsulation. Encapsulation is usually defined as one of two things:

- A mechanism by which information (code) is hidden
- A construct for bundling data together

A framework groups classes, resources, interface files, and more together in a hierarchical package; although you can view some of the resources inside the framework, the implementation of the classes, the key code, is hidden. Figure 9-1 shows the inside of the Map Kit framework you'll be working with in this chapter.

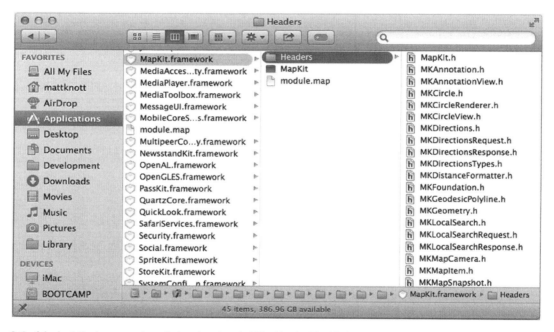

Figure 9-1. A look at the large number of class headers held inside the MapKit.framework

As you will learn later in this chapter, frameworks do not differ greatly in terms of definition from libraries, but the key difference is in how you define their purpose. Frameworks encapsulate a wide range of functions; Map Kit has a mass of classes and different resources, whereas libraries are intended to fulfill smaller, more specific tasks.

What frameworks provide is a way to unlock the features and functions of the operating system and the hardware.

Creating the Project

The project for this chapter will be called MapPin; it will show a number of pushpins on a map with a textual annotation. Many applications find innovative ways to use the Apple-provided Map Kit to display information in really interesting ways, and if this is something you want to add to your own applications, hopefully you'll be encouraged by how easy it is to add a Map View to your application and to get it displaying information with just a few lines of code.

1. Start by opening Xcode and creating a new project by clicking Create a new Xcode project from the Welcome screen or go to File ➤ New ➤ Project . . . (⌘ + Shift + N). Select the Single View Application template and click Next.

2. Name your project MapPin and ensure the Devices value is set to iPhone, not iPad or Universal. Configure the other values to your own preference, mine are shown in Figure 9-2; click Next.

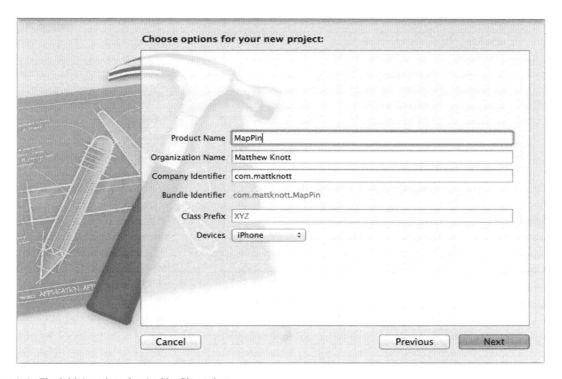

Figure 9-2. The initial settings for the MapPin project

3. You don't want to create a Git repository, so leave that option unchecked, and you don't want to add this to another project. With those options set, click Create.

4. You now have a blank slate project, a fresh canvas to which you only need to add a Map View. Open `Main.storyboard` and locate a Map View object in the Object Library. When you find it, drag it onto the View Controller in the design area, as shown in Figure 9-3.

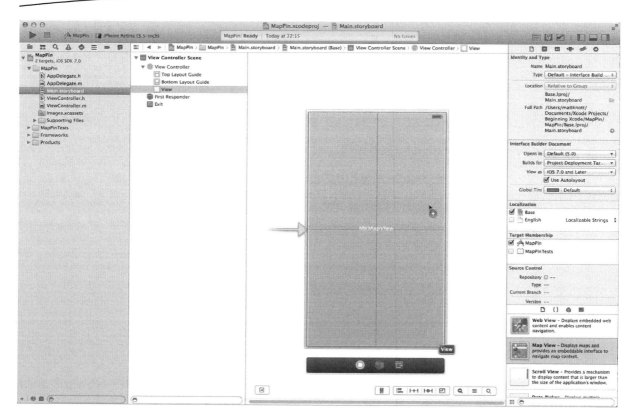

Figure 9-3. *Dragging a Map View object onto the View Controller*

The Map View represents an MKMapView object and is the only object needed to display maps in your application. Go ahead and run your application to see what happens after adding the object to the View Controller. The application will build successfully and launch in the Simulator before dropping back to Xcode with an exception, as shown in Figure 9-4, because the application has no knowledge of the MKMapView class; the prerequisite for adding a Map View to your applications is that you also need to add the Map Kit framework.

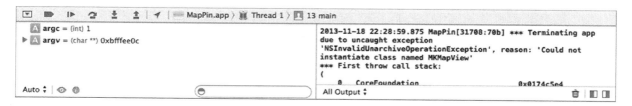

Figure 9-4. *The exception shown in the debug area when you add a Map View without the Map Kit framework*

Adding a Framework

So far in the book, you've had to add frameworks several times, and each time it was done the same way. But there are actually two different ways to add a framework to your project, and I'll cover both of them here. Both methods can be accessed from the same starting point, the project settings. Select the MapPin project in the Project Navigator, as shown in Figure 9-5.

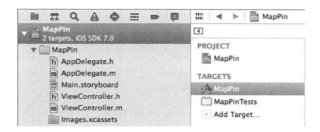

Figure 9-5. Selecting the MapPin project from the Project Navigator

On the screen that appears, select MapPin from the list of targets, then choose the General tab before scrolling down to the bottom of the page and the Linked Frameworks and Libraries section, as shown in Figure 9-6. This is how you've been instructed to add frameworks to your project in the past.

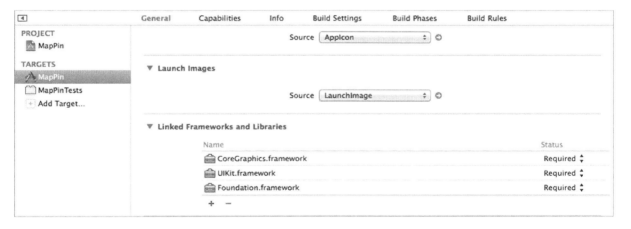

Figure 9-6. Showing the Linked Frameworks and Libraries area of your project's settings

As you know from previous projects in the book, you can add a framework to the current project by clicking the + symbol below the currently added frameworks. You won't do that here, this time I will show you an alternative method, which many iOS developers and many iOS development books refer to as it used to be the only way to do it, so it's good to be aware of its existence.

Select the Build Phases tab from the top of the project settings page. Build Phases allows you to manage the activities that take place when the project is compiled. One of those steps is Link Binary With Libraries; expand this section as shown in Figure 9-7.

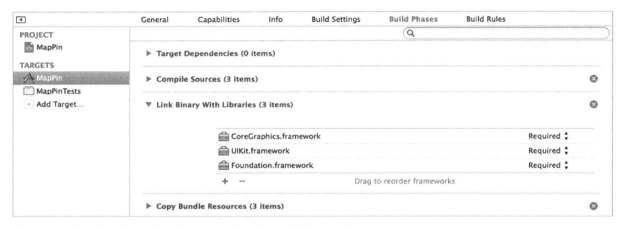

Figure 9-7. *The Link Binary With Libraries section of the Build Phases tab*

As with the other method for adding frameworks, select the plus symbol beneath at the bottom of the section, and you will be presented with the list of frameworks and libraries that can be added to the project. The list is quite large so rather that scrolling through the list, type the word "map" in the search box at the top of the list, as shown in Figure 9-8. Select MapKit.framework and click Add.

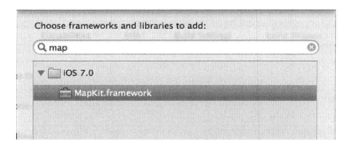

Figure 9-8. *Selecting the MapKit.framework*

You now have four frameworks linked to your project; if you expand the frameworks group in the Project Navigator, you will see that the framework has been added into the project's structure, as shown in Figure 9-9.

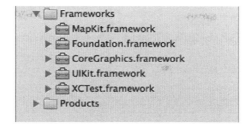

Figure 9-9. *The Frameworks group's contents within the Project Navigator*

Now that you have added the prerequisite framework for using a Map View, you're in a position to run the application again. Go ahead and run the application. You should now be greeted by a map showing North America, as shown in Figure 9-10.

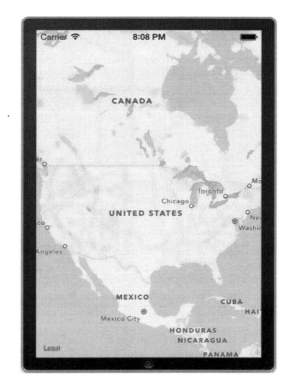

Figure 9-10. *The MapPin application displays an interactive map without even writing a line of code*

Manipulating a Map View

You haven't written a single line of code but already what the application does is fairly impressive; you can already pan and zoom the map. As a developer, you will instinctively want to add your own touches, setting the initial position of the map and adding some landmarks, which is what I will now explain.

In this application, you will be setting the region property to show a map of Wales, and then you will add some points of interest that display as pushpins. But before you do any of that, the first thing to do is to create an outlet for the Map View.

1.   Open `Main.storyboard` from the Project Navigator and enable the Assistant Editor; make sure that the selected file is `ViewController.h`.

Note   To quickly switch between the header and implementation files within the editor, you can use the Jump to next counterpart shortcut by holding Control + ⌘ and then pressing the up or down arrows.

2.   Control-drag a connection from the Map View to the header just above the @end line, as shown in Figure 9-11.

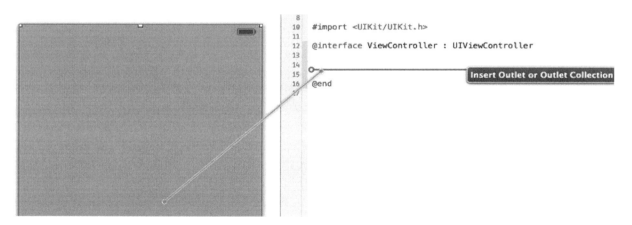

Figure 9-11. Dragging a connection from the Map View for an outlet

3.   Name the outlet mapView and then click Connect. You will be shown an error and a warning for the outlet because the import reference for the Map Kit framework hasn't been added to the View Controller's header file.

4. From the Project Navigator, open `ViewController.h` and switch the editor back to the Standard Editor. Import the Map Kit framework so that you have access to the Map View class and its associated classes. To do this, add the following code after the `#import <UIKit/UIKit.h>` line:

```
#import <MapKit/MapKit.h>
```

5. In order to manipulate the Map View from the View Controller, you will need to set it up as the delegate. Therefore, the next thing to do is add the `MKMapViewDelegate` protocol to the View Controller. Amend the `@interface` statement as follows:

```
@interface ViewController : UIViewController<MKMapViewDelegate>
```

6. That's all you need to do in the header; before moving on, check that your code matches that shown below:

```
#import <UIKit/UIKit.h>
#import <MapKit/MapKit.h>

@interface ViewController : UIViewController<MKMapViewDelegate>

@property (weak, nonatomic) IBOutlet MKMapView *mapView;

@end
```

7. You're finished with the header and are now ready to move on to the implementation file where you can start manipulating the map. Open `ViewController.m` from the Project Navigator. Start by scrolling to the `viewDidLoad` method.

8. You need to tell the Map View that the View Controller will be its delegate so that it obeys the instructions you send it. To do this you will use the `delegate` property of the `mapView` object and set it to `self`. In the `viewDidLoad` method, and after the `[super viewDidLoad];` line, add the following statement:

```
self.mapView.delegate = self;
```

9. To position the Map View in a specific position, you need to create a region, represented by the `MKCoordinateRegion`. Think of a region as an invisible window onto the map that can be set at a specific location and show a specific amount of the map. To create your region, you need two sets of values: the latitude and longitude for the center point of the region, and the north to south and east to west span values. Drop down a line and add the following three lines of code:

```
CLLocationCoordinate2D centerPoint = {52.011937, -3.713379};
MKCoordinateSpan coordinateSpan = MKCoordinateSpanMake(3.5, 3.5);
MKCoordinateRegion coordinateRegion = MKCoordinateRegionMake(centerPoint,
coordinateSpan);
```

> **Note**   You are probably familiar with longitude and latitude, but the span is a concept that is unique to Apple Maps. It consists of a latitude delta, which is a measurement in degrees north to south that equates to roughly 111 kilometers, and a longitude delta, which is also measured in degrees but unlike the latitude, the actual distance it equates to varies from 111 kilometers at the equator to 0 at either pole. So if you want to show a fixed zoom level where the location cannot be guaranteed, you would get more consistent results with the `MKCoordinateRegionMakeWithDistance` method.

10. Finally, you need to apply this region to the `mapView` object. Do this by calling two methods that apply the region in a way that ensures the map displays properly. Drop down a line and add the following code:

```
[self.mapView setRegion:coordinateRegion];
[self.mapView regionThatFits:coordinateRegion];
```

11. Go ahead and run the application, and when the map loads it should be focused over Wales, as shown in Figure 9-12. If your view doesn't match the figure, check that you set the delegate correctly and that your latitude and longitude values are spot on.

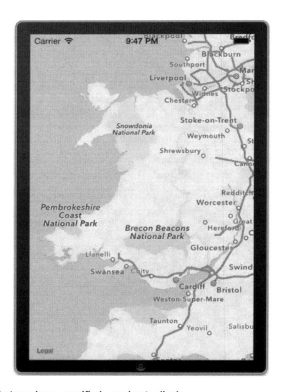

Figure 9-12. *The Map View now that you have specified a region to display*

Knowing how to move the map where you want it to be and setting the correct region to view are key skills when working with a Map View. But another key skill is marking locations on the map using pushpins.

You do this by creating instances of the MKPointAnnotation class and adding them to the map individually using the addAnnotation method. To instantiate an MKPointAnnotation, you will set three attributes: the title, subtitle, and coordinates.

1. Drop down a line in your viewDidLoad method and add the following code:

```
MKPointAnnotation *annotation1 = [[MKPointAnnotation alloc] init];
annotation1.title = @"Swansea Bay";
annotation1.subtitle = @"Beautiful Beaches";
annotation1.coordinate = CLLocationCoordinate2DMake(51.587736,-3.90152);

MKPointAnnotation *annotation2 = [[MKPointAnnotation alloc] init];
annotation2.title = @"Menai Bridge";
annotation2.subtitle = @"Fantastic Engineering";
annotation2.coordinate = CLLocationCoordinate2DMake(53.220527,-4.163561);

MKPointAnnotation *annotation3 = [[MKPointAnnotation alloc] init];
annotation3.title = @"Parc Y Scarlets";
annotation3.subtitle = @"Oh Dear";
annotation3.coordinate = CLLocationCoordinate2DMake(51.678809,-4.127469);

MKPointAnnotation *annotation4 = [[MKPointAnnotation alloc] init];
annotation4.title = @"Castell Coch";
annotation4.subtitle = @"A Fairytale Castle";
annotation4.coordinate = CLLocationCoordinate2DMake(51.535819,-3.2547);

MKPointAnnotation *annotation5 = [[MKPointAnnotation alloc] init];
annotation5.title = @"Arthur's Stone";
annotation5.subtitle = @"Rock Of Legend";
annotation5.coordinate = CLLocationCoordinate2DMake(51.593735,-4.179525);

[self.mapView addAnnotation:annotation1];
[self.mapView addAnnotation:annotation2];
[self.mapView addAnnotation:annotation3];
[self.mapView addAnnotation:annotation4];
[self.mapView addAnnotation:annotation5];
```

2. Go ahead and rerun your application now. You should see five annotations. Tap an annotation, as shown in Figure 9-13, to display the text associated with that pushpin.

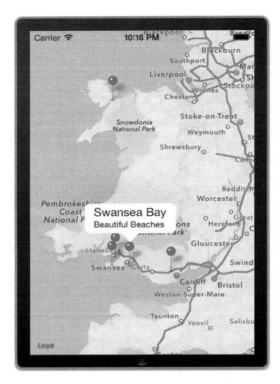

Figure 9-13. *The Map View, now with five annotations showing various attractions in Wales*

With very little code, you've made a really useful and interactive application! There are endless customizations you could make, such as replacing the pushpins with an image or adding controls to the callout that display the annotation text. I won't explain how to customize the pushpins any further, as the focus of this book is on Xcode. However, I will show you how to perform one of the key steps you would typically perform before any customization, which is subclassing the MKPointAnnotation class and then creating a custom initializer to simplify creation of the annotations.

Subclassing MKPointAnnotation

In order to demonstrate how static libraries work, as discussed later in this chapter, I want you to create a custom class that can be relocated inside a static library. As you are working with annotations, it makes sense to subclass the MKPointAnnotation class and replace the pushpin objects you just created with this new class, which you will call MyPin.

1. First, let's create the new class; select File ➤ New ➤ File (⌘ + N). Select Cocoa Touch from the left-hand menu and then select the Objective-C class template, as shown in Figure 9-14, and click Next.

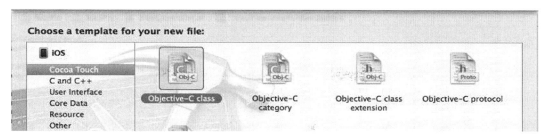

Figure 9-14. *Creating a new Objective-C class*

2. Name the class MyPin and set the subclass of value to `MKPointAnnotation` and click Next; accept the default save location and click Create.

3. You have now successfully created your custom class, but to make it work you need to make some modifications. Open `MyPin.h` from the Project Navigator.

4. You will now add a custom initializer to simplify the process of creating the annotation. The initializer will take the three parameters that are required: `title`, `subtitle`, and `coordinate`. Modify your header to match that shown below:

```
#import <MapKit/MapKit.h>

@interface MyPin : MKPointAnnotation

-(id)initWithTitle:(NSString *)title subtitle:(NSString *)subtitle
coordinate:(CLLocationCoordinate2D)coordinate;

@end
```

5. The implementation for this method will be really straightforward, open `MyPin.m` from the Project Navigator and add the highlighted code to the implementation file, as shown below:

```
#import "MyPin.h"

@implementation MyPin

-(id)initWithTitle:(NSString *)title subtitle:(NSString *)subtitle
coordinate:(CLLocationCoordinate2D)coordinate
{
    self = [super init];
```

```
        if (self)
        {
            self.title = title;
            self.subtitle = subtitle;
            self.coordinate = coordinate;
        }

        return self;
}

@end
```

6. With the custom initialization method now fully written, you can modify the annotations declared within the viewDidLoad method to use the new class. Open ViewController.m from the Project Navigator.

7. In order to reference the new class, you must include its header in the View Controller's implementation file, so after the #import "ViewController.h" line, add the following import statement:

```
#import "MyPin.h"
```

8. Now scroll back down to the viewDidLoad method where you created the five instances of MKPointAnnotation, and replace them with the highlighted code below:

```
- (void)viewDidLoad
{
    [super viewDidLoad];

    self.mapView.delegate = self;

    CLLocationCoordinate2D centerPoint = {52.011937, -3.713379};
    MKCoordinateSpan coordinateSpan = MKCoordinateSpanMake(3.5, 3.5);
    MKCoordinateRegion coordinateRegion = MKCoordinateRegionMake(centerPoint,
coordinateSpan);

    [self.mapView setRegion:coordinateRegion];
    [self.mapView regionThatFits:coordinateRegion];

    MyPin *annotation1 =
        [[MyPin alloc] initWithTitle:@"Swansea Bay"
                            subtitle:@"Beautiful Beaches"
                          coordinate:CLLocationCoordinate2DMake(51.587736,-3.90152)];

    MyPin *annotation2 =
        [[MyPin alloc] initWithTitle:@"Menai Bridge"
                            subtitle:@"Fantastic Engineering"
                          coordinate:CLLocationCoordinate2DMake(53.220527,-4.163561)];
```

```
    MyPin *annotation3 =
        [[MyPin alloc] initWithTitle:@"Parc Y Scarlets"
                            subtitle:@"Oh Dear"
                          coordinate:CLLocationCoordinate2DMake(51.678809,-4.127469)];

    MyPin *annotation4 =
        [[MyPin alloc] initWithTitle:@"Castell Coch"
                            subtitle:@"A Fairytale Castle"
                          coordinate:CLLocationCoordinate2DMake(51.535819,-3.2547)];

    MyPin *annotation5 =
        [[MyPin alloc] initWithTitle:@"Arthur's Stone"
                            subtitle:@"Rock Of Legend"
                          coordinate:CLLocationCoordinate2DMake(51.593735,-4.179525)];

    [self.mapView addAnnotation:annotation1];
    [self.mapView addAnnotation:annotation2];
    [self.mapView addAnnotation:annotation3];
    [self.mapView addAnnotation:annotation4];
    [self.mapView addAnnotation:annotation5];
}
```

Go ahead and rerun your application. You should find that all of the pushpins are still in place but you did this with a fraction of the code. In the next part of the chapter I will explain how to make the code easily reusable by using static libraries.

Static Libraries

After you've been writing software for a few years, you will find that there are custom classes and methods that you come back to time and time again. You can save the code in snippets or copy it from one project to another, but this isn't an efficient approach because if you refine or add new functionality to the code, you have to go back and change every instance of that function. A much more efficient approach is to save the code in a static library.

Static libraries allow you to group classes and resources together, and although there is no restriction or set pattern for what you include in your static library, it is generally a good idea to use them to group similar functions together, such as custom annotation classes for a Map View or different animation classes in a game.

Creating a Static Library

To create a static library, you will need to create a new project, but there is no need to close the MapPin project.

1. Go to File ➤ New ➤ Project . . . (⌘ + Shift + N), and this time select Framework & Library from the left-hand column of options under the iOS heading, and then select the Cocoa Touch Static Library option, as shown in Figure 9-15; click Next.

Figure 9-15. *Selecting the Cocoa Touch Static Library template*

2.　The project settings for a static library are slightly different from the settings when creating a project. There is no target device and no option for setting a class prefix. Set the Product Name value to MapAnnotation and leave the other settings as their default values, as shown in Figure 9-16. Then click Next.

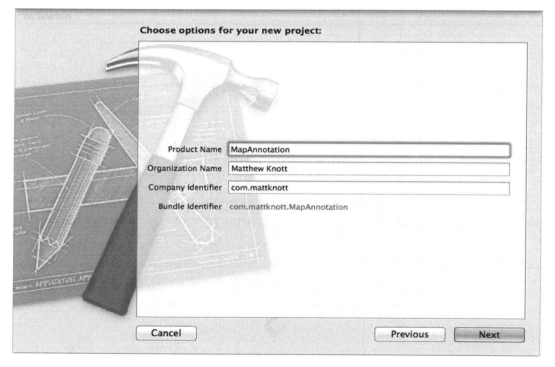

Figure 9-16. *The project settings for a Cocoa Touch Static Library*

3. You can leave the project location at its default setting, then click Create. Now you can start adding files to your library.

4. When the project was created, it added a generic MapAnnotation class to the project, which subclasses NSObject. As the only files the project needs to contain are the custom annotation files you just created, you may remove the default files from the project. In the Project Navigator. Select MapAnnotation.h and then hold the Command (⌘) key and click on MapAnnotation.m, as shown in Figure 9-17.

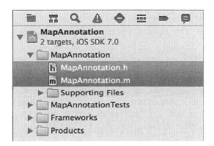

Figure 9-17. Selecting the generic MapAnnotation class files before removal

5. Now, to delete the files, press the Backspace key and you will be presented with the menu shown in Figure 9-18; choose the Move to Trash option.

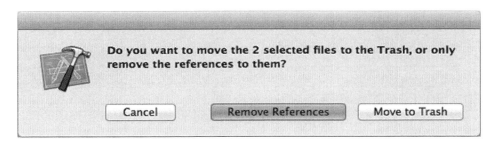

Figure 9-18. The file removal dialog, select Move to Trash to completely remove the files

6. With the project now empty, you need to add the class files from the MapPin project into this one. To do this, start by switching to the MapPin project; right-click the MyPin.h file, and select Show in Finder from the menu that appears, as shown in Figure 9-19.

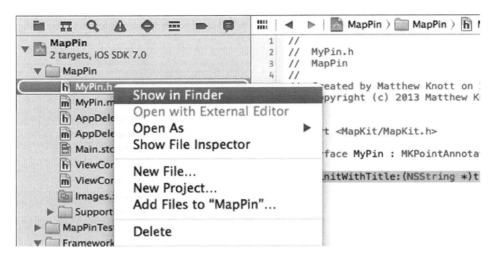

Figure 9-19. *The context menu that appears when right-clicking MyPin.h*

7. Minimize the MapPin Xcode project so that you're left with the Finder window and the MapAnnotation Xcode project. In the finder window, press and hold the ⌘ key and select both the `MyPin.h` and the `MyPin.m` files. Drag both of the files over to the MapAnnotation project group in the Project Navigator, as shown in Figure 9-20.

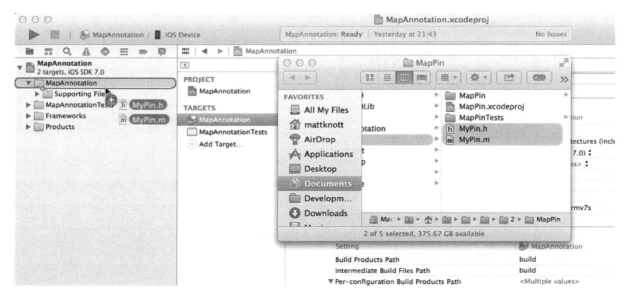

Figure 9-20. *Dragging the MyPin class files into the project group*

8. When you release the mouse, you will be asked to confirm the options applied when importing the files. It's important to ensure that Copy items into destination group's folder is checked and that the MapAnnotation target is also checked, as shown in Figure 9-21.

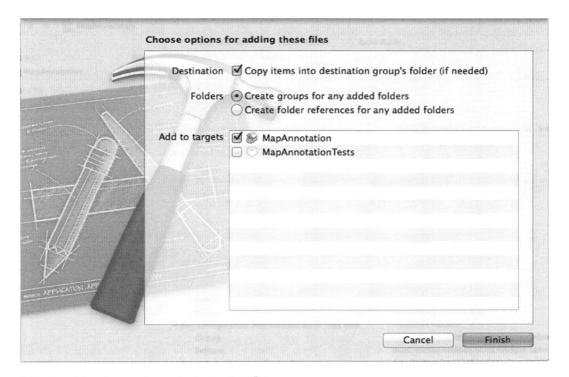

Figure 9-21. *The dialog shown after copying in the class files*

9. You've now copied the MyPin class files into the new MapAnnotation project. In order for those class files to work, you need to add the Map Kit framework into the project. To do this, select the MapAnnotation project at the top of the Project Navigator, and then the Build Phases tab, as shown in Figure 9-22.

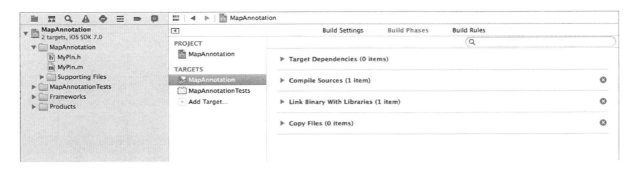

Figure 9-22. *The Build Phases tab of the MapAnnotation project*

10.   You'll add the framework to this project exactly as you did with the MapPin project. Expand the Link Binary With Libraries row and click the + icon. Select MapKit.framework from the menu and click Add.

Adding an Aggregate Target

I need you to stay in this area a little while longer. The next step in creating a static library is to add an Aggregate Target to the project so that both the simulator and a physical device can use the library.

1.   Click File ➤ New ➤ Target or click Add Target . . . underneath MapAnnoationTests (shown in Figure 9-22). Select Other under iOS from the left-hand menu and then select Aggregate, as shown in Figure 9-23. Click Next and set the Product Name to UniversalLib, leave the project as MapAnnotation and click Finish.

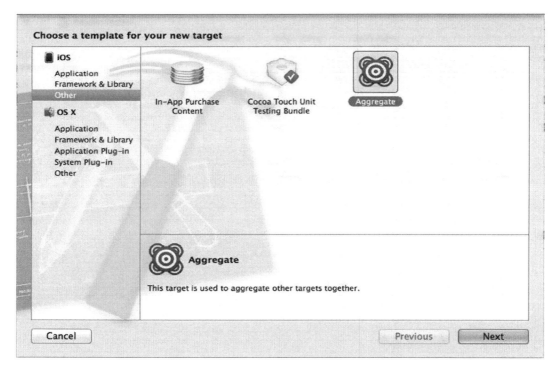

Figure 9-23. Selecting the Aggregate target

Note   Because the architecture of the simulator (i386) is different from that of an actual device (arm), you need to create a universal binary that runs on either system. The aggregate target binds these two versions together.

2. For the library to work correctly with the simulator, it needs to execute a script at build time. Select the new target, UniversalLib from the list of targets, then select Editor ➤ Add Build Phase ➤ Add Run Script Build Phase, as shown in Figure 9-24. If the menu is grayed out, reselect the Build Phases tab and then try the menu again or select another target and reselect UniversalLib.

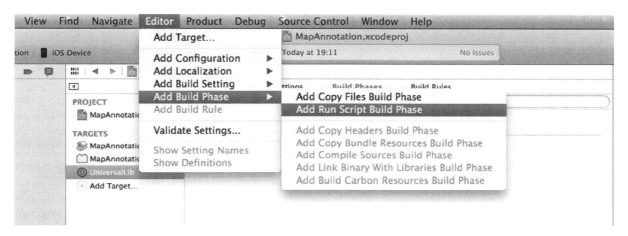

Figure 9-24. *Adding a Run Script Build Phase into the project*

3. The purpose of executing the script is to combine the simulator and physical device version of the library into a single universal binary using the `lipo` command. Expand the new Run Script phase and beneath the Shell property, there is a box that says Type a script or drag a script file from your workspace to insert its path. Click this box and type the code shown below exactly, your finished target should look like Figure 9-25.

```
UNIVERSAL_OUTPUTFOLDER=${BUILD_DIR}/${CONFIGURATION}-universal

xcodebuild -target MapAnnotation ONLY_ACTIVE_ARCH=NO -configuration ${CONFIGURATION} -sdk
iphoneos  BUILD_DIR="${BUILD_DIR}" BUILD_ROOT="${BUILD_ROOT}"

xcodebuild -target MapAnnotation -configuration ${CONFIGURATION} -sdk iphonesimulator
-arch i386 BUILD_DIR="${BUILD_DIR}" BUILD_ROOT="${BUILD_ROOT}"

mkdir -p "${UNIVERSAL_OUTPUTFOLDER}"

lipo -create -output "${UNIVERSAL_OUTPUTFOLDER}/lib${PROJECT_NAME}.a"
"${BUILD_DIR}/${CONFIGURATION}-iphoneos/lib${PROJECT_NAME}.a"
"${BUILD_DIR}/${CONFIGURATION}-iphonesimulator/lib${PROJECT_NAME}.a"

cp -R "${BUILD_DIR}/${CONFIGURATION}-iphoneos/include" "${UNIVERSAL_OUTPUTFOLDER}/"
```

Figure 9-25. *Your completed target's Build Phase tab*

4. Okay, before you try building the library, there are a few things you must check. Click the Build Settings tab, and with the UniversalLib target selected, make sure that Build Active Architecture Only is set to No for both Debug and Release, as shown in Figure 9-26, and then repeat this step for the MapAnnotation target.

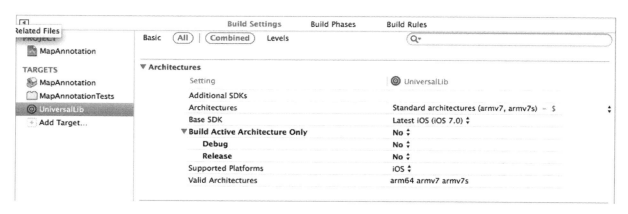

Figure 9-26. *Changing the Build Active Architecture Only setting to No*

5. Now reselect the Build Phases tab, but this time, select the MapAnnotation target. Creating a static library in Xcode can be tricky; one of the things you need to check is that Xcode is actively including the header file when the library is compiled. Expand the Compile Sources element and the Copy Files element, and ensure that they both contain MyPin.h, as shown in Figure 9-27.

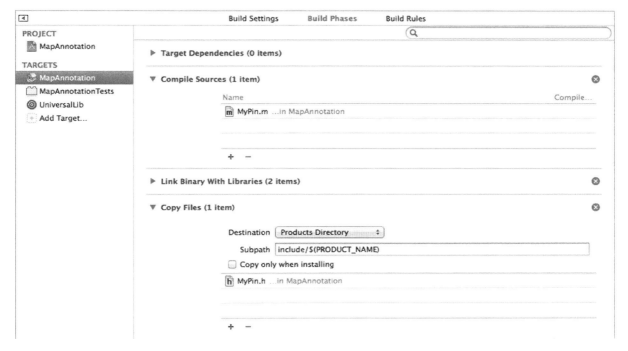

Figure 9-27. *How the Build Phases of the main target should look*

6. If MyPin.m is missing from Compile Sources or MyPin.h is missing from Copy Files, the library will cause you no end of headaches when you try to add it later. Click the + symbol at the bottom of the section and choose either MyPin.h or MyPin.m depending on the section, as shown in Figure 9-28, and then click Add.

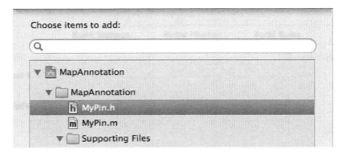

Figure 9-28. *Adding MyPin.h to the Build Phase sections*

7. You're just about ready to build the library, but before you do, you need to change the active scheme. To do this, click MapAnnotation in the Toolbar area, next to the Run and Stop buttons, and select UniversalLib, as shown in Figure 9-29; alternatively, select Product ➤ Scheme ➤ UniversalLib.

Figure 9-29. Changing the active scheme to UniversalLib

8. You're now ready to build the library. Click the Run button or use the ⌘ + B keyboard shortcut. Your library should build successfully; if there are any issues, try quitting Xcode and relaunching it, failing that, go back through the chapter and ensure you haven't accidentally missed a step.

> **Note**   If you get an error when building the project that says something along the lines of "-target: command not found. Command /bin/sh failed with exit code 127" then you need to quit Xcode and relaunch it before it will build correctly. It's not clear why this issue exists, but relaunching Xcode is the only solution.

Adding a Static Library to a Project

Now that your static library compiles correctly, all that remains is to link it with your MapPin project. You will do this by adding the Xcode Project file for the library into the MapPin project.

1. Add the library into the project by dragging and dropping `MapAnnotation.xcodeproj` into the MapPin project. To simplify this, right-click the project in Project Navigator and select Show in Finder, as shown in Figure 9-30.

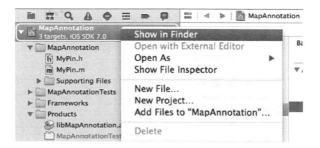

Figure 9-30. Locating the project file in the Finder

2. With the project file located, it's really important that you close the MapAnnotation project workspace completely. Bring back the MapPin workspace and then drag `MapAnnotation.xcodeproj` from the Finder onto the MapPin project item, as shown in Figure 9-31.

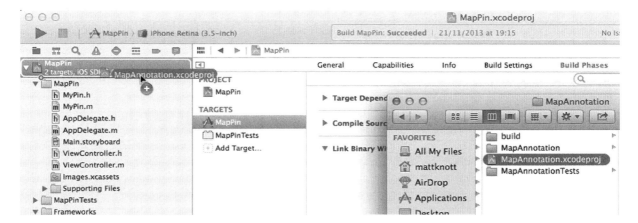

Figure 9-31. Dragging the static library project into the MapPin project

3. Release the mouse and the library will be added to the project. Before you continue, ensure your Project Navigator resembles that shown in Figure 9-32. If the `MapAnnotation.xcodeproj` entry doesn't show the three targets as it does in Figure 9-32, then remove the entry by highlighting it, pressing the Backspace key, and clicking Remove Reference.

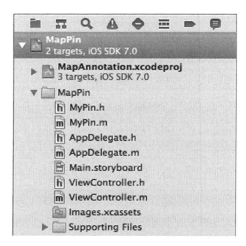

Figure 9-32. The MapAnnotation project located within our MapPin project

4. You can now start referencing the static library version of MyPin.h instead of the one inside the project. To do this, select the MapPin project from the Project Navigator and with the MapPin target selected, open the Build Phases tab, as shown in Figure 9-33.

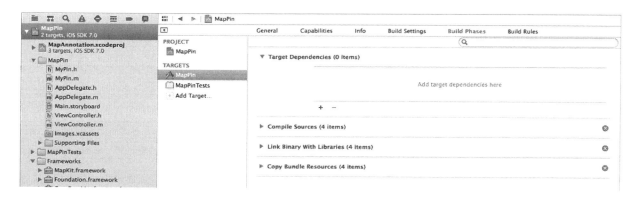

Figure 9-33. The build phases for the MapPin target

5. Expand Target Dependencies first and click the + symbol to open the Add Items dialog; select MapAnnotation, not UniversalLib, as shown in Figure 9-34 and click Add.

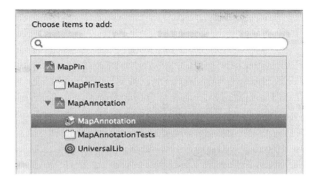

Figure 9-34. *Selecting the MapAnnotation target as a target dependency*

6. Next, just as you have done a number of times already in this chapter, expand the Link Binary With Libraries section and click the + symbol. This time, however, you will notice that there is a Workspace group that contains the library, `libMapAnnotation.a`. Select it, as shown in Figure 9-35, and click Add.

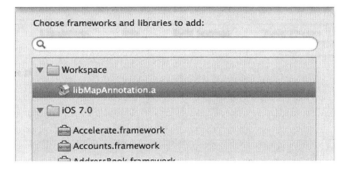

Figure 9-35. *Adding the library to the project*

7. With the library added to the project, all that remains is to implement it. To start with, select `MyPin.h` and `MyPin.m` from the Project Navigator and remove them from the project. Ensure that you select the class files from the MapPin project when removing the files and *not* from the newly added MapAnnotation library!

8. Open `ViewController.m` from the Project Navigator. You may find that Xcode is now showing an error against the line at the top of the file that says `#import "MyPin.h"`. This is because you have just removed that file, and you now need to reference the `MyPin.h` file from within the static library. To do that, change the line as follows:

```
#import "MapAnnotation/MyPin.h"
```

9. You may see a number of errors when you add this line in, but it should be temporary. Run the application and it should look exactly as it did back in Figure 9-13.

Static libraries are extremely important, and having a collection of commonly used features and functions will save you many hours over time as you find you no longer need to re-create those functions time and again. Now let's move on to the final part of this chapter and alter the functionality of the application based on the target selected.

Working with Multiple Targets

Hopefully when you finish this book, you'll be ready to start writing your own applications for the App Store. When you create an application that you're hoping to charge for, it's likely that you'll also want to create a free version with less features to tempt users into upgrading to the full version. You could create a new project and copy all of your code over to the new project, but then you've fallen into the pitfall of having to maintain two versions of the same code.

Through different targets, Xcode allows you to maintain different versions of the same application within the same project and then in code identify which version of the application is running and adjust the functionality to suit. For this example, let's create another target called MapPinSatellite that will display the map in satellite mode instead of the default standard mode.

Rather than creating a new target and going through and applying a lot of settings, let's just duplicate the existing MapPin target.

1. Start by selecting the MapPin project from the Project Navigator. When the project settings load, select the MapPin project and press the ⌘ + D keys or right-click the MapPin target and click Duplicate, as shown in Figure 9-36.

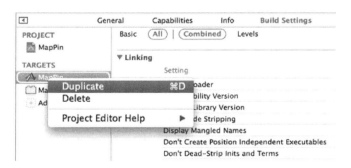

Figure 9-36. *Duplicating the MapPin target*

2. After choosing to duplicate the target, Xcode will detect that you're duplicating an iPhone-specific target and ask if you want to convert it for use with an iPad, as shown in Figure 9-37. In this instance, you just want to duplicate the target so select Duplicate Only.

Figure 9-37. Xcode will prompt you if you try to duplicate an iPhone-specific target

3. Xcode will duplicate the target and name it MapPin copy; this is great but not really what you want your target named. Click the MapPin copy target and then click it again so that you can edit the target name. Change its name to MapPinSatellite, as shown in Figure 9-38.

Figure 9-38. Renaming the new target

4. You now have to change a couple of the settings of the MapPinSatellite target to reflect its new name. With the MapPinSatellite target selected, open the Build Settings tab. You need to change two settings, but there are dozens of settings in this list! To make things much easier, use the search filter at the top of the page. First, change the Product Name property to MapPinSatellite; to do this, search for "product name" and then double-click the words MapPin copy and change them to MapPinSatellite, as shown in Figure 9-39.

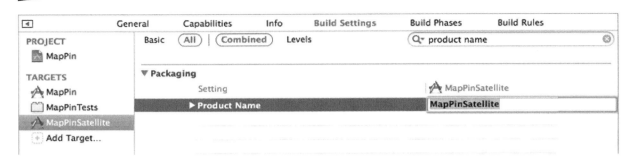

Figure 9-39. Changing the product name setting to MapPinSatellite

5. The next setting to change is the info.plist file; change the filter and then rename the value from MapPin copy-Info.plist to MapPinSatellite-Info. plist, as shown in Figure 9-40.

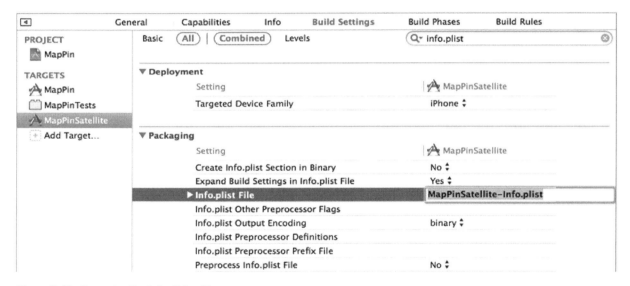

Figure 9-40. Renaming the info.plist setting

6. When you duplicated the target, it actually duplicated three things: the target was obviously duplicated but so were the info.plist file and the targets scheme. As you've just named it in the settings for your target, you should also change the info.plist file name next. In the Project Navigator, you may notice that at the bottom of the project there is now a plist file named MapPin copy-Info.plist. As you changed the target setting, you also need to rename this file to match. Highlight the file and press the Return key to begin editing and change the name to MapPinSatellite-Info.plist. Your Product Navigator should now resemble that shown in Figure 9-41.

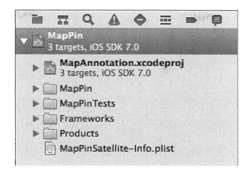

Figure 9-41. *The Project Navigator after renaming the file*

7. There is one final item to change: the scheme. Go to Product ➤ Scheme ➤ Manage Schemes and you will be presented with a list of the available schemes, as shown in Figure 9-42.

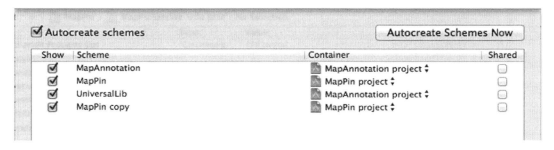

Figure 9-42. *Xcode's Manage Schemes view listing the available schemes*

8. Highlight the bottom scheme named MapPin copy and click the Return key. Change the scheme name to MapPinSatellite. You've now updated everything that needs to be updated to start taking advantage of your new target, click the OK button to close the window.

9. Open `ViewController.m` from the Project Navigator and scroll down to the `viewDidLoad` method. You first need to identify which version of the application is being run. You find this by looking at the bundle identifier of the application, which changes depending on which target scheme is being run. The bundle identifier is a combination of the Company Identifier specified in Figure 9-2 and the Product Name. Let's retrieve the bundle identifier and assign it to an `NSString` object and then use `NSLog` to output the identifier to the console. After the line `[super viewDidLoad]`, drop down a line and add the following code:

```
NSString *bundleID = [[[NSBundle mainBundle] infoDictionary]
                        objectForKey:@"CFBundleIdentifier"];
NSLog(@"Bundle: %@", bundleID);
```

10. Run the application, and you will see the bundle identifier reflected in the debug console, as shown in Figure 9-43.

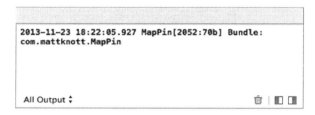

Figure 9-43. The bindle identifier reflected in the debug console

11. Let's change the scheme for this project from MapPin to MapPin satellite; this is no different from when you switched to UniversalLib when you created the static library. Select the MapPin scheme next to the Run and Stop buttons in the Toolbar area and select MapPinSatellite, as shown in Figure 9-44.

Figure 9-44. Changing to the MapPinSatellite scheme

12. If the Stop button is active, make sure you press stop to terminate the application running under the other scheme otherwise Xcode will throw an error about the simulator being in use. Run the application again with the new scheme and you'll see that the bundle identifier coming back in the debug area has changed to match the product name specified for this scheme, which will end with MapPinSatellite. You now have two distinct values that will allow you to implement differing functionality.

13. The different functionality in this project is going to be that the original target runs just as it is using the standard map type, but the satellite version runs with the satellite map type. In your `ViewController.m` file, after the line `self.mapView.delegate = self;` line, add the following code but change the text in the `if` statement to match your bundle identifier; remember that it's case sensitive:

```
if([bundleID isEqualToString:@"com.mattknott.MapPinSatellite"])
{
    self.mapView.mapType = MKMapTypeSatellite;
}
```

14. Run your application, once with the MapPinSatelite scheme and again with the MapPin scheme, to appreciate the difference, as shown in Figure 9-45. Remember to stop the application when switching schemes.

Figure 9-45. *The application running under both schemes*

Discovering Modules

One of the latest developments that are exclusive to Xcode 5 is a new feature called Modules. The Modules system allows you to write far more efficient applications by changing what happens when the compiler is asked to handle the importing a framework or library.

Within the MapPin application, your `ViewController.h` file has the following lines:

```
#import <UIKit/UIKit.h>
#import <MapKit/MapKit.h>
```

If you were using the Modules feature, you would write the same code like this:

```
@import UIKit;
@import MapKit;
```

The difference is subtle, the # symbol changes to an @, which for UK keyboard layouts makes life much easier. The other difference is that you now reference just the name of the library rather than writing the full path to the header. This is why it is also known as semantic importing.

At first glance you may assume that this change saves a few characters every time you import a framework or library, but the change goes far deeper than that. When you build your application, Xcode's LLVM compiler sees the `#import` directive and then adds the entire contents of that header into yours, thereby adding what can sometimes be tens of thousand of extra lines of code to each of your files and slowing the compile process.

When you use the Modules approach, the compiler doesn't add the contents of the header file into yours, but instead is far more efficient in how it encapsulates and processes the header.

Another benefit of using the Modules approach is that you can target a specific header within the framework. For example, in the `MyPin` class, you had to import the entire `MapKit` framework because you subclassed `MKPointAnnotation`. Because this was all you were referencing, you could have used the following import statement:

```
@import MapKit.MKPointAnnotation
```

Doing this would further improve the efficiency of the compiler. Finally, and this is a big one, when using frameworks and libraries, it's often very easy for forget to go through the process of linking the library to your project. With the Modules feature, you no longer have to manually add the frameworks to your project; if you write `@import MapKit` in your project, it will do the rest of the work for you and add the framework when you compile. Clearly this is a major time and effort saver, so you may well ask, why I'm first mentioning this now?

The reason I didn't mention this earlier is that many of the references you will buy today for developing using Objective-C won't use this approach. It's even absent from some iOS 7 specific development books. The reason for this is largely its newness, although the concept was first introduced in 2012, it wasn't until the release of Xcode 5 that it was added into the IDE.

Another reason is that you are benefiting from it already; every Xcode 5 project you create will have modules enabled by default. When Xcode 5 compiles your code, it implicitly converts `#imports` to `@imports`, but it will ultimately be good for you to adopt this as your approach and not rely on Xcode to do this for you. Unfortunately, however, Modules are only enabled by default on projects created with Xcode 5.

Enabling Modules for Older Projects

If you're working with an older project, it may not have Modules enabled. Thankfully, this is very simple to do. I will use the MapPin project to show you where the option to enable Modules can be found.

1. Start by going back into Xcode and selecting the MapPin project from the Project Navigator.

2. Next, select the MapPin target and choose the Build Settings tab.

3. Type "enable modules" in the filter, as shown in Figure 9-46.

Figure 9-46. The setting to enable or disable Modules for the project

You will see that under Apple LLVM 5.0 – Language – Modules is an option to enable Modules for the project, and currently it is set to Yes. In older projects that hadn't been updated in Xcode 5, this would be set to No. Once set to Yes, Xcode will take over and convert any `#import` statements automatically for you without you having to go back and update the code.

Summary

As you get further into the book, the topics will become more advanced. If you're serious about becoming an iOS or MacOS developer, then the skills you've learned in this chapter will allow you to show super efficient work, using libraries and custom initializers to good effect.

This chapter combined your knowledge of frameworks, static libraries, and targets to create a Map Kit–based application, which shows just a few of the many hundreds of points of interest in Wales. You learned how to add annotations to the Map View and then subclassed `MKPointAnnotation` to create a one-hit initializer for the annotation object.

Specifically in this chapter, you have:

- Learned about both ways of adding frameworks to a project
- Discovered Map Views and how to manipulate them in code
- Moved class files into a static library
- Learned about universal binaries and the use of aggregate targets
- Duplicated a target to create different sets of features from the same code
- Learned about the new Modules feature in Xcode 5 for importing frameworks

In the next chapter, you will learn how to mold Xcode into a more personalized development environment and how to get more out of Xcode as you learn new customizations that will make you a better and more efficient developer.

Chapter 10

Advanced Editing

Chapter 9 looked at how to add frameworks to a project and efficient ways of managing code through the use of libraries, as well as using multiple targets and aggregate targets. These skills were combined and developed as you created a basic Map Kit application that showed a selection of interesting points on a map of Wales, the country I live in. If you want to become an accomplished iOS or Xcode developer, either on your own or in a team of developers, then learning how to efficiently reuse code is essential.

This chapter will maintain the efficiency theme and focus on the code editor while creating a fun Sprite Kit–based application we will call AlienDev that will show our hero, the alien dev (Alien Cyborg Dev to give him his full name) surrounded by an increasing numbers of bugs (evil ones). I'll explain how small bits of reusable code can be saved as snippets, readily available to be dropped into your application as well as look at the many ways you can customize Xcode to work for you. It's a cliché, but everyone is different, and developers are no exception. Xcode is hugely customizable, from the font and colors used in the code editor to the way Xcode reacts to different events. There are so many ways you can tweak the IDE to be a better environment for you to code in. I'll also discuss how to work with large implementation files by using code folding and some of the subtle ways you can efficiently navigate your code using the jump bar and its pragma marks to bring order to your jump bar hierarchy.

Without further ado, let's get started on the project—let the bug wars commence!

Getting Started

The project for this chapter will be created using the Sprite Kit application template. As mentioned in Chapter 3, Sprite Kit is an exciting new framework that Apple introduced with Xcode 5 and iOS 7 to allow developers to easily create 2D animations and even games without having to use a third-party system such as Cocos2D or Unity.

1. Start by opening Xcode and creating a new project by clicking Create a new Xcode project from the Welcome screen or go to File ➤ New ➤ Project . . . (⌘ + Shift + N). Select the SpriteKit Game template and click Next.

2. Name your project AlienDev and ensure the Devices value is set to iPhone, not iPad or Universal. Configure the other values to your own preference, mine are shown in Figure 10-1; click Next.

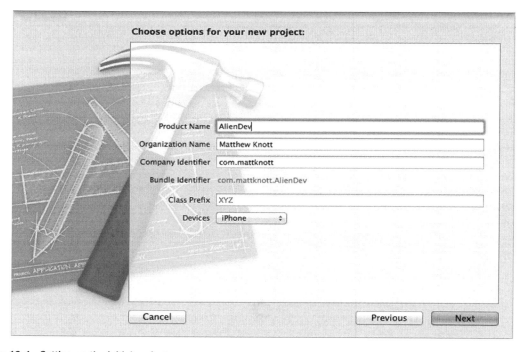

Figure 10-1. *Setting up the initial project*

3. By now you should be familiar with the process, you want to save in the default location and you don't want to create a Git repository, so just go ahead and click Create.

4. Xcode will take you straight into the project settings; you'll want the application to run in landscape mode only, so scroll down to the Deployment Info section. The default-supported orientations for an iPhone application are Portrait, Landscape Left, and Landscape Right; you need to untick Portrait so that only the landscape options remain, as shown in Figure 10-2.

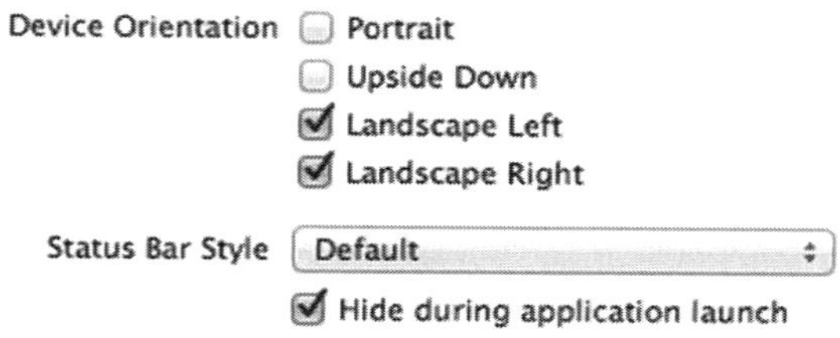

Figure 10-2. *Restricting the Device Orientation to landscape*

5. Before you go any further, let's stop to take a look at the assets for our application. Figure 10-3 shows the two characters you'll use; the hero—the alien dev—on the left and villainous bug on the right. One thing you should be able to gather is that I am *not* a graphic's artist; you can either download the files for this chapter from the Apress web site at www.apress.com or you can create your own characters. To account for standard and retina devices, each character will have two images:

Dev.png: A transparent png image, which is 21 pixels wide by 40 pixels high.

Dev@2x.png: The retina equivalent of dev.png, this image is twice the size at 42 pixels by 80 pixels.

Bug.png: A transparent png image, which is 54 pixels wide by 40 pixels high.

Bug@2x.png: The retina equivalent of dev.png, this image is twice the size at 108 pixels by 80 pixels.

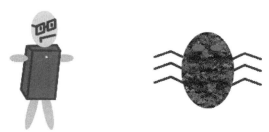

Figure 10-3. The hero and villain for this application

6. Once you have downloaded the images mentioned above or have created your own with the same names, go ahead and start dragging them from the Finder into the Supporting Files group in Xcode, as shown in Figure 10-4.

Figure 10-4. Dragging the image files into the Supporting Files group

7.   When you release the files over the supporting files folder, you must ensure that you check the Copy items into destination group's folder option, as shown in Figure 10-5, so that the files are physically copied into the project.

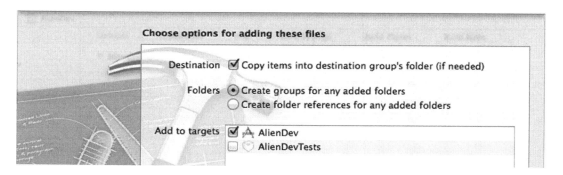

Figure 10-5. Selecting the import options for the images used in this project

With the assets in place, let's start to look at the code for the application, which is good because the rest of this chapter is dedicated to code: how to look at it, how to manage it efficiently, and how to quickly navigate it.

Efficient Editing

A good developer can be compared to a master craftsman, except that instead of a hammer and chisel, we have IDEs and compilers. Like a master craftsman, good developers take pride in their work, taking time to achieve perfection, adding the painstakingly small touches that set your product apart from the rest. Unlike a master craftsman though, when the tool isn't right, we don't have to pick up a different one because our tools are not static; Xcode's interface is an organic entity that can be tailored to your needs and made to work the way you want it to.

Changing Color Schemes

One of the things you will find when working in a team of developers is that everyone has a different way of working, whether it's how they write their comments or how they indent their code. But when you're working with a flexible IDE like Xcode, most developers will tailor the color scheme to meet their needs. You may not have realized it, but changing the color scheme can have a drastic effect on productivity; sometimes I find the lightness of the standard color scheme can cause migraines, so I switch to a dark background scheme with high contrast to make the code stand out without causing a migraine.

To start looking at what Xcode lets us change, open the Xcode preferences by selecting Xcode ➤ Preferences (⌘ + ,); when the preferences open, select the Fonts & Colors tab, as shown in Figure 10-6.

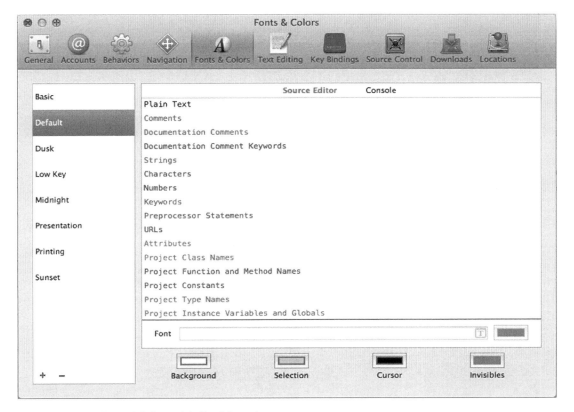

Figure 10-6. *The Fonts & Colors tab in Xcode's preferences*

The Fonts & Colors tab is divided into four key areas, as highlighted in Figure 10-7.

Theme List: This area lists the preset themes Xcode makes available. A theme is a predetermined combination of fonts and colors.

Detail View: The items listed in the detail view are known as Syntax Categories. These represent all of the conceivably customizable elements of code within either the source editor or console, depending which tab is selected at the top of the detail view.

Font Configuration: This area allows you to customize the font and color for the selected syntax category.

General Colors: The general colors control the background color, the selection color, which is used when highlighting text, the cursor color, and the "invisibles" color or instruction pointer if looking at the Console tab.

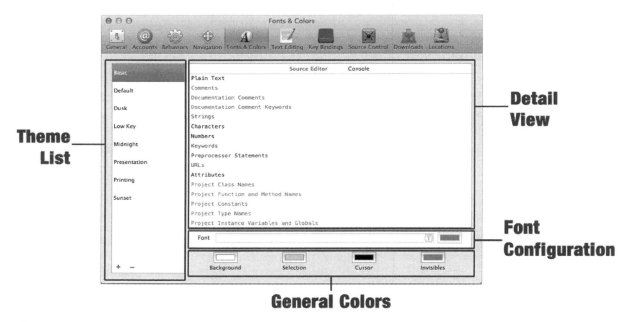

Figure 10-7. *The key areas of the Fonts & Colors tab*

Try changing the different themes, Dusk and Midnight are good if you want a high-contrast theme, whereas Low Key and Sunset are great if you want something that's a little washed out. There are specialist themes too, with Printing giving you a monochrome look and Presentation giving you an enlarged font size for when you're hooked up to a projector demonstrating your code.

Select the Default theme for now and then choose the Comments syntax category. The font configuration area will show you the key details about the selected syntax category, as shown in Figure 10-8. You can see that the font used for comments is Menlo Regular, size 11 and green. To change the font details, click the T icon as you would when setting font information for labels and text fields in Interface Builder. Unlike Interface Builder, however, you will be presented with the standard font selection dialog that will be familiar to anyone who has used Mac OS X for a period of time; this is shown in Figure 10-9.

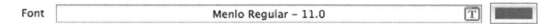

Figure 10-8. *The font configuration details*

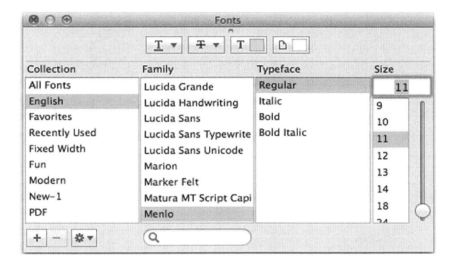

Figure 10-9. *The font selection dialog*

Creating a New Theme

Although it's easy to modify a theme, there is no *reset* button to revert your changes to the theme's original settings. If you modify your theme and want to get it back to its original state, the best way is to start over and create a new one based on one of the pre-set themes. This may sound drastic, but it's perfectly alright; all of the themes Xcode comes with as default are stored as templates within Xcode that can be re-created in a couple of clicks.

First, let's examine the Add button at the bottom of the theme list. Click the + symbol, as shown in Figure 10-10. You will be presented with a pop-up menu that effectively gives you two choices. You can either duplicate your current theme or create a new one from one of the default templates.

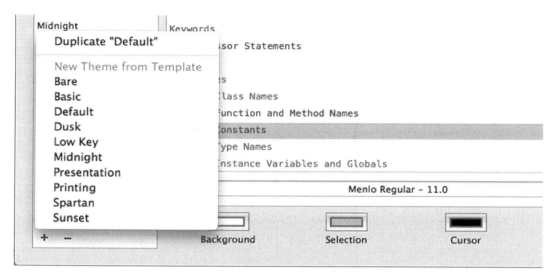

Figure 10-10. *The Add menu in the themes list*

Select Midnight and a new version of the Midnight theme will be added to your themes list, as shown in Figure 10-11. At this point you can change the name of the theme to anything you want, I'll name my theme Matt's Midnight; call your theme whatever suits your fancy.

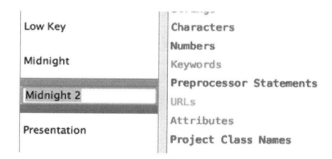

Figure 10-11. *The new theme, ready to be customized*

There may be a time where you get bored with your theme and want to remove it; this is done by clicking the minus symbol next to the + symbol in the themes list.

Sharing or Importing a Theme

You've spent hours customizing your theme to suit your preferences, fine-tuning every syntax category until the color and tone are perfect, and now you want to share it with the world. The good news is that this is really easy to do!

All the themes you create are stored on your computer in a dvtcolortheme file format; to locate these files, start by opening the Finder and then from the menu bar select Go. The option for Library is hidden by default, but if you press the Option (⌥) key you will see Library appear; choose Library and the user library will appear, as shown in Figure 10-12.

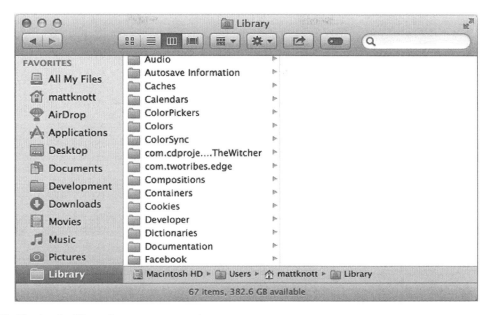

Figure 10-12. Viewing the Library for my user account

The path to the themes is quite deep within the library; start by selecting the Developer folder, then Xcode ➤ UserData ➤ FontAndColorThemes. In here, I have several custom themes, including Matt's Midnight.dvtcolortheme, as shown in Figure 10-13. From here, you can add themes you've downloaded from the Internet or copy them to share online.

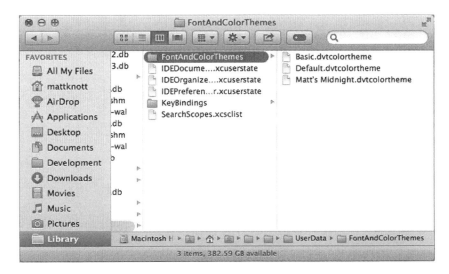

Figure 10-13. The contents of my FontsAndColorThemes folder

> **Note**   The FontAndColorThemes folder is only visible if you have duplicated a theme, so if you skipped the previous section, you may not see this folder.
>
> Whenever you make changes in this folder you must restart Xcode for those changes to take effect.

Now, back in Xcode, choose the theme you're happiest with and close the preferences by clicking the red ball in the top left corner. You now know everything there is to know about themes in Xcode! Next, I'll start delving into the code for AlientDev and show you how to make dealing with large amounts of code less of a chore.

Organizing and Navigating Code

You've now learned how to alter the visual appearance of code, so it's time to go a bit deeper and look at the fantastic shortcuts Xcode provides to help us be super efficient in how we code. In order to demonstrate some of the finer points of organizing and navigating through code, you'll first need to add that code. At this point, you've added the assets to display in the Sprite Kit scene, but if you were to run the application, it would still have all the behaviors of the default Sprite Kit template. The first thing you need to do is make some modifications to ViewController.m so that the stage is set for adding the hero and the villainous bugs.

Start by opening ViewController.m from the Project Navigator. Because you're using a landscape-only orientation and because of the point at which viewDidLoad is called, you need to create a method that performs the initialization once the view has been added to the stack. This method is called viewWillLayoutSubviews, and you need to add it in just after viewDidLoad, as shown below:

```objc
- (void)viewDidLoad
{
    [super viewDidLoad];

    // Configure the view.
    SKView * skView = (SKView *)self.view;
    skView.showsFPS = YES;
    skView.showsNodeCount = YES;

    // Create and configure the scene.
    SKScene * scene = [MyScene sceneWithSize:skView.bounds.size];
    scene.scaleMode = SKSceneScaleModeAspectFill;

    // Present the scene.
    [skView presentScene:scene];
}

- (void)viewWillLayoutSubviews
{
    [super viewWillLayoutSubviews];
}
```

Once you have created the new method with the single line of code, you need to move the bulk of the code from viewDidLoad into viewWillLayoutSubviews. Do this by highlighting all of the code after [super viewDidLoad], as shown in Figure 10-14, and using Edit ➤ Cut (⌘ + X) to cut the code and Edit ➤ Paste (⌘ + V) to paste the code into the method after the line [super viewWillLayoutSubviews].

```
13
14    - (void)viewDidLoad
15    {
16        [super viewDidLoad];
17
18        // Configure the view.
19        SKView * skView = (SKView *)self.view;
20        skView.showsFPS = YES;
21        skView.showsNodeCount = YES;
22
23        // Create and configure the scene.
24        SKScene * scene = [MyScene sceneWithSize:skView.bounds.size];
25        scene.scaleMode = SKSceneScaleModeAspectFill;
26
27        // Present the scene.
28        [skView presentScene:scene];
29    }
30
31    - (void)viewWillLayoutSubviews
32    {
33        [super viewWillLayoutSubviews];
35    }
```

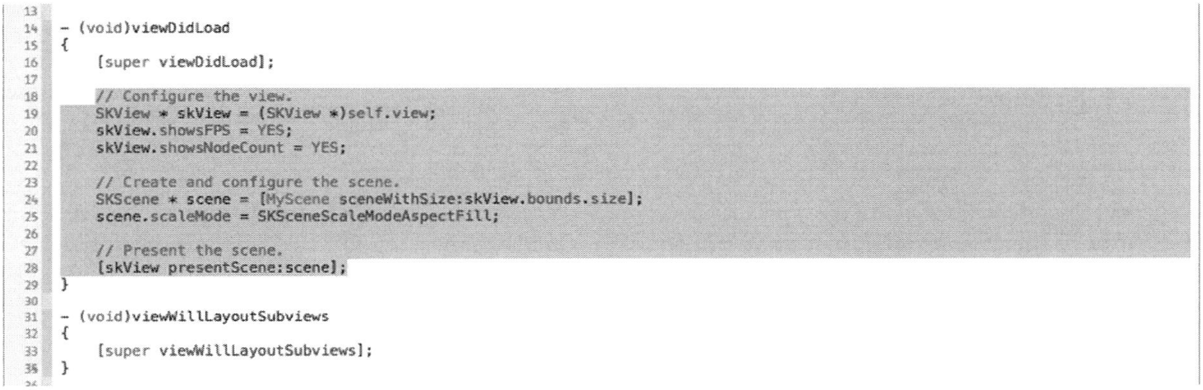

Figure 10-14. *Highlighting the code in the viewDidLoad method that needs to be moved*

After moving the code, the finished structure of the two methods should resemble the code shown below:

```
- (void)viewDidLoad
{
    [super viewDidLoad];
}

- (void)viewWillLayoutSubviews
{
    [super viewWillLayoutSubviews];

    // Configure the view.
    SKView * skView = (SKView *)self.view;
    skView.showsFPS = YES;
    skView.showsNodeCount = YES;

    // Create and configure the scene.
    SKScene * scene = [MyScene sceneWithSize:skView.bounds.size];
    scene.scaleMode = SKSceneScaleModeAspectFill;

    // Present the scene.
    [skView presentScene:scene];
}
```

The outcome of any code tutorial is usually a known entity, but in this case let's pretend we don't know what's going to happen as we develop this application. You've emptied all of the bespoke code from the override of the viewDidLoad method, because it was effectively just taking up space at this point, but you *might* need it in the future. So let's set a reminder to clean up the method if it doesn't get used.

Creating Code Reminders

Xcode provides several handy tags that can be added into code to help us remember to deal with different tasks such as adding code to a method, fixing something that isn't quite right but doesn't break the compiler, and sometimes just to add a general reminder to either research something further or double check whether you've added all the required elements to a view. Xcode has something for all of these eventualities in the form of tags that can be added into the code comments.

In Objective-C, you comment a single line of code by prefixing it with two forward slashes (//); if you then start your comment in one of the following four ways, Xcode will detect it and display it in the jump bar, which I'll explain shortly:

> // TODO: Todo reminders should be used when you want to create a quick reminder about a piece of work you haven't done. This can be great when you're writing a large method and you want to focus on the key functionality, but know that you need to come back later and write the error checking.

> // FIXME: I use fixme mainly when transitioning code between two versions of iOS. When iOS 7 came out, many of my iOS 6 applications developed small glitches. I pinpointed these glitches in one go, adding fixme comments to the errors of concern so that I could work through them one by one, ticking them off.

> // !!!: I don't often use this, but it is part of Xcode nonetheless; a good scenario where I have used it in the past is when I've used something that added a significant amount of memory usage onto my application. I commented it with this code in the same way a cleaner uses a yellow sign to signify a slippery floor, except I was highlighting slippery code.

> // ???: Finally, when you've done something either following a book or tutorial, or you've got some code you want to research further, mark it with ??? as a reminder to delve into the documentation when you have a spare minute.

Because this is something you'll want to look at later on, let's use the TODO mark to set a reminder. After the line [super viewDidLoad]; add your TODO comment so the method looks like this:

```
- (void)viewDidLoad
{
    [super viewDidLoad];

    //TODO: Cleanup if not used
}
```

> **Note**   These code words are case sensitive, if you use any lower case characters or fail to use the colon correctly, they will not display in the jump bar.

That's it, you've added a handy reference that will stand out in the jump bar like a sore thumb and remind you to tidy your code when you finish the application.

Using the Jump Bar

I've mentioned the jump bar several times, so now let's take a closer look at it. The jump bar is the series of items at the top of the code view, as shown in Figure 10-15. It's called the jump bar because, depending on which part you choose, it allows you to quickly jump between files, folders, and different areas of a code file.

Figure 10-15. The jump bar is located at the top of the code window

The very last block of the jump bar, which in Figure 10-15 says No Selection, is by far the most interesting. For many developers this *is* the jump bar, and it is the only part of the jump bar they will ever use. Select this block of the jump bar and you should see the effect of the added TODO comment, as shown in Figure 10-16. Although there are many comments in the code, the only one that appears in the jump view among the methods is the cleanup message.

Figure 10-16. The structure of the code outlined in the jump view

Notice in the jump bar that each of the methods is listed, as well as the class implementation. Selecting any of these will take you directly to the relevant portion of code.

Organizing Code with Pragma Marks

If you have any experience programming with a C-based language, you are probably familiar with the #pragma directive. Traditionally it is used to provide additional information to the compiler outside of what the language itself can express. It can also provide additional information to the IDE by using the #pragma mark directive to create sections for the methods in the jump bar.

Let's say we wanted to isolate the bottom three methods in the `ViewController.m` file, we could add a directive to indicate that these methods are not to be touched. Before the `- (BOOL) shouldAutorotate` method, type the following code:

```
#pragma mark Standard Methods : Ignore
```

Now go back and look at what the jump view shows for the code file and you'll see, as shown in Figure 10-17, the mark has been added to the hierarchy and now provides a heading for the bottom three methods.

Figure 10-17. *The mark appearing in the jump bar to isolate the standard methods*

These marks are incredibly useful, especially when you're working with dozens of methods. Grouping your methods together by area of function makes your life easier and also that of anyone else who needs to look at your code.

Building the Scene

Unlike other applications you have built so far in this book, a Sprite Kit application doesn't need much work within the View Controller, which just initializes the environment. All of the logic that controls what you'll see on the screen comes from the Scene. By default, the Sprite Kit application comes with two custom classes: `ViewController` and `MyScene`. Open `MyScene.h` and you will see that it subclasses `SKScene`.

In a Sprite Kit application, the scene is responsible for calculating what is shown on screen in each frame. Let's modify `MyScene` to add the alien dev hero onto the screen, before swamping him with bugs.

1.   If you haven't already, open `MyScene.h`. Start by creating an `SKSpriteNode` property called `alienDev`; you'll use this property to hold all of the information for the alien dev's character in the scene. Add the property into the scene so that the code resembles the following:

```
#import <SpriteKit/SpriteKit.h>

@interface MyScene : SKScene

@property (nonatomic, retain) SKSpriteNode *alienDev;

@end
```

2. With the property in place, let's switch to `MyScene.m`. Just as you did with the View Controller, let's remove all of the code and methods that are not needed, leaving a clean slate into which you can add your own logic and methods. Scroll down and remove the method called `touchesBegan`.

3. Next, let's make some changes to the `initWithSize` method. Remove all of the code within the `if (self = [super initWithSize:size])` brackets; your completed implementation file should resemble the following code:

```
#import "MyScene.h"

@implementation MyScene

-(id)initWithSize:(CGSize)size {
    if (self = [super initWithSize:size]) {

    }
    return self;
}

@end
```

4. Now let's start to set the scene for the application by setting the background color and initializing and adding the `alienDev` object. The `SKScene` object is always the root node hierarchy of Sprite Kit nodes; let's add the sprites into the scene to start creating the hierarchy. Inside the `if` statement, add the following code:

```
self.backgroundColor = [SKColor whiteColor];

self.alienDev = [SKSpriteNode spriteNodeWithImageNamed:@"dev"];
self.alienDev.position = CGPointMake(CGRectGetMidX(self.frame),
CGRectGetMidY(self.frame));

[self addChild:self.alienDev];
```

5. Go ahead and run the application. If everything works as it should, the lonely hero should stand alone in the middle of the screen, as shown in Figure 10-18, along with the node and fps (frames per second) counts. These two values are great for debugging poor performance in your animation and can help to identify choke points where you may have too many sprites (nodes) on the screen at any one time. They can also help you scale your application for different devices; more capable hardware can handle more sprites without a drop in performance, whereas an older device may need to have lower quality images and fewer sprites. When you're finished with them, you can disable them by changing the `showsFPS` and `showsNodeCount` properties of the `SKView` to NO in `ViewController.m`.

Figure 10-18. The AlienDev app in action, with the single, static sprite

6. The hero is a bit lonely on the screen, which looks quite sparse. Before you add his nemesis, the bug, let's add a title to the scene as another node, which will be an instance of the SKLabelNode class. Although this will be the only text you add, adding text nodes to the scene is a common requirement, so let's be efficient and create a method to add whatever text you send it to the scene. Start by dropping down a few lines after the initWithSize method and add the following method stub:

```
- (SKLabelNode *)createTextNode:(NSString *)text nodeName:(NSString *)nodeName
position:(CGPoint)position
{

}
```

7. This method returns an SKLabelNode object, so the first thing you should do is to declare and initialize an object of this class ready to be returned. Inside the method, add the following line of code:

```
SKLabelNode *labelNode = [SKLabelNode labelNodeWithFontNamed:@"Chalkduster"];
```

8. Next let's set the attributes of the labelNode object to set the text, size, color, and position of the label, as well as give it a name as an identifier. Once the attributes are set, you will return the label. Add the following code after the last line:

```
labelNode.name = nodeName;
labelNode.text = text;
labelNode.fontSize = 30;
labelNode.fontColor = [SKColor blackColor];
labelNode.position = position;

return labelNode;
```

Note   Sprite Kit applications do not use UIKit as our other solutions have, so in this instance you will use SKColor to set the color rather than UIColor. They are separate classes in separate frameworks but perform largely the same function.

9. Now that you have a method for generating labels, let's give the application a title. Go back to the initWithSize method and after the line [self addChild:self.alienDev]; add the following code:

```
SKLabelNode *title = [self createTextNode:@"Welcome to Alien Dev"
                                 nodeName:@"titleNode"
                                 position:CGPointMake(CGRectGetMidX(self.frame), 280)];

[self addChild:title];
```

10. Run the application again. This time it will look a little less sparse, as you can see in Figure 10-19.

Figure 10-19. *The application, now with two nodes, the dev and the title*

11. You've now got everything in this scene except the bugs that will plague the hero. In this application, the bugs will appear from the top of the screen and slide down toward the hero—the alien dev. To achieve this, let's create a method that adds a bug at a random position off screen. This will then be called by another method at a regular interval. Start by adding the stub for this method beneath the `createTextNode` method:

```
- (void)createBug
{

}
```

12. This will be a particularly large method, and as in previous chapters, I won't dwell too much on the actual code, just how Xcode ultimately makes it easy to manage and interact with this code. In pseudo code, let's create an `SKSpriteNode` as you did when you initialized the dev character. Let's set the bug to appear just off screen above the top of the screen, but then randomly determine where it "spawns" on the x (horizontal) axis. After adding the bug

to the scene, you'll indicate how long it should appear and then send it down the screen before it disappears and is removed from the scene. Add the following code into the createBug method:

```
- (void)createBug
{
    SKSpriteNode * evilbug = [SKSpriteNode spriteNodeWithImageNamed:@"bug"];

    int minX = evilbug.size.width / 2;
    int maxX = self.frame.size.width - evilbug.size.width / 2;
    int rangeX = maxX - minX;
    int finalX = (arc4random() % rangeX) + minX;

    evilbug.position = CGPointMake(finalX, self.frame.size.height + evilbug.size.
height/2);
    [self addChild:evilbug];

    int minDuration = 3.0;
    int maxDuration = 8.0;
    int rangeDuration = maxDuration - minDuration;
    int finalDuration = (arc4random() % rangeDuration) + minDuration;

    SKAction * actionMove = [SKAction moveTo:CGPointMake(finalX, -evilbug.size.height/2)
                                    duration:finalDuration];
    SKAction * actionMoveDone = [SKAction removeFromParent];
    [evilbug runAction:[SKAction sequence:@[actionMove, actionMoveDone]]];
}
```

Folding Code

The implementation file is really starting to fill out now, but there are still two methods and some instance variables to add in so that you can see the application in all its glory. Xcode kindly provides a way to make this file easier to navigate and modify in the shape of code folding.

Code folding isn't unique to Xcode and the concept exists in many popular IDEs and code editors, but it's maybe not as obvious how to access it in Xcode as it is in those other systems. Code folding is the concept of compressing code that is encapsulated by brackets, such as in methods and if statements, or some other logical structure into a single line, thus hiding the code from view and allowing the developer to focus on a specific segment of code. You can fold code within the editor itself as well as through menus and key combinations.

First, let's look at code folding and how it is done within the editor. Scroll to the top of the MyScene implementation file to the start of the initWithSize method. Move your mouse cursor to the gutter between the code and the line number just adjacent to the start of the method, as shown in Figure 10-20.

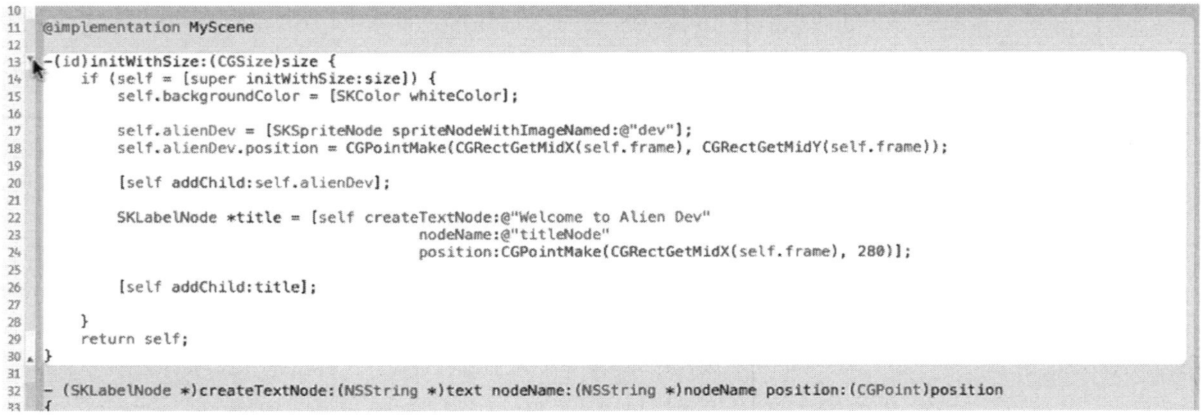

```
10
11  @implementation MyScene
12
13  -(id)initWithSize:(CGSize)size {
14      if (self = [super initWithSize:size]) {
15          self.backgroundColor = [SKColor whiteColor];
16
17          self.alienDev = [SKSpriteNode spriteNodeWithImageNamed:@"dev"];
18          self.alienDev.position = CGPointMake(CGRectGetMidX(self.frame), CGRectGetMidY(self.frame));
19
20          [self addChild:self.alienDev];
21
22          SKLabelNode *title = [self createTextNode:@"Welcome to Alien Dev"
23                                           nodeName:@"titleNode"
24                                           position:CGPointMake(CGRectGetMidX(self.frame), 280)];
25
26          [self addChild:title];
27
28      }
29      return self;
30  }
31
32  - (SKLabelNode *)createTextNode:(NSString *)text nodeName:(NSString *)nodeName position:(CGPoint)position
33  {
```

Figure 10-20. *Exposing the fold toggle in the code editor*

You will notice that a downward-pointing arrow appears and Xcode highlights all of the code that will be hidden if you click the mouse on that area of the gutter. The first line of the method is an `if` statement; move the pointer down one line and you will see Xcode adjust the highlighted area. Move the cursor back to the original position adjacent to the method declaration and click the mouse button. The entire method will be compressed, as shown in Figure 10-21. As you can see in the figure, the code shrinks to a single line, greatly reducing the visual clutter in the code. Notice that in the gutter you now have a right-pointing arrow. Click this arrow and your method will be restored.

```
8
9   #import "MyScene.h"
10
11  @implementation MyScene
12
13  -(id)initWithSize:(CGSize)size {⋯}
31
32  - (SKLabelNode *)createTextNode:(NSString *)text nodeName:(NSString *)nodeName position:(CGPoint)position
33  {
34      SKLabelNode *labelNode = [SKLabelNode labelNodeWithFontNamed:@"Chalkduster"];
35
36      labelNode.name = nodeName;
37      labelNode.text = text;
38      labelNode.fontSize = 30;
39      labelNode.fontColor = [SKColor blackColor];
40      labelNode.position = position;
41
42      return labelNode;
43  }
```

Figure 10-21. *The "folded" initWithSize method*

Folding one method at a time can be time consuming, which is where the menu options come into play. From the menu bar select Editor ➤ Code Folding. As you can see in Figure 10-22, Xcode gives us a number of options for folding the code in this file. There are the general Fold and Unfold options and an Unfold All option. Where Xcode separates itself from other lesser IDEs is that you also have the option to specifically Fold Methods & Functions or to Fold Comment Blocks. This fine level of control is really satisfying for developers who like to fold methods but not comments, rather than folding everything that could possibly be folded.

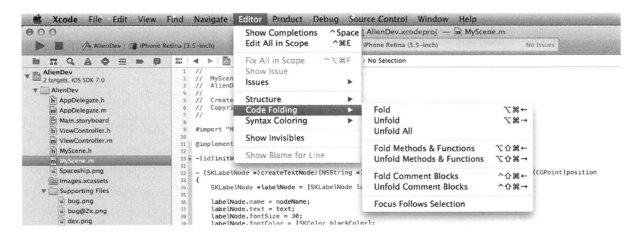

Figure 10-22. Options offered in Xcode's Editor tab

Select the Fold Methods & Functions option. Instantly, the implementation is compressed from 60 lines to just 10, as shown in Figure 10-23!

```
9    #import "MyScene.h"
10
11   @implementation MyScene
12
13 ▶ -(id)initWithSize:(CGSize)size {⋯}
31
32   - (SKLabelNode *)createTextNode:(NSString *)text nodeName:(NSString *)nodeName position:(CGPoint)position
33 ▶ {⋯}
44
45   - (void)createBug
46 ▶ {⋯}
60
```

Figure 10-23. The neatly folded implementation file

Now that there is some room to breathe in the implementation file, you can add the remaining two methods and the instance variables. The following code is actually provided by Apple as part of its Sprite Kit adventure template and it allows you to call the createBug method at a regular interval.

At the top of MyScene.m you'll need to add two instance variables, so let's modify the @implementation MyScene line to match the following code:

```
@implementation MyScene
{
    NSTimeInterval lastSpawnTimeInterval;
    NSTimeInterval lastUpdateTimeInterval;
}
```

These variables will be used to calculate the time elapsed between each frame. Next you will create one method stub and use one existing one to handle the updates: updateWithTimeSinceLastUpdate and update. The update method is a class method that gets called each frame and updateWithTimeSinceLastUpdate is a custom method that ensures the bugs are added at a constant rate. Add the updateWithTimeSinceLastUpdate method stub before the update method in the implementation file with the following code:

```
- (void)updateWithTimeSinceLastUpdate:(CFTimeInterval)timeSinceLast {
}

- (void)update:(NSTimeInterval)currentTime {

}
```

In the update method, add the highlighted code, which accurately calculates the elapsed time and calls the custom method:

```
- (void)update:(NSTimeInterval)currentTime {
    CFTimeInterval timeSinceLast = currentTime - lastUpdateTimeInterval;
    lastUpdateTimeInterval = currentTime;
    if (timeSinceLast > 1) {
        timeSinceLast = 1.0 / 60.0;
        lastUpdateTimeInterval = currentTime;
    }

    [self updateWithTimeSinceLastUpdate:timeSinceLast];
}
```

For the last method in this implementation file, let's look at another weapon in the efficient developers arsenal—code snippets.

The Code Snippet Library

The Code Snippet library is a collection of small pieces of code, like microtemplates, that allow you to quickly create commonly written blocks of code by simply dragging and dropping the code into the code editor. Code snippets, like code folding, is not a concept that is unique to Xcode, but like code folding, it is implemented in a clear and intuitive manner.

The Code Snippet library, shown in Figure 10-24, is located in the utilities bar and is accessed by clicking the { } icon (control + ⌥ + ⌘ + 2).

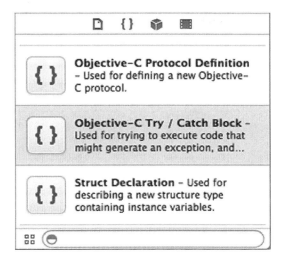

Figure 10-24. The Code Snippet library

Using Code Snippets

I'll explain how to create an `if` statement using a code snippet, but before you can do that, you'll need to add a line of code to the `updateWithTimeSinceLastUpdate` method. Add the following line to the method to update the `lastSpawnTimeInterval` object:

```
lastSpawnTimeInterval += timeSinceLast;
```

You'll want to spawn a bug every 1 second, so you need an `if` statement to check that the `lastSpawnTimeInterval` object, which counts milliseconds, is greater than 1. Look in the Code Snippet library for If Statement or type "if state" in the filter box, as shown in Figure 10-25.

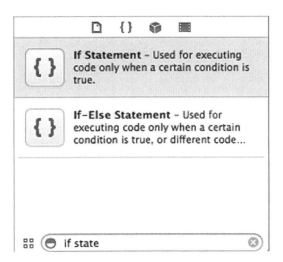

Figure 10-25. Filtering the Code Snippet library for an if statement

Create an empty line under the last line of code you added, and then drag the If Statement from the Code Snippet library, positioning just below that last line of code, as shown in Figure 10-26.

```
48
49     - (void)createBug
50  ▶  {⸱⸱⸱}
72
73     - (void)updateWithTimeSinceLastUpdate:(CFTimeInterval)timeSinceLast {
74
75         lastSpawnTimeInterval += timeSinceLast;
76     |
77     }          { }
78
79     - (void)update:(NSTimeInterval)currentTime {
80         CFTimeInterval timeSinceLast = currentTime - lastUpdateTimeInterval;
81         lastUpdateTimeInterval = currentTime;
82         if (timeSinceLast > 1) {
83             timeSinceLast = 1.0 / 60.0;
84             lastUpdateTimeInterval = currentTime;
```

Figure 10-26. Dragging an if statement from the Code Snippet library

When you release the snippet, it will create the outline of the if statement exactly as it does when you use the code completion method for creating if statements. Change the conditions placeholder to say lastSpawnTimeInterval > 1 and the statements to lastSpawnTimeInterval = 0; and then [self createBug];.

Your finished method code will look like this:

```
- (void)updateWithTimeSinceLastUpdate:(CFTimeInterval)timeSinceLast {

    lastSpawnTimeInterval += timeSinceLast;
    if (lastSpawnTimeInterval > 1) {
        lastSpawnTimeInterval = 0;
        [self createBug];
    }
}
```

Using code snippets to create an if statement isn't the most efficient way to use them, but look through the list of snippets—there are dozens of premade snippets for a wide range of scenarios.

Creating Code Snippets

Where code snippets come into their own is when you create them from your own code. You know better than anyone else the code you type time and again—whether it's a template for a web request or a pattern you use for error handling—so creating code snippets is a great way to simplify code reuse.

Now for the paradox of creating code snippets—it's as easy as drag and drop, but drag and drop isn't necessarily easy. To explain, you create a code snippet by highlighting the code you wish to save and dragging it into the Code Snippet library. Unfortunately, if you try this, you will probably find you just end up selecting different code when you try to drag; this is where the art of dragging code in Xcode comes into play.

Let's say you want to save the last two methods you created as they are the best way to perform a Sprite Kit action at a regular interval. Start by highlighting the code, as shown in Figure 10-27.

```
72
73   - (void)updateWithTimeSinceLastUpdate:(CFTimeInterval)timeSinceLast {
74
75       lastSpawnTimeInterval += timeSinceLast;
76       if (lastSpawnTimeInterval > 1) {
77           lastSpawnTimeInterval = 0;
78           [self createBug];
79       }
80   }
81
82   - (void)update:(NSTimeInterval)currentTime {
83       CFTimeInterval timeSinceLast = currentTime - lastUpdateTimeInterval;
84       lastUpdateTimeInterval = currentTime;
85       if (timeSinceLast > 1) {
86           timeSinceLast = 1.0 / 60.0;
87           lastUpdateTimeInterval = currentTime;
88       }
89
90       [self updateWithTimeSinceLastUpdate:timeSinceLast];
91   }
```

Figure 10-27. The highlighted code that you want to create a snippet from

Now, the technique—click and *hold* the mouse point in place until it changes from an I bar to a normal mouse cursor and drag the code to the Code Snippet library, as shown in Figure 10-28.

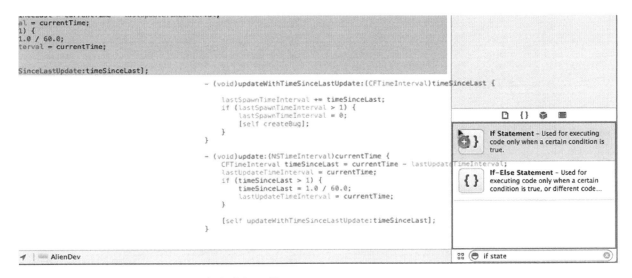

Figure 10-28. Dragging the code to the Code Snippet library

When you release the mouse, it will create an entry in the library called My Code Snippet. To save it from getting lost, it's important to name the snippet and set its attributes before you forget why you created it. Double-click the snippet to see a preview of the code, as shown in Figure 10-29; click the Edit button.

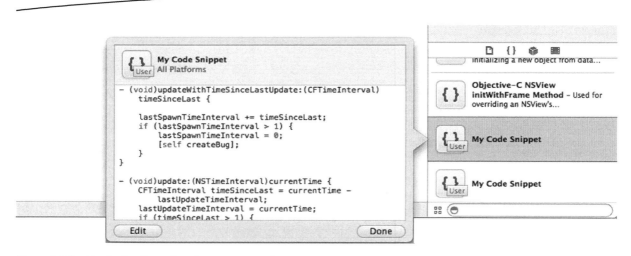

Figure 10-29. Previewing the code snippet you created

You can see that you can now edit the entire code snippet here, but what you want to do is set the Title to SKScene Update Methods, the Platform to iOS, and the Completion Shortcut to SKU, as shown in Figure 10-30, then click Done.

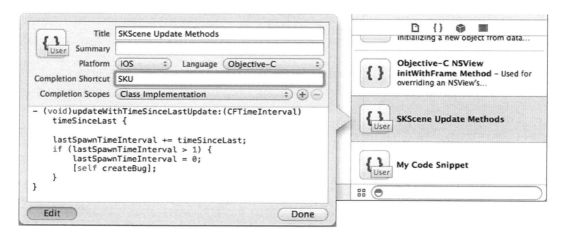

Figure 10-30. Setting the properties of the snippet

You can see as soon as the Title property is set, it is updated in the library. One important value you set is the Completion Shortcut. I mentioned earlier that an `if` statement isn't the most efficient use of a code snippet, but in fact the drag and drop of the code snippet wasn't efficient because you have learned that when you type `if` in the code editor, you can press the Tab key to complete the entire statement, which is faster than dragging the snippet. All that actually happens is when you type `if`, it sees that you have a snippet in your library with a completion shortcut of `if`. Go to your code editor and after the last method, type SKU. You will see that you can now quickly create the two update methods in your snippet simply by typing that completion shortcut, as shown in Figure 10-31.

Figure 10-31. *Quickly adding the snippet to the implementation file*

It's this feature that exemplifies how Xcode has many of the same features you will find in other IDEs, but Apple has taken the concept and refined it to make the developer's life so much easier. All that remains now is to run the application and watch the alien dev being bombarded by bugs, as shown in Figure 10-32.

Figure 10-32. *The completed AlienDev application*

Summary

This chapter used a Sprite Kit application as a backdrop to show the numerous ways Xcode can help reduce the overhead of writing code by streamlining how you code and by fine-tuning the development environment to suit your personal preferences.

Specifically in this chapter, you've learned:

- How to select a theme for the code editor
- How to customize a theme, share it, and import third-party themes
- Which keywords to use in code comments and when to use them
- How to use the jump bar to quickly navigate to a block of code or a comment
- How to fold blocks of code to allow you to focus on specific areas of the code
- How to create and use code snippets to allow you to reuse code

The next chapter will take a detailed look at how to debug issues in applications and how Xcode can give insight into what's going on behind the scenes.

Chapter 11

Debugging and Analysis

Chapter 10 looked at some of the ways Xcode could empower you to be a more effective and efficient developer, from tweaking the theme used to display your code to using the jump bar and code snippets to speed up development. You learned all of that by creating a Sprite Kit–based animation application where the hero, the alien dev, had bugs raining down on him from above.

This leads us nicely into this chapter, where you'll learn about debugging and analysis and hopefully answer the question "How can Xcode help when the bugs start raining down?" Xcode has a whole suite of tools dedicated to making your life easier when it comes to determining why your code throws an exception or why in some cases nothing happens at all. This chapter will take a detailed look at all of these reasons. Additionally, I'll discuss some of the lesser-known debugging tools that aren't integrated into Xcode but are essential as you explore the breadth of the features of iOS application development with Xcode.

This chapter will initially focus on three common debugging scenarios and how Xcode can be used to address them:

- *Logic errors*: Sometimes the hardest to debug, logic errors occur when your application doesn't do what you expect it to do, but it doesn't cause your application to trigger an exception or warning at either compile time or runtime. Examples of this would be a button that doesn't do anything or a Map View not displaying the specified area.

- *Runtime errors*: A runtime error is an error that is detected after the application has compiled and it is either launching or running. Unhandled runtime errors will usually be fatal to the application and cause it to crash.

- *Compile-time errors*: When you tell Xcode to Run or Build your application, it uses the compiler to take all of your code, linked files, and libraries and compile them into a binary. A compile-time error will stop your application from compiling into a binary, so it must be resolved before you can run the application.

This chapter will explain how to create an application that lists some of the European Union (abbreviated to EU throughout this chapter) member states in a Table View, which we will call EUStates. The Table View will use an array as its data source, which is traditionally a great way of demonstrating runtime and logic errors because of their precise nature (they have a set number of items, and going outside of those bounds can trigger a runtime or a logic error).

Building the Application

EUStates will be a very simple application to build. The focus here is on how to use Xcode to debug an application, so the code will be minimal. To create the EUStates application, let's start with a Single View Application template and add in a Table View Controller. Many of these steps will be familiar to you from when you created the Twitter client in Chapters 7 and 8.

1. To begin, start by opening Xcode and then create a new project by going to File ➤ New ➤ New Project … (⌘ + Shift + N) or, alternatively, Create a new Xcode project if you are on the Welcome screen (⌘ + Shift + 1).

2. Select the Single View Application Template and click Next.

3. Name the project EUStates, substitute your personal information for mine, and leave the other options as default, but ensure the device is set to iPhone, as shown in Figure 11-1. Click Next.

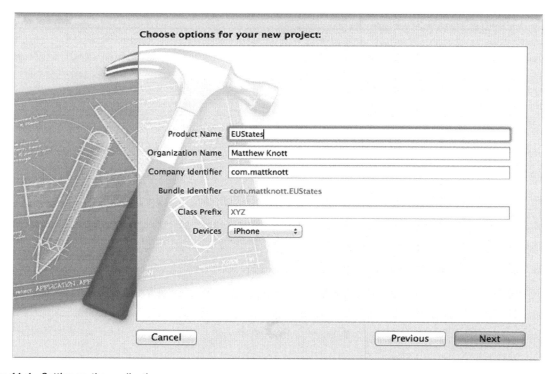

Figure 11-1. Setting up the application

4. The default save location is okay, so create the application by clicking
    Create. Next open `Main.storyboard` from the Project Navigator; this presents
    a single view on the Storyboard, select it and remove it so that you are left
    with a blank canvas, as shown in Figure 11-2.

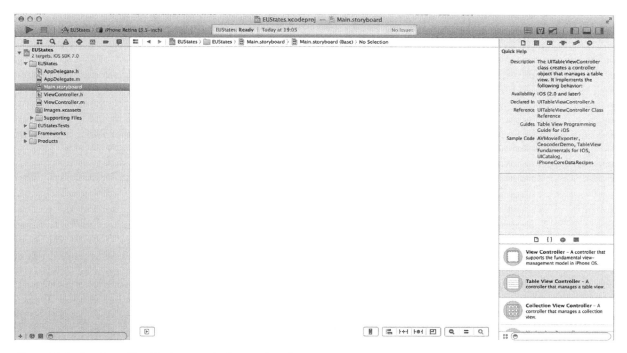

Figure 11-2. Starting with a blank canvas in the storyboard

5. To complete the initial set up of the application, select `ViewController.h`
    and `ViewController.m` in the Project Navigator and remove them either by
    pressing the Backspace key or by right-clicking them and selecting Delete
    and then Move to Trash when prompted.

6. The application is based around a single Table View Controller, so that means
    you need to subclass `UITableViewController` to create a custom view
    controller and then tie that into a Table View Controller on the storyboard.
    Start by selecting File ➤ New ➤ File ... (⌘ + N) and choosing Objective-C
    Class from the list of templates and click Next.

7. Set the Subclass of value to UITableViewController and the Class value to
    StatesViewController. Leave Targeted for iPad and With XIB for user interface
    unticked and click Next. Finally, accept the default location to save the new
    class files and click Create.

8.   Next, let's add the Table View Controller to the storyboard. Open
      `Main.storyboard` from the Project Navigator. Open the Object Library and
      locate the Table View Controller object near the top of the list.

9.   Drag a Table View Controller onto the storyboard's design area, as shown in
      Figure 11-3. When you release the Table View Controller, you will notice that
      the arrow indicating the initial scene in the storyboard appears automatically.

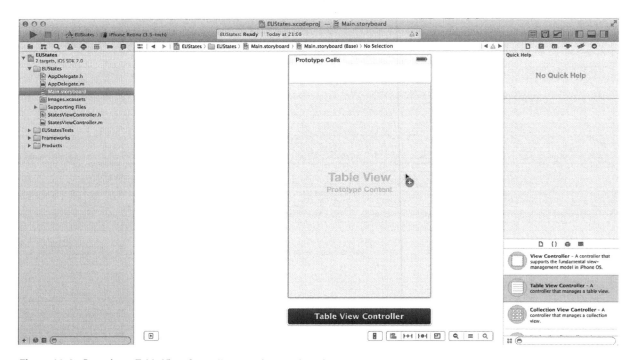

Figure 11-3. *Dragging a Table View Controller onto the storyboard*

10.   Next you'll specify the class for the new Table View Controller. If Table View
      Controller isn't select it, do so and then open the Identity Inspector. Change
      the Class value to StatesViewController, as shown in Figure 11-4.

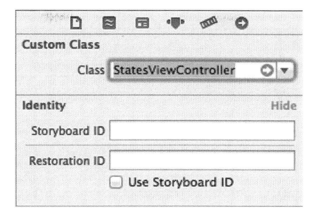

Figure 11-4. Setting the Class value for the Table View Controller to StatesViewController

11. With the structure of the application complete, it's now time to create the array that will hold the EU member states. This is done by creating an NSMutableArray as an instance variable and then populating it in a custom method. Open StatesViewController.m from the Project Navigator; to declare the instance variable, add the highlighted code to the implementation file as shown below:

```
@interface StatesViewController ()
{
    NSMutableArray *states;
}
```

12. Next you'll create a method to initialize the array and populate it with 15 EU member states. After the viewDidLoad method, let's create a new method called initStates, drop down a few lines and create the following method stub:

```
-(void)initStates
{

}
```

13. To initialize the NSMutableArray, you'll use that class's initWithCapacity method to specify how many items it can initially hold, then you'll add string values for the first 15 member states to the array. Add the highlighted code to the method:

```
-(void)initStates
{
    states = [[NSMutableArray alloc] initWithCapacity:15];
    states[0] = @"Austria";
    states[1] = @"Belgium";
    states[2] = @"Bulgaria";
    states[3] = @"Croatia";
```

```
            states[4]  = @"Cyprus";
            states[5]  = @"Czech Republic";
            states[6]  = @"Denmark";
            states[7]  = @"Estonia";
            states[8]  = @"Finland";
            states[9]  = @"France";
            states[10] = @"Germany";
            states[11] = @"Greece";
            states[12] = @"Hungary";
            states[13] = @"Ireland";
            states[14] = @"Italy";
        }
```

14. Now that you have a data source, all that remains is to use the states array to populate the Table View. You might recall from Chapter 8 that there are three methods that need to be altered: `numberOfSectionsInTableView`, `numberOfRowsInSection`, and `cellForRowAtIndexPath`. All of these methods sit beneath `#pragma mark - Table view data source`; click the jump bar and you will see that this pragma mark is used to neatly separate the Table View methods from the rest of the View Controller. Select -numberOfSectionsInTableView:, as shown in Figure 11-5.

Figure 11-5. *Selecting the –numberOfSectionsInTableView: method from the jump bar*

15. You'll be taken directly to the method. The first thing you need to do is remove the `#warning` preprocessor that is shown in Figure 11-6. Xcode adds the warning to this and the `numberOfRowsInSection` method to remind you to complete the set up of these critical methods. Remove the entire line and set the method to return 1 instead of 0.

```
63    #pragma mark - Table view data source
64
65    - (NSInteger)numberOfSectionsInTableView:(UITableView *)tableView
66    {
67    #warning Potentially incomplete method implementation.                    ⚠ Potentially incomplete method implementation.
68        // Return the number of sections.
69        return 0;
70    }
71
72    - (NSInteger)tableView:(UITableView *)tableView numberOfRowsInSection:(NSInteger)section
73    {
74    #warning Incomplete method implementation.                                ⚠ Incomplete method implementation.
75        // Return the number of rows in the section.
76        return 0;
77    }
78
```

Figure 11-6. Two key Table View methods with #warning elements to remind the developer they need to be completed

16.   Next, move down to the numberOfRowsInSection method; this method will dictate how many rows to render in the Table View's section. First, remove the #warning line and then focus on the number of rows to create. Because you want this to be the number of elements in your array, you'll simply return states.count. Your finished methods should now resemble the following code:

```
- (NSInteger)numberOfSectionsInTableView:(UITableView *)tableView
{
    return 1;
}

- (NSInteger)tableView:(UITableView *)tableView numberOfRowsInSection:(NSInteger)section
{
    return states.count;
}
```

17.   The final part of this implementation is to set the text of the table cell to the value of the corresponding index in the array. You'll use a string formatted to append the index number onto the table cell so that each cell will appear along the lines of 2: Bulgaria. Go to the cellForRowAtIndexPath method and remove the comment that says // Configure the cell.... In its place type the following code:

```
cell.textLabel.text =
        [NSString stringWithFormat:@"%i: %@", indexPath.row, states[indexPath.row]];
```

That's the last of the code you'll need to write for this application. Now you can run the application in the simulator. Unfortunately, when the application runs, not a lot happens, as shown in Figure 11-7. All the methods are set correctly, so where's the problem? To get to the bottom of this conundrum you're going to need to see what's happening behind the scenes, and to do that, you're going to need to use breakpoints.

Figure 11-7. *The application running in the simulator, but not doing very much*

Using Breakpoints to Resolve Logical Errors

You've now come across the first issue with the application and need to use Xcode's debugging tools to analyze the problem and understand what has gone wrong and what you need to do to fix it. The first tool in a developer's arsenal is the humble breakpoint.

Breakpoints allow you to specify a point in the application to pause the execution of the code and see what's happening behind the scenes. When a breakpoint is reached and the application pauses, you get to see the state of all of your objects and what values they contain. The application checks the numberOfSectionsInTableView and numberOfRowsInSection methods to set the parameters for the Table View, so these are good places to start the analysis. Because the numberOfSectionsInTableView method returns a fixed value, let's concentrate on the numberOfRowsInSection method first.

Setting a Breakpoint

If you've used other development environments in the past, you may find adding a breakpoint in Xcode is very familiar, and even if you haven't, you will find that the whole process is very intuitive. Scroll down to the `numberOfRowsInSection` method and click the line number next to `return states.count;` to place a breakpoint, as shown in Figure 11-8. When you add a breakpoint, a dark blue arrow will appear on top of the line number.

```
71
72     - (NSInteger)tableView:(UITableView *)
73     {
74         // Return the number of rows in th
75         return states.count;
76     }
77
78     - (UITableViewCell *)tableView:(UITabl
79     {
80         static NSString *CellIdentifier = (
```

Figure 11-8. The breakpoint added for a line of code

During runtime, when this line of code is reached, the application will pause and hopefully provide insight into why there isn't any information in the Table View. Try running the application now. The application will launch in the simulator and then you will be dropped back to Xcode with the Debug Navigator (Figure 11-9), showing the state of the application, and the Debug Area (Figure 11-10), showing a selection of objects that are relevant to where the application has paused.

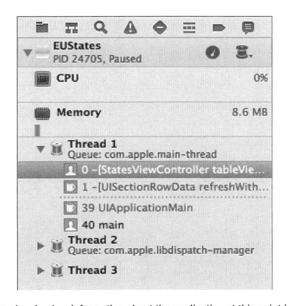

Figure 11-9. The Debug Navigator, showing key information about the application at this point in time

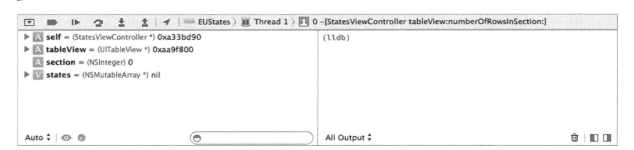

Figure 11-10. *The Debug Area showing a selection of objects relevant in the context of the breakpoint*

Before you look at why the application isn't working, let's examine both of these key areas in some detail to see what information each area provides.

The Debug Navigator

While the application is paused, the Debug Navigator, as shown in Figure 11-11, can be used to provide a live snapshot of the activities taking place within the application by displaying the application's performance in terms of resource usage and call stack of each thread in the thread list.

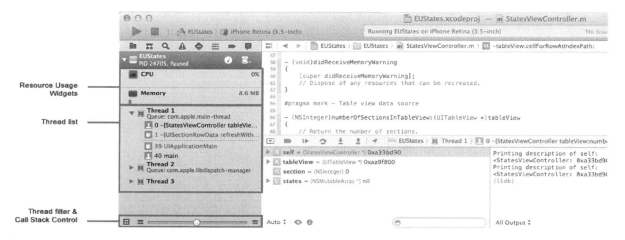

Figure 11-11. *The three key areas of the Debug Navigator shown while debugging an application*

The resource usage is the only portion of the Debug Navigator that shows while the application is running as well as when it's paused. When developing for iOS, memory management is essential, however, the task of ensuring objects are correctly disposed of has been automated to a large extent with the introduction of automatic reference counting (ARC) in iOS 5. Before Xcode 5, ARC could be turned on or off depending on your preference, but with Xcode 5 it is not even presented as an option and is enabled by default for all iOS application templates. ARC basically automates the disposal of objects when they are no longer needed, giving you a lot of insurance against memory leaks.

The thread list and the call stack within each thread show which methods are currently being executed by each thread. You can see from the expanded call stack for the main thread (thread 1) in Figure 11-12 that the currently executed method is the `tableView:numberOfRowsInSection:` method, which was called by [`UISectionRowData refreshWithSection:tableView:tableViewRowData:`]. This can make understanding the flow of your application much easier.

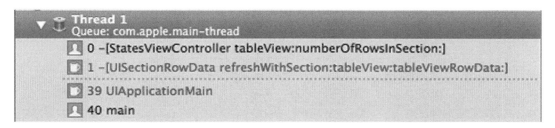

Figure 11-12. *A detailed look at the call stack of the main thread*

An icon adjacent to each thread reflects the status of the thread:

- *No icon*: The thread is running normally.

- *Yellow icon*: The thread is being blocked and is waiting for another thread to be unlocked or a certain condition to be met.

- *Red icon*: The thread has been suspended. While suspended, the thread will not execute any code when you proceed from the breakpoint.

If you refer back to Figure 11-11, you'll notice that the call stack control slider is in the center position. Sliding it to the right will display a more detailed call stack, whereas sliding it to the left will reduce the number of items shown. You can adjust this depending on the depth required for your debugging efforts.

The Debug Area

The Debug Area was covered in some detail in Chapter 3 so I won't go over old ground, but unlike in Chapter 3, the Debug Area has now come to life so you can actually interact with some of the controls and features you learned about earlier in this book.

Referring back to Figure 11-10 and indeed your own instances of Xcode use for a moment, you will notice that the main output of the Debug Area at this time is the list of four variables that are relevant in the context of the method you are paused on. Figure 11-13 shows the control bar for the Debug Area. I explained what each icon means in Chapter 3, but at that time you didn't necessarily have the ability to see what they would do. As you go through the rest of this chapter, feel free to click the buttons to see their effect and then stop and rerun the application to get back to the breakpoint.

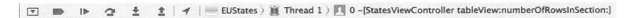

Figure 11-13. *The control bar for the Debug Area*

The buttons that appear in the Debug Area, listed left to right, are:

- *Hide button*: Show or hide the Debug Area.

- *Breakpoint toggle*: Currently in dark blue, clicking this will toggle all breakpoints between enabled and disabled.

- *Continue*: This resumes the execution of the application and then becomes a pause button.

- *Step Over*: This allows you to move out of the function being executed onto the next instruction.

- *Step Into*: This allows you to see in intricate detail each step of the application's execution. Think of this as a film on pause and each time you press Step Into, you move a single frame ahead.

- *Step Out*: Use this if you find that you've stepped too deep into your application's inner workings and want to see the next piece of code being executed.

- *Simulate Location*: I'll explain the functionality of this option later in the chapter.

Beyond these controls, the Debug Area also has its own jump bar. This jump bar shows the threads within the application and, in turn, each thread's call stack, as shown in Figure 11-14.

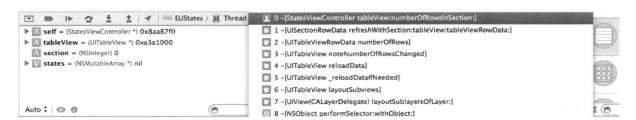

Figure 11-14. The Debug Area's jump bar

While trying to solve the current predicament, you essentially have two lines of investigation: one being the data source and the other being the application logic. Looking at the objects in the Debug Area, it's quickly obvious where the fault lies; the states array, instead of saying "15 objects" it says Nil, meaning it hasn't been initialized. Before you investigate why the array hasn't been initialized, there are a few more things to cover in relation to breakpoints, most importantly, the Breakpoint Navigator.

The Breakpoint Navigator

At this point you've only created a single breakpoint, which is fine for working through the current problem, but this is not necessarily the experience you will have when working in the real world. You will find you often set breakpoints on key pieces of logic and turn them on or off as required when flowing through your application. To manage these numerous breakpoints, you will need to take advantage of the Breakpoint Navigator (⌘ + 7), which is the seventh icon along in the list of Navigators and resembles the shape of a blue breakpoint indicator.

Figure 11-15 shows the Breakpoint Navigator as it stands for this application. Aside from giving you access to all of the breakpoints within the project from a single location, you can also use it to create an array of special breakpoints from the + symbol at the bottom of the navigator.

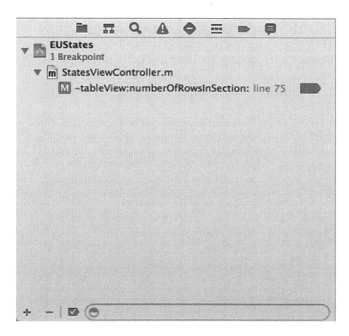

Figure 11-15. *The Breakpoint Navigator*

In addition to a standard breakpoint, Xcode will let you add the following breakpoints, which are used in specific scenarios:

- *Exception Breakpoint*: An Exception Breakpoint allows you to add a breakpoint that will trigger when any Objective-C or C++ exception is thrown or when a specific C++ exception is thrown.

- *Symbolic Breakpoint*: A Symbolic Breakpoint allows you to create a breakpoint that triggers when a specific method is triggered, which can be refined to a specific method in a specific class or even a specific function.

- *OpenGL ES Error Breakpoint*: These breakpoints are used when creating OpenGL ES-based applications, mainly games, and as with standard breakpoints, they can be configured to be conditional, which is something I'll explain shortly.

- *Test Failure Breakpoint*: The final type of breakpoint is the Test Failure Breakpoint, which is triggered when a unit test assertion fails, giving you an even greater level of granular analysis when testing.

Xcode also gives you a large degree of control over the behavior of your breakpoints. Right-click the breakpoint, as shown in Figure 11-16.

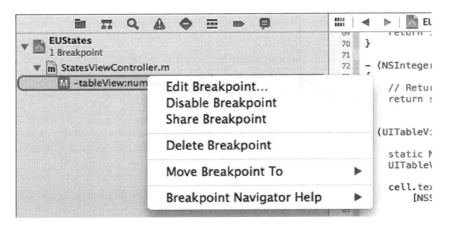

Figure 11-16. The contextual menu displayed when right-clicking a breakpoint in the Breakpoint Navigator

You can use this menu to *edit* the attributes of the breakpoint; you can also *disable* or *delete* the breakpoint. Sharing a breakpoint makes it available to other users of the same project. This menu also continues Xcode's great support for contextual help, providing numerous useful and relevant pages on the Breakpoint Navigator and its features. What you'll want to focus on here is the edit ability.

Click Edit Breakpoint … and you will be presented with a popover dialog, as shown in Figure 11-17. This dialog first shows the file and line number where the breakpoint has been added, and then provides several properties that can be set for the breakpoint.

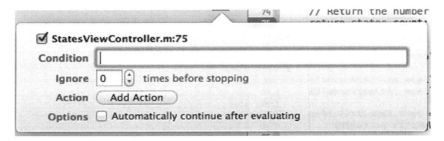

Figure 11-17. Editing a breakpoint

- *Condition*: A specific programming condition that must exist for the breakpoint to trigger such as the incremental number in a for loop being equal to 10.

- *Ignore*: The number of times that the condition needs to be met before it will trigger a pause.

- *Action*: The action menu exemplifies Xcode's flexibility as an IDE; when the condition of the breakpoint is met, Xcode can perform any number of combinations of the following actions:

  - Execute a piece of Applescript

  - Capture an OpenGL frame

- Issue a debugger command

- Log a message to the console or have it spoken to you!

- Run a shell command

- Play a sound

- *Options*: Although a plural word, this is only one option, which is to continue after the breakpoint has triggered. This may seem counterintuitive, but if you just want the actions you add to be executed and the program to continue, this saves you from having to manually resume the application.

Conditional Breakpoints

Conditional breakpoints only trigger when certain conditions are met. In this case it would be great if even after you fix the current issue the debugger notifies you anytime you get to a breakpoint and the states array is in a null state. Let's make the breakpoint conditional and add some humor to it at the same time (yes, breakpoints can be fun). Right-click the breakpoint in the Breakpoint Navigator and choose Edit Breakpoint.... In the Condition box, type `states == nil` and then click Add Action. Choose Log Message from the list and set the Message value to I've fallen and I can't get up. Finally, change the radio button selection from Log message to console to Speak message; your finished breakpoint should resemble that shown in Figure 11-18.

Figure 11-18. The customized breakpoint with a little added humor

Now rerun the application and you will be greeted by a synthesized voice saying "I've fallen and I can't get up." While amusing, the issue with the application, which is that the array is empty, still has not been resolved. Knowing this means that the `initStates` method isn't being called before it tries to build the table. The real issue is that the method isn't called *at all*.

Switch back to the Project Navigator and open `StatesViewController.m`. Go to the `viewDidLoad` method and add the highlighted code to the method:

```
- (void)viewDidLoad
{
    [super viewDidLoad];

    [self initStates];
}
```

Now rerun the application. The application will run and then you will be dropped back to Xcode. This isn't because of the breakpoint, as you should have noticed there was no voice expressing its need for assistance, but rather because of a runtime error.

Runtime Errors

Although logic errors are frustrating, runtime errors are far more destructive to your application and your reputation. Outside of your IDE, a runtime error will cause your application to crash, which will annoy your users to no end and will harm your reputation as a developer of bulletproof software. Because of this destructiveness, it's essential to thoroughly test your software for robustness.

The question to address here is how to address the issue. A runtime error is often one of the hardest to debug, but there is a wealth of information to get to the bottom of the issue. When the application crashed, it dumped the exception details and the call stack into the console in the Debug Area, as shown in Figure 11-19.

Figure 11-19. The console in the Debug Area after the runtime error has occurred

When you first look at this mass of detail, it can be quite daunting, but it is actually incredibly useful. Starting at the end of the message, you can see that the application threw a standard NSException, this isn't incredible helpful at this point. Then you have the call stack in reverse order, meaning you need to scroll up through the console to get to the point of failure. As you scroll up, look at item number 4, as shown below:

```
4   UIKit  0x0030eed3 -[UITableView dequeueReusableCellWithIdentifier:forIndexPath:] + 170
```

The call stack is like the black box flight recorder on an aircraft, and just like the real black box, it gives a detailed log of what happened leading up to a crash. Item 4 is significant because this is actually the last event that happened before Xcode starts reporting about the calls to the exception handlers in items 3 to 0, which can largely be discarded.

Item 4 is significant because it shows a call to the TableView class's dequeueReusableCellWithIdentifier:forIndexPath: method. If you open StatesViewController.m from the Project Navigator and scroll down to the cellForRowAtIndexPath method, you will see that this is the second line of the method.

Using Exception Breakpoints

To confirm the suspicions about this line, you can create an Exception Breakpoint to confirm the true source of the exception. Open the Breakpoint Navigator and click the + symbol at the bottom of the navigator, before selecting Add Exception Breakpoint..., as shown in Figure 11-20.

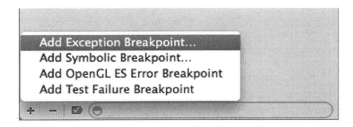

Figure 11-20. Adding an Exception Breakpoint

A new breakpoint to capture all exceptions will be added to the list of breakpoints, as shown in Figure 11-21. All that remains is to run the application and see what Xcode can tell you about this particular issue.

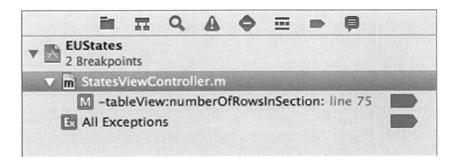

Figure 11-21. A breakpoint to capture all exceptions has been added to the Breakpoint Navigator

Run the application again; immediately the new breakpoint intercepts the exception and confirms the suspicions about the source of the exception, which is indeed the call to the dequeueReusableCel lWithIdentifier:forIndexPath: method, as shown in Figure 11-22.

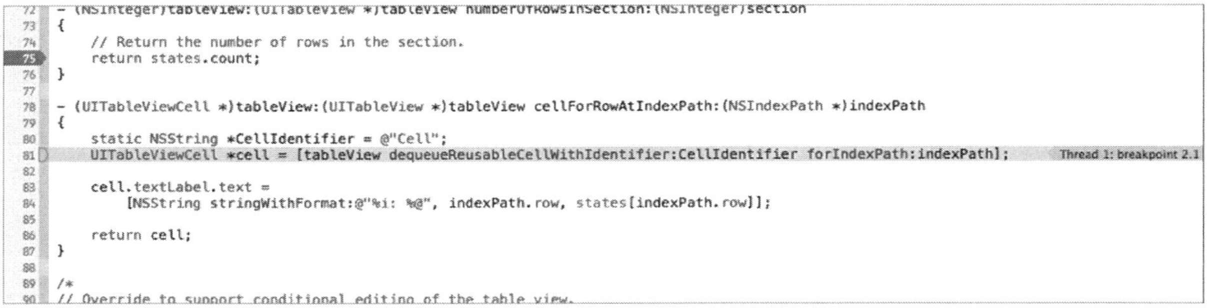

```
72   - (NSInteger)tableView:(UITableView *)tableView numberOfRowsInSection:(NSInteger)section
73   {
74       // Return the number of rows in the section.
75       return states.count;
76   }
77
78   - (UITableViewCell *)tableView:(UITableView *)tableView cellForRowAtIndexPath:(NSIndexPath *)indexPath
79   {
80       static NSString *CellIdentifier = @"Cell";
81       UITableViewCell *cell = [tableView dequeueReusableCellWithIdentifier:CellIdentifier forIndexPath:indexPath];    Thread 1: breakpoint 2.1
82
83       cell.textLabel.text =
84           [NSString stringWithFormat:@"%i: %@", indexPath.row, states[indexPath.row]];
85
86       return cell;
87   }
88
89   /*
90   // Override to support conditional editing of the table view.
```

Figure 11-22. The Exception Breakpoint pinpointing the source of the exception

So, now that you know the source of the exception, how do you begin to resolve it? In some cases it won't always be obvious, but in this case, Xcode gives all the answers needed to get the application up and running, what's more it's been there since the initial exception.

Click the breakpoints toggle button in the Debug Area to disable all of the breakpoints and then rerun the application. It will crash back to Xcode and again provide a mass of detail about the crash. This time scroll up through the details in the console until you reach the top and see the following line:

```
2013-12-08 14:29:35.821 EUStates[26196:70b] *** Terminating app due to uncaught exception
'NSInternalInconsistencyException', reason: 'unable to dequeue a cell with identifier Cell - must
register a nib or a class for the identifier or connect a prototype cell in a storyboard'
```

Roughly translated, this line is saying that you told the dequeueReusableCellWithIdentifier method to dequeue a cell called Cell, which indeed you did in the first two lines of the cellForRowAtIndexPath method:

```
static NSString *CellIdentifier = @"Cell";
UITableViewCell *cell = [tableView dequeueReusableCellWithIdentifier:CellIdentifier
forIndexPath:indexPath];
```

What it is saying is that you haven't set up a prototype cell in the Storyboard with the identifier of Cell, so it doesn't know what you're asking it to do. As you might recall from looking at Table Views in Chapter 8, you need to specify an identifier for each cell you want to reference, so now you can see what happens if you don't.

To resolve this exception and move one step closer toward a working application, open main.storyboard from the Project Navigator. Select the prototype cell from the Table View, as shown in Figure 11-23, and then open the Attributes Inspector.

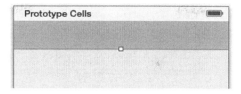

Figure 11-23. Selecting the prototype cell from our Table View in the Storyboard

In the Identifier attribute, match up the cell identifier to the code to set the value as Cell, as shown in Figure 11-24.

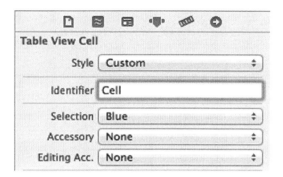

Figure 11-24. Setting the cell identifier

It's taken a while to reach this point, but it's finally time to rerun the application and see it in action. Click the run button, and your application should now run successfully, as shown in Figure 11-25.

Figure 11-25. The application, finally running!

Compile-Time Errors

So far this chapter has discussed logic errors, where the application ran but didn't work, and runtime errors, where the application ran but then crashed. In both situations, however, when Xcode was initiated to run the application, the compiler was happy that all of the code's syntax was correct and it compiled the application.

A compile-time error occurs when the compiler is processing the code and encounters an issue with either the syntax of the code or a problem with one of the linked files. The good news is that often compile-time errors are easily overcome, and many times Xcode will even help you overcome the issue by suggesting a solution.

Let's start to introduce some syntax errors into the application so you can see this in action. Open `StatesViewController.m` from the project and scroll down to the `viewDidLoad` method. After the `[super viewDidLoad];` line of code, let's specify a background color for the table. Add the highlighted code exactly as shown, the casing of words is extremely important:

```
- (void)viewDidLoad
{
    [super viewDidLoad];

    self.tableview.backgroundColor = [UIColour redColor];

    [self initStates];
}
```

Instantly, Xcode will show you that you have made a mistake by indicating the error with a red circle next to the line, as shown in Figure 11-26.

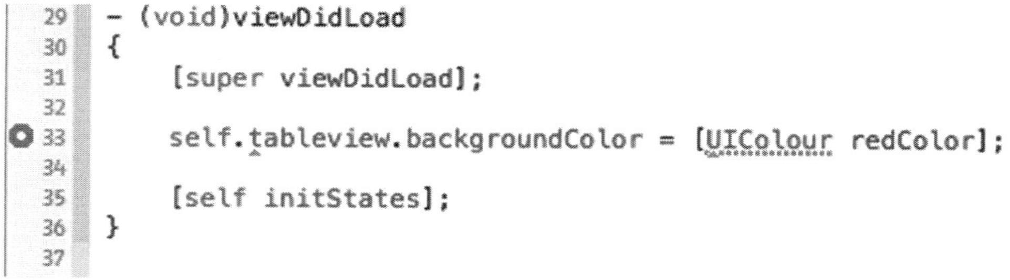

Figure 11-26. Xcode indicating an error with the syntax

Just to prove that you've created a compile-time error, try to run the application; it will fail and report the failure to build in the Activity Bar, as shown in Figure 11-27. As you will notice, the number of compile-time errors is reflected in the Activity Bar as a red circle with a white exclamation mark in it, next to the number of issues.

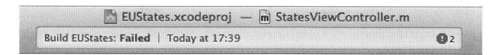

Figure 11-27. *The Activity Bar reflecting the two compile-time errors*

To get an overview of the issues, click on the red circle, which will take you to the Issue Navigator.

The Issue Navigator

You've created two errors in the single line of code, both of which Xcode can fix for you. To get an overview of any warnings or errors within the project, use the Issue Navigator (⌘ + 4), as shown in Figure 11-28.

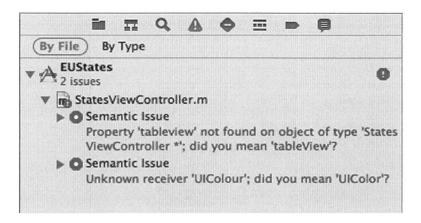

Figure 11-28. *The two issues listed in the Issue Navigator*

Issues that are highlighted with a white dot inside the red circle in the Issue Navigator can be fixed automatically by Xcode; select the first Semantic Issue in the list and you will be directed to the specific point in the code that Xcode feels is in error, as shown in Figure 11-29.

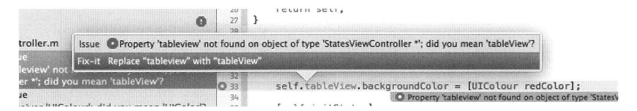

Figure 11-29. *The issue detail popover explaining the issue and offering to fix it*

As you can see, Xcode adds a popover explaining what the issue is, and it also gives a suggested fix. Click the Fix-it option and Xcode will correct the syntax issue. Repeat this for the other error in the Issue Navigator and immediately the Activity Bar will change from showing two errors to saying No Issues.

And that is how easy Xcode makes it to manage compile-time errors! There are times where you will find it slightly more challenging than this, such as when creating static libraries, which can be problematic if steps are missed, but on the whole, powerful code completion coupled with a highly responsive editor and debug system will stop errors or allow you to resolve them the second they crop up.

Tools to Help with Debugging

So far this chapter has looked at the debug tools that are built into Xcode, but there are a couple of extremely useful tools that you can access through the Simulator to help you debug your applications. Although these tools don't specifically debug anything, they allow you to test certain functions of your application in a way that can trigger an exception and therefore allow you to debug the error before you release your product.

In this final section of the chapter, I'll explain the tools you can use to help debug Map Kit–based applications and applications that have a print function. Rather than write another application to demonstrate these features, let's use the default iOS Maps application.

To access Maps, first make sure you stop EUStates, which will return the Simulator to the home screen, except not on the first page. To get to the first page of the home screen, open the Simulator and then use the mouse to slide the pages across until you reach the page with the Maps icon on it, as shown in Figure 11-30.

Figure 11-30. The main icons all appear on the first page in the Simulator

Run the Maps application from the Simulator. Depending on previous usage or both the Simulator and Xcode, you should see a view resembling that in Figure 11-31, which is a map with no user location and no movement.

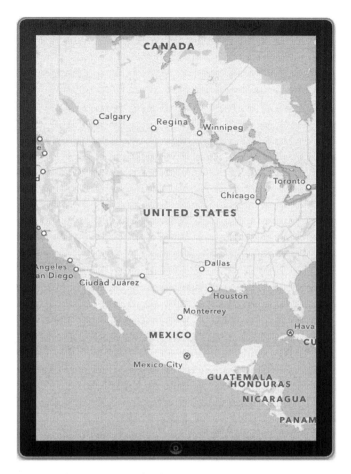

Figure 11-31. *The default starting point in the Maps application*

Debugging Location

The challenge when developing a Map Kit–based application is your location; unless you're commuting, using a physical device won't really help you develop your application because you will want to try the application in different locations, even at different speeds such as when driving or cycling, and using a Macbook while cycling is not advisable!

Because of this conundrum, Apple introduced location simulation in Xcode and the Simulator, which lets you use some preset locations and scenarios, or you can create your own. As shown in Figure 11-32, you can debug the location by selecting Debug ➤ Location and then select Apple. Almost immediately, a blue circle will appear over California; clicking the arrow in the bottom left-hand corner of the Maps application will zoom you to the Apple headquarters in Cupertino.

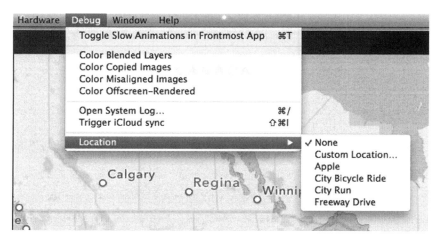

Figure 11-32. Accessing the options for debugging location from the Simulator

Next, return to the Debug ➤ Location menu and select Freeway Drive; the simulated position will start speeding around the Junipero Serra freeway, which is a great way to test an application that measures speed or distance.

Finally, to simulate a specific location, return to the menu and choose Custom Location...; from here you can specify a longitude and latitude as the user's location. Specify a longitude of 51.62228 and a latitude of -3.943491 to put the user in the middle of the city of Swansea. Simulating location is great for applications that use routing or perhaps that make recommendations based on a location.

Print Debugging with the Printer Simulator

Adding print functionality to your application is a great way to really enrich the capabilities of your application. Although the ability to print from within an application is not overly complicated, you need to be able to test the actual print functionality. If you don't have a printer that supports Air Print, the technology for printing from an iOS device, fear not, because the Printer Simulator can solve all your worries.

To access the Printer Simulator, go to the Simulator application and select File ➤ Open Printer Simulator. The Printer Simulator will launch as a simple console and will report that it has set up several types of printers, as shown in Figure 11-33.

[08/Dec/2013:19:40:41 +0000] Listening for connections on 0.0.0.0:8632.
[08/Dec/2013:19:40:41 +0000] Listening for connections on [::1]:8632.
[08/Dec/2013:19:40:41 +0000] [Printer Simulated InkJet] Registered "Simulated InkJet @ iMac" for LPD on port 0.
[08/Dec/2013:19:40:41 +0000] [Printer Simulated InkJet] Registered "Simulated InkJet @ iMac" for IPPS on port 8632.
[08/Dec/2013:19:40:41 +0000] [Printer Simulated InkJet] Registered "Simulated InkJet @ iMac" for IPP on port 8632.
[08/Dec/2013:19:40:41 +0000] [Printer Simulated 2-Sided InkJet] Registered "Simulated 2-Sided InkJet @ iMac" for LPD on port 0.
[08/Dec/2013:19:40:41 +0000] [Printer Simulated 2-Sided InkJet] Registered "Simulated 2-Sided InkJet @ iMac" for IPPS on port 8632.
[08/Dec/2013:19:40:41 +0000] [Printer Simulated 2-Sided InkJet] Registered "Simulated 2-Sided InkJet @ iMac" for IPP on port 8632.
[08/Dec/2013:19:40:41 +0000] [Printer Simulated Laser] Registered "Simulated Laser @ iMac" for LPD on port 0.
[08/Dec/2013:19:40:41 +0000] [Printer Simulated Laser] Registered "Simulated Laser @ iMac" for IPPS on port 8632.
[08/Dec/2013:19:40:41 +0000] [Printer Simulated Laser] Registered "Simulated Laser @ iMac" for IPP on port 8632.
[08/Dec/2013:19:40:41 +0000] [Printer Simulated Color Laser] Registered "Simulated Color Laser @ iMac" for LPD on port 0.
[08/Dec/2013:19:40:41 +0000] [Printer Simulated Color Laser] Registered "Simulated Color Laser @ iMac" for IPPS on port 8632.
[08/Dec/2013:19:40:41 +0000] [Printer Simulated Color Laser] Registered "Simulated Color Laser @ iMac" for IPP on port 8632.
[08/Dec/2013:19:40:41 +0000] [Printer Simulated Label Printer] Registered "Simulated Label Printer @ iMac" for LPD on port 0.
[08/Dec/2013:19:40:41 +0000] [Printer Simulated Label Printer] Registered "Simulated Label Printer @ iMac" for IPPS on port 8632.
[08/Dec/2013:19:40:41 +0000] [Printer Simulated Label Printer] Registered "Simulated Label Printer @ iMac" for IPP on port 8632.
[08/Dec/2013:19:40:41 +0000] [Printer Simulated 36" Roll Printer] Registered "Simulated 36" Roll Printer @ iMac" for LPD on port 0.
[08/Dec/2013:19:40:41 +0000] [Printer Simulated 36" Roll Printer] Registered "Simulated 36" Roll Printer @ iMac" for IPPS on port
[08/Dec/2013:19:40:41 +0000] [Printer Simulated 36" Roll Printer] Registered "Simulated 36" Roll Printer @ iMac" for IPP on port 8632.
[08/Dec/2013:19:40:41 +0000] [Printer Save Original to Simulator] Registered "Save Original to Simulator @ iMac" for LPD on port 0.
[08/Dec/2013:19:40:41 +0000] [Printer Save Original to Simulator] Registered "Save Original to Simulator @ iMac" for IPPS on port
[08/Dec/2013:19:40:41 +0000] [Printer Save Original to Simulator] Registered "Save Original to Simulator @ iMac" for IPP on port 8632.

Figure 11-33. The Printer Simulator running and providing a selection of printers

The Simulator might not be what you first expected, but it is extremely powerful and can simulate an incredible number of scenarios. To see an example of its power, click the Load Paper icon from the toolbar. A dialog will slide down showing all six of the simulated printers, with the options of customizing their functions and paper sizes; dismiss the dialog by clicking OK.

To use one of these virtual printers, return to the Maps application in the Simulator. Click the circled i icon in the bottom right corner of the toolbar, as shown in Figure 11-34.

Figure 11-34. The toolbar of the Maps application

From the Action Sheet that appears, select the option to Print Map. You will be presented with the standard iOS print dialog, as shown in Figure 11-35.

Figure 11-35. The iOS printer options

Choose the first option to select a printer. You are then presented with a list of simulated printers; choose Simulated Inkjet and click the Print button. After a brief pause, the Printer Simulator will spring to life, with details about the print job appearing in the console, before the Preview application appears showing the results of your print job, as shown in Figure 11-36, which I have rotated for easy viewing.

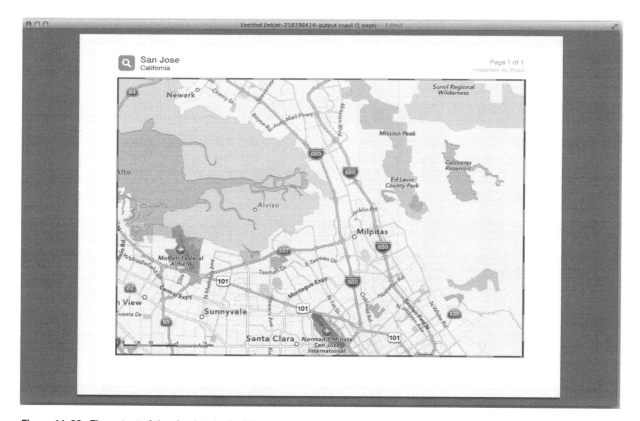

Figure 11-36. The output of the simulated print job

Setting up printing for your application is often done blind, with the developer having no visual indication of the output until they come to print, so being able to quickly test this functionality and debug any issues arising such as missing pages is invaluable. The depth offered by the Printer Simulator means that developers can test their print functionality on a range of device types at different resolutions and have a high degree of confidence in their finished product, and also not contribute to the erosion of the rainforests with reams of test prints.

Summary

Until IDEs develop artificial intelligence and can accurately predict what programmers intend to do in our code and automatically resolve any errors, there will be a need to debug code. It's rare to write something that works just fine the first time, so knowing how to debug an application in Xcode is an essential skill.

This chapter presented a detailed look at how Xcode can be used to resolve various issues with applications and also how you can use simulators to put the functionality of the application to the test when physically moving or when owning additional hardware would otherwise be required.

Specifically in this chapter, you learned:

- About the types of errors that can occur.
- How to use breakpoints effectively to investigate logic and runtime issues.
- How the call stack can be interpreted to lead to a solution to runtime errors.
- How the Breakpoint and Issue Navigators can help you efficiently debug an application.
- How to use the Location and Printer Simulation features to assist with testing and debugging an application.

We'll now move into the final part of the book: Final Preparations and Releasing. Chapter 12 will take a look at the fine level of integration Xcode has with the popular version control software called Git. You will find out how it can help you work better in a team of developers and give you the ability to roll back changes.

Part 3

Final Preparations and Releasing

Chapter 12

Version Control with Git

Chapter 11 focused on errors and exceptions and how you can use the tools within Xcode to root them out. You looked at the three most common types of errors and exceptions: logic, runtime and compile-time errors. You also looked at how to make sense of the call stack when your application crashes.

The focus of this chapter is version control, and specifically how Xcode integrates with the Git source code management system. Xcode stands out from other IDEs in this department. Its integration is so fine and complete that it is a joy to use and so intuitive you'll wonder why you haven't used it before.

As you work through the intricacies of version control, you will create a voice recorder application called HearMeNow. This application will have a record and a play button initially, but later on you will branch the project and modify it to play the voice back at half speed, perfect when trying to listen to people like me who talk too quickly. It's important to note that although the application will run without error in the simulator, you will need a physical device with a microphone to see it working with your recordings.

Why Use Version Control?

The question when it comes to version control is actually why not? Have you ever developed a solution, taken a vacation, and while you were away, a member of your team made a small change and suddenly there were a dozen other bugs as a consequence? If so, version control would have saved the day.

Version control software, also known as source control or revision control, allows you to track and manage changes made to code over time. If something suddenly stops working, you can compare it to an older version to see what's gone wrong. Version control makes it easy to see what's changed between releases, with changes to a file being highlighted, logged against a specific user, and even able to hold comments.

There are a wide variety of version control systems on the market, and unlike many software markets, some of the best systems are open source. Most software development houses use one of several tools for version control depending on the language they write in or preference, with the most popular systems being Git, Subversion (SVN), and Microsoft's Team Foundation Server (TFS). Xcode uses the extremely popular Git system to provide version control.

What Is Git?

If you're British, a Git is that person who steals your lunch, even though it had your name on it, written in capital letters using a black marker pen. The Git source control management system has very little to do with this vernacular; it is the brainchild of the principal developer of the Linux kernel, Linus Torvalds. When none of the version control packages available at the time supported his vision of robust distributed development of the Linux kernel, Torvalds wrote his own system, that system was Git.

Torvalds names all of his software after himself and has quipped that this one was no different, so read into that what you will. The actual software, however, is really quite amazing. Torvalds designed Git to be fast, efficient, and robust, and it excels at all three.

Git is notable as a system because it can be used either locally for version control or using a server to allow global collaboration on a piece of software. Online systems such as GitHub or Bitbucket provide free Git repositories so you can backup your project online and invite people to take a copy by cloning, branching, or forking your project. Another notable feature that separates Git from other similar systems is that when you make a change, Git snapshots the project, giving you a true point-in-time view of the project, rather than other systems that simply track changes on individual files. When talking about Git, there are many terms that might sound strange or complicated, so let's look at these terms to prove there's nothing to be afraid of.

- *Repository*: Also known as a repo for short, a repository is what encapsulates your project, storing the different versions of the files and folders in the project and tracking the changes.

- *Commit*: When you have made changes to a file and want to put them into the repository, you commit those changes.

- *Branch*: Branching a project allows you to work on a duplicate of that project within the repository without altering the original. Typically this is done when you want to add a new feature where you would branch off from the original project, make the changes, and then merge the branch back into the master branch or trunk.

- *Fork*: If you want to work on a project you have read-only access to or you want to send your project in a brave new direction, forking would be a good idea. This allows you to duplicate the repository, but is really something reserved for online services such as GitHub or Bitbucket.

Creating the Project

As it is suitable for the vast majority of iOS projects, you will yet again be using the Single View Application template for this project. The project for this chapter focuses on using the built-in microphone of an iOS device to allow you to record a voice or sound and play it back.

1. To begin the project, start by opening Xcode and then create a new project by going to File ➤ New ➤ New Project ... (⌘ + Shift + N) or, alternatively, Create a new Xcode project if you are on the Welcome screen (⌘ + Shift + 1).

2. Select the Single View Application Template and click Next.

3. Name the project HearMeNow, leave the other options as default and substitute your personal information, but ensure the device is set to iPhone, as shown in Figure 12-1. Click Next.

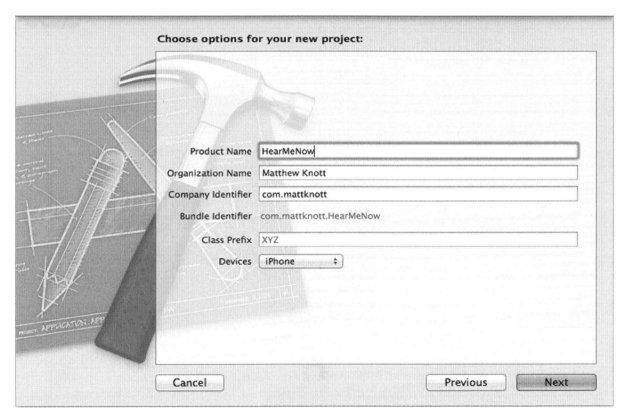

Figure 12-1. Setting up the initial properties of the project

4. Click the check box at the bottom of the save dialog where it says Source Control. This specifies that the project should use source control. Next, specify that you want to create a Git repository locally by choosing My Mac from the drop-down list, unless you have a server set up to house Git repositories. Ensure your settings match those shown in Figure 12-2 and click Create. Please note that if you don't see the Add to option, don't worry, this comes and goes depending on whether you have other workspaces open.

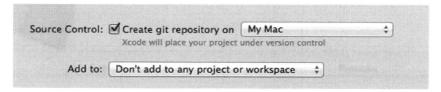

Figure 12-2. Choosing to create a Git repository locally on the Mac

Note   For this chapter you will be creating a local Git repository on the Mac. Many development teams choose to use a dedicated server or an online solution as this gives everyone access to all the team's projects and it greatly simplifies backups. Online solutions will be examined later in this chapter.

5. The project and a local Git repository have now been created for the project. Take a moment to select Source Control from the menu bar. This menu is where you will perform the different actions that are covered in this chapter. As you can see at the top of the menu in Figure 12-3, you will be working on the master branch, which is fine because you have just started the project.

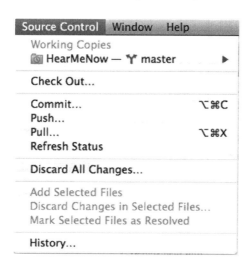

Figure 12-3. The Source Control menu

6. Select *History* ... from the Source Control menu. Figure 12-4 shows the history of the project in a source control context. When you created the project, a snapshot of that start point was automatically created and this is called the Initial Commit; click Done to close the dialog.

Project history: Q▾ Search commit messages

16 December 2013

Matthew Knott   eff9cc29ebbe
20:41   Show 18 modified files

Initial Commit

Done

Figure 12-4. The dialog showing the history of the project under source control

Note   Depending on the version of OS X, you may be prompted when opening the History dialog to allow access to contacts. This is so Xcode can try to identify who made changes to the project and the repository.

The project has been created and is now under source control, so you're ready to begin building the interface for the project and writing the code, which will make use of a framework called AVFoundation.

The AVFoundation Framework

Before you start an interface for the project, let's quickly take a look at what the AVFoundation framework is and what it lets us do. Although there are dedicated audio and video frameworks, AVFoundation, as its name might suggest, provides a powerful set of classes that underpin these other frameworks.

AVFoundation can be used in slightly varying forms in both iOS and OS X development, and its main purpose is to support the use of time-based audio and video functions, such as recording and playback of various media types.

In this application you will set the View Controller up as an AVAudioPlayerDelegate and also AVAudioRecorderDelegate, so that you can take advantage of the AVAudioPlayer and AVAudioRecorder classes, which are named to clearly indicate their purpose.

1. At this point, you will add the framework to the project. As you have in previous chapters, select the project HearMeNow from the Project Navigator.

2. Scroll to the bottom of the General tab of the Project Editor and click the + symbol in the Linked Frameworks and Libraries section.

3. Search the list for AVFoundation.framework and select it, as shown in Figure 12-5, then click Add.

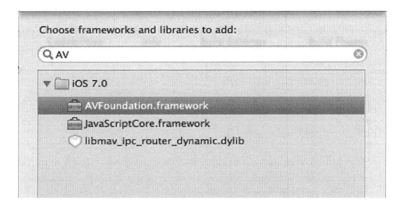

Figure 12-5. Selecting AVFoundation from the list of available frameworks and libraries

You will now have four entries in your list of linked frameworks and libraries, and you are ready to start building a simple interface for the HearMeNow application.

Creating the Interface

The interface for the application will be extremely simple; it will consist of a label and two buttons, one to record or stop recording and another to play back or stop playing back.

1. To begin building the interface, start by opening Main.storyboard from the Project Navigator.

2. As you created this project from the Single View Application template, you have a single view on the Storyboard. Drag in a Label from the Object Library and place it on the view, move it to the top of the view so that the blue guidelines appear, and then release it. Use the handles on either side of the Label to resize its width until it again reaches the left and right guidelines. Your label should resemble that shown in Figure 12-6.

Figure 12-6. *Positioning the Label within the view*

3. With the Label positioned, you will need to set its attributes; open the Attribute Inspector and change the Text attribute from Label to Hear me now ... and the Alignment to the center position, as shown in Figure 12-7.

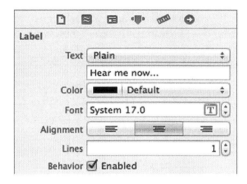

Figure 12-7. *Setting the attributes of the Label*

Now that the Label is configured, you can turn your attention to the two buttons. Drag in two Buttons from the Object Library, positioning them one beneath the other, as shown in Figure 12-8.

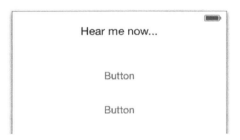

Figure 12-8. *Adding two Buttons to the view*

4. Resize both buttons in the same way you did with the Label, dragging the left and right sides until the guidelines display. Change the attributes for the buttons in the Attributes Inspector, setting the top button to be named Record and the bottom button to be named Play. Your finished interface should resemble that shown in Figure 12-9.

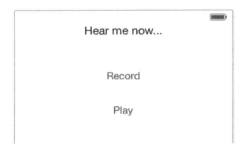

Figure 12-9. The completed interface for the application

5. The next task is to create an outlet and an action for each of the buttons. Open the Assistant Editor and ensure `ViewController.h` is selected alongside your Storyboard, instead of `ViewController.m`, the default option. Control-drag a connection from the Record button and create an outlet called `recordButton`, then create another outlet for the Play button and call it `playButton`. Once the outlets are created, repeat the control-drag process for each button but this time create an action for the Record button called `recordPressed` and one for the Play button called `playPressed`. Your header file should resemble that shown in Figure 12-10.

```
 9   #import <UIKit/UIKit.h>
10
11   @interface ViewController : UIViewController
12
13   @property (weak, nonatomic) IBOutlet UIButton *recordButton;
14   @property (weak, nonatomic) IBOutlet UIButton *playButton;
15
16   - (IBAction)recordPressed:(id)sender;
17   - (IBAction)playPressed:(id)sender;
18
19
20
21   @end
22
```

Figure 12-10. The outlets and actions created in the header file

6. Now that the outlets and actions have been created, it's time to add the final touches to the header file. Switch back to the Standard Editor and open `ViewController.h` from the Project Navigator. Earlier when I mentioned the AVFoundation framework, I mentioned two protocols you need to add to the View Controller: `AVAudioPlayerDelegate` and `AVAudioRecorderDelegate`. Add the highlighted code to the header to import the AVFoundation framework and apply the two protocols with the following code:

```
#import <UIKit/UIKit.h>
#import <AVFoundation/AVFoundation.h>

@interface ViewController : UIViewController<AVAudioPlayerDelegate, AVAudioRecorderDelegate>
```

```
@property (weak, nonatomic) IBOutlet UIButton *recordButton;
@property (weak, nonatomic) IBOutlet UIButton *playButton;

- (IBAction)recordPressed:(id)sender;
- (IBAction)playPressed:(id)sender;

@end
```

7. The header is now complete, and it's time to move on to the implementation file. Open `ViewController.m` from the Project Navigator. Aside from adding code to the `viewDidLoad` method and the two actions, there will be two delegate methods and a number of instance variables. First, you need to add the instance variables, as they are essential for all of the methods in the application. At the top of the implementation file, add two curly brackets after the line `@interface ViewController()`, as highlighted below, and then add the five instance variables:

```
#import "ViewController.h"

@interface ViewController ()
{
    BOOL hasRecording;
    AVAudioPlayer *soundPlayer;
    AVAudioRecorder *soundRecorder;
    AVAudioSession *session;
    NSString *soundPath;
}
```

You have just created five instance variables. Let's take a look at them and what they do:

Bool `hasRecording`: Determines whether or not a recording has been made.

`AVAudioPlayer *soundPlayer`: Handles all audio playback.

`AVAudioRecorder *soundRecorder`: Handles recording from the microphone.

`AVAudioSession *session`: Activates and deactivates the audio session.

`NSString *soundPath`: Holds the path for the recorded file.

8. Next, scroll down to the `viewDidLoad` method. In this method you will initialize the `session`, `soundPath`, and `soundRecorder` objects. As in previous chapters, I won't always go into detail about the code because that isn't the focus of this book; add the following highlighted code to your `viewDidLoad` method:

```
- (void)viewDidLoad
{
    [super viewDidLoad];
```

```
soundPath = [[NSString alloc] initWithFormat:@"%@%@",
                            NSTemporaryDirectory(), @"hearmenow.wav"];

NSURL *url = [[NSURL alloc] initFileURLWithPath:soundPath];

session = [AVAudioSession sharedInstance];
[session setActive:YES error:nil];

NSError *error;

[[AVAudioSession sharedInstance] setCategory:AVAudioSessionCategoryPlayAndRecord
                            error:&error];

soundRecorder = [[AVAudioRecorder alloc] initWithURL:url
                                        settings:nil
                                        error:&error];
if (error)
{
    NSLog(@"Error while initializing the recorder: %@", error);
}

soundRecorder.delegate = self;
[soundRecorder prepareToRecord];
```

}

9. With the soundRecorder object initialized, it's time to write the code for the recordPressed method. This method is called when the Record button is clicked. If the application is currently recording, it will stop the recording process and set the button title back to "Record," otherwise it will use the session object to check recording permissions and then either start recording, if granted, or use NSLog to log that the request was denied. Go ahead and add the following highlighted code to the method:

```
- (IBAction)recordPressed:(id)sender {
    if ([soundRecorder isRecording])
    {
        [soundRecorder stop];
        [self.recordButton setTitle:@"Record" forState:UIControlStateNormal];
    }
    else
    {
        [session requestRecordPermission:^(BOOL granted) {
            if(granted)
            {
                [soundRecorder record];
                [self.recordButton setTitle:@"Stop"
                                forState:UIControlStateNormal];
            }
```

```
        else
        {
            NSLog(@"Unable to record");
        }
    }];
    }
}
```

10. You've written the method for the Record button, so now you need to write one for the Play button, which calls the `playPressed` method. In this method the action is determined from three possible states: first, if the `soundPlayer` object is currently playing back the audio file, it will pause it; second, if the `hasRecording` object is set to `Yes` or `true`, then the application will play the recorded file; and finally, if neither of the other two states were met, the method checks to see if the player is initialized, which means it is being asked to resume from a paused state. Add the following highlighted code to the `playPressed` method:

```
- (IBAction)playPressed:(id)sender {
    if (soundPlayer.playing)
    {
        [soundPlayer pause];
        [self.playButton setTitle:@"Play" forState:UIControlStateNormal];
    }
    else if (hasRecording)
    {
        NSURL *url = [[NSURL alloc] initFileURLWithPath:soundPath];
        NSError *error;
        soundPlayer = [[AVAudioPlayer alloc] initWithContentsOfURL:url error:&error];
        if (!error)
        {
            soundPlayer.delegate = self;
            [soundPlayer play];
        } else {
            NSLog(@"Error initializing player: %@", error);
        }
        [self.playButton setTitle:@"Pause" forState:UIControlStateNormal];
        hasRecording = NO;
    }
    else if (soundPlayer)
    {
        [soundPlayer play];
        [self.playButton setTitle:@"Pause" forState:UIControlStateNormal];
    }
}
```

11. The final task in the implementation of this application is to write two delegate methods that are called when the recording and playing is finished to change the text of the relevant button and, in the case of playing the audio back, to set the hasRecording object to no or false. Add the following two methods just after the playPressed method:

```
- (void)audioRecorderDidFinishRecording:(AVAudioRecorder *)recorder successfully:(BOOL)flag
{
    hasRecording = flag;
    [self.recordButton setTitle:@"Record" forState:UIControlStateNormal];
}

-(void)audioPlayerDidFinishPlaying:(AVAudioPlayer *)player successfully:(BOOL)flag
{
    [self.playButton setTitle:@"Play" forState:UIControlStateNormal];
}
```

With those last two methods in place, the application is now ready to be run. As I mentioned at the beginning of this chapter, you will need a physical iOS device to test the application's full functionality, although you can test for compile-time errors and runtime errors to some extent without one. To select a physical device vs. the currently selected simulator, click the simulator name next to the scheme, as shown in Figure 12-11, and select your physical device if you have one. Physical devices are separated from the various simulators and are represented by the device's icon. In order for your device to appear in the list, it must be connected to your Mac via the USB cable and must be prepared for development, which is something I will cover in Chapter 14.

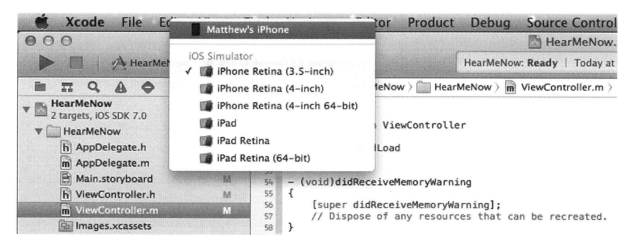

Figure 12-11. *Selecting a physical device from the list of available devices*

Run the application and you should find that you have a plain, but effective sound recorder. Tap the record button and speak. When you click stop, the sound will be saved onto the device and is available for playback. Record as many times as you like, but the application will only use a single filename and therefore overwrite the file every time you click record. Figure 12-12 shows the application running on a physical device.

Figure 12-12. *The application running on a physical device*

Once you've played with this great little application you've just created, stop it and return to Xcode. Take a look at the Project Navigator, every item that has been changed since the project was created (i.e., the project settings and the View Controller files) has an M symbol next to it, as shown in Figure 12-13. This icon indicates that the project item has been modified since the last time the project changes were committed to the Git repository.

Figure 12-13. *The Project Navigator places an M next to each project item modified since the last commit*

Committing Changes

When making changes to a project under source control, just as with any other project you've created going through this book, the changes take effect locally as you save the files or run the application, so why is Xcode pointing out that some of the files and settings in the project have been modified? The reason is that although the changes are being applied, they are not being saved into the Git repository until you perform an action called a commit. A commit action creates an updated snapshot of the project within the Git repository, and you are creating a point in time reference for your project that you can go back to at any time.

Because you have created the first goal for the project, this is a good time to commit the project and update the Git repository. Select Source Control ➤ Commit (⌘ + ⌥ + C); you will be presented with a wealth of information about the files that have changed, as shown in Figure 12-14.

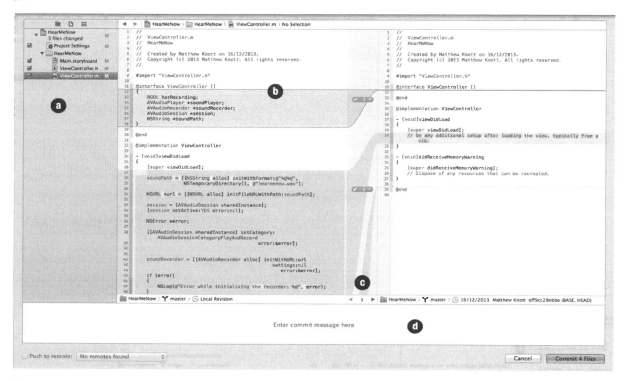

Figure 12-14. The Commit screen, detailing all changes made within the project since the last commit

In this instance I have selected ViewController.m as it received the greatest modification, and as indicated on Figure 12-14, there are four key points of interest.

1. *List of modified items*: This area lists all items within the project that have changed. You have three options for viewing this list: the default which is Project View; File View, which shows modified files in the context of their folder structure within Finder; and Flat View, which simply lists the items with no structure around them. It is important to note that each item has a check box next to it that can be unticked if you wish to exclude it.

2. *Highlighted changes*: When selecting an item, you are shown the changes that have occurred within that item since the initial commit, unless it is a new item. Each change is highlighted and you can see the point at which the original file became modified.

3. *Change numbering*: Within each modified item, Xcode dynamically identifies and groups changes to make it easier for you to ignore specific changes at the time of the commit or to discarding them entirely. Clicking the numbered item in this area will present these options, as shown in Figure 12-15. At the bottom of the list is a number that represents the number of changes that can be affected in isolation along with stepper controls that allow you to jump between the changes in sequence.

Figure 12-15. When clicking one of the numbered changes you can choose to ignore or discard that change

4. *Commit message*: When committing the modifications to Git, it's important to add a message explaining what has been changed. Another user will be able to see what's physically changed, so here you can explain why you made the changes and what your thinking behind each change was.

Add a comment into the commit message box to explain what's changed and click the button in the bottom right-hand corner that says Commit 4 Files. After a brief pause, you will be returned to Xcode. Note that there are no longer any M icons in the Project Navigator, meaning that the project has not been modified from the version currently stored in the Git repository.

For an alternative view of what you have just done, go back to Source Control ➤ History ... and note that you now have two entries: the initial commit and the commit you just made, as shown in Figure 12-16.

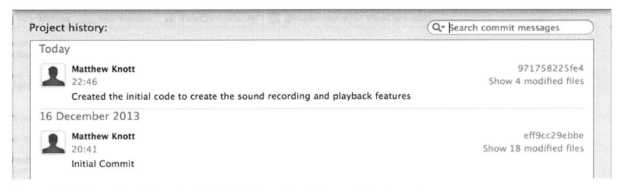

Figure 12-16. The project history showing the initial commit and the one just performed

The details of the last commit appear at the top, with previous changes appearing below in reverse chronological order. Hopefully you can see the value of adding the comments now, as they help provide a rich picture of how and why the application has changed, especially if you are working as part of a team, where understanding who did what is critical. Although this view gives you a good deal of information about the changes made with each commit, Xcode has a number of ways you can compare multiple version of a file and the changes within that file.

Examining Changes with the Version Editor

One of the most enticing aspects of version control is that it gives you a safety net in which you can have multiple people working on a single project. When something stops working between commits, however, it's important to be able to look back at what's changed and even determine who is to blame for breaking the code. As well as the Standard and Assistant Editors, Xcode provides you with a third editor called the Version Editor. As you may remember from Chapter 3, the Version Editor is the third icon in the group of different editors, as shown in Figure 12-17. You may also have noted the small downward pointing arrow, which indicates the editor has multiple views: Comparison, Blame, and Log.

Figure 12-17. The Version Editor is the third icon in the group of editors

The Comparison View

To begin, select `ViewController.h` from the Project Navigator, and then select the Version Editor icon within Xcode. The Comparison view is the default view that will be presented. The Comparison view will be immediately familiar to you, it forms the major part of the commit process, except that within the Version Editor it has far more flexibility. The difference in the view can be found on the bar at the bottom of the editor, as shown in Figure 12-18.

Figure 12-18. The bar beneath the editor provides the core functionality in the Comparison view

You can configure either the left or right pane to show any available version of the file you have selected in the Project Navigator. Because the left and right sections have identical functionality, I will focus on the left side for a moment. You will have three segments: in this case they are HearMeNow, which represents the projects within the workspace, master, which represents the selected branch, and Local Revision, which represents the selected version of the file to be displayed. On the right, almost the exact same information is displayed except that it is showing the version from the last time the file was committed.

From the right-hand pane, select the master branch item in the bar and you will see the available versions of the file that can be compared, as shown in Figure 12-19. To review again what changed since the initial commit, select the bottom item, which will be the oldest one available.

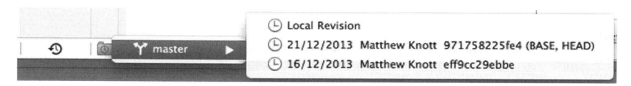

Figure 12-19. The list of available revisions in the selected branch

Once you select the older version, the code comparisons will appear, highlighting what has changed between the two selected versions, as shown in Figure 12-20. I've already highlighted the functionality available when selecting a numbered change in the previous discussion of the commit process, so I won't go into that again. However, it is worth noting that unlike when you commit, you don't have the option to exclude code from the commit because it is already committed, which makes sense.

```
HearMeNow ›  HearMeNow ›  h  ViewController.h › No Selection
```

```
1   //                                                              1   //
2   //  ViewController.h                                            2   //  ViewController.h
3   //  HearMeNow                                                   3   //  HearMeNow
4   //                                                              4   //
5   //  Created by Matthew Knott on 16/12/2013.                     5   //  Created by Matthew Knott on 16/12/2013.
6   //  Copyright (c) 2013 Matthew Knott. All rights reserved.      6   //  Copyright (c) 2013 Matthew Knott. All rights reserved.
7   //                                                              7   //
8                                                                   8
9   #import <UIKit/UIKit.h>                                         9   #import <UIKit/UIKit.h>
10  #import <AVFoundation/AVFoundation.h>                          10
11                                                                 11  @interface ViewController : UIViewController
12  @interface ViewController : UIViewController<                  12
        AVAudioPlayerDelegate, AVAudioRecorderDelegate>            13  @end
13                                                                 14
14  @property (weak, nonatomic) IBOutlet UIButton *recordButton;
15  @property (weak, nonatomic) IBOutlet UIButton *playButton;
16
17  - (IBAction)recordPressed:(id)sender;
18  - (IBAction)playPressed:(id)sender;
19
20  @end
21
```

```
HearMeNow ›  master › Local Revision          HearMeNow ›  master ›  16/12/2013  Matthew Knott  eff9cc29ebbe
```

Figure 12-20. *Comparing the current local revision with the oldest version available*

One neat feature that Xcode provides to allow you to compare different version of a selected file is the Version Timeline. If you have ever used Time Machine on your Mac to restore a file, you will find this very familiar. Start by clicking the timeline viewer icon, which is in the center of the bar shown as a clock in Figure 12-18. The central area between the two panes will then be replaced with the Version Timeline, as shown in Figure 12-21.

Figure 12-21. *The timeline viewer icon opens the Version Timeline*

At the bottom of the timeline are two default options: local and base. Local will show you the current version of the file, and base will show the last committed version. Comparing base to local versions can be useful if you started making changes and made a mess of things. You can identify the offending code and revert it back to how it was in the previous version.

Above base is a reverse chronological order of the previous commits to the repository. As Figure 12-22 shows, as you move the cursor over an entry in the timeline, it will show the key details about the commit, such as date and time, the comment, and the name of the person who performed the commit.

Figure 12-22. Each entry in the timeline shows the commit comment, date, and the name of the person who committed the project

Arrows on the left and right of the timeline indicate what is being displayed in the corresponding pane, giving you extremely fine control over which revisions are being compared.

The Blame View

All of the Xcode integration with Git is done so that you don't really have to worry about what happens behind the scenes. As with many of Apple's products, it just works, but behind the scenes Xcode is actually firing off command line messages to the Git system to perform the action you have just asked Xcode to perform. There are a whole host of commands, including `git blame`, which is what the Blame view bases its display upon.

Blame is an unfair term, because often you are not looking to actually blame anyone for anything, you just want to know who changed what in a project so you can ask them a bit more about it. It's also unfair because it adds a negative term to one of the coolest views when using Xcode's source control.

To turn on the Blame view, click the Version Editor button again and a menu will appear, as shown in Figure 12-23; select Blame.

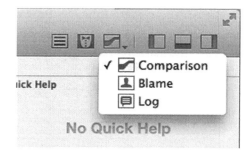

Figure 12-23. Clicking the Version Editor button when it is selected will let you choose from three views

Once you have opened the Blame view, you will see why it is so powerful in a team environment. Figure 12-24 shows the detailed analysis of every change in the selected file, when it was made, and by whom. If a colleague wrote a method that you're not quite sure about, you will know who to talk to about it.

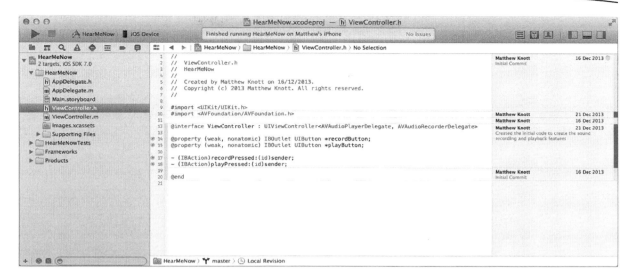

Figure 12-24. The Blame view in action

In the detail area to the right of the code, if you move your cursor over one of the blocks, a circled i symbol appears. Clicking this will cause a popover to appear giving you further information, and also the option to analyze the change further in the Comparison view, as shown in Figure 12-25.

Figure 12-25. Clicking the i icon in the details area will give you more information about the change

The Log View

The third and final view offered as part of the Version Editor is the Log view. Selecting the Log view will give you a Standard Editor along will an additional bar, as shown in Figure 12-26, that details the change history for the current file along with any comments. The Log view is the most simple of the different views of the Version Editor, and as such you will find you use either the Comparison or Blame views more.

Figure 12-26. The Log view within the Version Editor

Branching Within a Repository

When you're developing a project that is under version control with Git, the master branch or trunk should always be used to hold the version of your project that is ready for release. When you want to add new features, you could just continue working on the master branch, but if you need to modify the code to fix a bug, you're in a situation where you have no good version to update and the development process starts falling apart. In this situation, you can create a branch from the master. This will allow you to work in total isolation from the master branch. Once you are happy that your branch is complete and you're ready to add the changes into the release version, you can simply merge your branch back into the master.

To add some new functionality to the HearMeNow application, you will be creating a new branch called SlowDown, as shown by Figure 12-27. The master branch will remain untouched and all of your work will now be done on the new branch. Within this new branch you are going to modify the playback routine to slow down playback to half of normal speed, which is actually quite a useful feature when typing up dictation or just trying to understand someone who either talks quickly or in a language you are trying to learning.

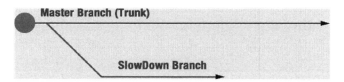

Figure 12-27. A branch allows you to work in isolation from the master branch

To create a new branch, go to Source Control ➤ HearMeNow – Master ➤ New Branch . . . . You will then be presented with a dialog asking you to name the branch, as shown in Figure 12-28. Name it SlowDown and click Create.

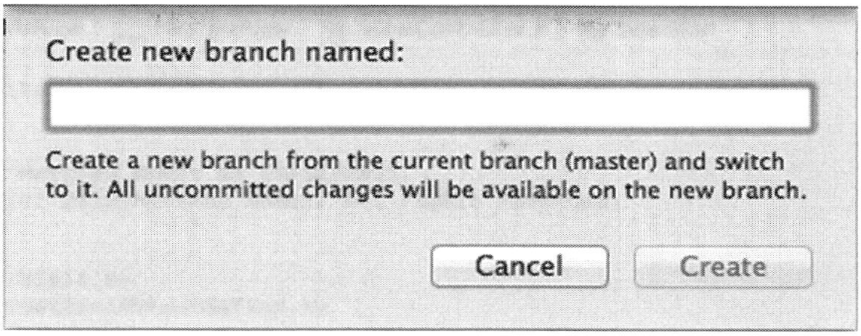

Figure 12-28. The new branch dialog asking you to name the branch

Xcode will create the new branch and automatically switch you to it. Open ViewController.m from the Project Navigator and ensure you are still on the Log view. Notice that as Figure 12-29 shows, you are now working on the SlowDown branch instead of the master.

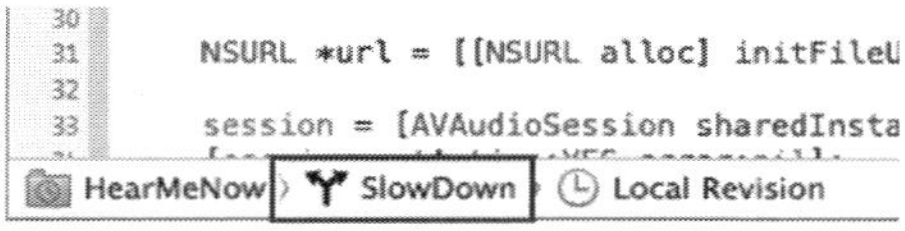

Figure 12-29. The branch has changed from the master to the new SlowDown branch

Now that there is a separate branch, you are free to alter the code without fear of breaking the original and working project, which will safely remain in the master branch. You can now add the code needed to reduce the speed of the playback, which can be achieved with only two lines of code.

If it is not already open, select the Standard Editor. Now open ViewController.m from the Project Navigator. Scroll down to the playPressed method; you will be changing the rate property used by the soundPlayer object. Add in the highlighted code to the second if statement just after you set the player delegate:

```
else if (hasRecording)
{
    NSURL *url = [[NSURL alloc] initFileURLWithPath:soundPath];
    NSError *error;
    soundPlayer = [[AVAudioPlayer alloc] initWithContentsOfURL:url error:&error];
    if (!error)
    {
        soundPlayer.delegate = self;
        soundPlayer.enableRate = YES;
        soundPlayer.rate = 0.5;
        [soundPlayer play];
    } else {
        NSLog(@"Error initializing player: %@", error);
    }
    [self.playButton setTitle:@"Pause" forState:UIControlStateNormal];
    hasRecording = NO;
}
```

Before you commit the changes to the current branch, run the application to test the new functionality. When the application runs, record yourself saying something and play it back. If all goes well, you should come across as sounding slightly tired or a little drunk, but importantly the sound is half of normal speed.

Once you are satisfied with the change, commit the changes in the same way as you did earlier in the chapter, and remember to add a suitable comment. You are now well on your way to mastering Git, but now that you have changed this branch of the application, how do you apply those changes to the master branch? With unbelievable ease, as it happens.

Merging Branches

You've been able to develop your changes without affecting the working solution that you created in the master branch, but now that you've successfully made the changes to the SlowDown branch, it's time to merge this arbitrary branch with the master branch and release another version of the application.

Merging is incredibly simple to do, so before you merge the two branches, take a moment to compare the ViewController.m file between the two branches. Open the Version Editor and the default Compare view and then select ViewController.m from the Project Navigator.

By default, Xcode will present you with the local revision on the left and the last committed version on the right. This tells you nothing because they are effectively the same at this point. At the bottom of the right-hand pane, click SlowDown and a menu will appear. Hover over master and then select the most recent version, as shown in Figure 12-30. This will load the version of ViewController.m that you committed the first time.

Figure 12-30. Selecting the version of ViewController.m from the master branch for comparison

When the other version of the file appears, scroll down to where you modified the playPressed method. As Figure 12-31 shows, Xcode has singled out the change you made, so now you can clearly see that the code you just wrote does not exist in the master branch.

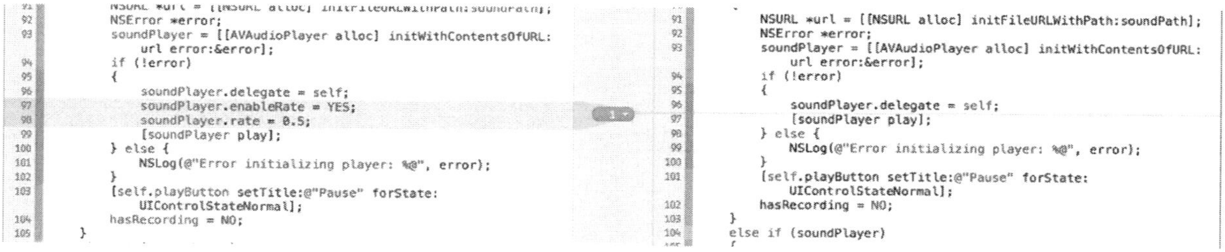

Figure 12-31. Xcode showing the difference between the ViewController.m file in both branches

Now that you are certain that there is a difference between the files, you should be able to merge the branches and see the code added into the master branch. Open the Source Code menu again and hover over the HearMeNow – SlowDown item. As you can see in Figure 12-32, Xcode gives you two options for merging branches: Merge from Branch ... and Merge to Branch .... Which branch you are currently working on will influence your choice here.

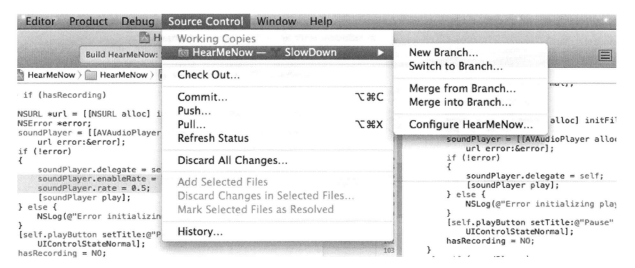

Figure 12-32. Examining the options for merging branches

- Use Merge from Branch if you are currently working on the target branch, the one you want to add the changes to. You can then select a source branch that has the changes you wish to merge from.

- Use Merge into Branch if you are currently working on the source branch, the one that holds the changes, as you currently should be. You can then select the branch you want to use as the target to merge into.

Based on these two cases, it is the later that is needed in this scenario. Choose Merge into Branch ... and as shown in Figure 12-33. You will be presented with a screen to select a target for merging into.

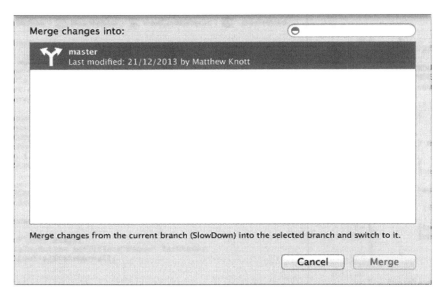

Figure 12-33. Selecting a target branch

> **Note**   There is a small glitch that you may encounter here. You may find that when the list of available branches appears, the merge option is grayed out, even when you click the branch. Click in the white space below the branch name to deselect it and click the branch name again; the merge button will become available again.

Select the master branch and click Merge. You will again be presented with the code Comparison view, as shown in Figure 12-34, just as when you went to commit the changes, however, this time the options are different. Notice that in between the left and right panes, you will have a switch instead of the numbered option that appears when you commit changes. This is the direction slider that determines how you merge the files. Because you have been disciplined and not modified the master branch, only the SlowDown branch, you need to merge the changes from the right to the left as is currently selected.

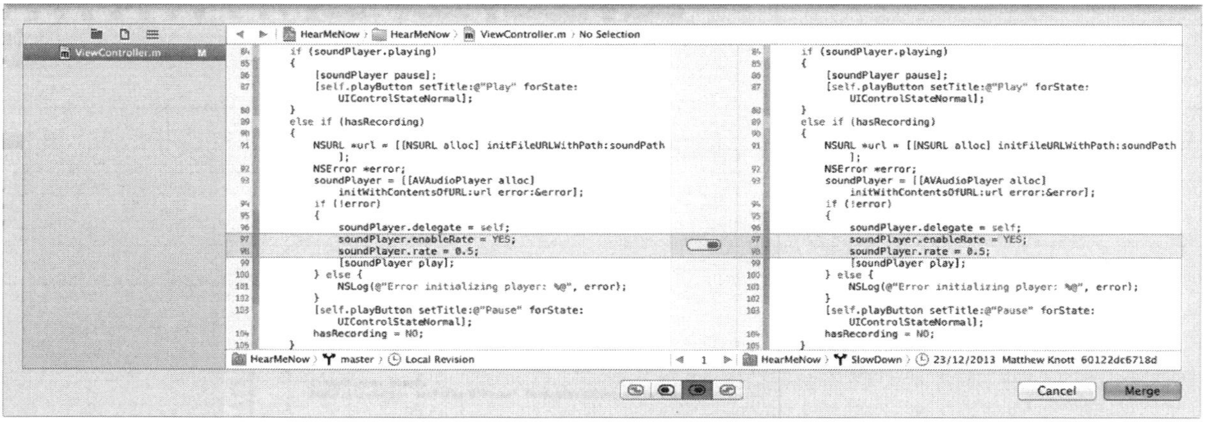

Figure 12-34. The code comparison view shown before merging

You could very realistically have a scenario where both yourself and a colleague have separate branches where you are adding new features independently of each other. In this scenario, you might want to merge the two branches before merging them into the master branch. Alternatively, you may wish to merge one of the branches with the master, create a new master branch, and have your colleague merge his or her branch with the new branch for testing purposes before ultimately merging that branch into the master.

Once you are happy that the dark part of the switch is pointing to the newer SlowDown branch as the source, click Merge. At this point, there is a good chance you will be prompted to enable or disable snapshots. I tend to disable snapshots. I have Time Machine configured on my Mac and because I am committing code to the Git repository, I am fairly comfortable that I don't need snapshots, however, the choice is yours to make.

Once you have made your choice, the merge operation will be complete and you will return to Xcode and the ViewController.m file within the master branch. If you now run the application, you will find that the application being built from the master branch has the half speed playback you added in the SlowDown branch, neat!

Removing a Branch

Now that you have successfully merged your branches, it would be considered good housekeeping to remove the SlowDown branch as it is no longer needed. Go to Source Control ➤ HearMeNow – Master ➤ Configure HearMeNow … and select the Branches tab, as shown in Figure 12-35.

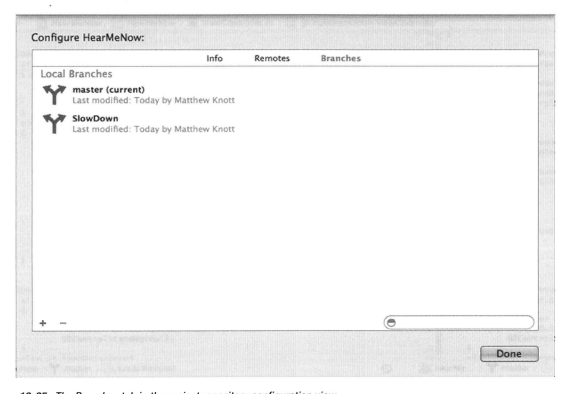

Figure 12-35. The Branches tab in the project repository configuration view

Select the SlowDown branch from the list and then click the – icon in the bottom left corner. You will then be prompted to confirm the removal, as shown in Figure 12-36, so click Delete Branch. The branch will be permanently removed, leaving you with a neat and tidy repository.

Figure 12-36. Xcode prompting to delete the branch

Using a Remote Repository

Up until this point, this chapter has been concentrating on using a local Git repository, but as I've already mentioned, it is not the only option available. There are a number of online solutions available to you for hosting or backing up your Git repository online, such as with the massively popular GitHub, Bitbucket, and a number of others.

With these services, you get all the benefits of a local Git repository, with the added benefits of it being available for collaboration with the rest of the online world. If you don't have all the expertise you need to finish your application or game, you can push your repository online and enlist your friends' help in adding those killer features.

In this era of open source software, more and more people are turning to online Git repositories to share their source code with the world. Making your software publically available can be incredibly rewarding when you see people making interesting new applications based on your code. Being online doesn't have to mean being open to everyone, however. You can create a private repository and restrict access to it based on your preferences.

To finish this chapter, I am going to take you through signing up for a GitHub account and sharing your repository online, and it's unbelievably simple.

Registering for GitHub and Creating a Repository

Registering for a GitHub account is made extremely simple because of the clever way the web site has been designed. Start by heading to http://github.com. As you can see in Figure 12-37, the registration form is right on the front page. Fill in the username, e-mail, and password boxes and click the Sign up for GitHub button.

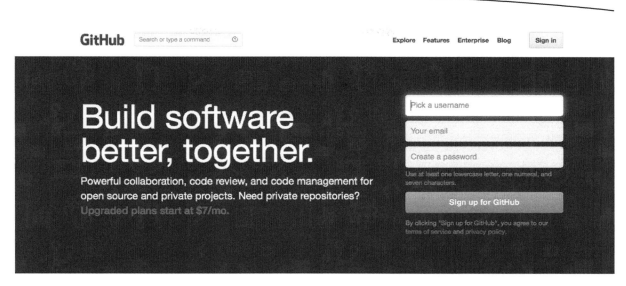

Figure 12-37. *The GitHub home page*

If you already have an account, click the Sign in button in the top right-hand corner.

Once you've signed in to GitHub, you will be presented with the launch page shown in Figure 12-38. The first thing you need to do is create a repository to add into Xcode. I have highlighted the New repository button, so go ahead and click this.

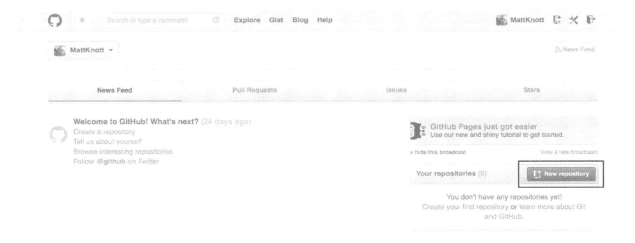

Figure 12-38. *The GitHub launch page*

Creating a new repository in GitHub is super easy. Just give the repository a name, as shown in Figure 12-39, and choose whether you want the repository to be public or private. I have named my repository HearMeNow after the project, but you can name it anything within reason. Once you have added a name, click the Create repository button.

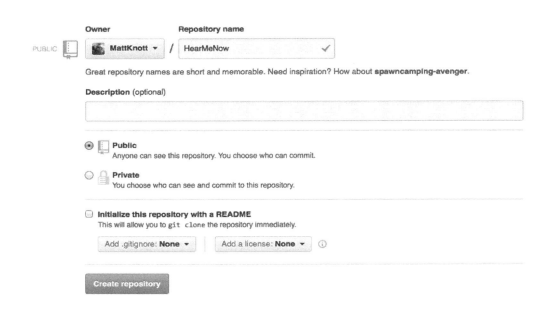

Figure 12-39. *Creating a new GitHub repository*

Once you have created the repository, you will be taken to the repository page, which is effectively empty at this point. But there are some key details you need to make note of. Figure 12-40 shows the Quick setup box, which holds the HTTP address for the repository. At the end of the address is a Copy to clipboard button. Click it to copy the repository address ready for adding into Xcode.

Figure 12-40. *The Quick setup box on the GitHub repository page*

Adding a GitHub Repository to Xcode

If you've worked with Git before or if you're trying it for the first time, hopefully one thing that's apparent to you is how easy Apple has made their interface into this fantastic technology. Linking with the remote repository you just created is no exception, and Apple gives you two ways to do it.

Adding a Remote Repository in Repository Configuration

First, you can quickly add a link to a remote repository by going to Source Control ➤ HearMeNow – Master ➤ Configure HearMeNow … and select the Remotes tab. Click the + symbol in the bottom left-hand corner and click Add Remote … .

Figure 12-41. *Adding a remote repository in the repository configuration's Remotes tab*

Give the remote repository a reference name and then paste in the address you copied from the Quick setup box in GitHub. Your completed configuration should resemble that shown in Figure 12-42. Click Add Remote to add the reference into Xcode.

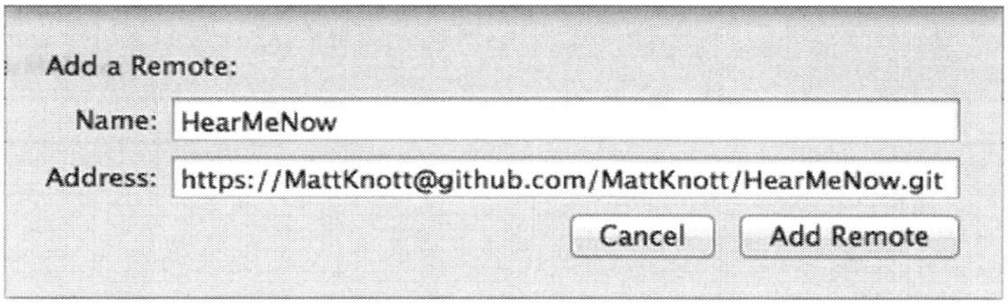

Add a Remote:

Name: HearMeNow

Address: https://MattKnott@github.com/MattKnott/HearMeNow.git

Cancel | Add Remote

Figure 12-42. *Configuring a reference to a remote repository*

One of the limitations with this method is that it doesn't present us with the ability to add in the GitHub username and password that is required to write to the repository, which brings me nicely to the second way of adding a remote repository.

Adding a Remote Repository with Xcode Preferences

The second method for adding a remote repository is my preferred way and often the quickest way to get your repository ready for action. For this method you will need to access Xcode's Preferences, the area of Xcode you went to when you customized the Xcode interface in Chapter 10. To access the preferences, go to Xcode ➤ Preferences … (⌘ + ,). When the preferences appear, select the Accounts tab, as shown in Figure 12-43. You will see the reference to the GitHub repository you just added in the left-hand column, so go ahead and select it.

Figure 12-43. The incomplete reference for the GitHub repository

You will see that there are fields for User Name and Password, this refers to your GitHub credentials. Take this opportunity to enter your credentials now. Once you enter the user name and click into the password box, Xcode will try to validate the details online. When you have entered the details, click the red dot in the top left corner to close the preferences.

> **Note**   A word of caution when entering your credentials; if you make a mistake with the User Name field, you will have to remove the repository reference and then add it again. It's not clear why Xcode locks the field, but it does and it cannot be edited.

You have now successfully added a remote repository into Xcode. Next I will show you how to push your entire repository to the cloud in your GitHub repository.

Pushing to a Remote Repository

You've successfully set up a remote repository and linked it into Xcode, so now all that remains is to somehow duplicate your repository onto GitHub. Because Git was developed with this type of working in mind, there are two features designed specifically for working with remote repositories: Push and Pull.

Issuing a Push command will copy the entire repository over to your GitHub repository, and it is incredibly easy to do now that you have added the repository into Xcode. To push the local repository to GitHub, go to Source Control ➤ Push … and you will be presented with the dialog shown in Figure 12-44 to choose which remote repository you want to push to.

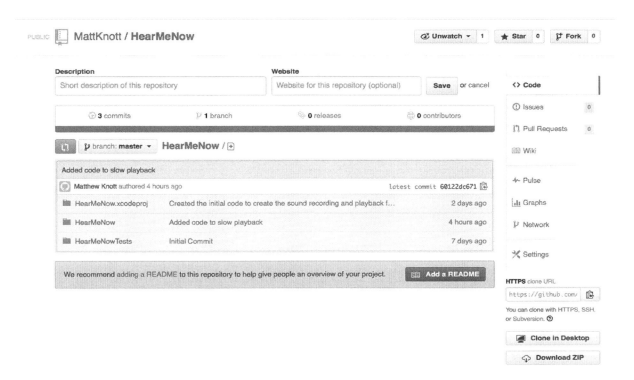

Figure 12-44. *Selecting the remote repository*

As you only have a single repository available, the choice here is simple, so click the Push button. Xcode will spend a few moments depending on your connection speed as it sends the entire repository to GitHub. When the process is complete, the dialog will automatically close.

Now for the exciting part! Head back to your web browser and the GitHub web site, refresh the page on your repository, and the contents of your project will appear, as shown in Figure 12-45.

Figure 12-45. *The files from the project are now also hosted on GitHub*

In just a few quick steps you have taken a piece of work that was stuck in the confines of your Mac and shared it with the world. Now anyone can look at your code if you let them, they can copy it to their own Git repository or offer to update yours, and you will come to learn the collaborative joy that is Git version control.

Updating the Remote Repository

Now that you have pushed your code to a remote repository, you will need to think about maintaining it as your project continues to develop locally. Xcode makes linking your local and remote updates a piece of cake.

To demonstrate this, you will need to make a small modification to one of the files in the project so open `ViewController.m` from the Project Navigator and ensure you are using the Standard Editor.

There is no need to make a drastic change; the only goal is to differentiate the file somehow from the last committed version. To do this I added a line to the comments at the top of the file to say that this is the implementation file. Modify your implementation file in a similar way to this highlighted code:

```
//  ViewController.m
//  HearMeNow
//
//  Created by Matthew Knott on 16/12/2013.
//  Copyright (c) 2013 Matthew Knott. All rights reserved.
//  This is the view controller implementation file
```

Once you have done that, commit the change to the repository by going to Source Control ➤ Commit … . Before clicking the button to commit the files, take a look in the bottom-left corner of the Commit view and note the Push to remote check box. Check this as shown in Figure 12-46 and your GitHub repository will automatically appear.

Figure 12-46. *Electing to also push to the remote repository*

You may notice that the Commit button has now changed to read Commit 1 File and Push. Add in a commit message as the button suggests, then push it to see what happens. After a brief pause, the view will close and the operation is complete.

To verify what happened in the remote repository, go back to your web browser and the page for the GitHub repository you created. Once you have refreshed the page, you will note that as shown in Figure 12-47, the number of commits shown is now listed as 4.

4 commits	1 branch	0 releases	0 contributors

branch: **master** ▾   **HearMeNow** / ⊞

Figure 12-47. *The number of commits on the repository now shows as 4*

To see the level of replication between the local and remote repositories, click the number of commits, and you will be taken to a page showing the commit history, as shown in Figure 12-48. As you will see, it has all of the previous commits and their comments exactly the same as the local repository does.

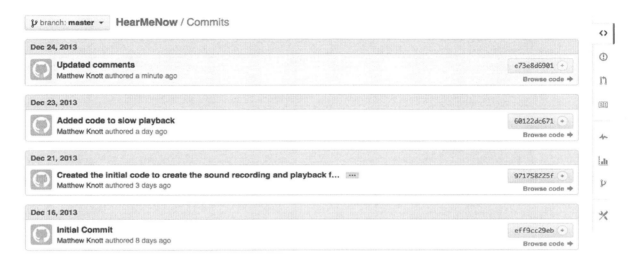

Figure 12-48. The GitHub commit history matches the local repository

Summary

In this chapter, you've learned the ins and outs of software version control in Xcode using Git while writing a basic voice recorder application. Specifically you have:

- Created a local repository

- Learned about committing changes to the repository

- Looked at the Version Editor and seen how it allows you to compare files and roll back changes

- Made and merged branches

- Added and used a remote repository

One of the reasons that I started writing this book is because I have always loved trying to encourage people to code, and I know so many people who found that programming was their artistic outlet after years of trying to express themselves. My son is only five now, but one day I dream about us working on projects together, and it's because of technology like Git that wherever in the world life might take my son, that dream doesn't have to die.

Whatever your hopes for Git, you now have an excellent grounding in all the skills needed to make the most out of it. In the next chapter, you will be learning about localization with Xcode and how to make your application support multiple languages in a single version.

Chapter 13

Localization

Chapter 12 looked at how Xcode used Git to create some of the finest version control ever seen in an IDE. You created a simple voice recorder under Git source control, and then branched the repository to add extra functionality without altering the original and then merged the two branches together.

This chapter will look at the localization of an application. Localization is the term given to the ability of a single application to appear in multiple languages. Making your application available in multiple languages is a key step to maximizing your success on the App Store as you can offer your application in the native language of every country you choose to advertise in.

> *If you talk to a man in a language he understands, that goes to his head. If you talk to him in his language, that goes to his heart.*

—Nelson Mandela

Localization works best when the user doesn't even have to make a language selection, the application simply detects the language the user has set for their operating system and the correct language files are loaded. In the past with other programming languages and IDEs, this could create massive development overheads, but developing applications for iOS and OS X with Xcode makes this process so simple, requiring minimal development, and once you've created your application in one language, you'll be amazed how easy it is to add more.

In this chapter you will be creating an interesting application called Castles. This application will be the kind of app a tourist board might develop to highlight one of the great features of a country, and in this case it will show a number of photos from different castles in Wales.

In addition to localizing the application and making it available in Italian, you will also be using two new controls, a Scroll View (`UIScrollView`) and a Page Control (`UIPageControl`), to create a gallery of images that the user can swipe through to the left and right. Figure 13-1 shows the finished application running in both English and Italian.

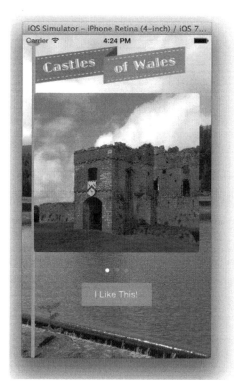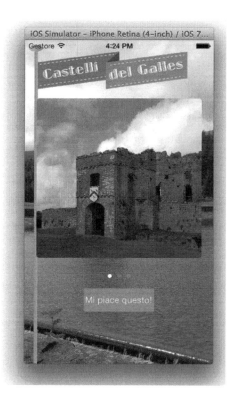

Figure 13-1. *The finished application running in English and Italian*

Another point about the Castles application is that it is the last application you will be creating in this book. For the final two chapters, you will be using this application to explore the functionality before seeing how you would go about submitting it to the App Store, so be sure to keep it handy when you finish this chapter.

Creating the Castles Application

One thing about localization that I've always found to be true is that you should do it at the end of the development process. This doesn't necessarily mean that you shouldn't write your application with localization in mind, such as by using the NSLocalizedString macro for all user-facing strings, but it's not essential. When you are starting out with Xcode, focus on getting your code right and your application working the way you want it. This is the approach I'm going to take with the Castles application. You will write the code in a familiar way, and then once the application is finished and working, you will start to localize the strings in your code, Images, and the Storyboard.

1. Start by opening Xcode and then create a new project by going to File ➤ New ➤ New Project ... (⌘ + Shift + N) or, alternatively, Create a new Xcode project if you are on the Welcome screen (⌘ + Shift + 1).

2. The Castles application is going to be based on the Single View Application template, so select this and then click Next.

3. Name the product Castles, and ensure that the Devices option is set to iPhone, substitute your own personal information, leaving the other settings as they are shown in Figure 13-2, and then click Next.

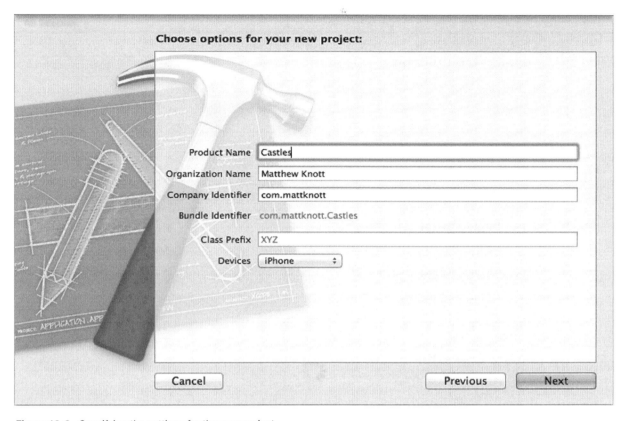

Figure 13-2. *Specifying the settings for the new project*

4. On the next screen, ensure that the Source Control option is ticked, as shown in Figure 13-3, and click Create. Using source control, you will then be able to commit the changes once you have a working application before embarking on the localization of the application, where your application may become unstuck.

Figure 13-3. *Choosing to create a Git repository*

5. After clicking Create, you will be taken to your new project and the settings for this project. Within the settings, look for the section titled Deployment Info; because this application only needs to operate in portrait mode, uncheck the Landscape Left and Landscape Right options, as highlighted in Figure 13-4.

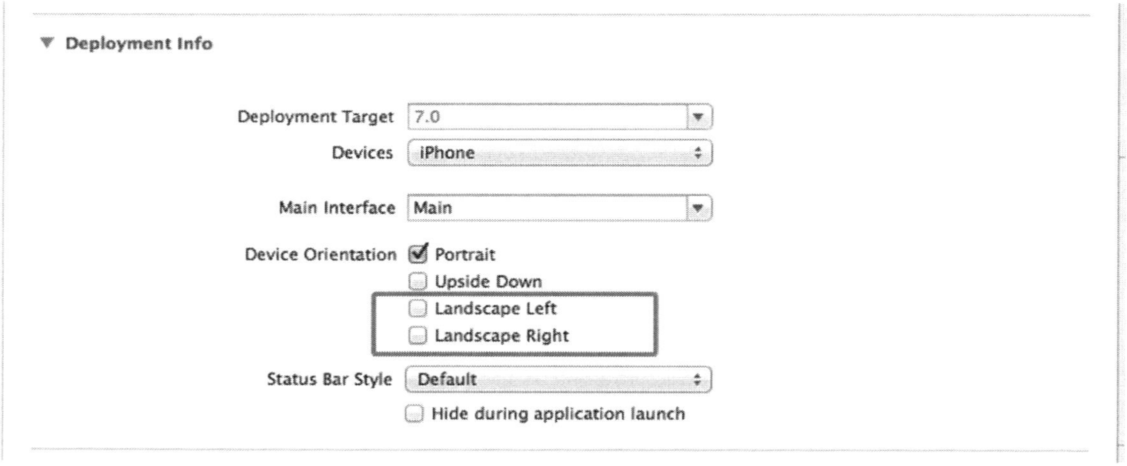

Figure 13-4. *The Landscape options unticked in the project settings*

Great! The project is now ready to be assembled, but before you do that, there are a number of pre-prepared resources you really need to download and add to your project.

Adding the Resources

For this chapter more than any other, I recommend you download the source code and resources file available from `apress.com`. To get the source code, go to the Apress web site and then the page for this book, or go directly to `www.apress.com/9781430257431`.

Once on the page, scroll down until you see a series of tabs, one of which will be Source Code/Downloads. On this tab you will find a link to download all of the resources for the book, as shown in Figure 13-5. Click the Download Now link to begin the download.

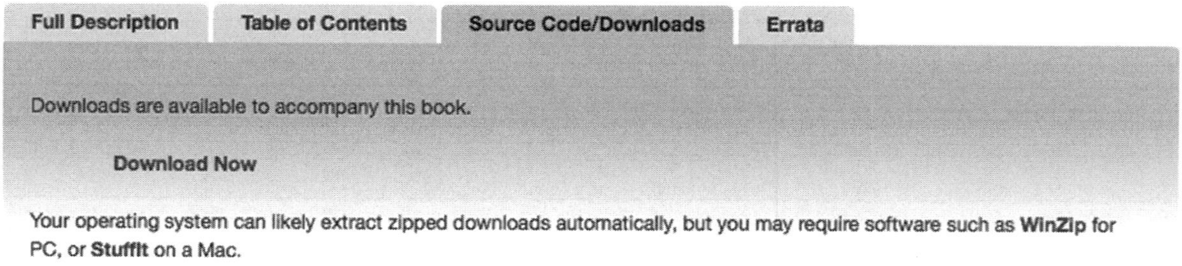

Figure 13-5. *The area of this book's page on* `apress.com` *where you can download the resources for the book*

Once the zip file has downloaded, your Mac is capable of opening the file without any additional software. Open the Finder and navigate to the downloads folder for whichever browser you are using. Open the file you just downloaded and the Mac will extract it automatically. Within the extracted file, go to the Chapter 13 folder, and then the Resources folder, as shown in Figure 13-6.

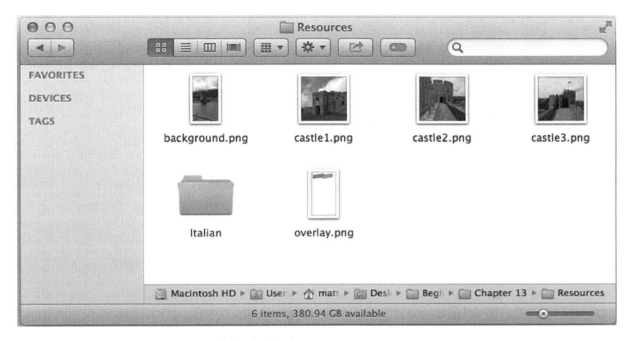

Figure 13-6. The contents of the resources folder for this chapter

With the exception of the contents of the Italian folder, you need to add all of these resources into Xcode before you go any further. The destination for every one of these images is going to be the Images.xcassets Asset Catalog.

1. Back in Xcode, select Images.xcassets from the Project Navigator to open the Asset Catalog.

2. You will be creating five new image sets to hold these resources. Thankfully, you don't have to create each image set individually. Start by having both Xcode and the Finder window with the resources for this chapter open.

3. Select the background, overlay, castle1, castle2, and castle3 images within the Finder and drag them over to the list of assets, as shown in Figure 13-7.

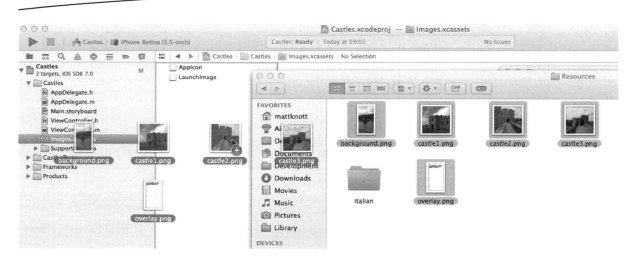

Figure 13-7. Dragging in the resources for the application to create image sets

You will be left with five new image sets that are already named exactly as they need to be, and unlike when you add an image in the traditional fashion, you don't have to explicitly specify whether or not to copy the image into the project, that is done automatically! Ensure that your Asset Catalog resembles that shown in Figure 13-8 and then you can begin to create the application's interface.

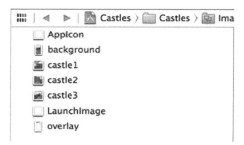

Figure 13-8. The contents of the Asset Catalog after adding the five images for the project

Creating the Application Interface

Now that your project is configured and has all of the required resources, all that remains is for you to create the interface and write a relatively small amount of code to create a working application.

In Figure 13-1, I gave you a preview of the application's user interface. It consists of two Image Views, a Scroll View, a Page Control, and a Button. Select `Main.storyboard` from the Project Navigator to start building the interface.

Compositing with Transparent Images

Before you start adding the different controls onto the Storyboard, it's worth taking a moment to explain an important technique you will often use when developing applications in Xcode, which is the use of transparent PNG files to create composite images, which is an image made up of more than one file.

To explain this a bit better, take a look at Figure 13-9. This image shows two of the images you just added to the project: `background.png` and `overlay.png`.

| background.png | overlay.png | Combined in final application |

Figure 13-9. The background and overlay images from this project, used to create a composite effect

`Background.png` is a regular photograph, whereas `overlay.png` is special because it has a transparent background. In Xcode, you combine these images by first creating an Image View for the background and then adding a second Image View on top containing the overlay image. Because `overlay.png` has a transparent background, the Image View containing `background.png` is still visible through it, however, in the finished application, it gives the illusion of being a single image.

You may wonder why you would want to take this approach? Well, in this situation where the application that is being developed is going to be available in another language, you can produce multiple overlay images for each language without having to include the background in the file every time, ultimately reducing the file size of your completed application. Another benefit is that you may want to alter the background at a later date, either by changing the included image or by programmatically alternating between multiple images that do not then need to include the foreground portion of the image.

1. Now that that's clear, you're ready to start creating the composite effect. Drag an Image View from the Object Library onto the View in the Storyboard, as shown in Figure 13-10 and let it fill the entire view.

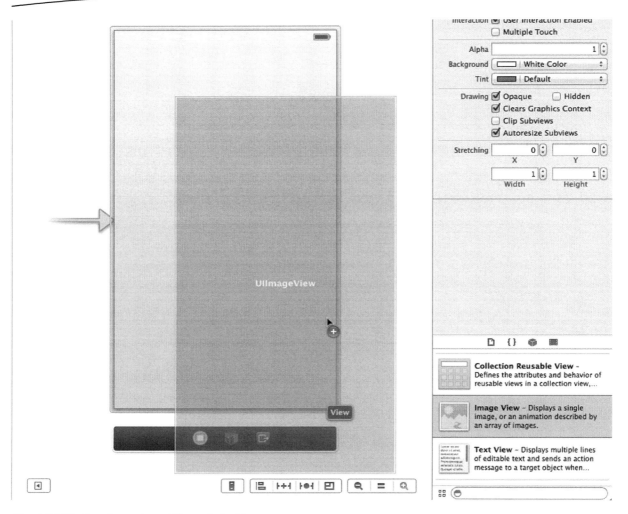

Figure 13-10. *Dragging an Image View onto the View*

2. Once the Image View is in place, open the Attributes Inspector and in the list for the Image attribute, select Background.

3. Because this Image View is the correct size and shape, it makes sense to duplicate it for the overlay image. To do this, first click the background Image View, and then go to Edit ➤ Duplicate (⌘ + D), which will create a replica of the image, as shown in Figure 13-11.

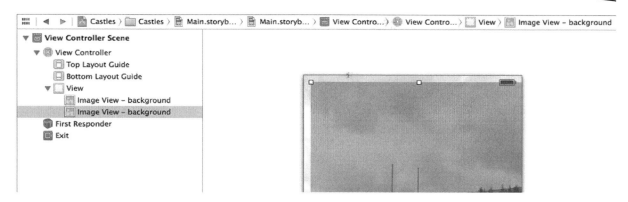

Figure 13-11. The duplicated Image View, slightly offset from the original's position

4. The duplicated Image View is offset slightly from the original's position, but you can correct that easily. First, open the Attributes Inspector and change the Image attribute from background to overlay and then position the image back in the top-left corner, as shown in Figure 13-12.

Figure 13-12. Repositioning the overlay Image view in the top-left corner

That's it! You have successfully composited your first image in Xcode. Now to move on to the next two elements of the interface: a Scroll View and Page Control. This is the first time you have come across the these two controls within this book, however, if you've ever used an iOS device before, you will be more than familiar with them.

Adding a Scroll View

Scroll Views are a bit of an unsung hero of iOS development, they are everywhere but unless you're an iOS developer, you wouldn't know it. Before I started writing iOS applications, my background was in web development, where you can just keep adding content onto your page, knowing that the browser will allow the user to scroll through that content and all you as a developer needed to be concerned with was that the content was there.

When developing for iOS applications, you don't have that luxury. If you want the user to scroll through content that isn't in a Web or Text View, or other such control, then you need to use a Scroll View. The Scroll View itself is a fixed size and does not move, but within the Scroll View is a content area that can move in any direction or can be fixed to move only in a vertical or horizontal direction.

Figure 13-13 tries to explain how a Scroll View works by illustrating what goes on behind the scenes in the finished application. As you can see, the Scroll View is positioned in the middle of the parent View and doesn't move, but within the Scroll View highlighted in gray is a large content area containing the three castle image views that extend way off screen.

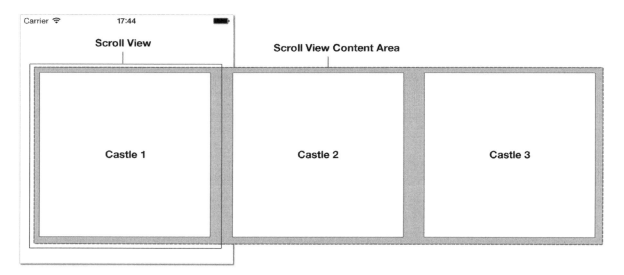

Figure 13-13. *An illustration highlighting what goes on behind the scenes in a Scroll View*

The Scroll View automatically recognizes swipe gestures and allows the user to position the content area by positioning it with their finger. When the paging attribute is enabled on the Scroll View, it will automatically calculate a "page" size and snap to those pages as the user scrolls through. You will be enabling paging and feeding back that position into a Page Control that reflects the user's position within the scrollable content.

That's it for the theory, now it's time to add the Scroll View into the user interface.

1. Drag in a Scroll View from the Object Navigator and position it loosely in the middle of the View, as shown in Figure 13-14. Don't worry too much about the positioning for now, because of the need for precise positioning you will be adjusting the size and position in the Size Inspector.

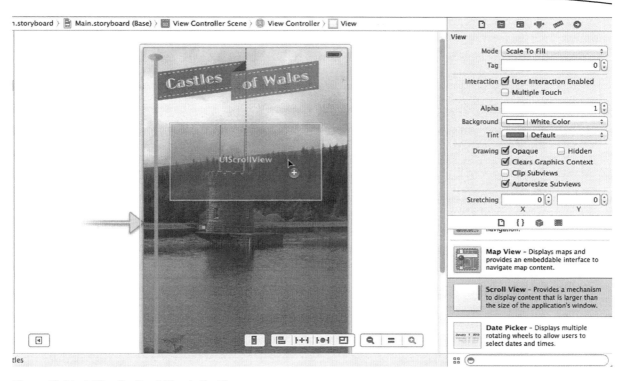

Figure 13-14. *Adding the Scroll View to the View*

2. Once the Scroll View has been added to the scene, open the Size Inspector. Scroll down to the View section and set the X value to 20, Y value to 100, and Width and Height to 280; your completed values should resemble those shown in Figure 13-15.

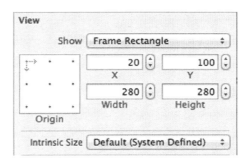

Figure 13-15. *The precise positioning and sizes of the Scroll View*

3. Now that the Scroll View is positioned, open the Attributes Inspector. There are a number of attributes to configure, so I'll take you through in groups. First, because this Scroll View will only move horizontally, uncheck the Shows Vertical Indicator box.

4. Next, in the Scrolling section, tick the box for Paging Enabled. I previously mentioned that the Scroll View will be using paging, so this is the attribute that controls it.

5. For this last attribute, I decided I didn't want the swiping to feel too rigid, so to counter this, tick the box for Bounces Horizontally in the Bounce section. Now when the user swipes left and right, the image will have an elastic appearance and will snap into place. The Attributes Inspector should match those shown in Figure 13-16.

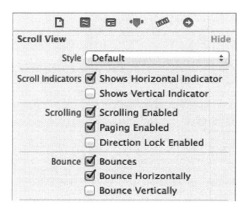

Figure 13-16. *The attributes of the Scroll View*

6. In previous chapters, you set the delegate for various controls within the code of the implementation file, but it is possible to also set it through Interface Builder. Control-drag a connection from the Scroll View down to the yellow View Controller icon, as shown in Figure 13-17.

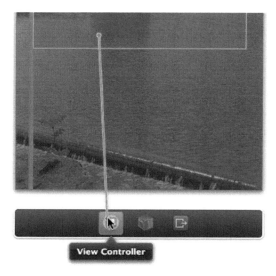

Figure 13-17. *Creating a connection between the Scroll View and the View Controller*

When you release the mouse, you will have a single option of delegate. Select this, and you have now specified that the View Controller is acting as the delegate for the Scroll View, just as if you had specified `MyScrollView.delegate = self`.

Because you will be using paging with the Scroll View, it automatically calculates page dimensions, so it's really important to think through the size of the content items so they are evenly distributed and to set the Scroll View dimensions appropriately, which is what you've just done. Next, you will add the Page Control to the scene.

Adding a Page Control

Page Controls provide a visual representation in the form of a series of horizontal dots to show the user's position in any paged object, in this case a Scroll View, and traditionally the number of dots shown represents the number of pages within the object. Page Controls are also interactive, and often a user can select a dot to go to the respective page in the paged object. A Page Control in an iPhone or iPod touch application can hold around 20 dots before they are clipped. If you are likely to have more than 20 pages, it may not be worth displaying a Page Control, so think about the user's experience before settling on a Page Control.

Page Controls can be found throughout iOS, even on the home screen, as shown in Figure 13-18. As you add additional pages of app icons to the home screen, the number of dots will increase to reflect the number of pages.

Figure 13-18. The Page Control as shown on the iOS home screen

Now that you know what a Page Control is and what it does, it's time to go ahead and add one onto the View. Locate the Page Control object in the Object Library and drag it onto the View, positioning it centrally and just below the Scroll View, as shown in Figure 13-19.

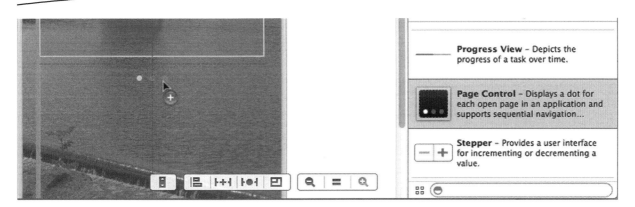

Figure 13-19. Adding a Page Control onto the View

There are no attributes that need configuring for the Page Control, so now you can complete the interface for this application by adding and configuring a button and creating the outlets and actions.

Completing the Interface

To complete this application, you will be adding a Button that says "I Like This!" and when tapped it will thank the user for liking castle number x, with x being the current page number.

1. Start by dragging in a Button from the Object Library and positioning it just below the Page Control for now, as shown in Figure 13-20.

Figure 13-20. The new button added to the View, although slightly hard to see

2. It will be quite hard to see the blue Button text against the background, so open the Attributes Inspector and change the Title text to I Like It! and the Text Color attribute to White Color. Your attributes should match those shown in Figure 13-21.

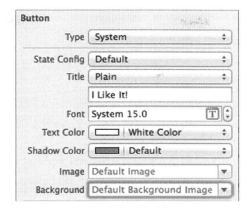

Figure 13-21. The top section of the Button attributes

3. Next, scroll further down the list of attributes until you reach the View section. Find the attribute called Background and change the color to one of your choosing; I went for an orange color but you can choose anything you like for your button.

4. By now you probably think your button looks ridiculous compressed and unreadable, and you'd be right. As Figure 13-22 shows, drag the left and right sides of the Button out to greatly increase its size. Be generous, because when you translate the Button's text later on, you'll be glad for the extra space.

Figure 13-22. Resizing the I Like It! Button

5. With your button a respectable size, you can now create the outlets and actions so that you can begin writing the code for this application. Start, as usual, by opening the Assistant Editor and ensuring that ViewController.h is selected from the jump bar, as shown in Figure 13-23.

Figure 13-23. Selecting ViewController.h from the jump bar

6. First, you are going to create the outlets for each item. Start by holding down the Control key and dragging a connection from the Scroll View to the header just below the @interface in the header file and create an outlet called scrollView.

7. Next, control-drag a connection from the Page Control to just below the last outlet and create a new outlet called pageControl.

8. Finally, you need to create an action for the I Like It! Button. Control-drag a connection from the Button to just below the outlets and change the Connection property to Action and set the name of the action as likeCastle.

That's it for the user interface. Everything else in this application will be done using code. Before moving on, ensure that your header code matches the code below and then switch back to the Standard Editor.

```
#import <UIKit/UIKit.h>

@interface ViewController : UIViewController

@property (weak, nonatomic) IBOutlet UIScrollView *scrollView;
@property (weak, nonatomic) IBOutlet UIPageControl *pageControl;

- (IBAction)likeCastle:(id)sender;

@end
```

Writing the Code for the Castles Application

You are extremely limited in what you can achieve with a Scroll View using Interface Builder. To create anything purposeful with them, you need to write some code and create the contents dynamically. Although it isn't glamorous and can be complex at times, creating a working Scroll View with paging can be really rewarding.

In the implementation file, you can set the dimensions of your content area because this is a known value, and then you will create a custom method to initialize and populate your Scroll View, before adding a Scroll View delegate method to update the Page Control position.

1. As you may have suspected, you need to start by opening the ViewController.m file from the Project Navigator.

2. The first code you will write in the implementation file is to create an instance variable to keep the width dimension of the content area so that other methods can reference it. Add the highlighted code below just beneath the line @implementation ViewController:

```
@implementation ViewController
{
    CGFloat dimension;
}
```

3. Next, scroll down a little to the viewDidLoad method; here, you are going to specify the dimension of the content area for the Scroll View. This is done by setting the contentSize property of the scrollView object. This property is a CGSize type, and you can set it by using the CGSizeMake method that takes a width and height parameter, which will be based on the height of the scroll view and three times the width. Once the content size is set, you will take the width and use it to set the dimension instance variable. Add the highlighted code into your viewDidLoad method:

```
- (void)viewDidLoad
{
    [super viewDidLoad];

    _scrollView.contentSize = CGSizeMake(_scrollView.frame.size.width * 3,
                                    _scrollView.frame.size.height);
    dimension = _scrollView.bounds.size.width;
}
```

4. You have now set the Scroll View's content area size; if you were to refer to Figure 13-13, the dark shaded area is the content area and if you were to run the applications now, even though you can't see it, this is the size of the content area. Next you need to start on the method that will populate your Scroll View with images of castles, createPages. After the viewDidLoad method, drop down a line and create the method with the following code:

```
- (void) createPages
{

}
```

5. Within this method, you are going to create and position three UIImageView objects within the Scroll View. Because the code for doing this is repeated, you are going to use a for loop that will repeat three times, each time adding an extra UIImageView to the content area, as was shown in Figure 13-13. Within the createPages method, add the following highlighted code to create your for loop:

```
- (void) createPages
{
    for (NSInteger i = 0; i<3; i++)
    {

    }
}
```

As I mentioned previously, each time this loop runs, a UIImageView will be added into the Scroll View. When this happens, you need to supply an x (left to right) and y (top to bottom) position for the UIImageView; the y position will always be 0 (i.e., the top of the content area), but the x position increases by the width of the Scroll View each loop. To calculate the x position, you are going to multiply the Scroll View width by the value of I from the for loop. The Scroll View width is 280, so every time the for loop fires, the x position will be calculated as follows:

- *Loop 1:* I = 0, 280 * 0 = 0. x = 0
- *Loop 2:* I = 1, 280 * 1 = 280. x = 280
- *Loop 3:* I = 2, 280 * 2 = 560. x = 560

Based on these figures, the Image Views will be positioned along the x axis, as shown in Figure 13-24.

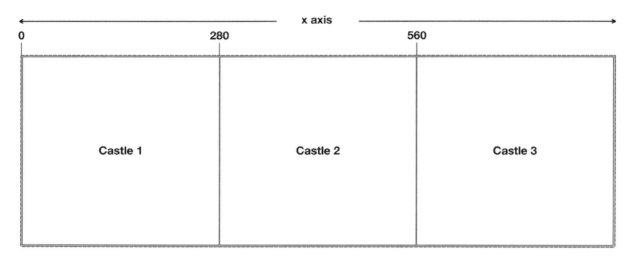

Figure 13-24. *The position of the three Image Views along the x axis of the Scroll View*

6. If all of that seemed quite complicated, the implementation is very straight forward; add the following highlighted code into your for loop:

```
- (void) createPages
{
    for (NSInteger i = 0; i<3; i++)
    {
        NSInteger xPosition = 0;
        NSInteger yPosition = 0;

        xPosition = _scrollView.frame.size.width * i;
    }
}
```

7. With the coordinates for each image now known, you can start to create the UIImageView using the initWithFrame method, which will allow you to supply a CGRect parameter that consists of an x position, y position, width and height. Just as with the CGSize type, there is a CGRectMake method. Add the highlighted code to your method to declare and initialize the UIImageView:

```
- (void) createPages
{
    for (NSInteger i = 0; i<3; i++)
    {
        NSInteger xPosition = 0;
        NSInteger yPosition = 0;

        xPosition = _scrollView.frame.size.width * i;

        UIImageView *castleView = [[UIImageView alloc]
                                initWithFrame:CGRectMake(xPosition,
                                                        yPosition,
                                                        _scrollView.frame.size.width,
                                                        _scrollView.frame.size.height)];

    }
}
```

8. Now that you have declared and initialized your UIImageView, you need to dynamically fetch the image in the shape of a UIImage to be displayed and apply it to castleView using the setImage method. Add the following highlighted code into the method:

```
- (void) createPages
{
    for (NSInteger i = 0; i<3; i++)
    {
        NSInteger xPosition = 0;
        NSInteger yPosition = 0;

        xPosition = _scrollView.frame.size.width * i;

        UIImageView *castleView = [[UIImageView alloc]
                                initWithFrame:CGRectMake(xPosition,
                                                        yPosition,
                                                        _scrollView.frame.size.width,
                                                        _scrollView.frame.size.height)];

        NSString *imageName = [NSString stringWithFormat:@"castle%li",(i+1)];
        UIImage *img = [UIImage imageNamed:imageName];
        [castleView setImage:img];
    }
}
```

9. With the position, dimensions, and image set, all that remains is to add the UIImageView into the Scroll View. This is done by using the addSubView method of the scrollView object. Add the final highlighted line of code to complete the method:

```
- (void) createPages
{
    for (NSInteger i = 0; i<3; i++)
    {
        NSInteger xPosition = 0;
        NSInteger yPosition = 0;

        xPosition = _scrollView.frame.size.width * i;

        UIImageView *castleView = [[UIImageView alloc]
                                initWithFrame:CGRectMake(xPosition,
                                                        yPosition,
                                                        _scrollView.frame.size.width,
                                                        _scrollView.frame.size.height)];

        NSString *imageName = [NSString stringWithFormat:@"castle%li",(i+1)];
        UIImage *img = [UIImage imageNamed:imageName];
        [castleView setImage:img];

        [_scrollView addSubview:castleView];
    }
}
```

> **Note** Depending on whether you are building for a 32-bit or 64-bit architecture, you may receive a warning about your use of %li suggesting you change it to %i. This is because integers are 32-bit and longs or long integers are 64-bit and therefore it is more efficient to use the type the best suits your environment. In this case, stick with whichever option suits your target architecture.

10. Next, you will write a function that specifies the position of the dot in the Page Control as the user flicks back and forth between the pages. The best way to do this is by using the Scroll View delegate method scrollViewDidEndDecelerating, which is called when the Scroll View settles on a page. Add the following code after the previous method to set the pageControl object's currentPage property:

```
- (void)scrollViewDidEndDecelerating:(UIScrollView *)aScrollView
{
        _pageControl.currentPage = floor(_scrollView.contentOffset.x / dimension);
}
```

11. Finally, to complete the application, you need to add some code into the
     likeCastle action method that is called when the I Like It! Button is tapped.
     All that will happen in this method is that an Alert View will be displayed,
     thanking the reader for liking the selected castle picture. Add the following
     highlighted code into the method to complete the application:

```
- (IBAction)likeCastle:(id)sender {

    UIAlertView *likeAlert =
    [[UIAlertView alloc] initWithTitle:@"Thanks!"
                                    message:[NSString stringWithFormat:@"You like castle
number %li",(_pageControl.currentPage+1)]
                                delegate:self
                        cancelButtonTitle:@"Okay"
                        otherButtonTitles:nil];

    [likeAlert show];
}
```

12. All of your methods are now in place, but there is one tiny detail left to add
     in. You created the createPages method but you haven't called it, so nothing
     will happen when you run the application. To rectify this, scroll back up to the
     viewDidLoad method. Add in the highlighted code to call your method:

```
- (void)viewDidLoad
{
    [super viewDidLoad];

    _scrollView.contentSize = CGSizeMake(_scrollView.frame.size.width * 3,
                                    _scrollView.frame.size.height);
    dimension = _scrollView.bounds.size.width;

    [self createPages];
}
```

You're now finished building the application, so go ahead and run it. When the application launches
in the Simulator, use the mouse to act as a digital finger and try to swipe through the three different
images. Click the I Like It! button and see the message appear, as shown in Figure 13-25.

Figure 13-25. *The application running nicely in the simulator*

If everything has been entered correctly, you should now have a working Scroll View in your application. You should be proud of yourself, but the journey is only half complete. This chapter is about localization, and right now you only have a single language in the application, so now the real work begins.

Localizing the Application

So, you may be wondering what's involved in taking your single-language application and turning it into a multilanguage super app? It's easy to have a sense of foreboding at this point, but the process is surprisingly simple. With Xcode 5 and iOS 7, Apple has further refined the steps you need to go through to localize an application, making life much easier for you, the developer. But before you dive in with both feet, take a moment to think about all the elements in this application that are user facing and will need to be translated for each language you localize to:

- Overlay image
- Button text
- Alert View text

Thankfully this application is small, so it won't take a huge amount of effort to localize, but don't think you're missing out on anything. I purposely selected this variety of elements because each one needs to be handled in a completely different way to the others.

Before going any further though, hopefully you kept Source Control enabled as requested when you created the Castles application, so go ahead and commit the changes into the repository through Source Code ➤ Commit (⌘ + ⌥ + C). Add an appropriate comment and click the Commit Files button.

Enabling Localization

Just like a number of other development platforms, when developing apps for iOS 7 in Xcode 5, localization is already enabled for the default language, which in this case is English. Localization isn't something you strictly enable as a principle. Your application is ready and waiting to be localized, all you need to do is specify which languages you want to make it available in.

To see what I mean, in Xcode and as shown in Figure 13-26, select the Castles project from the Project Navigator (step 1), and then select Castles from the Project heading in the sidebar (step 2), instead of Castles under the Target heading.

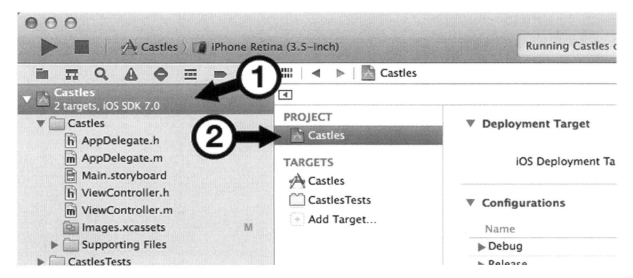

Figure 13-26. Accessing the Project Settings

Within the Project settings, and specifically the default Info tab, you will find all of the details about the different languages that have been added to the project in the Localization section, as shown in Figure 13-27.

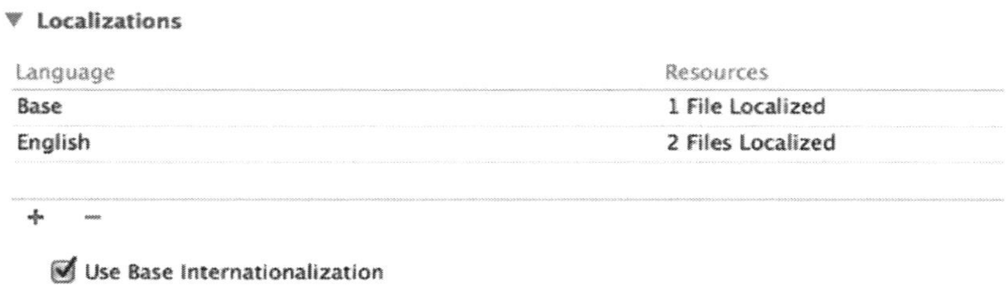

▼ **Localizations**

Language	Resources
Base	1 File Localized
English	2 Files Localized

+   —

☑ Use Base Internationalization

Figure 13-27. *The default localization settings*

As you can see, there are two items showing under the Language heading: Base and English; where do they speak Base? Base actually refers to the Base Localization feature and isn't unique to Xcode but it is a great concept. Basically, base localization is your fallback, your catch all, and while this will become clearer once you begin adding another language, the base language should represent your default language and contain all your strings and localized information.

By adding all of the strings into your base language files, if you miss a translation for some reason, the application will display the base translation instead of a reference or, worse, an error. Once you're happy that your base localizations are right, that's when you move on to adding other languages to the project.

For the sake of building progressively toward the end goal of a localized application with more than one language, you will be creating the strings for the base language at the same time as the Italian translation in some sections, but ordinarily you would get your base translation right before adding any additional languages.

Adding Another Language

Now that you understand what the base language is, it's time to add another language into the project, which as I've already stated, will be Italian.

1. To add a new language, click the + symbol shown at the bottom of the Localizations section shown in Figure 13-27. When you do, a list of available languages will appear as shown in Figure 13-28; select Italian from this list.

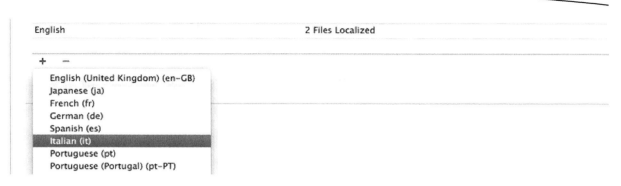

English   2 Files Localized

+ —

    English (United Kingdom) (en-GB)
    Japanese (ja)
    French (fr)
    German (de)
    Spanish (es)
    Italian (it)
    Portuguese (pt)
    Portuguese (Portugal) (pt-PT)

Figure 13-28. *Selecting the Italian language to add to the project*

Once you select the Italian language, a popover will appear, as shown in Figure 13-29, listing all of the files that will be localized, their reference language, and, if applicable, the file type.

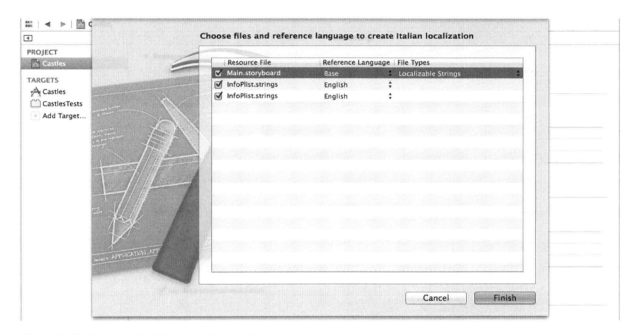

Figure 13-29. *Choosing the files to localize to Italian*

This is actually the most important part when adding a new language. You must ensure that it is using the correct reference language for each resource file. In this case the files are sourced from the only languages they are available in, but if you are adding multiple languages, you have a degree of variability, so ensure the settings are correct. Finally, the Main.storyboard row has a destination File

Types option that can be changed from the default Localizable Strings option to Interface Builder Cocoa Touch Storyboard. To help you understand the differences in these:

- *Localizable Strings*: Selecting this option means you only have a single base Storyboard, and each additional language uses a strings file that holds the translation for every element in the Storyboard rather than a completely separate Storyboard, which can make changing the Storyboard needlessly complicated.

- *Interface Builder Cocoa Touch Storyboard*: This option will create an entirely separate Storyboard that is unique to this locale. Ordinarily you wouldn't want to do this because of the administrative headache you would be creating for yourself. There are occasions where this option might be beneficial if, for example, you needed the application to be pieced together in a drastically different fashion for the new language area.

Based on these explanations, you will definitely want to leave the file type as Localizable Strings, which is the first area you will be translating once the Italian localizations are added.

2. Because the default options are absolutely fine, click the Finish button. You will be returned to the project settings with three languages appearing in the list, as shown in Figure 13-30.

▼ **Localizations**

Language	Resources
Base	1 File Localized
English	2 Files Localized
Italian	3 Files Localized

+ −

Figure 13-30. The list of localizations now features the Italian language

Storyboards and Localization

The additional language that has appeared in your project settings wasn't the only change that's happened when you added the Italian localization. The three files listed in Figure 13-29 have all been duplicated or had a strings file created, as is the case with the Storyboard.

If you look at the Project Navigator, you will notice that Main.storyboard now has a disclosure indicator next to it. Click the arrow and you will see that it is hiding Main.storyboard (base) and Main.strings (Italian), as shown in Figure 13-31, with the base Storyboard being a reference to the true Storyboard and the Main.strings file containing all of the strings that can be found within the Storyboard.

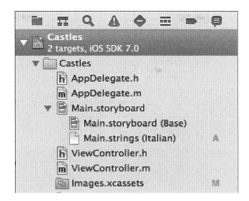

Figure 13-31. *Expanding the disclosure indicator against Main.storyboard exposes the localization strings*

Click `Main.strings` to examine its contents. Your file should contain two lines similar to the following:

```
/* Class = "IBUIButton"; normalTitle = "I Like It!"; ObjectID = "oOI-Ml-ozT"; */
"oOI-Ml-ozT.normalTitle" = "I Like It!";
```

The first line is a comment, and the second is a key/value pair that links the translation to the button's text. The first part of the key `oOI-Ml-ozT` points to the button's unique Object ID that is automatically assigned when the button is added to the Storyboard, and the second part `normalTitle` indicates that the text will be the title for the button's normal state.

Note Your button's Object ID will be different from mine as the value is randomly generated when the object is added to the Storyboard.

The value of I Like It! is taken directly from the base translation and is the part you need to change. So change the text to `Mi piace questo!` as in the following code:

```
"oOI-Ml-ozT.normalTitle" = "Mi piace questo!";
```

Now that you have translated one of your localized items, it's time to see how this takes effect when the application is run in the Simulator.

Testing Localizations in iOS 7

Once you have begun to localize your application, it's a good idea to test it regularly to make sure everything is still as it should be. You can be dealing with a large number of resources and strings, so don't underestimate the potential for making a mistake.

In order to test your translations, however, you need to change the language in the Simulator or device to the one you're localizing to. This is done through the Settings application.

1. Start by stopping your application if it is running and open the Simulator. To get to the home screen, go to Hardware ➤ Home (⌘ + Shift + N) and then select the Settings icon, as shown in Figure 13-32.

Figure 13-32. The icon for the Settings application

2. To access the language selection, choose General ➤ International ➤ Language, as illustrated in Figure 13-33. Once on the language selection, choose Italiano. You will see a message in Italian and then be taken back to the home screen.

Figure 13-33. Accessing language selection by choosing General ➤ International ➤ Language

3. Go back into Xcode and run your application. Although some of the interface will still appear in English, importantly the Button text has now changed to the Italian variation, as shown in Figure 13-34!

Figure 13-34. Your Button, now in Italian!

This is a great start, but there are still two items that need to be localized, so next up, you will look at localizing Images.

Localizing Images

So far, localization has been fairly painless. You have successfully added a new language and added a translated string into the Storyboard strings files to change the text on your button. It's now time to localize the overlay.png file, which is more complicated because of the Asset Catalog.

Asset Catalogs are great, but they haven't been integrated into the localization system as well as other resources have within Xcode. Although Asset Catalogs can be duplicated, it simply isn't worth it when you've got a single image in your catalog that needs a localized version. This is because the process to localize the catalog involves duplicating it in its entirety, which isn't really practical. The easiest way to localize an image in Xcode 5 is to simply remove it from the Asset Catalog and flag it as being localized to both the base and Italian languages.

1. Start by selecting Images.xcassets from the Project Navigator, right-clicking the overlay item, and choosing Remove Selected Items, as shown in Figure 13-35.

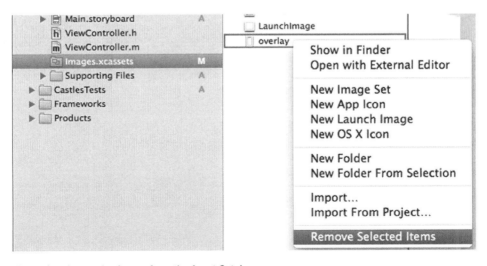

Figure 13-35. Removing the overlay image from the Asset Catalog

With the image removed, you will need to re-add it to the project and then fix the Storyboard, which right now will look a mess.

2. Start by opening Finder and then navigating back to the resources for this project. Drag in overlay.png again, but this time, drag it to the Supporting Files folder, as shown in Figure 13-36.

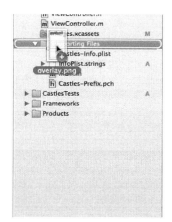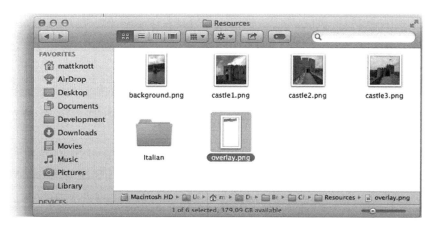

Figure 13-36. Dragging overlay.png into the Supporting Files folder

3. When you release the file onto the Supporting Files folder, the familiar popover will appear. Remember to check the box to Copy items into destination group's folder, as shown in Figure 13-37, and then click Finish.

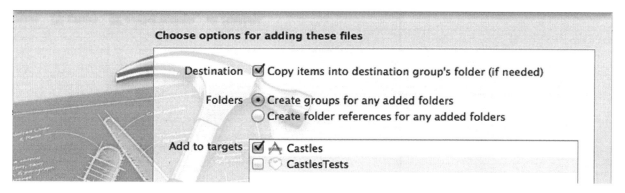

Figure 13-37. Setting the options for adding overlay.png to the project

4. With the overlay image a part of the project again, it's time to correct the gaping hole it left in the Storyboard. Open Main.storyboard from the Project Navigator. As shown in Figure 13-38, the Image View is clearly having issues finding the overlay image.

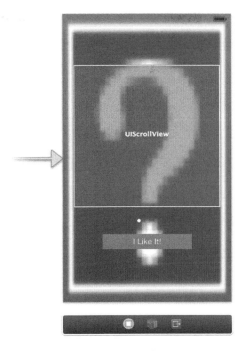

Figure 13-38. The Image View in the Storyboard can't find the overlay image

5.   To fix this, select the Image View and then open the Attributes Inspector; click the Image drop-down and select `overlay.png`, as shown in Figure 13-39.

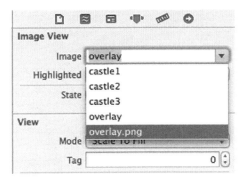

Figure 13-39. Selecting overlay.png as the new source image

6.   Once you have selected the `overlay.png`, order will be restored and the image will appear once again in the Image View. Now you need to look at localizing the file; start by selecting `overlay.png` from the Project Navigator.

7.   Once you have the file selected, open the File Inspector by going to View ➤ Utilities ➤ Show File Inspector (⌘ + ⌥ + 1). You will see that contained within the File Inspector sidebar is a button called Localize..., as shown in Figure 13-40.

Figure 13-40. The Localize button found within the File Inspector

8. Click the Localize button, and you will then be prompted which language you wish to localize to, as shown in Figure 13-41. Leave the selection as the default base language and click Localize.

Figure 13-41. Selecting the Italian language as the target for localization

9. Once the dialog has closed, the area that contained the Localize button in the File Inspector has changed to reflect the languages available for localization. Select Italian, as shown in Figure 13-42. There is no need to tick the English box because English is also the base language, so you would be doubling up needlessly.

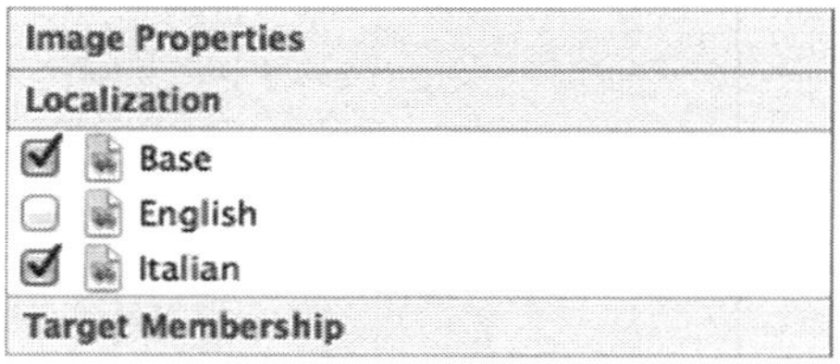

Figure 13-42. Selecting Italian as a localization option

10. If you look at the `overlay.png` image in the Project Navigator, just as with the Storyboard, there is now a disclosure indicator alongside the image. Expand this and, as shown in Figure 13-43, you now have two versions of the image, base language and Italian.

Figure 13-43. The overlay.png file now has two language versions

A Peek Behind the Scenes

As with many things, Xcode does a great job of masking what goes on behind the scenes within your project, presenting you with a nice, easy-to-use interface. To see what Xcode is working with, right-click the project name in the Project Navigator in Xcode and select Show in Finder.

As you can see in Figure 13-44, if you select the `Castles` folder, you will notice that now there is an `it.lproj` folder in addition to the `base.lproj` and `en.lproj` folders that you will normally find in an iOS 7 project folder. Within this folder are all of the files that are localized to Italian, including `overlay.png`. It's here that you will replace the overlay image, currently written in the English language, overwriting it with an Italian version.

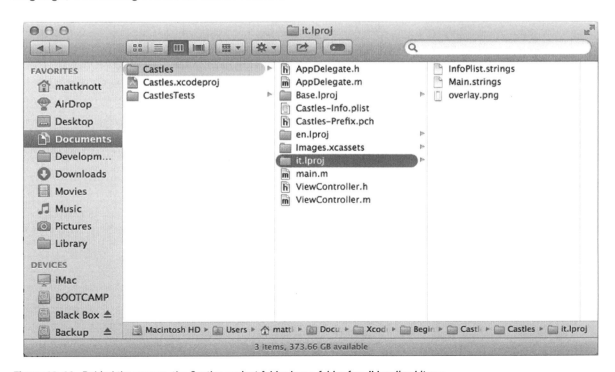

Figure 13-44. Behind the scenes, the Castles project folder has a folder for all localized items

Replacing overlay.png

Your sneak peek into the project folder has shown you that when you localized `overlay.png`, Xcode added a copy of the file to the `it.lproj` folder. Your goal now is to replace this with a version that has Italian text within it.

1. Start by opening an additional Finder window. To do this, within Finder, go to File ➤ New Finder Window (⌘ + N).

2. Next, within your new Finder window, navigate to the resources for this chapter, and open the Italian folder, which contains a single file: `overlay.png`. Drag this file over to the `it.lproj` folder, as shown in Figure 13-45.

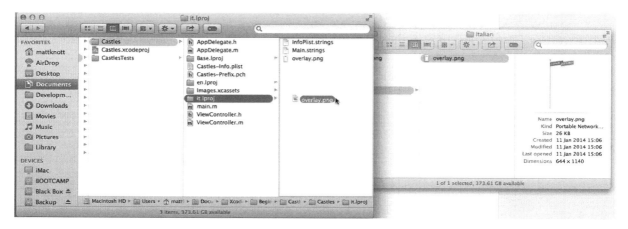

Figure 13-45. *Dragging the Italian overlay.png over to the it.lproj folder*

3. When you release the file, you will be told that the file already exists, and asked how you want to handle the duplicate files, choose Replace. Now, return to Xcode and run your application. It should look like that shown in Figure 13-46.

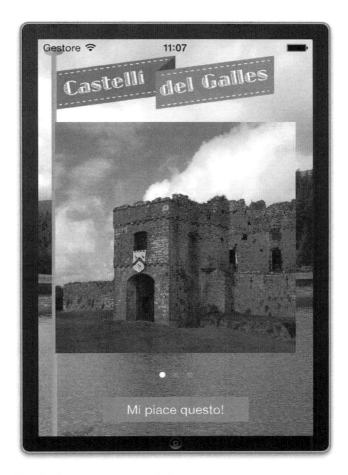

Figure 13-46. *The Button and Overlay image now appear in Italian*

You have now learned how to localize a Storyboard and a project resource, in this case an image file. All that remains is to look at localizing the strings that appear in your Alert View.

Localizing Code with Localizable.strings

The last area of application localization I will be covering in this chapter is code localization. When localizing code, you don't have to translate all of your code, just the strings that are used within the code. Below, I have highlighted all of the strings within the code that appear when you declared the UIAlertView in ViewController.m:

```
UIAlertView *likeAlert =
        [[UIAlertView alloc] initWithTitle:@"Thanks!"
                              message:[NSString stringWithFormat:@"You like castle number %i",
                                      (_pageControl.currentPage+1)]
                              delegate:self
                    cancelButtonTitle:@"Okay"
                    otherButtonTitles:nil];
```

As you can see, there are three strings here that need to be translated. There are actually a number of ways to localize these strings, but all of them use the same method of retrieving the localized string: NSLocalizedString. In this instance, you will be using NSLocalizedString to retrieve a localized string value from a file you haven't created yet: Localizable.strings.

Creating Localizable.strings

The Localizable.strings file, like the Main.strings file for the Storyboard, holds localized strings in a key/value format. Unlike Main.strings, Xcode hasn't created this file for you automatically; you need to create it yourself.

1. Creating a strings file is a quick and easy task, so let's take a moment to create the file. Start by selecting the Supporting Files folder in the Project Navigator, and then going to File ➤ New ➤ File ... (⌘ + N).

2. When the new file popover appears, select the Resource category under iOS on the left, and then choose the Strings File template on the right, as shown in Figure 13-47, then click the Next button to continue.

Figure 13-47. Selecting the Strings File template from the Resources category

3. Now, you need to name the file correctly within the Save As box, ensuring that you name the file Localizable, as shown in Figure 13-48. Click Create to add the new strings file to the project.

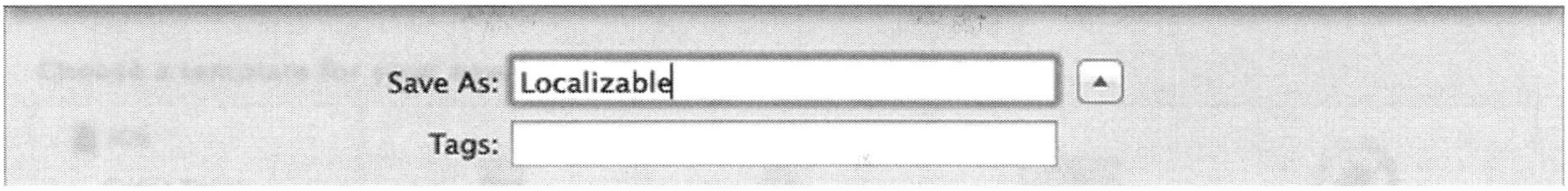

Figure 13-48. *Naming the new strings file*

4. Within your Project Navigator, you should now see a `Localizable.strings` file. Select the file and it will appear in the code editor. Currently the file is empty apart from the opening comments. Beneath the comments, add the following code:

```
"THANKS" = "Thanks!";
"CASTLE_LIKED" = "You like castle number %li";
"OKAY" = "Okay";
```

The first item in quotes is the *key*, this is the value you reference from within to retrieve the *value*, which is the item on the right. This is illustrated in Figure 13-49. Although there isn't a specific convention for naming your keys, it's good to think semantically and name the key as either the whole word or a part of the sentence.

Figure 13-49. *Illustrating the structure of Localizable.strings*

Localizing Localizable.strings

When you created `Localizable.strings`, it wasn't associated with any language, so in order to have a language-specific version of the file, you need to localize the file just as you did with the overlay image.

1. Start by selecting the `Localizable.strings` file in the Project Navigator and then open the File Inspector by going to View ➤ Utilities ➤ Show File Inspector (⌘ + ⌥ + 1).

2. Look for the Localize … button within the File Inspector (refer to Figure 13-40 if you can't find it) and click it. Just as before, once you click it, leave the language as Base and click Localize.

3. Again, the Localize button will be replaced with a list of available languages with check boxes. Tick the box next to Italian, just as was shown in Figure 13-42. This will create a base and Italian version of the file.

4. Expand the disclosure indicator shown next to Localizable.strings in the Project Navigator and select the Italian version, as shown in Figure 13-50.

Figure 13-50. Selecting the Italian version of Localizable.strings

5. Within the code editor, you should find that the contents are exactly the same as the base version of the file. Change the values highlighted in the following code to their Italian counterparts:

```
"THANKS" = "Grazie!";
"CASTLE_LIKED" = "Ti piace il numero castello %li";
"OKAY" = "Bene";
```

6. Great! You now have a base and Italian version of your Localizable.strings file, fully translated and ready to go, so all that remains is working the contents into your application's code.

Retrieving Localized Strings with NSLocalizedString

With the localized strings in place for both languages, all that remains is to retrieve the values from the Localizable.strings file using the NSLocalizedString macro. To do this you replace the static strings that you have already written with the NSLocalizedString macro. NSLocalizedString does all of the hard work in retrieving the correct strings for the selected language, meaning all you as the developer need to do is supply the correct key.

NSLocalizedString requires you to supply it with two arguments: first, the key that corresponds to the string you want to display, and second, a comment, which allows you to add context but is completely optional; in this instance the comment argument will be nil.

Open ViewController.m from the Project Navigator and scroll down to the likeCastle method. Replace the highlighted parts of the UIAlertView code with the following code:

```
UIAlertView *likeAlert =
    [[UIAlertView alloc] initWithTitle:NSLocalizedString(@"THANKS", nil)
                message:[NSString stringWithFormat:NSLocalizedString(@"CASTLE_LIKED", nil),
                                    (_pageControl.currentPage+1)]
              delegate:self
    cancelButtonTitle:NSLocalizedString(@"OKAY", nil)
    otherButtonTitles:nil];
```

That was really easy, you've now replaced the three strings that were there with a call to the NSLocalizedString macro, so whenever your application runs, the value from the Localizable.strings file will be displayed. Now all that remains is to run the application and see whether there are any errors. If all goes well, your application will run as it did the last time, but this time when you click the button, the Alert View text will appear in Italian, as shown in Figure 13-51.

Figure 13-51. *The Castles application now fully translated into Italian*

Summary

That's it! You now know how to make your application appear in any of the supported languages. You started out creating a single-language application with a cool paged Scroll View and ended with the excellent multilanguage application you set out to make. You could test your skills by taking the project further and adding another language to the application.

Specifically in this chapter you:

- Learned about Page Controls and Scroll Views
- Added multiple images to an Asset Catalog
- Programmatically configured your Scroll View
- Added an additional language to the project
- Localized the Storyboard and modified its strings file

- Learned about the difficulties of localizing an Asset Catalog

- Localized an image file

- Saw what happens to the project behind the scenes

- Created a `Localizable.strings` file and populated it with string for both languages

- Implemented `NSLocalizedString` to pull in the string values

You've achieved a lot in this chapter, learning some really important skills that will cement your application's success in the App Store. Before you move on, here's a hint: keep the Castles application handy because you'll be using it with the next two chapters as you learn about the Organizer, before moving on to publish an application in the App Store!

Chapter 14

The Organizer

Chapter 13 taught you about localization and how you can enable your application to appear in multiple languages with minimal effort. To learn about localization, you built the Castles application, where you applied a Scroll View and a Page Control to create a sliding photo gallery.

The Castles application, despite being really quite cool, is going to be used in both this and the next chapter as you step away from coding and focus on Xcode's functionality. This chapter will explain the Organizer, which is one of the key aspects of Xcode that you need to be familiar with when looking to manage a physical device and to prepare it for having applications deployed.

Chapter 1 showed you how to register for an Apple Developer Account, and in this chapter I will be explaining how to upgrade this to a fully paid Developer Account, allowing you to deploy applications to a physical device and also in preparation for Chapter 15, where you will be publishing to the App Store. This chapter delves into the real nitty-gritty of Xcode's Organizer and explains many advanced activities such as obtaining crash logs, capturing screenshots to your computer from a device, and learning about derived data and snapshots.

> **Note** To make the most of this chapter, you will need a physical iOS device such as an iPhone, iPad, or iPod Touch running iOS 7. If you don't have one of these devices, then it will be hard for you to follow some of what is shown in this chapter.

What Is the Organizer?

The Organizer in Xcode 5 has been streamlined somewhat since Xcode 4, where the Documentation element of the Organizer and the ability to view repositories used for source control have been removed. This doesn't diminish the importance of the Organizer in any way, however, and it is still an absolutely essential area of Xcode with which you should be familiar.

The Organizer itself doesn't really do anything, but instead it groups a bunch of incredibly useful functions into a single location. In Xcode 5, the Organizer is broken into three distinct areas:

- *Devices Organizer:* Manages the devices used with the Mac and prepares them with provisioning profiles and much more.

- *Projects Organizer:* Not just a list of projects, but rather a place where you can delve into any snapshots that have been created for a project with the ability to remove any associated or derived data.

- *Archives Organizer:* This area represents one of the ways you can publish an application to the App Store.

The Organizer is accessed from the menu bar by going to Window ➤ Organizer (⌘ + Shift + 2), which will load the Devices Organizer by default, as shown in Figure 14-1. Because so much of this chapter revolves around devices that are enrolled in the iOS Developer Program, it makes sense to go through the enrollment process before looking at the Organizer further.

Figure 14-1. The Organizer, specifically the Devices Organizer

Preparing Xcode for Deploying to a Device

Deploying an application to a physical device allows you to take your developments with you and test them in the real world. This and many of the topics in this chapter and Chapter 15 require that you be a paid up member of the iOS Developer Program and that your Developer Account is fully integrated with Xcode.

The first thing you will need to do is to enroll in the iOS Developer Program and become a fully fledged iOS Developer.

Enrolling in the iOS Developer Program

If you want to publish to the App Store or test you software on a physical iOS device, then you must be enrolled in the iOS Developer Program. Although everything that has been covered in the book to this point could be done with the free account, this chapter requires enrollment in the Developer Program, which costs $99 per year (at the time of writing). If you're not ready to enroll in the Developer Program just yet, I recommend you still read through this chapter just to have a feel for things, especially in relation to the Organizer.

There's nothing wrong with holding back on enrollment into the program. When I started developing for iOS I signed up immediately and then didn't make full use of it until my second term, so it might make financial sense for you to hold back until you've got an application you want to test on a physical device before release to the App Store.

There's much more to the Developer Program than just being able to publish apps and test on a device. You also get access to beta versions of iOS, Xcode, and Apple TV firmware, which gives you a head start on adapting any existing apps for the new versions of iOS but it also allows you to show off all the new features Apple is bringing to their devices months before Joe Public gets a look in.

1. To begin the process, go to the iOS Dev Center in your web browser at `https://developer.apple.com/devcenter/ios`. Once on the web site, click the Log In link in the top right-hand corner, as highlighted in Figure 14-2, and enter your Apple Developer Account details.

Figure 14-2. Click the Log In link and enter your Developer Account details

2. Next, once you've entered your details and you're returned to the iOS Dev Center, you will notice a box on the right-hand side promoting the iOS Developer Program, as shown in Figure 14-3. Either click the Learn More link or visit `https://developer.apple.com/programs/ios`.

Figure 14-3. An advertisement for the iOS Developer Program

3. The landing page for the iOS Developer Program is shown in Figure 14-4. This page holds lots of information about what the program enables you to do, and this is where you start the enrollment process. Click the Enroll Now button when you're ready.

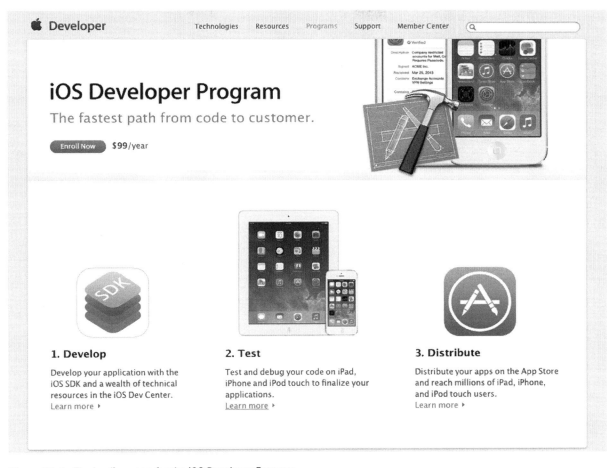

Figure 14-4. The landing page for the iOS Developer Program

4. Next, you will be provided with information about how the whole enrollment process works, as shown in Figure 14-5. I will take you through registration as an individual; if you're registering as a business in the United States, you will need to supply your D-U-N-S® Number, or if you're in another part of the world, you will be asked for alternative information for validation. Once you have read this information, click the Continue button near the bottom of the page.

Enrolling in Apple Developer Programs

Get everything you need to develop and distribute apps for iOS and OS X.

It's easy to get started.

✓ **Choose an enrollment type.**

Individual: choose this option if you are an individual or sole proprietor/single person business.

Company/Organization: choose this option if you are a company, non-profit organization, joint venture, partnership, or government organization.

✓ **Submit your information.**

Provide basic personal information, including your legal name and address. If you're enrolling as a company/organization, we'll need a few more things, like your legal entity name and D-U-N-S® Number, as part of our verification process.

✓ **Purchase and activate your program.**

Once we verify your information, you can purchase your program on the Apple Online Store. After you have completed your purchase, we'll send you an email within 24 hours on how to activate your membership.

Figure 14-5. The process for enrollment explained

5. Next, you need to choose whether to use the account you signed in with or if you want to create a whole new account, as shown in Figure 14-6. This is obviously a choice that you must make; the process of registering for an Apple Developer Account was covered in Chapter 1, but if you're going to register for a new account at this point, feel free to refer back in the book for guidance and then come back here to continue. For the majority of you who are logged in with the account you want to use for the program, click Continue.

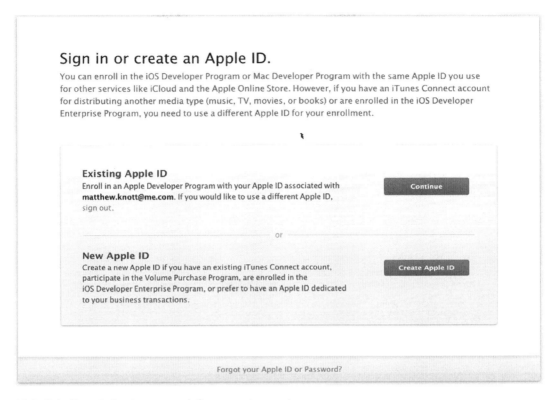

Figure 14-6. *Selecting whether to use an existing account or create a new one*

6. On the next screen you select whether you want to register as an individual or as a company. As I have already mentioned, I will be going through the process for an individual, so scroll to the bottom of this page and click the button on the left labeled Individual.

7. You will now be presented with options for each of the available programs: iOS, Mac, and Safari. Check the box next to the iOS option, as shown in Figure 14-7, before scrolling down to the bottom of the page and the click the Continue button on the right.

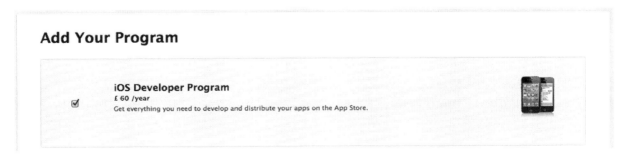

Figure 14-7. *Selecting the iOS Developer Program*

8. With your options for enrollment set, you will then be shown a summary of
    the proposed purchase, as shown in Figure 14-8. At this point the price of
    enrollment will adjust to your local currency. If you are ready to do so, click
    the Continue button in the bottom-right corner.

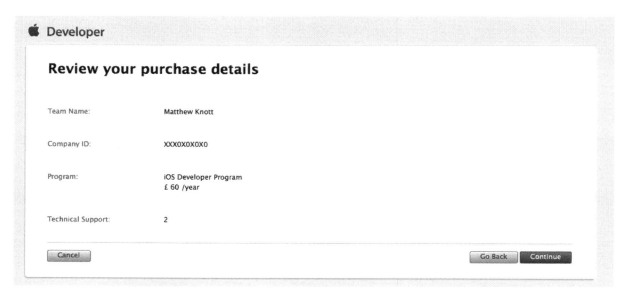

Figure 14-8. Reviewing the details of the enrollment

9. You're almost at the end of the process. Apple will now present you with
    the license agreement. Contrary to how you may usually approach such
    things, these are legally binding and if you are planning to take iOS app
    development seriously, I recommend you read these through and save
    a copy. There is a link to a PDF version of the agreement, which I have
    highlighted with a box in Figure 14-9. This document protects you as much
    as it protects Apple, so get a copy for your records. When you are ready,
    check in the disclaimer box below the license agreement and click the I
    Agree button in the bottom-right corner.

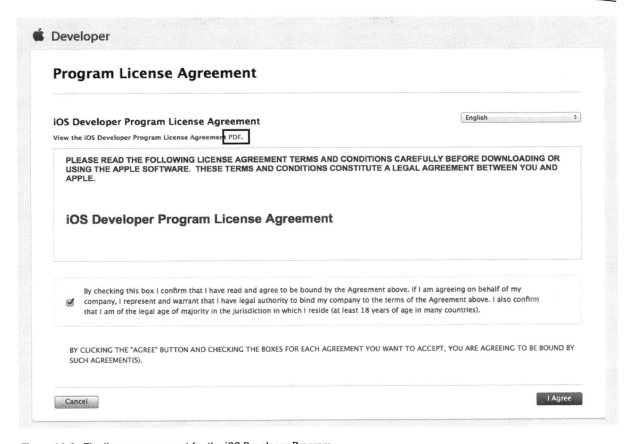

Figure 14-9. The license agreement for the iOS Developer Program

10. The final part of the enrollment process comes when you are prompted to add your personalized iOS Developer Program item to the cart for the Apple Store, as shown in Figure 14-10. Click the Add to cart button and you will be taken to the Apple Store for your region, where you can go through the checkout process and pay for your purchase.

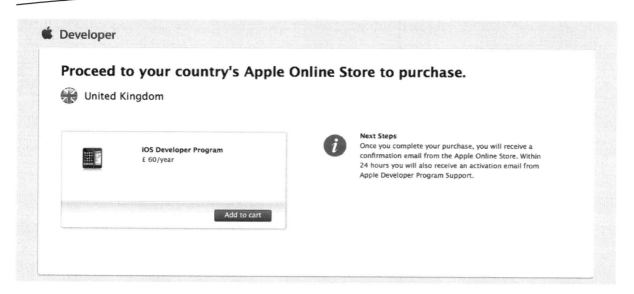

Figure 14-10. Getting ready to purchase your iOS Development Program

I won't step you through the specifics of the checkout and payment process, however, once you've completed the purchase and your enrollment is approved, you will receive an e-mail confirming that you are a part of the Developer Program! But before you begin to start writing your first hit app, remember that you haven't actually learned anything about the Organizer, so read on to the end of the chapter to learn all about one of Xcode's most important but least praised tools.

> **Note** If your live in a country that has no online Apple Store, the process for paying is very different from that shown in this chapter. You can still sign up, it just takes a little longer.

Adding Your Developer Account to Xcode

Being enrolled in the iOS Developer Program is one thing, but if Xcode doesn't know that you have a Developer Account, then you won't be able to take advantage of any of the extra functionality that this gives you. You may have already added your Developer Account details through your own experiences with Xcode, but if not, I will guide you through adding the account details, and then it's on to the Organizer.

1. Start by opening Xcode and from the menus select Xcode ➤ Preferences (⌘ + ,) then once you're in the Preferences, select the Accounts tab, as shown in Figure 14-11.

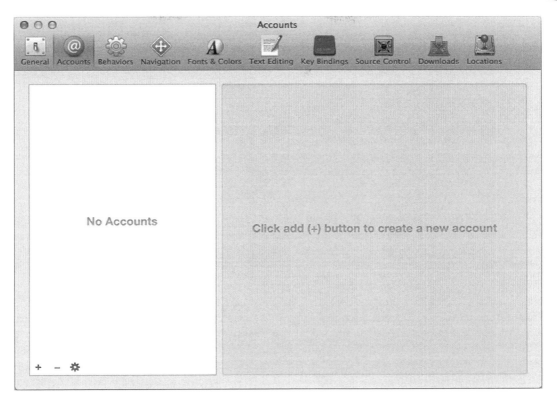

Figure 14-11. *The Accounts tab in Xcode*

2. This is the same area you came to in Chapter 12 when you added the remote Git repository, but this time you are going to be adding an Apple ID. As you see in Figure 14-11, I cleared out all of my accounts, leaving the area blank. Xcode is now directing me how to add a new account, so just as Xcode says, click the + symbol at the bottom of the left page and select Add Apple ID ..., as shown in Figure 14-12.

Figure 14-12. *Selecting the option to add an Apple ID into Xcode*

3. A popover will appear asking for your Apple ID and password, as shown
    in Figure 14-13. Enter your credentials and click the Add button to link this
    account with Xcode. Notice the Join a Program ... button—this is an alternative
    way to start your enrollment into any of the Apple developer programs.

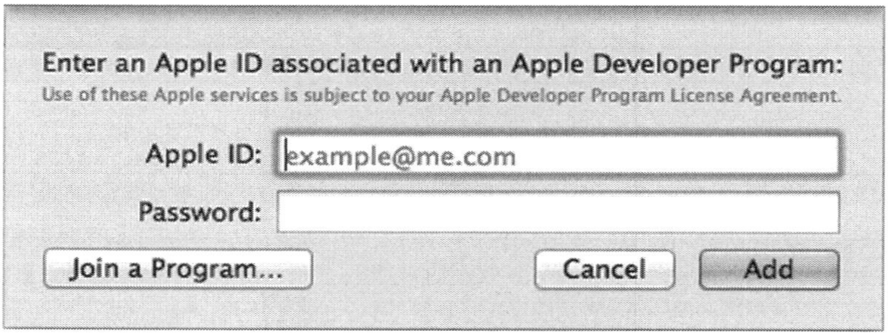

Figure 14-13. Enter your Apple ID and password to integrate the account with Xcode

When you return to the Preferences, you will see that your Developer Account now appears in the
left pane of the account preferences. Your Developer Account is now added to Xcode, however,
there are a few more steps you need to go through before you can deploy your application onto a
device. This is a great opportunity to get familiar with the Devices Organizer, which will allow you to
finish preparing your device for deployment.

The Devices Organizer

Now that the preparatory work has been done, you're all set to begin your exploration of the various
parts of the Organizer and you will start this journey with a thorough look at the Devices Organizer as
you prepare your device to be user for development. The Devices Organizer is the first of the three
tabs in the Organizer; if you haven't already, close Xcode's Preferences and open the Organizer by
going to Window ➤ Organizer (⌘ + Shift + 2).

The Devices Organizer allows you to manage your physical hardware in great detail. With an iOS
device you can access crash logs, take screenshots, add provisioning profiles, and view the device's
console data.

Assuming you have a physical iOS device that meets the requirements laid out at the start of the
chapter, go ahead and connect it to your Mac using the USB cable. Your device will then appear
on the sidebar; select it and you will be presented with an overview of all of the information that
is relevant to you as a developer, as shown in Figure 14-14, which highlights the key areas you
can see.

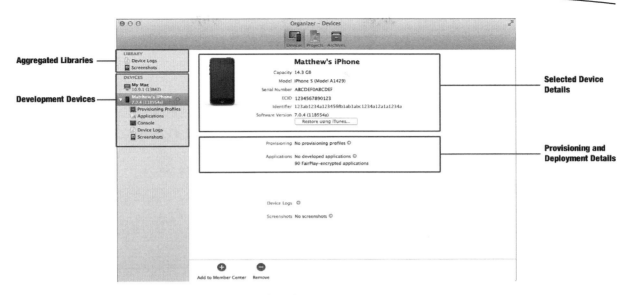

Figure 14-14. *The Devices Organizer with a device selected*

- *Aggregated Libraries:* These libraries aggregate data from all of your devices into a single location. Selecting Device Logs, for example, will give you access to all of the crash logs from every device, just as Screenshots collates any screen captures you've created using the Organizer.

- *Development Devices:* Under the Devices heading in the sidebar, you will find all of the devices that are, or have been, connected to the Mac and used for development. Currently connected iOS devices will display a green circle next to their name.

- *Device Details:* In this area you can view important information that is unique to your device such as the serial number and the unique identifier.

- *Provisioning and Deployment Details:* Here you can see any provisioning profiles that have been created on the device and also any applications that you have deployed directly to the device.

Preparing a Device for Development

Because of the secure and robust way iOS manages development devices, iOS requires that you first register your device for development and link it to your Developer Account. In older versions of Xcode, this was a bit of a chore. You had to use the Devices Organizer to obtain the unique identifier for your device and manually add it to the Provisioning Portal within the iOS Developer web site.

In Xcode 5, Apple has refined the process of preparing your device for deployment nearly as far as they possibly could, so that now it can be done with just a couple of clicks.

1. Start by clicking the + icon that is labeled Add to Member Center at the bottom of the Device Organizer, as shown in Figure 14-15.

Figure 14-15. *The Add to Member Center button used for registering a device*

2. A popover will appear listing any available development teams. If you have completed enrollment to the iOS Developer Program and have added your account, then your default team name should show up here. Check the box next to your chosen team, as shown in Figure 14-16, and click the Choose button.

Figure 14-16. *Selecting a Development Team to associate your device with*

3. At this point, if you haven't used your Mac with this account and deployed to devices before, you will be prompted to create a development certificate, as shown in Figure 14-17. This is another part of the process of enabling your device for development that Apple has refined. Click the Request button and Xcode will generate the required development certificates automatically and upload them to Apple.

Figure 14-17. *Xcode conveniently asks if you want it to do the hard work of generating a certificate*

At this point, you will be returned to the Devices Organizer and a candy stripe progress indicator will appear while the certificate is being created and uploaded to Apple, before retrieving a Team Provisioning Profile, which will be added to your devices, as shown in Figure 14-18. After a few seconds, this should disappear. You're now ready to go ahead and run the Castles application on your own device.

Figure 14-18. It will take a few seconds to send the certificates and retrieve a Team Provisioning Profile

Deploying an Application to an iOS Device

If you have had any experience in preparing an iOS device for development with version 3 or 4 of iOS, then you fully appreciate the work Apple has put into Xcode to make the process you just went through as easy as it was. Unbelievably, in just a handful of clicks you've registered your device on your Developer Account and can now deploy your applications to it!

When you first run your code on a physical device, a provisioning profile is created on the device, authorizing the code to run. A provisioning profile brings together a number of digital elements that tie your Developer Account and device to an authorized iOS Development Team. It's worth noting that a single device can contain multiple provisioning profiles. Now, let's select a physical device to run the application on.

1. Close the Organizer window for a moment and go back to Xcode. Make sure you have the Castles project open and then click the currently selected destination for deployment. As shown in Figure 14-19, your device will appear atop the list of available destinations, click it to select it.

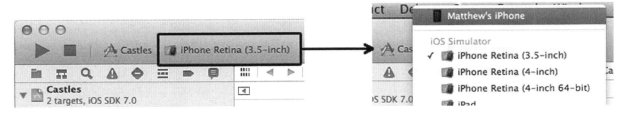

Figure 14-19. Selecting a physical device from the list of destinations

2. With your device now selected, all that remains is to run the application. When you click the Run button, Xcode will take a moment to prepare your device, at which point you may be prompted for Xcode's code signer to be able to access your keychain, as shown in Figure 14-20. If you are prompted, it's easiest to choose the Always Allow option.

Figure 14-20. You may be prompted for access to your keychain

Note   If you use a pin lock or other lock type, you will need to unlock your device before the application can run. If you do try to run while the device is locked, it will fail and warn you that you need to unlock the device before continuing.

3. Once you've gotten over the sheer awesome elation of seeing something you made running on an actual piece of Apple hardware, head back into Xcode and reopen the Organizer. Click back on the device you ran the application on. You will notice that now your device overview shows that you have a provisioning profile specified and also that the Castles application is installed on the device, as highlighted in Figure 14-21.

Figure 14-21. Your device overview will now include a Provisioning Profile and an Application

The thrill of seeing your work appear on an actual device for the first time is an incredible feeling that will really add to your sense of achievement that comes so easily when developing applications using Xcode. You've added an application to your device with the help of the Devices Organizer, but there is much more you can do using the five different areas contained within your device.

- *Provisioning Profiles:* You can remove any provisioning profiles from your device here or manually add a provisioning profile from the file system.

- *Applications:* Within the applications area, you can remove or manually add applications to your device if you have them in an IPA file format. You can also add and remove sandbox files.

- *Console:* View the debug console of your device in real time. Not only is this useful for debugging your own applications but it can also be used to identify issues with Wi-Fi and other facilities on the device.

- *Device Logs:* When an application on your phone crashes, it creates a crash log with a full stack trace and other meta data that will help you identify why there was an issue.

- *Screenshots:* Capture screenshots from your device directly to your Mac. You can also export the screenshots, turn them into Launch Images, and compare them for differences.

Capturing a Screenshot from a Running Application

As you will learn in Chapter 15, getting screenshots is not only good for posterity, but it's a prerequisite for submitting your application to the App Store. You can take a screenshot of your application from within the Simulator by going to File ➤ Save Screen Shot (⌘ + S), and you may already know that you can take a screenshot on a physical device by pressing the Home and power buttons simultaneously, but then you have the hassle of organizing and copying files. Through the Devices Organizer, Xcode gives you the ability to capture full resolution screenshots directly onto your Mac.

1. In the Organizer sidebar, make sure that the disclosure indicator next to your device is pointing downward and select the Screenshots option, as shown in Figure 14-22.

Figure 14-22. *Selecting the Screenshots option for the connected device*

> **Note**   Make sure you don't click the top-most Screenshots item under Libraries when looking to capture screenshots, this will not give you the same functionality.

2. Ensure the Castles application is running on your device and then click New Screenshot, found on the right of the toolbar at the bottom of the Organizer window, as shown in Figure 14-23.

Figure 14-23. *The button for taking a new screenshot is found on the right of the toolbar*

Instantly, the screenshot will appear in the main area of the device's screenshots, with all of the technical details such as title and resolution, and also a preview of the image, as shown in Figure 14-24.

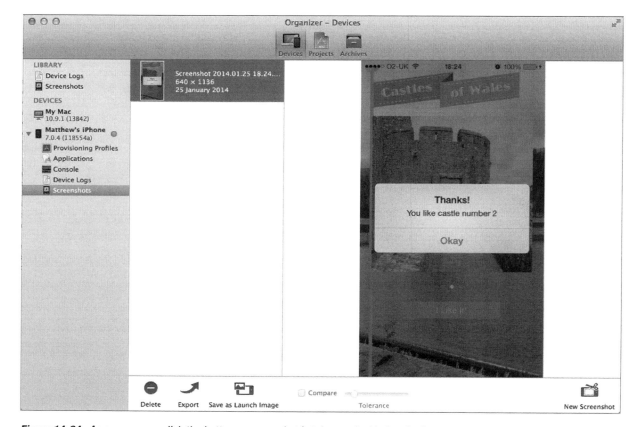

Figure 14-24. *As soon as you click the button, a screenshot is taken and added to the list*

Although taking a screenshot may not seem like an important function, as I've mentioned previously, it is essential for when you submit your application to the App Store, as Apple requests that you supply screenshots of the application in action. Furthermore, Apple has bundled some really great features for developers into the Screenshots area.

As you saw in Figure 14-23, the toolbar contains a number of options that were grayed out initially, but now that you have a screenshot selected on your device, most of these options have now become enabled.

- *Delete:* Along with the Backspace key on your keyboard, this allows you to remove the selected screenshot. A word of caution, however, once you delete an image, it's gone for good; it will not be sent to the Trash but will be completely erased.

- *Export:* This effectively allows you to duplicate the screenshot, which is already held within your computer file system, and save it to another location.

- *Save as Launch Image:* A Launch Image can be used to give the user the impression that your application has launched quickly by displaying a screenshot of the running application while it is still launching.

- *Compare:* This is one of the more interesting functions of the screenshot facility. It allows you to compare two or more images for differences, and the tolerance slider then allows you to vary the highlighted difference.

Using a Screenshot as a Launch Image

When you run your application, you have the option of displaying an image while the application finishes launching. This is called a Launch Image and it is a required asset for any application you hope to release to the App Store. Choosing a Launch Image is a very personal thing that comes down to your own personal preference. You may want to display a splash screen, advertising technologies used or maybe partner companies or sponsors. However, the intended use of a Launch Image is to trick the user into thinking the application has finished loading, even though it hasn't. This technique is achieved by taking a screenshot of the application running and setting it as the Launch Image, thus giving the impression of near-instant launching.

If you do not set a Launch Image, then when the user first runs the application they will see a black screen before the application launches and appears. This doesn't create a great first impression, but worse than that, Apple will not accept your application into the App Store, so it's always important to remember to use a Launch Image. Xcode makes it really simple to use a screenshot captured from with the Devices Organizer as your Launch Image, as you're about to find out.

> **Note**   Only the iPad currently supports separate portrait and landscape orientation Launch Images. For more information on device support and naming conventions, open the Documentation Viewer and search for "App Launch (Default) Images."

1. Run the application on your device and click the I Like It! button to trigger the Alert View.

2. Go back to the Organizer, select Screenshots for your device, and click the New screenshot button so that you end up with something similar to the image I captured in Figure 14-24. Ordinarily this wouldn't be a good choice for a Launch Image because it differs from how the application looks when it finishes launching, but this way you can appreciate how long the image could be on screen and understand the value of the illusion it creates.

3. Next, with your screenshot captured, highlight it and click Save as Launch Image on the toolbar. A popover will appear and you will be prompted to name the file.

4. Xcode will suggest a name of `Default@2x.png` for your Launch Image, but depending on the device you are capturing from, this may not be correct. `Default@2x.png` is meant to indicate an image for a 3.5-inch retina device, yet my screenshot was captured from an iPhone 5! Apple's documentation stipulates that Launch Images for the 4-inch retina devices (R4) should be named `Default-568h@2x.png`. Go ahead and set the appropriate name for the file, as shown in Figure 14-25.

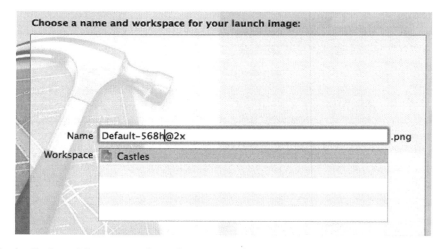

Figure 14-25. Naming the Launch Image according to its source device

5. If you have multiple projects open, these will all be listed as available workspaces, so ensure that beneath your file name, Castles is selected. The Organizer won't know which project you intend on adding the image for, so you must ensure that this is correct. Click Next.

6. You will now be prompted to select which targets you wish to add the image file to, as shown in Figure 14-26. In this case, the default selection is correct, so go ahead and click Finish.

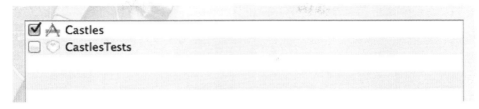

Figure 14-26. *Selecting the targets to add the Launch Image to*

7. Upon clicking Finish, you will be taken back to the Organizer, close it for now and return to your project workspace. Looking at the Project Navigator, you will notice that it now includes your Launch Image, which was added to the root of the project structure, as shown in Figure 14-27.

Figure 14-27. *The root of your project structure now includes the Launch Image, in my case Default-568h@2x.png*

8. It's not good practice to leave images kicking about in the project structure so drag the Default-568h@2x.png file or whatever you named it to the Supporting Files folder within the Project Navigator.

9. Open the Images.xcassets Asset Catalog and you will find an item called LaunchImage. This is an Image Set that Xcode created for you when you created the project. Click LaunchImage and you will notice that it has two image wells (placeholders), as shown in Figure 14-28.

Figure 14-28. *Selecting the LaunchImage Image Set*

10.   If you captured your image from a retina 3.5-inch device, drag the
      default@2x.png file to the @2x image well, otherwise drag default-568h@2x.png
      to the R4 image well, as I have in Figure 14-29.

Figure 14-29. Dragging the Launch Image to its relevant image well in the set

Ideally at this point you would also be adding a screenshot captured from the Simulator for the other
resolution Launch Image if you do not have a physical device for that resolution, so that all devices
are provided for and your application has a greater chance of being accepted into the App Store on
first submission. Because you are just testing this particular function, you can skip it for now and run
the Castles application on your device and watch closely what happens.

You will notice that almost immediately, the specified Launch Image appears, before the application
finishes loading and dismisses it. If you had used a screenshot of the application once it had loaded,
then at the point where the user taps the applications icon, they would be fooled into thinking the
app was ready to use, giving that all important impression of speed and professionalism.

Try repeating this exercise but using a screenshot of the initial state of the application. Apply it to the
LaunchImage Image Set and see how it can changes your impression of the application instantly.

If you intend to manually create your Launch Image, it's essential that you know the correct
resolutions for each device you intend on supporting. Table 14-1 shows the range of Apple devices
and the resolutions required for the Launch Images.

Table 14-1. Resolutions of Launch Images for Various Devices

Device Family	Portrait Resolution	Landscape Resolution
iPhone 5 and iPod touch (5th generation)	640 × 1136 pixels	N/A
Earlier Retina iPhones and iPod Touches (3.5 inch)	640 × 960 pixels	N/A
Non-Retina iPhones and iPod Touches	320 × 480 pixels	N/A
Non-Retina iPad and iPad Mini	768 × 1024 pixels	1024 × 768 pixels
Retina iPad and iPad Mini	1536 × 2048 pixels	2048 × 1536 pixels

Now that you've taken a look through some of the useful functions available within the Devices Organizer, it's time to move on and examine the two remaining tabs: the Projects and Archives Organizer.

The Projects Organizer

The Projects Organizer is accessed through the second tab at the top of the Organizer window, which is labeled Projects. The main purpose of the Projects Organizer is to list all of the projects and workspaces that you have opened on your Mac, and then provide you with a number of actions you can perform against each project or workspace.

If you want to create snapshots of your projects using Xcode's integrated snapshot facility, then you will likely find the Projects Organizer invaluable for the amount of control you have over the project's snapshots. A snapshot is as the name suggests, a complete snapshot of your project at a specific point in time. Don't be fooled into thinking that if you are using Xcode's Git-based source control then you don't need snapshots! They can still offer valuable protection from mistakes between commits.

If you don't want to use the snapshots, then you will find the ability to hunt down a project you've opened and view its location invaluable at some point in time. Figure 14-30 gives you an overview of the key areas of the Project Organizer.

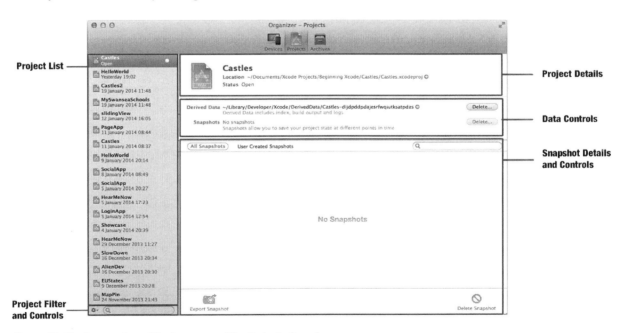

Figure 14-30. An overview of the key areas of the Projects Organizer

Using the Project and Workspace List

The sidebar in the Projects Organizer is dedicated to listing all of the projects or workspaces that you have ever opened on your Mac. Each project is sorted in reverse chronological order based on the last time you opened the project, which is why Castles appears at the top in Figure 14-30. Any projects listed in red are projects that you have opened but have since been removed from the Mac.

To make sense of the list, you can filter the contents with the filter search box at the bottom of the sidebar, which is illustrated in Figure 14-31. Typing "cas" would quickly narrow the listed items to show the Castles project, for example.

Figure 14-31. *Type in the filter box to restrict the projects and workspaces that are listed in the sidebar*

Directly adjacent to the filter bar is a small cog icon, which allows you to perform a set number of actions for the selected project or workspace. You can see this icon on the left of the filter in Figure 14-31. The options displayed are also available by right-clicking a project or workspace, as shown in Figure 14-32, with the added benefit of Xcode's contextual help menu being available.

Figure 14-32. *Right-clicking a project reveals some useful options*

- *Open:* This option opens the project or workspace in Xcode.

- *Reveal in Finder:* Use this option to track down the projects folder in the file system.

- *Remove from Organizer:* This will remove the project from the Project Organizer and delete what is known as derived data, such as snapshots and indexes, but will leave the project itself intact in its folder.

Using Snapshots

Snapshots in Xcode is a great feature that lets you save and archive not just the project files and folders, but also the workspace settings and configuration. A snapshot, as the name implies, is like a photograph, it is an image of a point in time that allows you to roll back your project to the time of the snapshot in the event of a major issue.

Automatically Creating Snapshots

One of the most effective ways you can use snapshots is by configuring a behavior within Xcode so that a snapshot is created when you perform a set task, such as a successful build of your application. If you have followed this book to the letter so far, then in Chapter 4 you may recall that you were prompted to set up snapshots, which I advised against at that point so that you could look at the end-to-end snapshot process now.

1. To set up the snapshot behavior, start by accessing Xcode's Preferences by selecting Xcode ➤ Preferences (⌘ + ,) from the menu, and then choosing the third tab, labeled Behaviors.

2. The left-hand column of the Behaviors tab lists all of the events that can have their behaviors configured. The aim here is to configure Xcode so that it creates a snapshot every time you successfully build the project. The first group in the left column is labeled Build, and the third option within that group is Succeeds. Choose Succeeds, as shown in Figure 14-33.

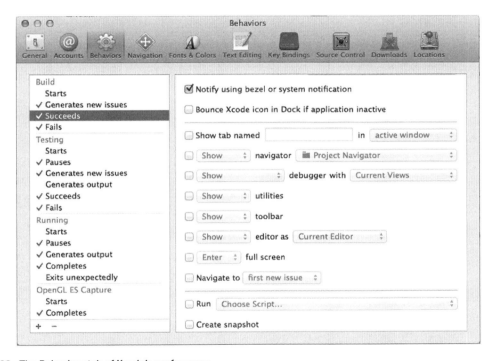

Figure 14-33. The Behaviors tab of Xcode's preferences

3. When you select Succeeds, the right-hand pane will display all of the behaviors that can be configured. Scroll to the bottom of the list and tick the box next to Create snapshot.

4. Close the preferences and return to Xcode. Now run your application once more, either on your device or in the Simulator, or alternatively, as the criteria for an automatic snapshot that your project builds successfully, you would go to Product ➤ Build (⌘ + B).

Once the application is running, or your build completes, then, assuming it was successful, you will now have a snapshot. Before you confirm this, it's important to note that in addition to automatic snapshots, you can also create manual snapshots.

Manually Creating a Snapshot

Have snapshots automatically created when your build event is successful is really useful because if it all goes wrong, you know you can go back to the last known good configuration and start again without too much heartache.

Sometimes though, you may want to capture an interim snapshot if you feel you're about to attempt something that may cause some issues, such as refactoring large amounts of code. In this instance, the best thing to do is to create a quick snapshot and annotate it to explain why you created it and what you were about to do.

To create a snapshot manually, simply go to File ➤ Create Snapshot (⌘ + Control + S). You will be presented with a popover, as shown in Figure 14-34, where you can add a title for the snapshot and provide some descriptive text. Fill out both text fields and click Create Snapshot. It's a testament to the way Xcode has been developed that the snapshots are created so quickly and subtly! Now it's time to go back to the Project Organizer to see what's been happening behind the scenes.

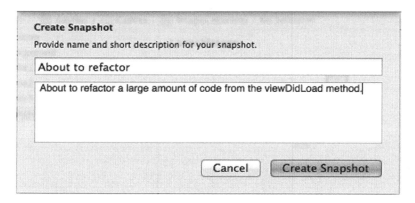

Figure 14-34. Adding a title and description for the manually created snapshot

Managing Snapshots

Now that you have created a couple of snapshots, you will be able to see more of what the Project Organizer can offer you. Reopen the Organizer and reselect the Project Organizer tab. With the Castles project selected, you will now be able to see your two snapshots listed, as shown in Figure 14-35.

Figure 14-35. The two snapshots listed in reverse chronological order within the Project Organizer

Although it isn't completely apparent, snapshots are stored in a single archive on your Mac. To see this archive, just above the list of snapshots is a line titled Snapshots that indicates the full path to the snapshot archive for this project. Next to the path, and highlighted in Figure 14-36, is an arrow that will take you straight to the archive path. Click that arrow to see your snapshot archive in the Finder.

Figure 14-36. The folder containing the snapshot archives can be navigated to by clicking the highlighted arrow

When you navigate to the folder containing the snapshot archive, you should take note of the size. On my system it sits just under 30 megabytes. This will rapidly increase as you continue to develop and build your application, which will have an impact on available storage and backup times, so managing your snapshots and disposing of older snapshots are important maintenance tasks.

Deleting Snapshots

Deleting a snapshot is very straightforward, but be careful how you do it. In Figure 14-36, you will notice that next to the highlighted arrow is a Delete button. Clicking this button will delete *all* snapshots on the system, not just one, so be careful.

1.   To delete a single snapshot, start by highlighting the bottom most snapshot, titled Before succeeds, as shown in Figure 14-37.

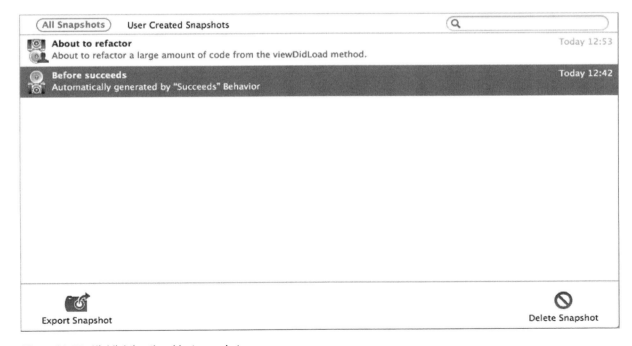

Figure 14-37. Highlighting the oldest snapshot

2. You will now be able to use the Delete Snapshot button in the bottom-right corner, also shown in Figure 14-37.

3. You will be prompted whether or not you wish to delete the snapshot, click Delete and the snapshot will be removed, leaving you with just a solitary snapshot in the list.

Exporting Snapshots

An alternative to restoring your project from a snapshot is to use the Project Organizer's Export functionality. Exporting a snapshot doesn't export the archive; it allows you to extract the full project from the archive to a separate folder on your system.

1. To export a snapshot, select the single remaining snapshot within your list of snapshots and click the Export Snapshot button on the left side of the toolbar, as shown in Figure 14-37.

2. You will be presented with the standard Mac OS Save dialog, as shown in Figure 14-38. Locate the folder you want to export to and click the Export button.

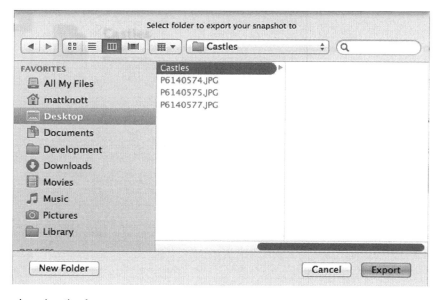

Figure 14-38. Choosing a location for export

Once complete, you will receive a notification advising you that the export has finished; click OK and you will be returned to the Project Organizer, at which point you could now navigate to your exported project and run that instance in parallel with the current one.

Restoring from a Snapshot

The main purpose of creating snapshots is that you have something to fall back on if something goes horribly wrong. Therefore, it makes sense that at some point you may need to restore your project from a snapshot.

1. Because the Organizer is effectively operating independently of any workspaces you may have open, you cannot trigger a restore from the Project Organizer. Instead, return to your project in Xcode and go to File ➤ Restore Snapshot.

2. A popover will appear, as shown in Figure 14-39, asking you to select the snapshot to restore. In this case you're limited for choice with a single snapshot; select it and click the Restore ... button.

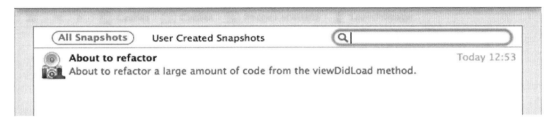

Figure 14-39. *Selecting a snapshot to restore*

3. If you haven't made any changes to the project since the snapshot was created, you will receive a warning advising you that no changes have been made, as shown in Figure 14-40. This is great because it means that Xcode has compared the snapshot with the current project status and detected no changes, instead of simply overwriting the files blindly.

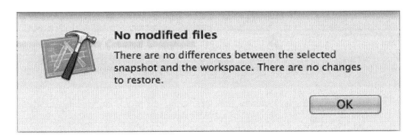

Figure 14-40. *Rather than blindly overwriting the files, Xcode compared the snapshot and detected no changes*

If you had made changes to the project, they would have been removed and you would now be exactly where you were when the snapshot was created. You now know everything there is to know about using snapshots with Xcode, meaning that with Git version control and snapshots, you should never be in a situation where you lose large chunks of your project.

The Archives Organizer

The Archives Organizer represents one of a couple of ways that you can submit your application to the App Store. Because App Store submission is the topic of Chapter 15, I will focus here on how you can create an archive of your application and then use the Archives Organizer to analyze it.

Right now, your Archives Organizer probably looks quite empty, as does the example in Figure 14-41, because it contains no actual archives at this point. In order to make more sense of the Archives Organizer and its capabilities, the first thing you will do is archive the Castles application.

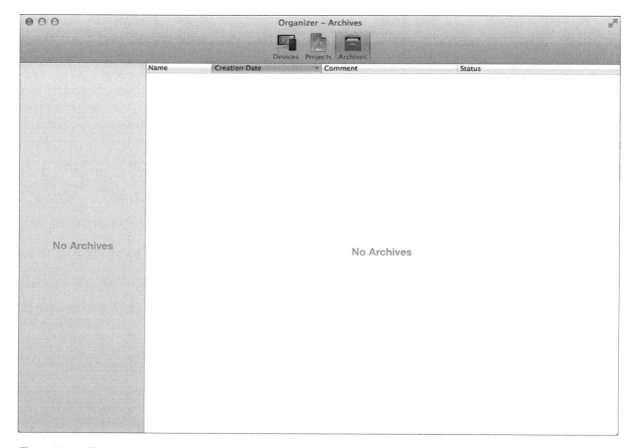

Figure 14-41. *The Archives Organizer, minus any archives*

Archiving Your Application

When you archive your application, it is compiled ready for release and then compressed into an Xcode archive file (.xcarchive) on your computer. The actual archiving process takes two clicks of the mouse, so rather than starting with that, I'll take you behind the scenes so you have a better understanding of what happens when you ask Xcode to archive your application.

First, when you choose to archive your application, you are performing an action that is customizable as part of the currently active scheme.

To see how the action is configured, close the Organizer and go back to Xcode. Next, go to Product ➤ Scheme ➤ Edit Scheme (⌘ + <) and select the Archive action from the left-hand column, as shown in Figure 14-42.

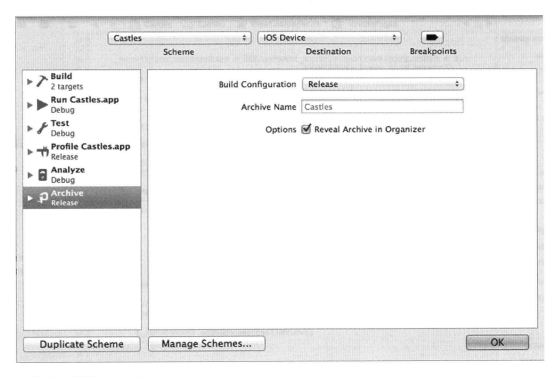

Figure 14-42. The Edit Scheme dialog

You can see that by default, the action is configured to use the release build configuration, that it uses the default name of Castles, and, finally, that upon completion, it will launch the Archives Organizer. You can customize any of these options, however, for how best they would suit you. Click OK to dismiss this dialog; it's time to try archiving the Castles application.

To actually archive your application, simply go to Product ➤ Archive. At this point Xcode will go through a build process before reopening the Archive Organizer, which will now contain an archive, as shown in Figure 14-43.

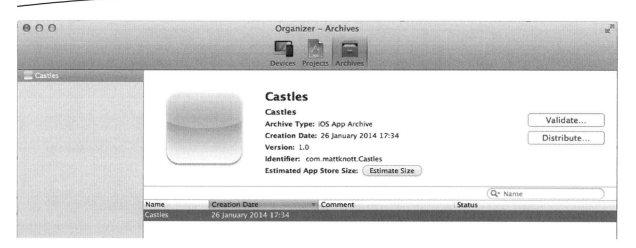

Figure 14-43. The Archives Organizer, looking far less dull with some actual content

The main information pane now shows the application version and bundle identifier, which is useful for differentiating between multiple archives. The Validate and Distribute buttons will be covered in Chapter 15, which leaves several small pieces of functionality to cover here.

First, application file size is something you should try hard to reduce. You will notice that next to Estimated App Store Size in the information pane is a button labeled Estimate Size. Clicking this will show you the expected size of your finished application. Think about the end user when adding resources to your project; the smaller the application the more likely it is that people will download your application over their mobile data connection. Optimize your assets as much as possible by using a photo editor to size and encode your images appropriately for your application.

Second, if you right-click the archive, as shown in Figure 14-44, you will be able to perform actions and access contextually relevant help files.

Figure 14-44. Right-clicking the archive exposes several options

Choosing Show in Finder will launch a Finder window in the folder containing the selected archive. This archive can then be distributed to other users within your development team.

Finally, choosing Delete Archive … will remove the archive from the file system. Before removal, you will be prompted whether or not you wish to delete the archive, and in this instance you would simply confirm the action by clicking the Delete button.

That's as far as I can take you through the Archives Organizer without encroaching into the next chapter, where I will show you how to validate your application and submit it to the App Store from this very window.

Summary

It may not be the most exciting facet of Xcode, but if you don't know about the Organizer then you will be seriously limited in what you can achieve with Xcode. As it stands, you've looked in detail at the key areas of the Organizer and seen how it can be used to take your applications to the next level.

Specifically in this chapter you have:

- Learned how to sign up as a paid member of the iOS Development Program
- Registered a physical device, prepared it for development, and deployed your application to it
- Captured an application screenshot and used it as a Launch Image
- Discovered how to create snapshots of your application
- Archived your application ready for distribution on the App Store

In the next, and final chapter, you will complete your knowledge by publishing an application to the App Store!

Chapter 15

Building, Sharing, and Distributing Applications

Chapter 14 looked at the Organizer and the vast array of actions it lets you perform, from managing iOS devices and project snapshots to preparing archives for submission to the App Store.

This chapter will be continuing that theme of looking at the App Store as you learn about how to take your finished application and submit it for hosting on Apple's App Store, the single storefront for both free and paid applications for iOS.

You will be adding the final touches to the Castles application that you first created in Chapter 13, by adding an icon to the project. You will then move online, where I will introduce you to the iTunes connect portal, a one-stop shop for publishing to the App Store and also reporting on download amounts and revenue. You will use the iTunes connect portal to prepare for publishing, creating a profile for your application with all of the text and images that are required for submission.

Finally, this chapter will look at how you can distribute your application and two ways of uploading your application to iTunes Connect, before submitting the application and all of the required files to Apple for approval. I'll give you some hints and tips along the way to improve the likelihood of first-time acceptance, and then that's it! Once you've completed this chapter, you'll be ready to dive into writing and sharing your own apps and games!

It's worth noting that being enrolled in the paid iOS Developer Program is essential before you start on this chapter. I covered enrollment in Chapter 14, so if you need to go back and get registered, now is a good time.

Final Checks Before Publishing Your Application

Before I take you through the process of submitting the Castles application to the App Store, you need to add a final touch of polish to complete the application. One of the focal points of this chapter is ensuring that your application has everything it needs to get through the Apple review process and be published to the App Store the first time. One key element that is currently missing from the Castles application that is an absolute prerequisite is an icon.

If you haven't already downloaded the collective resources for the book, then head to this book's page on the apress.com web site and download the resources file. Inside the Chapter 15 folder you will find all of the icons needed for both the application and the iTunes Connect portal. The icon provided for the Castles application is shown in Figure 15-1.

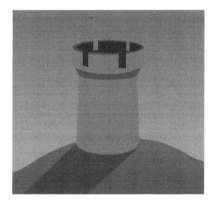

Figure 15-1. The icon you will be using for the Castles application

I have already covered the process of setting an application icon in Xcode, but because that was back in Chapter 2, I'll take you through it again because here you will be setting three icons, not just one. Each of the icon files are named according to their resolution, so the main application icon, for example, is named icon120.png because it is 120 pixels × 120 pixels.

1. Start by opening the Castles project in Xcode.

2. Open Images.xcassets from the Project Navigator.

3. Select the AppIcon image set, as shown in Figure 15-2. You will notice that there are three image wells, all of which will hold an icon used in differing locations within iOS 7.

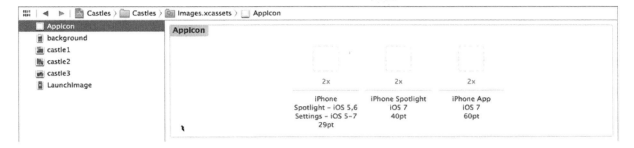

***Figure 15-2.** Select the AppIcon image set from the images Asset Catalog to see the three image wells in the set*

Note   Only one of these sets is a requirement, but you will set them all for the sake of completeness. Another thing to note is that as this is an iOS 7 only application and only for iPhone or iPod Touch, all of the image wells are subtitled with 2x, indicating that they are all retina images. This is because all of the devices in the iPhone form factor that run iOS 7 have retina screens. If you were creating an application that was backward compatible with iOS 6.1 and earlier, or a universal application, then there would be a far greater number of icons to set.

4. Open a Finder window and navigate to the resources for this book. Inside the Chapter 15 folder you will find all of the icons listed. Into the first image well that is labeled iPhone Spotlight iOS 5, 6 Settings – iOS 5-7, drag the file named icon58.png, as shown in Figure 15-3.

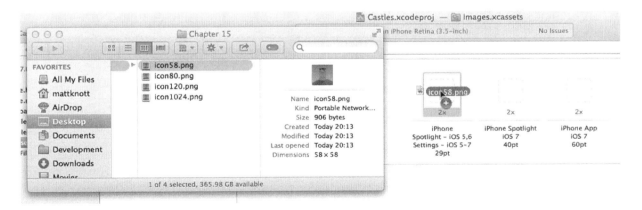

***Figure 15-3.** Dragging the first of three icons into the AppIcon image set*

5. Now repeat this action, dragging icon80.png into the second image well labeled iPhone Spotlight iOS 7, and icon120.png into the third image well labeled iPhone App iOS 7.

With your three icons in place, run the application, either on a device or in the Simulator, to ensure there are no warnings regarding the icons. If you add the wrong resolution icon into an image well, then when you build and run the application you will receive a warning similar to that shown in Figure 15-4. If you do receive this warning, ensure you have added the correct image into the correct well.

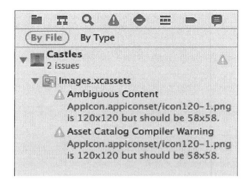

Figure 15-4. *Xcode will warn you if your icons are the wrong resolution*

If you're running your application in the Simulator, go to Hardware ➤ Home (⌘+ Shift + H) or if using a physical device, just press the Home button to return to the home screen with all of the application icons. You should see that the icon for the Castles application has now been set, also searching in Spotlight within iOS will use the 80 × 80 pixel image for the application, as shown in Figure 15-5.

Figure 15-5. *The Castles application, now completed with an icon*

Now that you have added the final touches to the Castles application, it's time to look at the iTunes Connect portal where you will prepare for uploading the Castles application.

Discovering iTunes Connect

You will now be leaving Xcode behind for a moment and focusing on the functionality available through the iTunes Connect portal where you will create a profile for your application and set some initial details about the application and its audience.

A large portion of this chapter relies on you having an Internet connection and a web browser. I use the default Safari browser, but you should be able to use almost any modern web browser and achieve the same results.

To access iTunes Connect, you can go directly to `https://itunesconnect.apple.com` or alternatively from the iOS Dev Center you were introduced to in Chapter 14. You will find the iOS Developer Program on the right of the page, as shown in Figure 15-6.

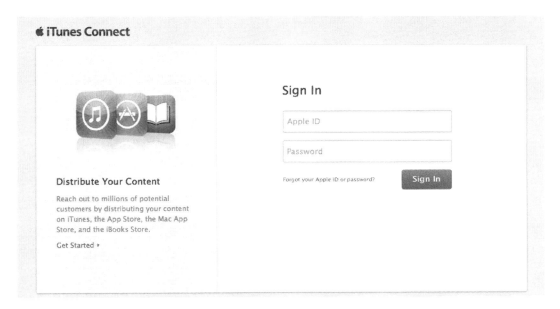

Figure 15-6. *There is a link to the iTunes Connect tool from the iOS Developer portal*

When you first arrive at the iTunes Connect portal, you will be asked to sign in. Because of the highly sensitive nature of the content within iTunes Connect portal, your connection will time out if left unattended for a short while, so you will be seeing a lot of the screen shown in Figure 15-7. Enter your iOS Developer ID details and click the Sign In button.

Figure 15-7. *Accessing the iTunes Connect portal for the first time*

If this is your first time accessing the iTunes Connect portal, you will be asked to review and agree to a separate set of terms and conditions, as shown in Figure 15-8. As with other terms and conditions presented to you, it's a good idea to review them before accepting them.

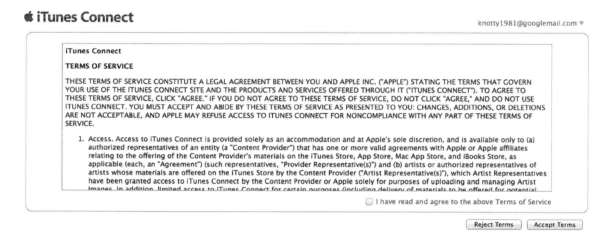

Figure 15-8. *iTunes Connect has separate terms and conditions that must be agreed to*

Once you have agreed to the terms and conditions, you will arrive at the iTunes Connect dashboard, as shown in Figure 15-9.

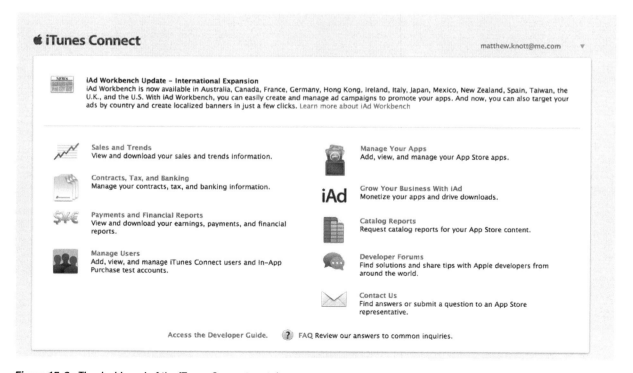

Figure 15-9. *The dashboard of the iTunes Connect portal*

As you can see, there are numerous sections available from this dashboard:

- *Sales and Trends:* Report on the level of downloads for a particular timeframe.

- *Contracts, Tax, and Banking:* View your tax details and request contracts in relation to the developer program. You can also view any transfer agreements you may have in place.

- *Payments and Financial Reports:* Get a detailed breakdown of payments and also view trends on your app-generated earnings.

- *Manage Users:* Give others access to the iTunes Connect portal. You can control permissions, restricting users from the financial aspects, for example.

- *Manage Your Apps:* As far as this chapter is concerned, this is where it all happens. Create and manage your application profiles and control how they appear on the App Store.

- *Grow Your Business With iAd:* Get started here if you want to make iAds for your products or if you want to include them in your application.

- *Catalog Reports:* Here you can generate a tab-delimited report for download that shows key metrics for all of your App Store content.

- *Developer Forums:* This links back to devforums.apple.com, a great community where you can discuss issues with your applications and find help.

- *Contact Us:* This step-by-step process allows you to send a message to Apple regarding a range of issues you might be having.

From this vast array of feature, you need to click Manage Your Apps so that you can begin creating an application profile for the Castles application. You will be taken to an empty list (assuming you haven't created any applications already), as shown in Figure 15-10, that invites you to create a new app. Do so by clicking the Add New App button in the top-left corner.

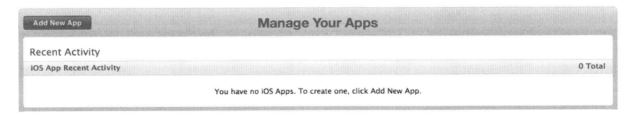

Figure 15-10. The Manage Your Apps page in iTunes Connect

If you have already enrolled in both the Mac OS and the iOS Developer Programs, then at this point you will be prompted to choose which platform you are creating a new app for: as you probably suspect, in this instance you need to click the iOS button.

If you're not a member of the Mac OS Developer Program, then you will go directly to the App Information screen where you need to specify some basic information about your application, as shown in Figure 15-11. The Default Language is English, the App Name field should contain the name of the application as you want it to appear on the App Store; I chose Castles of Wales. The SKU Number field is for you to specify an identifier that is unique for you that will help you differentiate this app from others you may publish; I chose CastlesOfWales.

App Information

Enter the following information about your app.

Default Language [English]
App Name [Castles of Wales]
SKU Number [CastlesOfWales]
Bundle ID [Select]
You can register a new Bundle ID here.

Does your app have specific device requirements? Learn more

Cancel   Continue

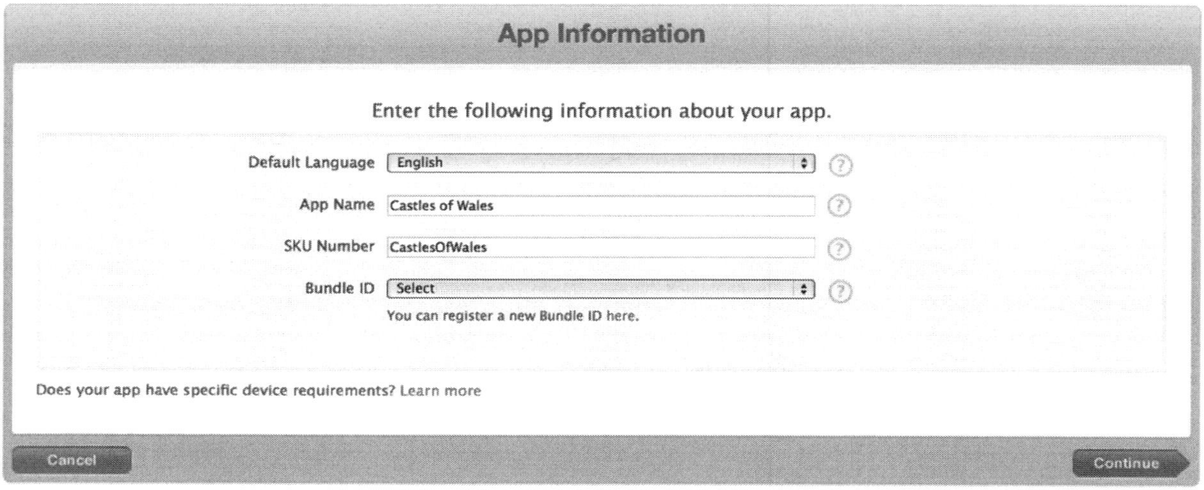

Figure 15-11. Setting the basic app information

When it comes to the Bundle ID select list, you will have a wildcard app id listed there already, but depending on what you want your application to do now and in the future, it is worthwhile thinking about this very carefully.

Below the select list you will see the text "You can register a new Bundle ID here." Click the word "here" and the Developer Portal will open in a new window or tab on the New App ID page.

Creating an App ID

An App ID links your application into Apple services such as iCloud, Game Center, and Pass Book and it also allows you to enable push notifications. There are two types of App ID, and the services you want your application to access both now and in the future will influence the type of App ID you use.

Start by giving the App ID the name Castles, as shown in Figure 15-12.

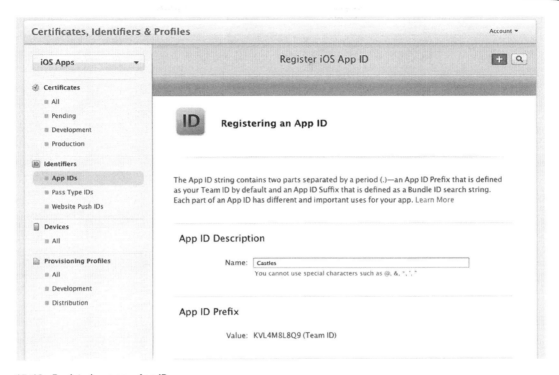

Figure 15-12. Registering a new App ID

Next, you will need to specify the type of App ID you want to register; I've briefly explained each one below:

> *Wildcard App IDs:* Can be shared between multiple applications. You will be able to enable Data Protection, iCloud, Inter-App Audio, and Passbook services with a Wildcard App ID. This type of App ID is useful if you have a series of really basic applications that don't need access to the full range of Apple services.

> *Explicit App IDs:* Gives you access to all Apple services that are available to the Wildcard ID but with the addition of Game Center, In-App Purchase, and Push Notifications. If you aren't sure about what you want to do with your application in the future, choose an Explicit App ID to reduce future hassles.

In this instance, choose Explicit App ID and enter the Bundle ID that you set for the Castles application when you created it in Xcode in Chapter 13, which in my case was com.mattknott.Castles, as shown in Figure 15-13.

⊙ **Explicit App ID**

If you plan to incorporate app services such as Game Center, In-App Purchase, Data Protection, and iCloud, or want a provisioning profile unique to a single app, you must register an explicit App ID for your app.

To create an explicit App ID, enter a unique string in the Bundle ID field. This string should match the Bundle ID of your app.

Bundle ID: com.mattknott.Castles

We recommend using a reverse-domain name style string (i.e., com.domainname.appname). It cannot contain an asterisk (*).

Figure 15-13. Setting the Bundle ID value for the Explicit App ID

If you can't remember the Bundle ID you specified, then you can find out quickly by going back into Xcode and selecting the Castles project in the Project Navigator, before choosing the Castles target and the General tab. Figure 15-14 shows that following this path, you will see the Bundle Identifier value that was specified when you created the application, so enter this same value as the Bundle ID in your web browser.

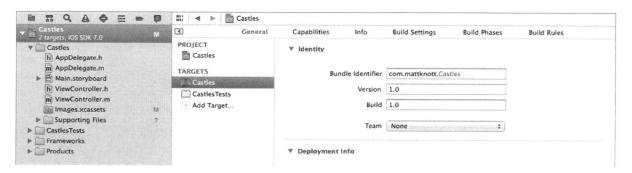

Figure 15-14. Checking the Bundle Identifier is quick and painless

Note   If you want, you can change the bundle identifier at this point within the target. For simplicity sake, let's keep it the same for now.

There is no need to enable any additional services, so scroll to the bottom of the page and click the Continue button.

On the next screen you will be shown a summary of the App ID details including which services are enabled, as shown in Figure 15-15. Don't worry that Game Center and In-App Purchase are enabled, this is the case for every Explicit App ID and you don't have to use them. When you're happy with everything, click the Submit button at the bottom of the page.

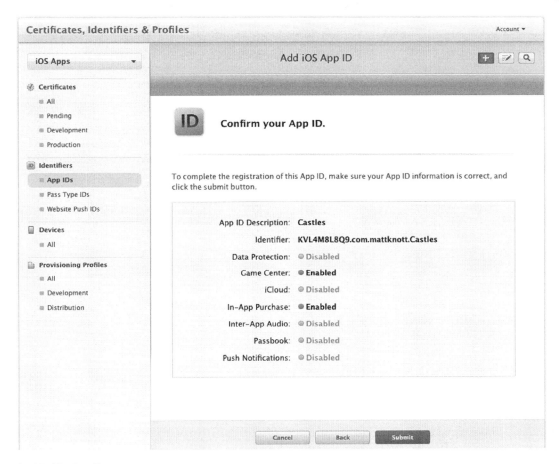

Figure 15-15. *The App ID summary page*

You will be taken to a repeat summary page, and the App ID has now been created. Click Done to return to the list of App IDs, which will now contain your Explicit App ID. That's it, you now have everything you need to go through and create an application profile.

Creating an Application Profile

It's frustrating when you have to rip something up and start again, but in this case, at least you only typed a couple of words. Go back to the iTunes Connect window or tab you were using in your browser and click the Back button, then once again click the Add New App button that was shown in Figure 15-10.

Once again, specify the Default Language as English, the App Name as Castles of Wales, and the SKU Number as CastlesOfWales. This time, when you click the Bundle ID select list, you will see your new App ID in the list; select this as shown in Figure 15-16 and click Continue.

Figure 15-16. *Selecting the explicit App ID you created*

On the next screen, you need to set a release date and the pricing tier for your application, as shown in Figure 15-17. The release date is aspirational to some extent; it will default to the current date, but it could take some weeks to be approved, so if you want it to be released once approved, leave the current date selected.

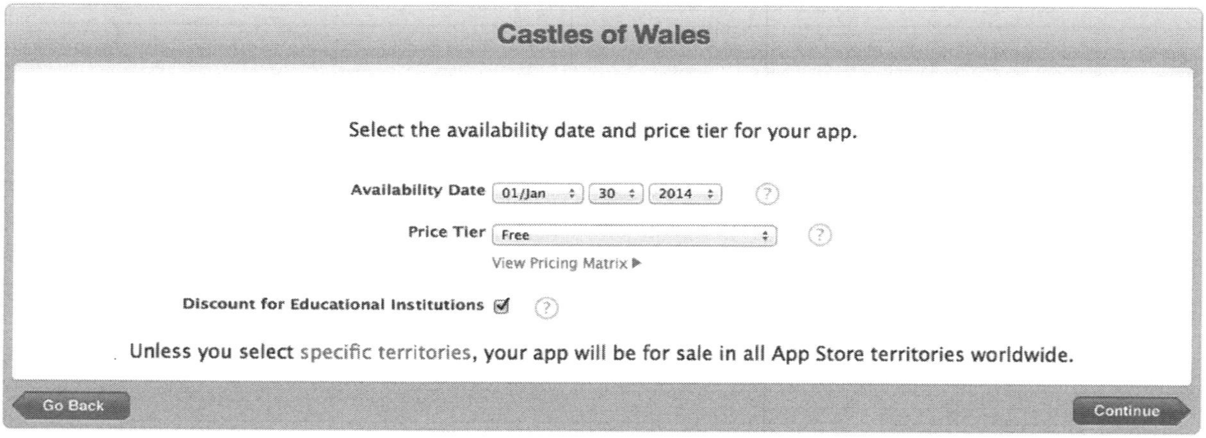

Figure 15-17. *Specifying a release date, pricing tier, and whether or not to discount for educational institutions*

For the pricing tier, well this is up to you. I have selected Free, but with your own applications, this is obviously a choice that you need to make. If you opt for one of the pricing tiers, then it's good to click the View Pricing Matrix link below the Price Tier select box so you can see what the retail price of the app is and the proceeds for each territory the App Store is available in.

> **Note** If you do choose to release a paid-for application, you will be asked to supply your bank account details and also accept the iOS Paid Applications Agreement, which sets out your rights and entitlements. The temptation is to skip through these agreements, but you should always save anything you agree to, because it's legally binding.

Finally, you will be asked if you want your application to be discounted for educational institutions that can benefit from a discount when buying your application in bulk. As someone who works in the education sector, I can tell you that the cheaper you can make your application for schools and colleges, the more likely it is that they will buy in bulk if they like what they see. The specifics of the discount might change, so check the specifics of the discount in the Paid Application Agreement that you accepted when you joined the iOS Developer Program to make sure you're happy with what you're agreeing to. Once you have finished making your selections, click Continue.

This next page is critical, and large. There are a lot of fields on this page, and there is no option to save and return later, you must complete all required fields to some degree. The good news is that once you have created your application's profile, you can edit the information you enter here before you submit to the App Store.

The first section of this page asks you to supply version information for your application and to set the categories it will appear under within the App Store. As this is the first version of your application, you would use 1.0 as the version number, so go ahead and enter this in the Version Number. In the Copyright field, you would usually enter the year and your name or company; as you can see in Figure 15-18, I have entered the year and my name.

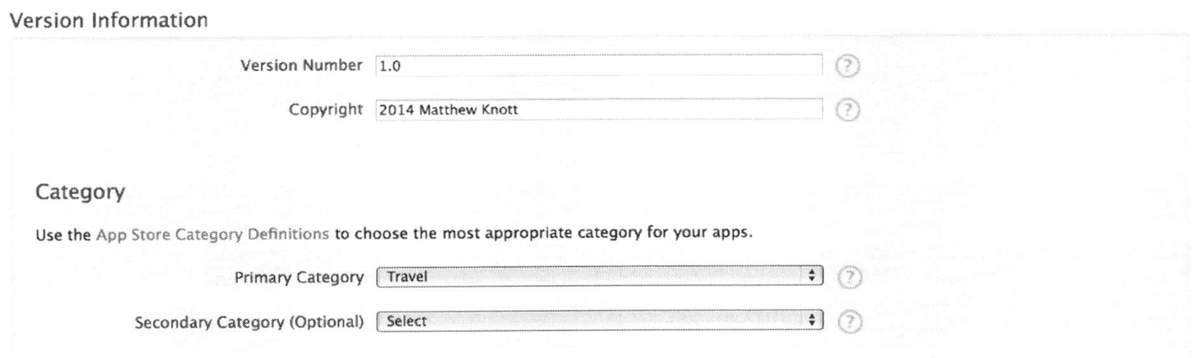

Version Information

Version Number 1.0

Copyright 2014 Matthew Knott

Category

Use the App Store Category Definitions to choose the most appropriate category for your apps.

Primary Category Travel

Secondary Category (Optional) Select

Figure 15-18. Setting the version information

When setting the categories, you have two options to look at: primary and secondary. Looking at the options within the Primary Category select list, you will see that the categories shown reflect those available within the App Store. You need to set a primary category, so I've gone with Travel, because it is most appropriate for this application. Choosing a second category means that your app will have greater visibility to users browsing the apps in the App Store.

With your categories selected, scroll down to the ratings area, as shown in Figure 15-19. Here you must specify the types of content that may appear within your application so that an appropriate content warning may be given to the user downloading the application. The Castles app doesn't have any of the listed content types, so I've selected the None value for all of them.

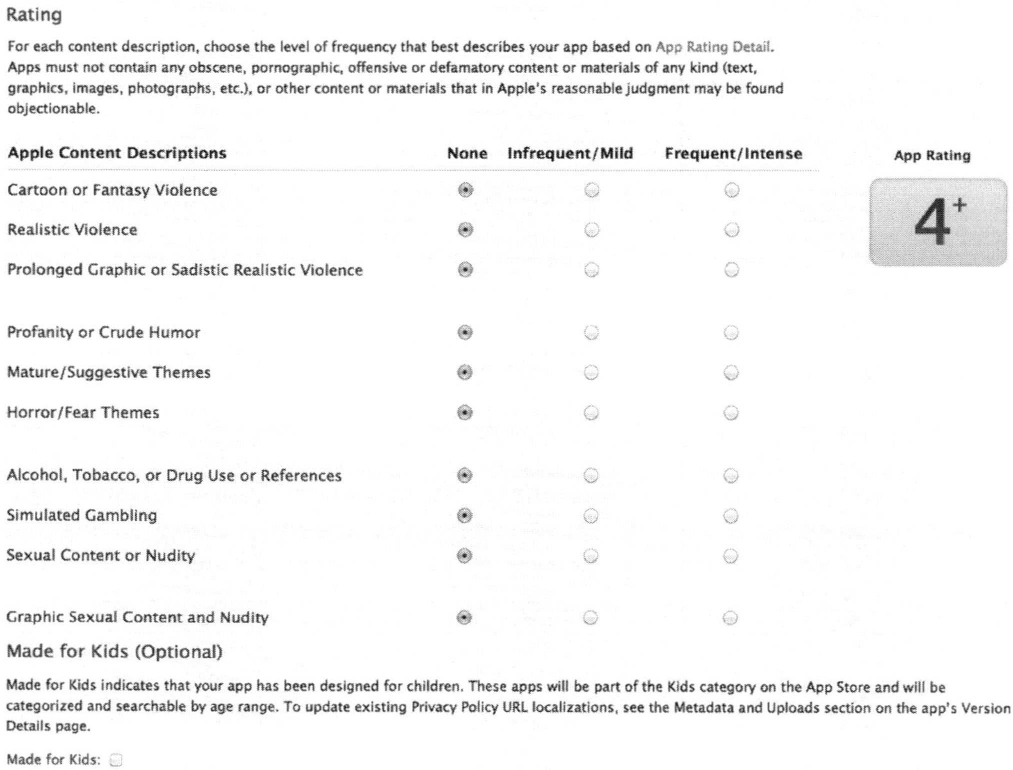

Rating

For each content description, choose the level of frequency that best describes your app based on App Rating Detail. Apps must not contain any obscene, pornographic, offensive or defamatory content or materials of any kind (text, graphics, images, photographs, etc.), or other content or materials that in Apple's reasonable judgment may be found objectionable.

Apple Content Descriptions	None	Infrequent/Mild	Frequent/Intense	App Rating
Cartoon or Fantasy Violence	●	○	○	**4⁺**
Realistic Violence	●	○	○	
Prolonged Graphic or Sadistic Realistic Violence	●	○	○	
Profanity or Crude Humor	●	○	○	
Mature/Suggestive Themes	●	○	○	
Horror/Fear Themes	●	○	○	
Alcohol, Tobacco, or Drug Use or References	●	○	○	
Simulated Gambling	●	○	○	
Sexual Content or Nudity	●	○	○	
Graphic Sexual Content and Nudity	●	○	○	

Made for Kids (Optional)

Made for Kids indicates that your app has been designed for children. These apps will be part of the Kids category on the App Store and will be categorized and searchable by age range. To update existing Privacy Policy URL localizations, see the Metadata and Uploads section on the app's Version Details page.

Made for Kids: ☐

Figure 15-19. Specifying the types of content found in the Castles app

Scroll to the next section titled Metadata, as shown in Figure 15-20. In this segment you have five pieces on information you can specify, two of which are optional:

- *Description:* This will appear on the App Store page for your application and should focus on the app's purpose and its key features.

- *Keywords:* These are words that help your application show up when users search the App Store. You can have 100 characters worth of keywords, which you separate with a comma.

- *Support URL:* This is the primary support URL for your application. You must have a web site set up to support users with your application. The site doesn't have to be specifically about your application and can be your personal or business web site.

- *Marketing URL:* This is optional, but a Marketing URL is displayed to users on the App Store so they can discover more about your app before they purchase or download it.

- *Privacy Policy URL:* If your application collects user data in any way, you should help your users feel confident that you won't abuse their information by publishing a link to your privacy policy page on the Internet.

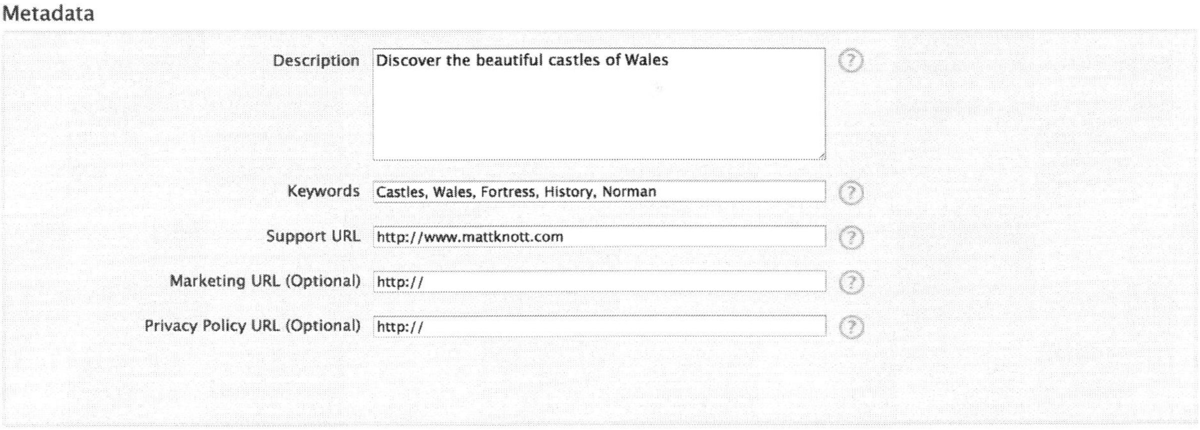

Metadata

Figure 15-20. *The Metadata area contains searchable information and key URLs for the Castles application*

Enter the values you feel are relevant, as long as you provide a description, at least one keyword and a support URL.

The next section on this page is for your contact information, which isn't automatically pulled from your developer account. As shown in Figure 15-21, enter your First Name, Last Name, Email Address, and Phone Number (including the country code). This information is used if there are any queries regarding the application during the approval process.

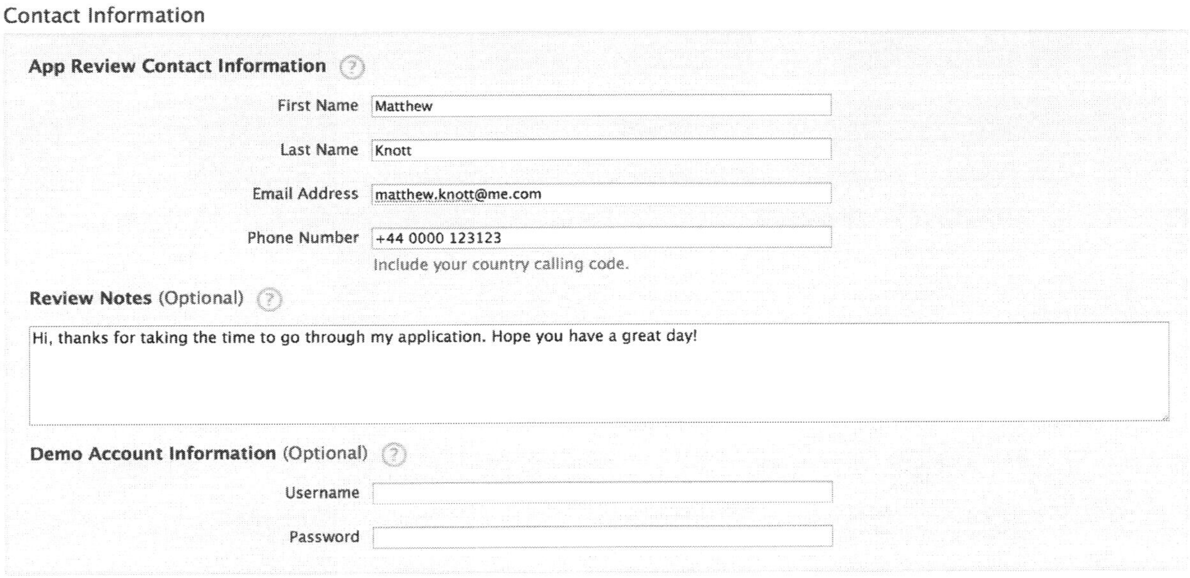

Contact Information

Figure 15-21. *Setting the contact details, review notes, and any demo account information*

The next field, Review Notes, is entirely optional, however, many people, including myself, have found that adding a kind word for the person reviewing your application can have a hugely positive impact on your application being accepted the first time. I always thank them for their work and hope they have a great day, and so far all of my app submissions have gone through the first time, so I recommend you take the time and write your own positive message.

Lastly, for the Demo Account Information segment, if your application is secured with a username and password and you have a test account set up, then provide it here so that the person testing your application submission can test all of the functionality.

The final segment is where you upload any required images and files for the application, as shown in Figure 15-22. There are five separate fields you can upload to, and in each one, clicking the Choose File button will allow you to select a file for upload:

- *Large App Icon:* This is where you upload the high-resolution application icon that will appear on the App Store. The image should be 1024 × 1024 pixels. Upload the file titled `icon1024.png` from the resource files you downloaded for the chapter.

- *3.5-Inch Retina Display Screenshots:* Here you can upload multiple screenshots of your application running on a 3.5-inch retina display. If you don't want to take a screenshot yourself, I have included one in the `screenshots` folder for this chapter's resources called `screen35.png`.

- *4-Inch Retina Display Screenshots:* Here you upload screenshots of your application running on a 4-inch retina display. Again, if you don't wish to use your own image, in the resources for this chapter, use the file called `screen4.png`.

- *iPad Screenshots:* Upload screenshots of your application running on an iPad if it is supported by the application. The Castles application is design exclusively for the iPhone and iPod Touch, so you don't need to upload files here.

- *Routing App Coverage File:* New for iOS 7 and Xcode 5, you can develop applications that allow them to be used when planning routes in the iOS Maps application. This is where you would upload the associated coverage file that indicates the areas your application covers.

Uploads

Large App Icon (?)

[Choose File]

3.5-Inch Retina Display Screenshots (?)

[Choose File]

4-Inch Retina Display Screenshots (?)

[Choose File]

iPad Screenshots (?)

[Choose File]

Routing App Coverage File (Optional) (?)

[Choose File]

Figure 15-22. *The file uploads area*

Once you have uploaded the three images, scroll down and click the Save button at the bottom of the page. Congratulations, you have just completed your first application profile within iTunes Connect!

Uploading an Application to iTunes Connect

You've now completed your application's profile, but there are still some key steps to go through in order to submit your application to the App Store. In a sense, all of the information you just entered is metadata; it's there to support the real thing you want to share, which is the binary file for your application.

Getting Ready to Upload

When you saved the application profile, you were shown the application details, as shown in Figure 15-23. If you look to the right of the large app icon, you will see that the application's status is Prepare for Upload. Before you can supply iTunes Connect with a binary for your application, you need to change that status to Ready for Upload.

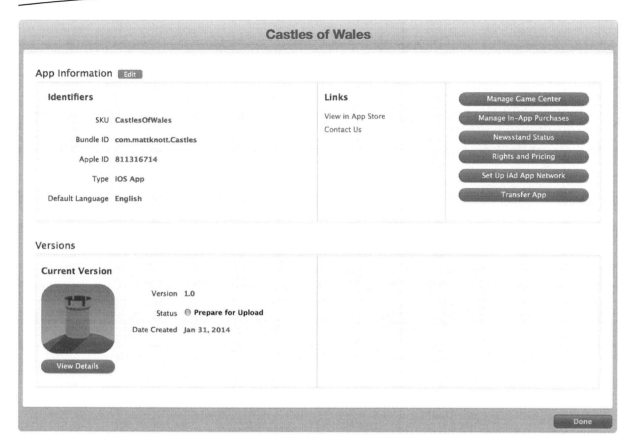

Figure 15-23. *The application details page with the status shown as Prepare for Upload*

Below the large application icon, click the button labeled View Details. The page you are taken to is where you can edit the details of your application before submission to the App Store. If you look in the top right corner you will see a button, as shown in Figure 15-24, called Ready to Upload Binary. This is where you start to enable your application template to be uploaded.

Figure 15-24. *The Ready to Upload Binary button in the toolbar*

Click the Ready to Upload Binary button and you will be presented with an export compliance check, as shown in Figure 15-25. The Castles application does not contain any cryptography, so select No and click the Save button.

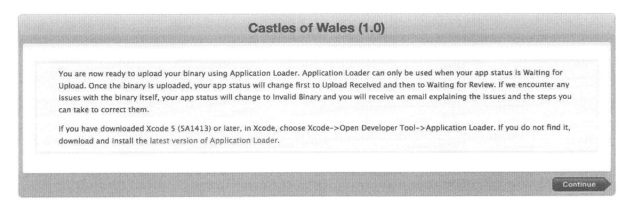

Figure 15-25. *The Export Compliance check*

That's it! Your application has been marked ready for upload. You will be shown the confirmation as shown in Figure 15-26 explaining that you can upload your application with the Application Loader. Application Loader is an application Apple bundled with Xcode to allow you to upload the binary of your application to iTunes Connect, but there are a couple of things you need to look at before you use this application.

Castles of Wales (1.0)

You are now ready to upload your binary using Application Loader. Application Loader can only be used when your app status is Waiting for Upload. Once the binary is uploaded, your app status will change first to Upload Received and then to Waiting for Review. If we encounter any issues with the binary itself, your app status will change to Invalid Binary and you will receive an email explaining the issues and the steps you can take to correct them.

If you have downloaded Xcode 5 (5A1413) or later, in Xcode, choose Xcode->Open Developer Tool->Application Loader. If you do not find it, download and install the latest version of Application Loader.

Continue

Figure 15-26. *Confirmation that your app is ready for upload*

Creating a Distribution Certificate and Profile

In order to prove that you are the owner of the binary file you are uploading, you need to build and sign your binary using an iOS Distribution certificate. This is something a paid up member of the iOS Developer Program is able to do, and the creation process is quick and relatively painless.

1. Start by going to Xcode, then from the top menu go to Xcode ➤ Preferences (⌘ + ,) and then select the Accounts tab.

2. Select the Developer Account from the left-hand column, and then click the View Details … button in the bottom right corner to display a popover containing details about your Developer Account and any linked Signing Identities and Provisioning Profiles, as shown in Figure 15-27.

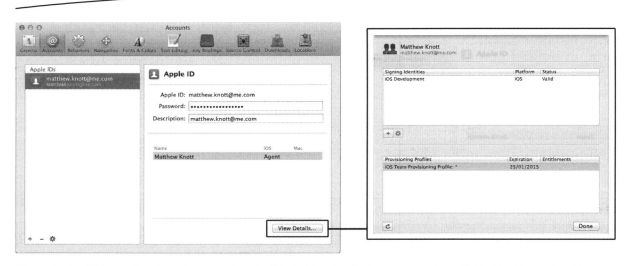

Figure 15-27. With your Developer Account selected, click the View Details button to see the available identities and profiles

3. Beneath the list of Signing Identities, there is a + icon and a cog icon next to it, click the + icon and then choose iOS Distribution from the subsequent menu, as shown in Figure 15-28.

Figure 15-28. Creating an iOS Distribution Signing Identity

4. At this point, Xcode will communicate with Apple while it generates the relevant certificates on their servers before confirming that the identity has been created. Click the OK button.

5. You will be returned to the Accounts details area, which will update to include a distribution identity alongside the development identity. Click the Done button to dismiss the popover and close the Preferences.

Great, you're finished with Xcode for a moment! It's time to go back online and set up a Distribution Provisioning Profile with the certificate you just created. If you think this is a lot of hassle, you're probably right, but the good news is that setting up the signing identity for distribution only has to be done once, but you need to create a provisioning profile for each application you submit to the App Store.

1. In your web browser, go back to the iOS Dev Center at http://developer.apple.com/ios. Once you have signed in, choose the Certificates, Identifiers & Profiles link from the navigation block on the right; refer to Figure 15-6 if you're not sure what you're looking for.

2. You will be taken to a page with three columns: iOS Apps, Mac Apps, and Safari Extensions. Under the iOS Apps heading, click Provisioning Profiles. This will take you to a list of all the provisioning profiles created for your account, as shown in Figure 15-29.

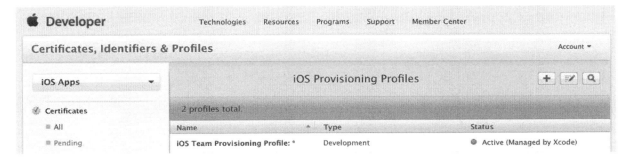

Figure 15-29. *Listing all provisioning profiles*

3. Next to the title iOS Provisioning Profiles is a + icon, which is shown on the right in Figure 15-29. Click this icon; you will be presented with a form for creating a new provisioning profile. Select the App Store option, as shown in Figure 15-30, and click Continue.

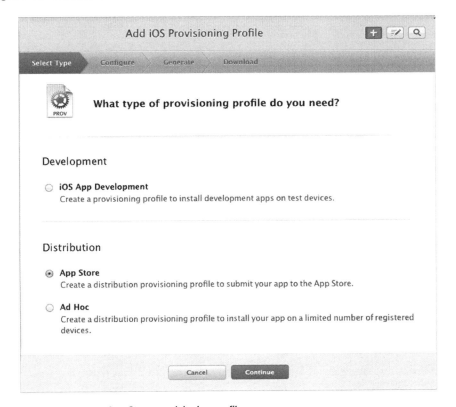

Figure 15-30. *Opting to create a new App Store provisioning profile*

4.   Next, you will be asked to select an App ID; if you've followed the steps so far, then you should see Castles appear, as shown in Figure 15-31, if not, then select it from the list. When you're happy with the selection, click Continue.

Figure 15-31. *Selecting the App ID that the provisioning profile is for*

5.   You will now be prompted to select a certificate; listed here should be the iOS Distribution certificate you just created within Xcode. It is not selected by default, so click the radio button next to the certificate to highlight it, as shown in Figure 15-32, and click Continue.

Figure 15-32. *Selecting the certificate to use with this provisioning profile*

6. The last step in generating a provisioning profile is to give it a name. Because this is specific to the application, type Castles in the Profile Name field, as shown in Figure 15-33, and then click Generate.

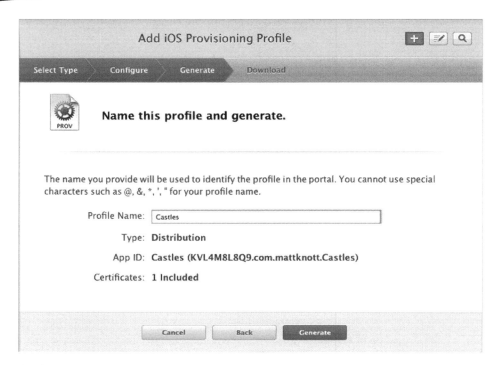

Figure 15-33. Naming the profile Castles is the last step before generating the profile

7. It will take a moment for your profile to be generated, but eventually you will be taken to a confirmation page, as shown in Figure 15-34. Click the Done button at the bottom of the page and return to Xcode.

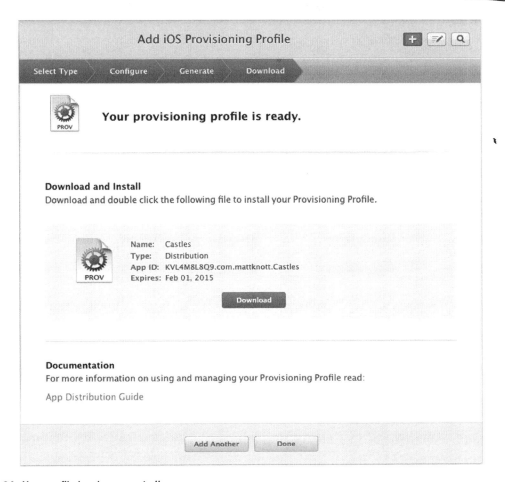

Figure 15-34. Your profile has been created!

> **Note**   You could download and install the profile at this point by clicking the button marked Download and then running the downloaded `Castles.mobileprovision` file. However, it is a good demonstration of Xcode's flexibility in fetching missing information to just let it handle the whole thing.

Setting a Code Signing Identity

Now that you have created a code signing identity that is suitable for distributing iOS applications, you need to tell Xcode to use this identity for signing your applications when it builds a version for release, such as when you archive the project.

1.   To do this, simply go back to Xcode and select the project from the Project Navigator.

2. Next, select the Castles item listed under Project and then select the Build Settings tab.

3. Scroll down the list of settings until you reach the Code Signing section.

4. Within this area you will have an item called Provisioning Profile, as highlighted in Figure 15-35.

Figure 15-35. *The code signing settings for the project*

5. Click where it says None next to the Provisioning Profile item and, as shown in Figure 15-36, you will be presented with all of the available provisioning profiles. Select the one titled Castles. This will automatically ensure that the correct code signing identities are used. If you don't see the correct information, always try restarting Xcode.

Figure 15-36. *Setting the code signing identity*

6. Now that Xcode is properly configured to sign release versions of your application, you can test this new setting by archiving your project, which is considered a Release build. From the menu bar, go to Product ➤ Archive to archive your project.

Note   If the Archive option is grayed out, check that the target of your build that appears next to the run button is not the Simulator, but that it says iOS device or the name of your actual device.

7. You will be presented with a dialog, as shown in Figure 15-37, which alerts you to the lack of a provisioning profile for distribution; click the Fix Issue button.

Figure 15-37. Xcode will warn you that it can't find a provisioning profile for distributing applications

8. Now you will be asked to select a development team; if you're the only member of the team, then your name will be listed, otherwise select the team associated with your provisioning profile for the Castles application and then click Choose, as shown in Figure 15-38.

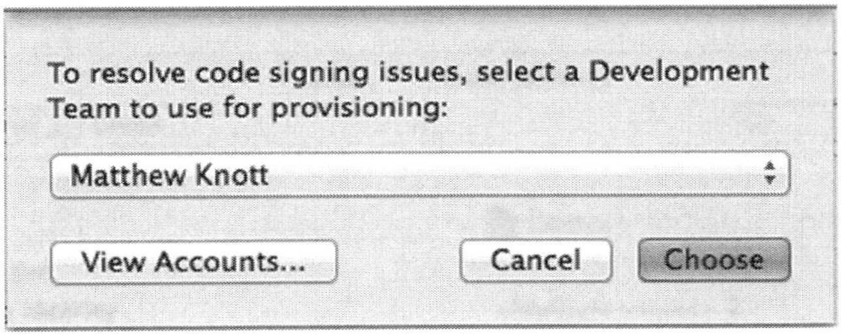

Figure 15-38. Selecting a Development Team

Xcode will now download the provisioning profile and then it will archive your application, eventually opening the Archive Organizer. You're nearly ready to upload your application and submit it to the App Store for approval, but before doing so, it's a good idea to validate the application and its settings to improve your chances of being accepted the first time.

Validating Your Application

You may remember that in Chapter 14 I discussed the Archives Organizer in some detail, but I didn't cover the Validation or Distribute features available for an archived application because they form an essential part of the uploading process.

By validating your application in Xcode before submission, you will find out if it meets the minimum standards for the App Store. If it does, great, but if not, then you've just spared yourself a good 2-week wait, only to find that Apple rejected your submission. Validating your application doesn't take long at all.

1. Within the Archives Organizer, select the newest archive for Castles, as shown in Figure 15-39, and click the Validate … button.

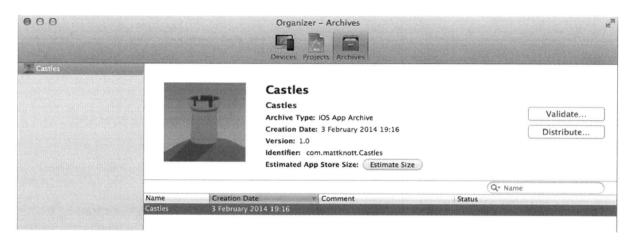

Figure 15-39. *The Archives Organizer has a validation feature built in*

2. You will be prompted for your iTunes Connect credentials, enter these and click Next.

3. Once Xcode has validated your credentials, you may be presented with the screen shown in Figure 15-40. If this happens, then you should click the Download Identities button and follow the steps, which are exactly the same as when Xcode fetched the provisioning profile for archiving.

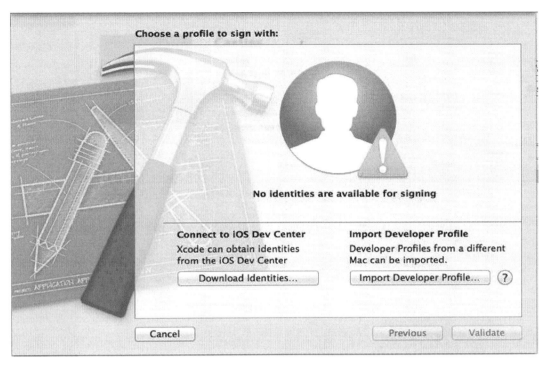

Figure 15-40. *Xcode will prompt to download an identity if none are found*

Note   It's possible that you may find Xcode takes you around in circles at this point, constantly returning you to the screen shown in Figure 15-40. If this happens, go to Xcode ➤ Preferences and choose the Accounts tab. Click your Developer Account and then the View Details button as you did toward the beginning of this chapter and let the provisioning profiles update. Now close the preferences and try again.

4. Finally, select the provisioning profile called Castles, as shown in Figure 15-41, and click Validate. This will take a moment, and if prompted to allow permission to the keychain, ensure it is given.

Figure 15-41. *Selecting the Castles provisioning profile for validation*

If everything has gone to plan, Xcode will come back with a clean bill of health, as shown in Figure 15-42. Click the Finish button, and then as Xcode just told you, it's time to submit this application to the App Store! If there are any issues with your submission and you aren't clear on the reason for rejection, then head to the developer support site where you will find all the information you need to set about correcting the issue.

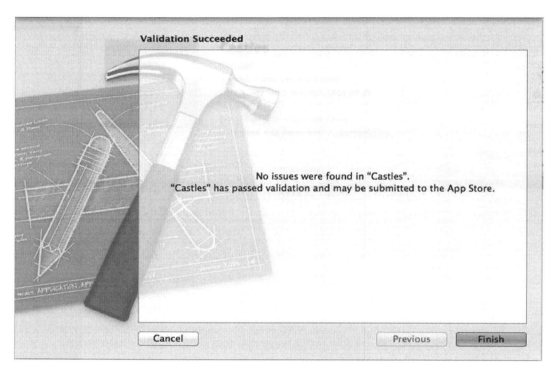

Figure 15-42. Your application has been validated and can be submitted to the App Store!

Submitting Your Application to the App Store

After all of the buildup, it's finally the moment of truth, it's the culmination of 15 chapters of learning and growing as a developer, now you're ready to submit your application to the App Store. Let's get to it!

You will actually look at two ways of submitting your application to the App Store, and I will explain why later on in the chapter, for now let's take a look at the first method for submission.

Submitting Applications Using Archives Organizer

You should be quite familiar with the Archives Organizer by now, so it's time to wring the last bit of functionality out of it, which is using the Distribute feature to complete your submission to the App Store.

1. You will be using the same archived application you just validated, so within the Archives Organizer, with the archive selected, click the Distribute ... button that is just below the Validate ... button. You will then be prompted to choose how you want to distribute your application, as shown in Figure 15-43.

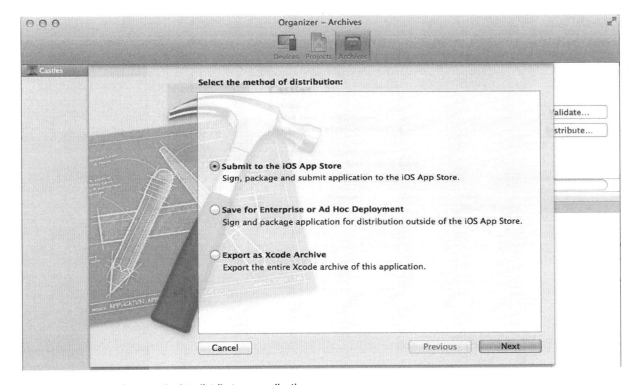

Figure 15-43. Selecting a method to distribute an application

Submit to the iOS App Store: This option will upload your digitally signed application to iTunes Connect and the application will then head off for review by Apple.

Save for Enterprise or Ad Hoc Deployment: Choosing this option will allow you to save a signed .ipa file to your Mac ready for distribution. If you wanted a friend or colleague to test your application, you could send the file to them and it can then be installed on their devices via iTunes on either a Mac or Windows computer.

Export as Xcode Archive: In Chapter 14 you discovered the .xcarchive format that Xcode saves your application in when it is archived. This option simply creates a separate .xcarchive file for you.

Note If you send a friend or colleague your .ipa file, their device's unique identifier must be registered on your provisioning portal.

2.   In this instance, you should ensure that the first option, Submit to the iOS App Store, is selected, and then click Next.

3.   You will then be asked to enter your iTunes Connect credentials as you were during validation, do this and click Next.

4.   Now, as shown in Figure 15-41, select the Castles provisioning profile. This time, click Submit.

Your application will take a moment to upload before Xcode presents you with the message shown in Figure 15-44 that confirms your submission has been made and your application is pending review. That's right, as soon as the binary file for your application has been uploaded, the review process begins whether you had intended it to or not.

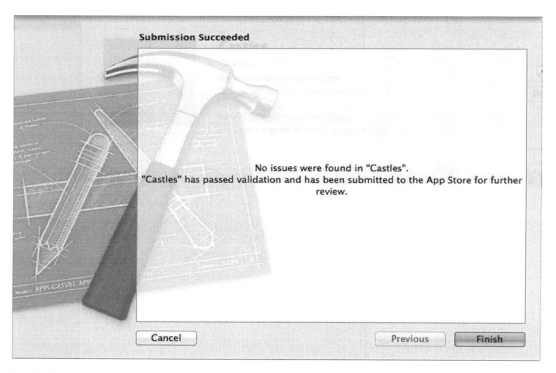

Figure 15-44. Your application has finally been uploaded to iTunes Connect and the App Store

Canceling Your Submission

If you've followed this chapter to the letter, then your version of the Castles application is now waiting to be reviewed by one of the Apple engineers who process all App Store submissions. If you want to cancel this process for any reason, it's not immediately obvious how you would do this, but fear not, I'll take you through canceling the review so you can see a second way to submit your application to the App Store.

1. To start, go to the iTunes Connect portal, sign in, and go to your list of applications.

2. Click the Castles application; notice that the status has now changed to Waiting for Review. On the right you will see a link that says Binary Details, which has been highlighted in Figure 15-45.

Figure 15-45. Selecting Binary Details for the Castles application

3. At the top of the Binary Details page is a button that says Reject This Binary, as shown in Figure 15-46. Click the button and you will be prompted to confirm whether or not you want to delete the binary. Select Reject Binary and the application will be put into the Developer Rejected status.

Figure 15-46. The Reject This Binary button is hidden in the title bar of the Binary Details page

4. To put the application back into the awaiting upload status, refer to Figure 15-24 and click the Ready to Upload Binary button.

Submitting Applications Using Application Loader

Here I will take you through using the Application Loader. You may be wondering why you may need to use it after what should have been a fairly painless upload process using the Archives Organizer. Well, in truth, the Archives Organizer isn't always a painless process. When I submitted my very first application to the App Store, my elation at finally being ready to submit turned to despair as for some reason, the upload process refused to work behind the corporate firewall and nothing I tried would get around it, which is when I turned to the Application Loader.

Application Loader is distinctively different visually from other parts of Xcode, and although it can be downloaded separately from the Developer Portal, it is bundled within the Xcode package. It can be used to upload applications to the App Store, but also to create in-app purchase packages. Rather than uploading the binary file from an archive, Application Loader uploads a presigned .ipa file to the App Store.

Some organizations have a specific person who is responsible for App Store submissions, so the fact that you can use this as a standalone application makes that process far simpler, because this person only needs to contend with one simple application rather than working through different Xcode screens and projects files.

Ironically, before I can show you how to use the Application Loader, you need to create an .ipa file for the Castles application, and to do that you will use the Archives Organizer. You can probably already guess how to do this from when you submitted your application using the Archives Organizer.

1. With the Castles archive selected, click the Distribute button. This time, when presented with the options shown in Figure 15-43, choose the middle option Save for Enterprise or Ad Hoc Deployment and click Next.

2. As you have done several times, select the Provisioning Profile for the application and click Export.

3. You will be prompted to save your file somewhere; ensure that the Save for Enterprise Distribution is *not* checked and click Save. You have now created the .ipa file ready for the Application Loader.

4. To launch the Application Loader, go to the menu bar and select Xcode ➤ Open Developer Tool ➤ Application Loader.

5. When the Application Loader first loads, you will be presented with a terms and conditions page, and then asked to log in. Enter your credentials and click Next.

6. Once your information has been verified, click Done. You will now be looking at the screen shown in Figure 15-47; this is the Application Loader.

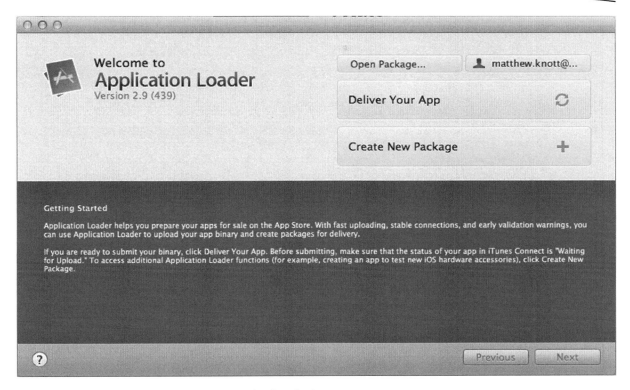

Figure 15-47. Enter your iTunes Connect account details to log in

7. Click the button labeled Deliver Your App. After a moment, you will be presented with a list of available applications; select the Castles of Wales app, as shown in Figure 15-48 and click Next.

Figure 15-48. Selecting the Castles App

8. The next screen will give you key details about the application. In the bottom right-hand corner of the window is a button labeled Choose …. Click this to open a file dialog. Browse until you find the .ipa file you created a moment ago, as shown in Figure 15-49, and click Open.

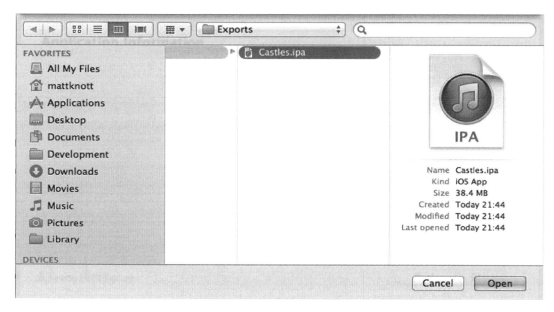

Figure 15-49. Selecting the .ipa file you created to submit to the App Store

9. You will be shown a screen titled Adding Application. At this stage nothing is actually happening despite the misleading title. Click the button labeled Send that is in the bottom right-hand corner and the window will spring to life as it uploads your application to the App Store.

When it has finished uploading, you will be presented with a large green tick icon. Your application has now been put into the Waiting for Review status. Click the Done button and you will be shown a thank you message. That's it, now you just need to sit back and wait for the app to be approved by Apple's engineers, which most developers find happens in around 10 working days.

Summary

In this chapter, you've added the last feather into your cap and you can now use Xcode to a high standard. Where you go from here is up to you, but you have all the skills necessary to become a professional iOS developer.

Specifically in this chapter you:

- Finished the Castles application by adding icons
- Set up an application profile within iTunes Connect

▣ Used Xcode to create a distribution certificate

▣ Created a provisioning profile in the Dev Center

▣ Learned how to verify your application separately from the upload process

▣ Uploaded your application two different ways

Next Steps

You're now armed with an excellent knowledge of how to use Xcode, and you've used the Objective-C language to create a number of really neat little applications. Now it's time to take what you've learned and put it into practice.

If you're wondering where to go from here, Apress has publish a wide array of titles that will help you go to the next level, whether that's iOS, OS X, or Game Development. As I mentioned at the start of the book, iTunes U is also a great source of material to help and inspire you. There is so much help available online, start small and build up to grander projects, you're more likely to succeed.

My sincerest hope is that you've found this book useful and that it's given you the confidence to try something yourself. If it has, I'd love to hear from you, or if you have any questions or suggestions on how I might improve a future edition, please send me an e-mail at `matthewknott@me.com`. I might not be able to reply right away, but I will certainly do my best.

Finally, please remember, if you feel like you need a holiday after finishing this book, come to Wales for the best people, food, sport, history, and countryside in the whole world, not that I'm biased!

Index

Get the eBook for only $10!

Now you can take the weightless companion with you anywhere, anytime. Your purchase of this book entitles you to 3 electronic versions for only $10.

This Apress title will prove so indispensible that you'll want to carry it with you everywhere, which is why we are offering the eBook in 3 formats for only $10 if you have already purchased the print book.

Convenient and fully searchable, the PDF version enables you to easily find and copy code—or perform examples by quickly toggling between instructions and applications. The MOBI format is ideal for your Kindle, while the ePUB can be utilized on a variety of mobile devices.

Go to www.apress.com/promo/tendollars to purchase your companion eBook.

Apress®
THE EXPERT'S VOICE™

Made in the USA
Middletown, DE
21 October 2014